Wanda De

Office Informatio

Concepts and Applications

Office Information Systems

Concepts and Applications

Third Edition

Sharon Lund O'Neil
Associate Professor, Business Education/Technology
Technical Education Department, College of Technology
University of Houston
Houston, Texas

A Gregg Publication

Glencoe/McGraw-Hill
A Macmillan/McGraw-Hill Company

Mission Hills, California   New York, New York

Sponsoring Editor: Marilyn Sarch
Cover Design and Art Supervisor: Penina M. Wissner
Production Supervisor: Mirabel Flores

Development and Production Management: Cole and Associates
Developmental Editor: Annette Gooch
Production Manager: Lorna Cunkle
Photo Researcher: Carolyn Chandler
Cover Photograph: David Wagner/Phototake
Artist: Joseph Maas, Advanced Presentations
Typography: G & S Typesetters, Inc.

Library of Congress Cataloging-in-Publication Data

O'Neil, Sharon Lund.
Office information systems: concepts and applications / Sharon Lund O'Neil.—3rd ed.
p. cm.
ISBN 0-07-047818-X
1. Office practice—Automation. 2. Business—Data processing. 3. Electronic office machines. I. Title
HF5548.057 1990
651.8—dc20 89–25945
CIP

The manuscript and artwork for this book were prepared electronically.

Send all inquiries to:
Glencoe/McGraw-Hill, 29th floor
1221 Avenue of the Americas
New York, NY 10020

ISBN 0-07-047818-X

1 2 3 4 5 6 7 8 9 0 VNH VNH 9 8 7 6 5 4 3 2 1 0

To the Student

The revolutionary technological advances of the last few decades have made today's office environment a dynamic, exciting workplace. Your future as an information specialist in an office information system can be just as dynamic and exciting.

This text, *Office Information Systems: Concepts and Applications*, has been designed with you in mind. Its purpose is to give you the greatest amount of information in the clearest and most easily understood manner to prepare you for a rewarding career in a modern office information system. As you progress through the text, you will discover the new technology and the automated equipment that make accomplishing office work easy and efficient. You will learn about the impact of change and the importance of managing and distributing information. You will also learn that the effectiveness of an information system in an organization depends on *you*. You are the most important resource a business has in providing information to the right people at the right time for effective decision making to take place.

Begin your study of *Office Information Systems: Concepts and Applications* by reviewing the table of contents, noting the variety and progression of topics you will be studying. Then, as you start studying each chapter, note how the opening vignette "sets the stage" for the concepts you will learn in the chapter. Key terms appear in the vocabulary list at the end of the chapter and again, with definitions, in the glossary at the back of the book. Use the end-of-chapter vocabulary list, chapter summary, and chapter questions to reinforce the concepts you have learned in each chapter. Also, the case study at the end of each chapter will give you an opportunity to apply what you have learned to a realistic situation.

In a separate section near the end of the book are 65 "hands-on" applications to help you learn and practice information processing skills on automated equipment. These exercises move you through a progression of common functions that are vital in processing a wide range of office documents in a modern office. For many applications, you will be asked to record the steps you must take to complete the application. Take careful notes because your notes are your "reference guide"—a valuable resource to use as you progress through the applications, as well as for later reference.

You alone hold the key to your career and future as a competent information specialist. By learning the concepts and applications presented in this text, you can build your confidence and develop expertise as a productive worker in an information system. You will soon find that there are many career paths for skilled office information workers. If you make the decision now to become the kind of competent worker businesses want, you can build the skills needed for a productive, rewarding, and exciting career in a modern office information system.

About the Author

Sharon Lund O'Neil, Ph.D., is a Professor of Business and Office Education in the College of Technology, University of Houston. Dr. O'Neil's extensive teaching, research, consulting, and business experience has been concentrated in occupational survival and office information systems. She has written numerous journal articles and has been a contributing author and editor for several books. Her widely disseminated works have brought her national recognition.

Taking an innovative approach to curriculum development, Dr. O'Neil has initiated curriculum and research projects that serve as models for today's classroom. Her 20 years of classroom experience and curriculum development form the basis of a "tried and tested," common-sense approach to teaching that has earned her praise from students and colleagues and awards for teaching excellence.

Dr. O'Neil also is active at the local, state, and national levels of business education. She has made countless presentations at conventions, seminars, and workshops throughout the country. Among the professional organizations in which she has held many leadership roles are the American Vocational Association, National Business Education Association, Delta Pi Epsilon, and the Association for Information Systems Professionals.

Dr. O'Neil received B.A. and M.A. degrees from Walla Walla College in Washington, and a Ph.D. degree from the University of Illinois.

About the Reviewers

Bridget I. Archer is a Systems Analyst for the School of Public Health at the University of Illinois in Chicago.

Eddie Espinosa is the Director of Off-Campus Credit for the Department of Continuing Education at Front Range Community College in Arvada, Colorado.

Deborah Hinkle is an Instructor and Department Head for the Department of Secretarial Science at Catawba Valley Community College in Hickory, North Carolina.

Evelyn Maddux is a Systems Manager for Vial, Hamilton, Koch & Knox in Dallas.

Catherine Smith is an Instructor and Chairperson for the Secretarial Department at American Institute of Business in Des Moines, Iowa.

Carol Williamson is an Instructor of Business Administration at Daytona Beach Community College in Daytona Beach, Florida.

Photo Credits

Chapter 1 **1** Sharp Electronics Corporation. **3** Will Faller (left); Bank of America (right). **4** The Bettmann Archive (left); Bull Information Systems (right). **5** IBM Corporation. **6** AT&T Archives. **7** IBM Corporation. **8** IBM Corporation (above); Hattori Seiko Co., Ltd. (below). **9** AT&T Archives. **10** Apple Computer, Inc. (above left); IBM Corporation (above right); San Francisco Convention Facilities (below). **22** Unisys Corporation.

Chapter 2 **25** Hewlett-Packard Company. **36** Will Faller. **37** IBM Corporation. **39** Aetna Life & Casualty. **40** NCR Corporation. **42** Hewlett-Packard Company.

Chapter 3 **47** Dictaphone Corporation. **50** Will Faller. **52** Stenograph Corporation. **53** Dictaphone Corporation. **54** Will Faller. **57** Dictaphone Corporation. **58** Dictaphone Corporation. **59** Will Faller. **60** Dictaphone Corporation. **61** International Voice Products, Inc. **64** New Dest Corporation. **66** Lockheed Corporation. **67** AT&T Archives.

Chapter 4 **71** IBM Corporation. **73** IBM Corporation (above); CPT Corporation (below). **74** Lanier Business Products. **75** IBM Corporation. **76** Canon U.S.A., Inc. **77** IBM Corporation. **79** Sharp Electronics Corporation. **81** Radio Shack, A Division of Tandy Corporation (above); Compaq Computer Corporation (below). **83** Radio Shack, A Division of Tandy Corporation. **89** Apple Computer, Inc. **93** CPT Corporation (left); Lanier Business Products (right). **95** BASF Corporation. **98** MiniScribe Corporation. **99** Hewlett-Packard Company.

Chapter 5 **104** AT&T Archives. **110** Copyright 1984, 1987 Ashton-Tate Corporation. **120** Internal Revenue Service, Photo by Janet Klise. **122** Unisys Corporation. **127** Apple Computer, Inc.

Chapter 6 **133** Xerox Corporation. **136** Okidata, an OKI AMERICA company. **137** Qume Corporation. **139** Hewlett-Packard Company. **141** Hewlett-Packard Company (above); Xerox Corporation (below). **142** Texas Instruments (above); Qume Corporation (below). **143** The Hedman Corporation. **144** TAB Products

Co. **146** Dennis Barna. **147** Canon U.S.A., Inc. **149** Sharp Electronics Corporation. **151** Xerox Corporation. **153** AGFA Compugraphics. **155** Xerox Corporation. **156** Dennis Barna. **157** VeloBind Incorporated (above); Michael Business Machines (below). **158** Will Faller.

Chapter 7 **163** Western Union. **166** Federal Express. **168** TAB Products Co. **171** AT&T Archives. **176** Apple Computer, Inc. **186** ComDate Corporation. **189** Unisys Corporation (above); AT&T Archives (below).

Chapter 8 **195** IBM Corporation. **201** Dennis Barna. **204** Brian Griffin. **206** Microseal Corporation. **207** 3M Document Systems Division. **209** Dennis Barna. **211** 3M Document Systems Division.

Chapter 9 **226** IBM Corporation. **231** IBM Corporation. **232** Apple Computer, Inc. **243** Racal-Milgo.

Chapter 10 **251** Steelcase Incorporated. **253** IBM Corporation (above); Will Faller (below). **262** Steelcase Incorporated. **265** American Ergonomics Corporation. **267** American Ergonomics Corporation. **272** Steelcase Incorporated.

Chapter 11 **276** Heald Colleges. **278** CenterCare, Incorporated. **283** WordPerfect Corporation (above); Heald Colleges (below). **287** IBM Corporation.

Chapter 12 **291** Aetna Life & Casualty. **296** Will Faller. **298** IBM Corporation. **301** Will Faller. **303** WordPerfect Corporation. **304** IBM Corporation (above and below). **305** Genicom Corporation. **308** Apple Computer, Inc. **309** Will Faller.

Office Automation **I** IBM Corporation (above and below). **II** Hewlett-Packard Company (above and center); IBM Corporation (below). **III** Hayes Microcomputer Products, Inc. (above); IBM Corporation (below). **IV** AT&T Archives (above); IBM Corporation (below).

Computer Graphics **V** Lotus Development Corporation (above, center and below). **VI** IBM Corporation (above and below). **VII** IBM Corporation (above and below). **VIII** IBM Corporation (above); Zenith Data Systems (below).

The Human Interface With Technology **IX** IBM Corporation (above); Texas Instruments (below). **X** Hewlett-Packard Company (above); IBM Corporation (below). **XI** IBM Corporation (above); Monica Suder & Associates (below). **XII** Esprit.

Advances in Technology **XIII** IBM Corporation (above); Control Data Corporation (below). **XIV** Compaq Computer Corporation (above); Hewlett-Packard Company (below). **XV** IBM Corporation (above); Hewlett-Packard Company (below). **XVI** U.S. Sprint (above left); Commodore Electronics, Ltd. (above right); AT&T Archives (below).

Contents

Chapter 12 You and Your Career 291

Hands-On Applications 314

CHAPTER 1

Information Systems and You

Jackie Holmes awakens, turns off the music from her digital clock radio, and turns on her TV set with a remote-control unit. She gets out of bed and showers. As she dresses, she listens to the news over the electronic speaker system connected to her TV. In the kitchen of her apartment, she pours a glass of orange juice, butters a roll, and puts freeze-dried coffee into a cup of water she heated in her microwave. After breakfast, Jackie checks her appointment calendar on her home computer, gathers her coat and attaché case, and turns on the automatic security alarm for her apartment. She then leaves for work.

The morning routine of a typical office worker only a few decades ago would have been quite different from Jackie's. The information and the technology accessible to Jackie, such as the digital clock radio, remote-control television, home computer, and microwave oven, simply did not exist. These technology-based conveniences, all fairly recent, affect the daily lives of working people today—people like you, who recognize the effect of modern technology on almost every aspect of your daily life.

Technology and the Information Industry

Technology has made a major contribution to the amount and type of information you have at your fingertips. It has also had a vast impact on the information industry, the largest and fastest growing in the world. As you will see, information is something people cannot live without.

Knowledge Workers

Because the amount of information is growing so rapidly, more and more workers, like Jackie, are becoming **knowledge workers** (people who use information to make decisions in doing their work). Knowledge workers are mainly white-collar workers. They make up about 60 percent of our work force. Typically, knowledge workers are managers, administrators, and other professionals who rely on technology and automation to help them make good decisions in completing their job tasks. More than likely they use electronic and automated machines to help them complete their work.

Knowledge workers are **information specialists** who know how to obtain, use, and pass on information. They depend on many components of today's technology such as word (text) and data processing, graphics and imaging, electronic and desktop publishing, telecommunications and voice messaging, facsimile and electronic data interchange—information components and technologies explored in this text.

Workers who intend to compete and survive in a business office must become proficient information handlers. They must know how and where to get the right information at the right time. They must know how and when to use automated equipment. They must know how to plan, think, and take appropriate action. They must be knowledge workers within businesses and information-based organizations.

Technology and You

Do you think of yourself as a knowledge worker who can compete in an information-based organization? Consider for a moment how information and modern technology affect almost every aspect of your daily life. For example, you may be one of millions of people who own a pocket- or credit card-sized calculator. With a hand-held calculator, you can quickly balance your checkbook or personal budget, compute interest on a credit card purchase, or determine monthly payments on a fitness club membership. The opportunities for using a hand-held calculator in some way nearly every day are almost limitless.

There are many other ways you may use information and technology in your daily life. If you are one of the growing number of people who have a home computer, you may be able to pay your bills without ever writing a personal check. Your computer may enable you to communicate directly with a bank computer that transfers money from your own account to a creditor's account. Or you may use an **automated teller machine (ATM)** to do your personal banking. These conveniently located machines permit you to deposit money, withdraw cash, and review the balance of your account without coming in contact with another person.

Because you have technology and information close at hand, your daily activities may be somewhat different today than they were before some of the more recent electronic developments. You probably take many of these developments for granted: electronically controlled traffic lights, electronic trouble-sensoring devices in cars, miniature radios and cassette players, camcorders and video recording machines with instant replay devices, home tele-

Computers have become a part of our everyday lives.

phone answering and fax machines, portable computers and home copiers, digital wristwatches, and large-screen television sets. Some of these are luxuries, some are considered necessities, but all of them help make your daily life more enjoyable, comfortable, or safe.

The Changing Office

The developments and inventions of the past 100 to 150 years have changed your personal life just as they have changed the way work is done in offices. The office of today contains machines that did not exist even a few years ago. It is important to know about these new machines—what they are, how they work, and how to use them to originate, process, and communicate information. Learning about office machines will be one of your main goals in using this book. But first let's look at some of the inventions that are influencing the way we work and live today.

Consider what it might have been like to visit an office in the mid-1800s, with its big wooden desks, quill pens, and inkstands—and no air conditioning. All correspondence was written by hand—by men, because women had not yet entered the work force. Information moved around, in, and out of the office at a rate that was extremely slow by today's standards. Businessmen trusted most daily transactions to memory. A small number of office clerks and people who functioned as secretaries were responsible for items that had to be committed to paper. Letters were dictated by one person directly to another. Documents were copied by hand at an average speed of ten words a minute. The file cabinet was not yet a necessity, so papers were stacked on desks, stuck on desktop spikes, or tacked to the wall. But all of this changed with the invention of typing machines.

Contrast the nineteenth-century office with the office of today.

Electronic typewriters have become faster and more efficient during the last half-century: Shown here are the IBM Model 01, introduced in 1935 as the first commercially successful typewriter in the United States; the IBM Selectric, introduced in 1961; and the new IBM Wheelwriter 70 Series II.

The Invention of the Typewriter

During the early to mid-1800s, more than 50 patents were issued to European and American inventors for their machines with keyboards that operators could use to print a letter. Credit for the typewriter, however, goes to C. L. Sholes, a Milwaukee newspaperman, who was issued the fifty-second patent for a typewriter. It was Sholes's 1869 invention that F. Remington and Sons purchased and began mass producing in 1875. What a shock it must have been to many office workers in the late 1800s to share a desk with a noisy machine that dramatically changed virtually all their work procedures. No doubt there was resistance to this drastic change even though printed documents could be turned out at least three times faster than handwritten ones. In addition, typewritten documents were much easier to read. Nothing could stop the typewriter from becoming an indispensable office tool.

Typewriters gradually became faster and less bulky. By 1900, inventors and manufacturers had agreed on a standard arrangement of three rows of letters and a top row of numbers. This **standardization** permitted trained typists to move from one office to another, easily transferring their skills to any kind of typewriter. (**Standardization of equipment** is the process by which manufacturers agree on a basic design for a specific piece of equipment.)

In 1964, when IBM introduced the Magnetic Tape Selectric Typewriter (MT/ST), the term **word processing** also was introduced. The MT/ST recorded keystrokes on magnetic tape. Corrections and changes were made by overstriking—the same principle you use when you record music and voice on a tape recorder. Who would have guessed that Sholes's typewriter would lead to word processors and electronic typewriters, to high-speed equipment for scanning, duplicating, printing, and copying, let alone to the powerful computers of today?

The Telephone and Its Impact

Can you imagine how people communicated before Alexander Graham Bell's invention of the telephone in 1876? The invention of the telegraph in 1836 by Samuel Morse allowed people to communicate with Morse code, which was much faster than word of mouth or writing a letter. But even with telegraph lines connecting every part of the United States and extending across the Atlantic by 1866, the telegraph was not practical for offices and homes. In the 40 years prior to the invention of the telephone, only a limited number of people used the telegraph.

Telephones of yesterday and today.

Since its development in the 1880s, the telephone has evolved into one of the most important pieces of office (and home) equipment. For example, it can be used as a one-to-one, person-to-person, or station-to-station link. Conference calls can be made easily using switchboards and other technology that link several parties or offices. On many phones, merely pressing one digit can instantly connect you with a person or office whose number you frequently dial. You can also speak by phone to people who are traveling by car, train, airplane, or walking on the street if they have the proper kind of phone receiver.

Many executives use the telephone to dictate to secretaries, who are free to transcribe the information at a later, more convenient time. Businesses communicate both written and graphic information over telephone lines.

The telephone has played an important role in the development of a variety of equipment (including facsimile) and carrier services available today. For example, the deregulation of the telephone industry and the 1982 AT&T Modified Final Judgment allowed greater competition in the telecommunications long-distance market. Communications have expanded rapidly beyond telephone wires into systems utilizing networks of cables, satellites, microwaves, and fiber optics. Many of these technological advances and their effect on you are discussed in later chapters.

The Computer and Its Significance

To complete the census of 1880 took nearly the entire decade. In 1880, the census takers used handwritten data sheets to count and classify everyone living in the United States. The time required to complete the 1880 census caused the U.S. Bureau of Census to be concerned about taking the census in 1890 (with 13 million more people than ten years earlier). A mechanical solution to this problem was needed. Dr. Herman Hollerith, a statistician from Buffalo working at the bureau, provided a technical solution to this problem: a mechanical counting or tabulating machine. His invention read and sorted data from **punched cards** (a heavy card that can be punched with coded information). You can imagine the relief at the bureau when the 1890 census was completed in less than three years using Hollerith's tabulating machine.

Hollerith, however, is not credited with inventing the first computer; Charles Babbage is considered the father of computers. Prior to Hollerith's invention, several mathematicians had experimented with ways to solve complicated mathematical problems. One such English mathematician and professor, Charles Babbage, designed an analytical engine that used the **binary number system** (a number system based on zeroes and ones as compared to the ten-part decimal system). The concepts of his designs formed the beginning of the computing machine industry in 1871.

Today computers can process hundreds of times faster than when the first business computer was installed in 1954. They are now more compact and versatile and continue to decrease in price while their capabilities increase. In contrast to the large systems of the past, the microcomputer-based networked system of today can fit on the corner of your desk at home. Such a system can analyze, compute, communicate, and transmit at speeds that surpass all comprehension. These developments will be explored later in this text. The following is a brief history of the computer and related developments:

1836 Telegraph—invented by Samuel Morse

1869 Typewriter—invented by C. L. Sholes

1842 Facsimile—crude machine developed by Alexander Bain

1876 Telephone—invented by Alexander Graham Bell

1888 Dictating machine—developed by Bell and others

1889 Strowger switch—automatic telephone dial and connect

1913 Triode vacuum tube—developed by Lee De Forest

1937 Electrophotographic process—first copy of a document, made by Chester Carlson

1946 ENIAC (Electronic Numerical Integrator and Computer)—an 18,000 vacuum tube system needing 1500 square feet

1947 Transistor—developed by Bell Laboratories

1951 UNIVAC (Universal Automatic Computer)—first large-scale commercial computer

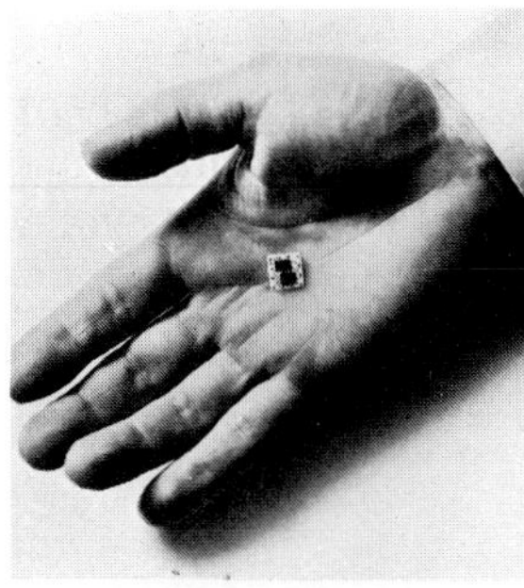

Tiny silicon chips used in today's computers enable them to outperform the huge computers of the past, such as ENIAC.

ENIAC (Electronic Numerical Integrator and Computer), the earliest electronic digital computer, filled an entire room.

1957 FORTRAN—first high-level programming language released; developed by IBM employee John Backus and others

1958 Integrated circuit (IC)—the silicon chip developed by Jack Kilby at Texas Instruments

1960 Dry-print office copier—first plain-paper copier introduced by Xerox

1962 Telstar—first international communications satellite placed in orbit

The first wrist computer, developed in 1984, included a wristwatch and a unit for programming and printing.

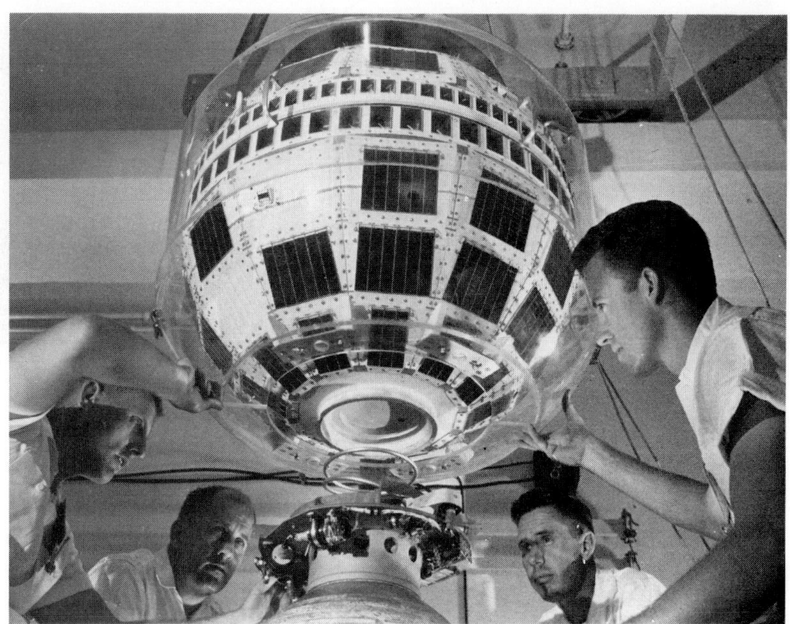

Telstar, the first international communications satellite.

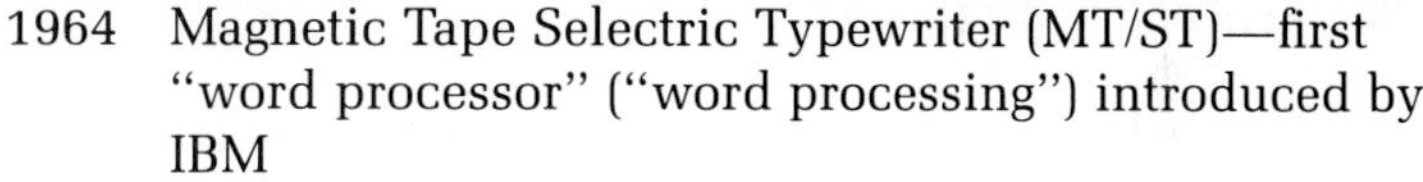

1964 Magnetic Tape Selectric Typewriter (MT/ST)—first "word processor" ("word processing") introduced by IBM

1970 Optical fiber—developed by Corning Glass Works for long-range communications

1971 Microprocessor—a CPU on a silicon chip developed by Ted Hoff at Intel Corp.

1974 Altair 8800—first microcomputer (marketed in a kit)

1976 Apple Computers—started by Steven Jobs and Stephen Wozniak; popularized educational computing

1977 Microcomputer mass marketing—by Radio Shack (Tandy Corp.), Commodore, and Apple Computers

1980 Cray-1—first supercomputer developed by Seymour Cray

1984 Seiko DATA 2000—first wrist computer

1985 Canon NP-9030—first digital copier

1987 Desktop publishing (DTP)—and several software tools to use with PageMaker and Ventura software

1988 Self-service, credit card-accessed facsimile—developed by the FAXplus Corp.

1989 Pacific link—first fiber-optic link between the United States and Japan

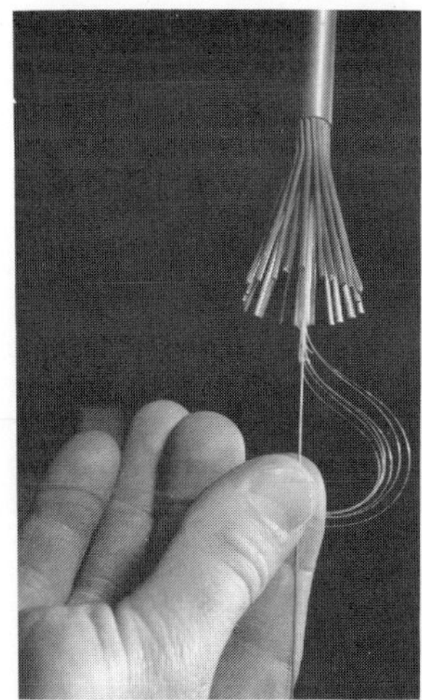

Optical fibers have made possible the first fiber-optic telecommunications link between the United States and Japan.

The design of this portable computer makes it easy to carry and use almost anywhere it is needed.

Desktop publishing software, introduced in 1987, can be used to produce documents that combine text and graphics, as shown in this real estate ad.

The Automated Office

Working in an office today involves performing essentially the same kinds of office tasks performed in the past. However, **electronic** or **automated equipment** permits you to streamline the flow of work and provides a greater choice of ways to do it. This is why we refer to the modern office as the **automated** or **electronic office.** In such an environment, **automation** (a system of production with "self-acting," or automatic machines) utilizes new technologies to make office work fast, efficient, and accurate.

Many automated machines have several things in common even though many manufacturers, or **vendors**, have added their own technological improvements to stay competitive. For example, computers, **microcomputers** (small-sized computers), and similar machines have a **central processing unit (CPU)**—the "brains" of the operation—that allows certain production steps to take place. Sets of instructions **(software programs)** are vital to computer operation and can be stored in a computer. Vendors have created a wide range of software programs (instructions that computers read to allow them to perform a variety of automated operations) that also can be stored in a computer.

New equipment is displayed at trade fairs.

Disk storage has made it possible to keep many documents in a small space—considerably less space than a filing cabinet requires. In addition to the flexible plastic **magnetic disk** (sometimes called a **floppy diskette**), a variety of other storage media (such as hard disks and laser disks) have become popular.

An equally important innovation standard to most computers is a **video display terminal (VDT)**. A VDT is sometimes referred to as a visual display or video screen. The VDT is similar to a TV screen on which copy (frequently referred to as **soft copy**) is displayed on the screen as you key text. Early video displays had a special **cathode-ray tube (CRT)** that was designed to show clear, readable text. More recent VDT developments include the light-emitting diode (LED), liquid crystal display (LCD), gas plasma, vacuum fluorescent, and electroluminescent screens or displays.

An Information System

An **information system** is a combination of all the separate and interrelated elements of doing business that make an organization operate effectively. That is, an information system should result from connecting and integrating all the components of a business operation. This usually involves people using **standardized procedures** (doing things in the same way) to share resources, technology, and information. A common goal is to work together in a productive way so that management and operations are effective.

An information system is only as strong as "the weakest link in the chain"—that is, it is only as effective as the combination of technology, people, procedures, and related elements that make up the system. Thus, for efficient management of information, all the elements of the system must be strong. Each of these elements and how **office automation** helps you become a more efficient and productive office employee are explored throughout this text.

Information Defined

Information in an office environment consists of facts arranged in an orderly and useful form so as to make them accurate, timely, complete, and concise. To create information, you start with facts that you classify or organize. Information can be categorized in several ways. You may wish to think of these categories as information "parts" that are often intertwined and essential for completing work in an automated office environment:

Data—information in numeric form that usually can be calculated by a computer

Words (text)—information in text form (mainly words and numbers) that can be arranged in various ways, usually using an electronic typewriter, word processor, or computer

Graphics—information in the form of data and words that is keyed into a computer and displayed on a screen in a graph, chart, table, or other visual form that makes the information easy to comprehend

An information network enables people to use and manage different types of information efficiently.

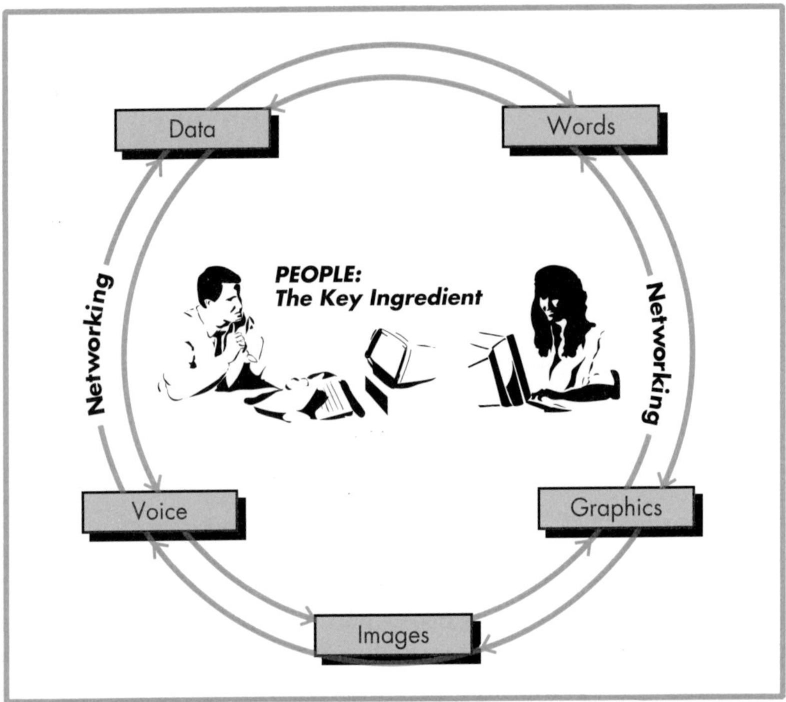

Images—information in the form of pictures or photographs that is entered into the computer and shown on the screen (many times in an enhanced form)

Voice—information in the form of the spoken word that is changed into written form

Information (data, words/text, graphics, images, and voice) is of little value unless it can be communicated and used by people. For this to happen, it must be closely associated with two additional elements:

People—human decision makers who, with the assistance of electronic equipment, communicate and distribute information

Networking—linking computers and other office equipment together electronically for communicating and transmitting information

The value of information depends partly on how easily and quickly it can be communicated. An information network that helps people and machines communicate and interact in a timely manner further expands the possibilities for using and managing information. Networking is a common way to share resources for maximum cost-effectiveness and nonduplication of effort.

Thus, technology is useful only if it can be applied and used to help people. Helping people make good decisions and be more productive are major goals of office automation within an information system. Whatever equipment a company uses or whatever information it processes and communicates, the key ingredient of a business is people. People make decisions. The most effective decisions are those based on accurate and complete information.

The Information Processing Cycle

You have learned that an information system refers to the way an office functions to handle information for the efficient operation of the business. It is the sum of all the interrelated and interconnected parts (or subsystems) that help a business operate smoothly. For the parts to interact in a meaningful way, they must be properly processed. Thus, a key function of any organization is processing information.

Information Processing Defined

Information processing involves coordinating people, equipment, and procedures for organizing information in a meaningful way within an information system. Information processing is a vital subsystem of an information system. Its purpose is to make sure that essential information is received by office workers, managers, and customers who require it to make informed decisions.

Information Processing and Word Processing

Information processing has become a common term referring to the automated processing of all the various categories of information (data, words/text, graphics, images, and voice). Because the categories of information are becoming less separate and distinct, *word processing* no longer means the same thing as when it was first introduced. Words/text still have a major role in information processing, but terms such as *word processing, text processing*, and even *word/information processing* are giving way to *information processing*. This term is widely accepted today because it encompasses the work flow of an office. You will see how broad and important information processing is as you continue through this book. Also, *data* is used more and more frequently to refer to facts and words/text rather than only to numbers. Thus, **data processing** also may be included under the "information processing" umbrella. Many of these changes are due simply to changing times.

Stages in the Information Processing Cycle

The **information processing cycle** consists of several steps completed during five important phases or stages. These steps occur and recur frequently in processing the types of information typi-

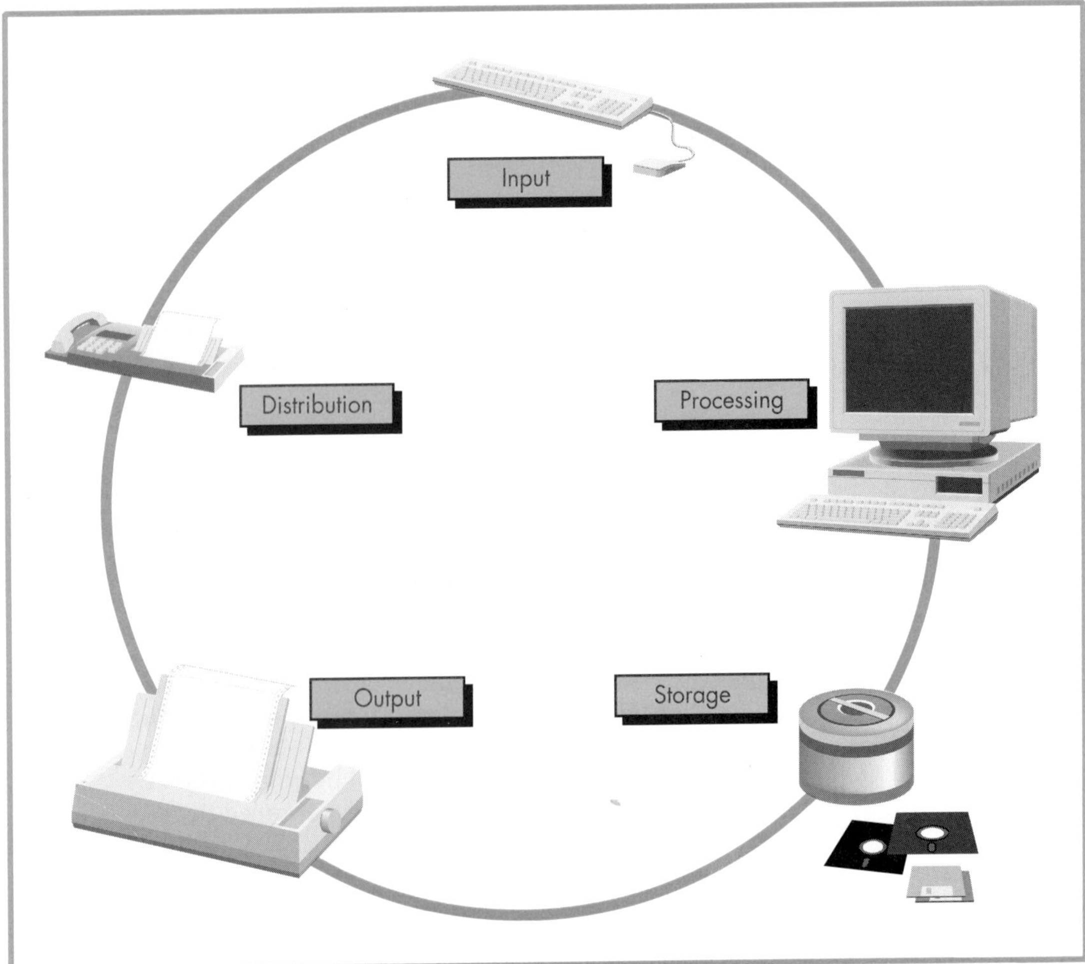

The information processing cycle has five stages: input, processing, storage, output, and distribution.

cally found in offices, such as letters and memos. The five stages of the information processing cycle are

1. Input
2. Processing
3. Storage
4. Output
5. Distribution

Note that storage is an important part of the cycle as you input, output, and distribute information. You can store and retrieve information at any time in the cycle. The effectiveness of these stages depends on people, equipment, and procedures. Good communication is essential for the cycle to work efficiently. Let's take a closer look at this cycle by following a specific example through each of the information processing stages.

Input Grady Washington, an underwriting agent at the Mutual Insurance Company, receives an application for a life insurance policy from May Lew. The application is a printed form Ms. Lew has filled out.

To the Mutual Insurance Company, this application is a form of **input**. Input, one stage of the information processing cycle, consists of facts or data entered into a system for processing. Input can come from several sources that originate either outside or within the office. Input can also come in several forms: **numeric** data, such as Ms. Lew's age and date of birth (for instance, "10/6/70" for October 6, 1970); **alphabetic** data, such as F for "female" and S for "single"; and **alphanumeric** data, such as Ms. Lew's address.

Input might also be in the form of **graphics**, such as charts and graphs. An electronics company, for example, might have input in the form of bar charts showing industrywide sales in such areas as watches and video cassette recorders (VCRs).

A large percentage of the paper input received in an office is in the form of **images**—photocopies, pictures, signatures, and logos. In the personnel department of a company, standard personnel data includes photocopies of resumés, acceptance letters, letters of recommendation, and contract agreements.

Still another kind of input is **voice**. This might be in the form of a telephone call from a client placing an order for a product, dictation for a letter, a recording of a business meeting, or a voice message left on a machine (voice mail).

Thus, the input stage in the information processing cycle can consist of almost any data that comes into or originates in the office. Depending on the type of input, it will be processed manually or with the help of electronic equipment. **Keyboarding** (pressing keys on a keyboard) is a popular a way of inputting facts. Scanning devices, such as **OCRs (optical character recognition** equipment), frequently are used to input and record a document into the computer's storage unit.

Processing Another stage of the information processing cycle is **processing**. In this stage, input is organized to become information. Processing makes it possible for information to be sorted, classified, edited, distributed, or stored. Sales reports, for example, may be sorted by geographic region and further classified according to the type of product sold. Mathematical calculations or other logical processes may be performed. Information may be summarized, checked, and so on.

Machines play an important role in the processing stage of the information processing cycle. The kind of processing will depend on the input. In most cases, you can manipulate the soft copy on the screen as much as you want—changing, deleting, rearranging, and inserting new text—until it is exactly the way you want it and arranged in appropriate **format** or style (page setup, including margins, indentions, line spacing). When the document is correct, you can use a few keystrokes to store it indefinitely on disk or print a **hard copy** (paper copy) of it. Few changes have been made in basic editing (the "cut and paste" concept) since the early days, except that programs have become easier to use, are more powerful, and have many more options for nearly every application.

In the processing stage, Mr. Washington goes over Ms. Lew's application, verifies the facts or data, and applies certain prescribed rules that Mutual has for processing insurance policies.

In processing Ms. Lew's application, Mr. Washington will need to determine whether she has previously applied for an insurance policy from Mutual. Then he can use his microcomputer to calculate how much risk Mutual will take if it insures someone of Ms. Lew's age, medical history, and occupation.

At this point, Mr. Washington will have a formal policy prepared for Ms. Lew. Assembling the information of Ms. Lew's policy is a job for automated equipment. An insurance policy consists of paragraphs of text that state what the insurance company will do under specified circumstances. Many of these paragraphs are the same from policy to policy. These paragraphs can be stored on disk in Mr. Washington's microcomputer, retrieved easily, and inserted into a policy for a specific person.

Storage Another stage of the information processing cycle, **storage** is extremely important when information is to be accessed later. The storage stage includes all records of management activities in an office, such as storing, retrieving, maintaining, and even destroying files.

If you worked in the Records Department of Mutual Insurance Company, you would have the copy of Ms. Lew's policy to put in the file for new or pending policyholders. Depending on the kind of equipment Mutual has, you might file a paper copy of the policy, such as a photocopy, or you might keep a copy on some kind of magnetic medium.

Output Once the policy has been assembled, it enters another stage of the information processing cycle known as **output**. At the output stage, a readable form of copy is produced. This copy may be keyed (typed) or produced on a printer attached to the word processing equipment. In some offices, this stage includes pro-

Office Automation

Office automation encompasses six major technologies: data processing, word processing, graphics, image, voice, and networking. These technologies are illustrated here.

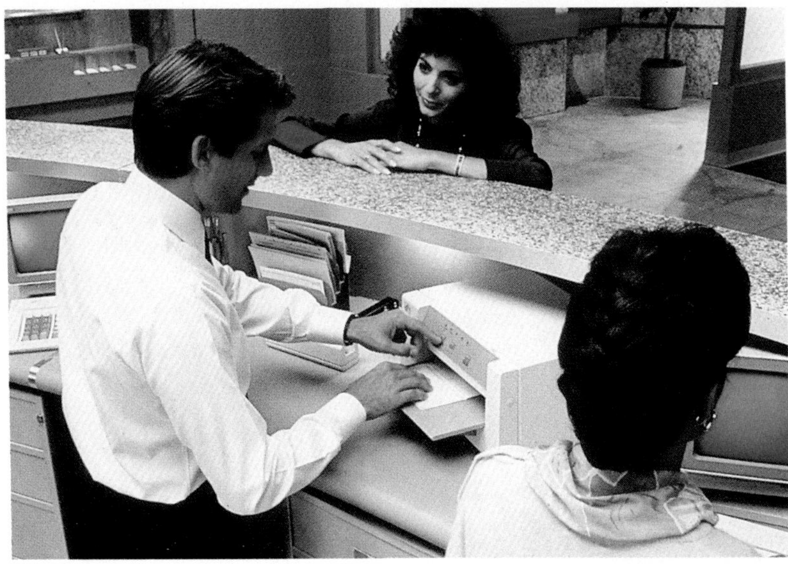

Automated equipment for data processing increases the efficiency of many business operations.

Word processing equipment and software are important features in today's office environment.

Using graphics is often an effective way to convey information.

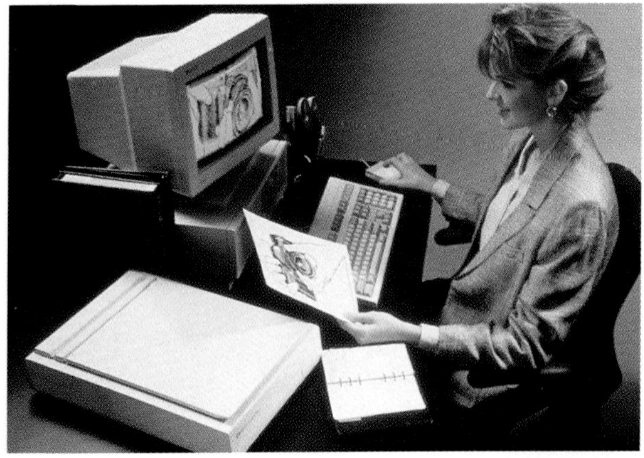

A scanner can reproduce images for use in word processing and desktop publishing applications.

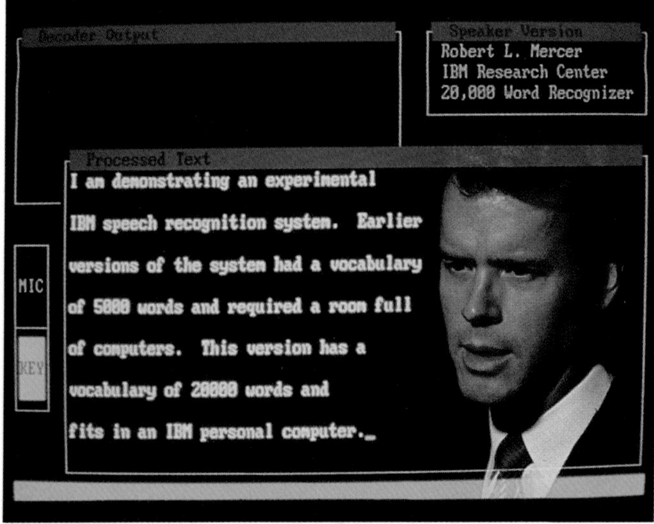
Decoder Output
Speaker Version
Robert L. Mercer
IBM Research Center
20,000 Word Recognizer
Processed Text
I am demonstrating an experimental
IBM speech recognition system. Earlier
versions of the system had a vocabulary
of 5000 words and required a room full
of computers. This version has a
vocabulary of 20000 words and
fits in an IBM personal computer._
MIC
KEY

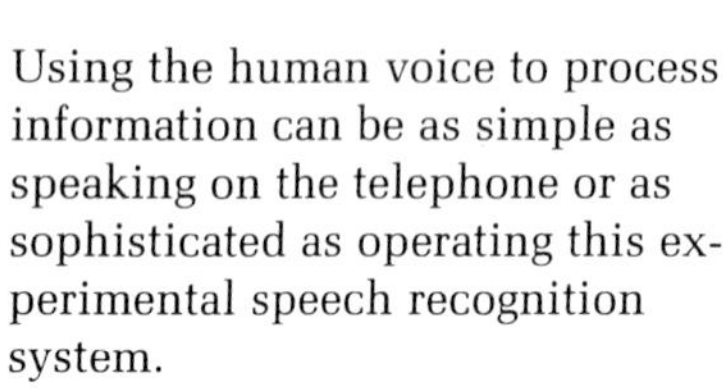

Using the human voice to process information can be as simple as speaking on the telephone or as sophisticated as operating this experimental speech recognition system.

Networking—linking computers and other office machines used for processing information—expands the possibilities for managing information efficiently.

A modem links the computer in this department store (above) to other computers in the store's headquarters (below).

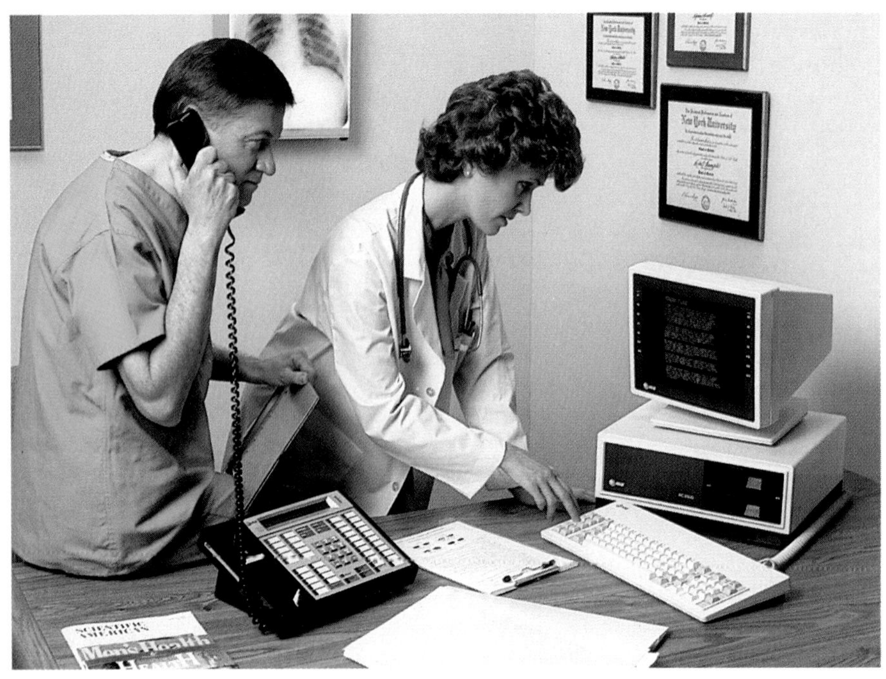

Through networking, the people and equipment in this medical office (above) can communicate and interact with people and equipment in this laboratory (below).

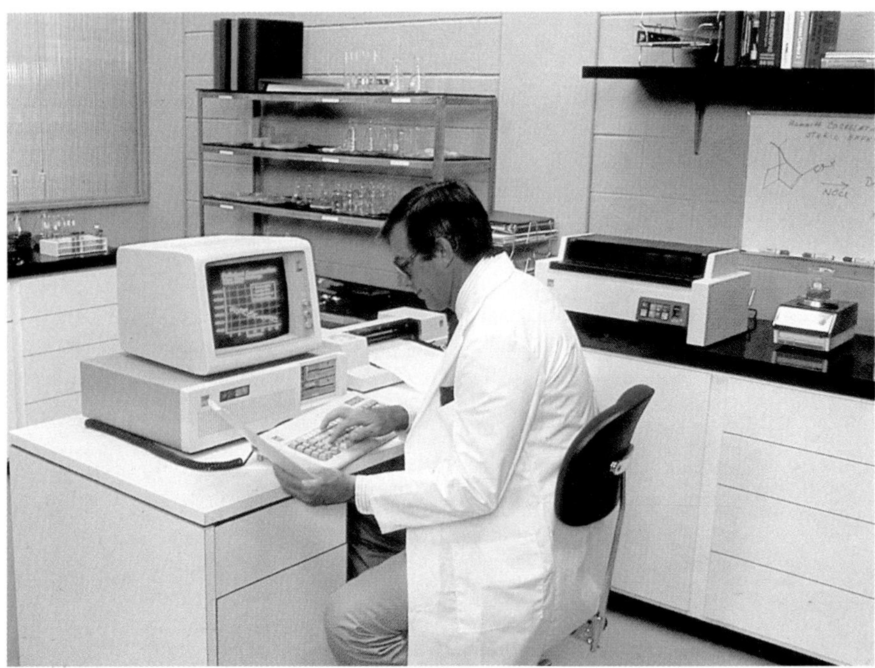

ducing **microforms** (making smaller or **miniaturizing** the output), typesetting, or printing documents.

Output also includes making multiple copies, although sometimes the only output is a corrected, keyed copy with a carbon. The number of copies and the method of reproduction **(reprographics)** depends on how many people must receive the information, what kinds of duplication or copying equipment the office has, and the cost of reproducing the information.

In the case of Ms. Lew's insurance policy, four copies will be made—two for Ms. Lew (one of which she will sign and return), one for Mutual's Records Department, and one for Mr. Washington's files. These copies will be produced on a carbon pack policy form consisting of five reprinted forms (one original and four copies), interleaved with carbon paper and bound at the top and perforated. The operator inserts the carbon pack into the **printer** (a machine that produces a hard copy), keys in the command to print, and the information pertaining to Ms. Lew's policy is printed in the appropriate places on the policy form. When the entire form has been printed, the operator removes the carbon pack from the printer, tears it along the perforated line at the top, and removes the carbon paper. The copies are then ready for distribution.

Distribution Another stage of the information processing cycle usually is **distribution.** The purpose of distribution is to make sure the information is communicated to the people who need it. Before automated equipment was available, distribution usually consisted of giving people their copies by interoffice mail, messenger service, or the postal system. Today you can distribute information in several different ways, depending on the format (the way information in a document is organized) that is needed and where the recipients are located. Ms. Lew's policy will probably be sent to the Records Department of Mutual Insurance Company by interoffice mail to be **microfilmed** (photographically making and recording a smaller image of the document on film) for Mutual's **archives** (permanent file). Ms. Lew's copy will be sent to her via the U.S. Postal Service.

In some offices, this stage may involve sending or **transmitting** the document to another location. Because Ms. Lew's policy includes her signature, an exact reproduction of the document may need to be sent. If time is a factor, the policy may be transmitted by **facsimile** (**fax** is a fast way to electronically send an exact copy of a hard copy) or even by one of several express mail or air services. You will learn more about these transmission methods, as well as their advantages and disadvantages, later in this text.

Now you have followed a document through the five main stages of the information processing cycle. The document followed an established and commonly recurring path. The term **work flow** refers to this path from the start to the finish of a task. Beginning with Ms. Lew's application form, you observed the logical flow of information from input to processing to storage to output to distribution.

Because these stages are constantly being repeated in the office and what is stored may be retrieved and reprocessed at any stage, the whole operation must be viewed as a cycle. Also, keep in mind that some documents return to one or more of the stages during their lifetime or even bypass one of the stages as they are revised, printed, stored, retrieved, distributed, and communicated. In each of these stages some processing must occur, and cycle effectiveness depends on communication and networking of people, equipment, and procedures.

Keeping Paperwork Under Control

Business success depends largely on how efficiently a firm manages the information that is important to it. As the amount of information increases, businesses occasionally find themselves searching for ways to keep paperwork under control. Business offices in the United States create, print, and store a staggering amount of information on paper every day. It has been estimated that for the average office worker, 30 to 40 pages of computer printout are produced, 20 to 30 photocopies are made, and 15 to 30 pieces of paper are filed every business day. This adds up to about 300 trillion computer printouts and 225 trillion photocopies made every year by office workers. And these figures do not include printing, retrieving, or refiling office documents. Yet these and other office tasks continue to increase. With an estimated 200 trillion documents being filed each year (enough paper to wrap around the entire earth about two dozen times), it is difficult to take seriously the suggestion that computer storage will make file cabinets obsolete in a few years.

The growing amount of information we handle is, in large part, the result of the capability of machines to create and process it. Studies have shown that the amount of time spent on each business operation 30 to 40 years ago has been reduced today by about 1000 percent, mainly because of the use of computers. Yet the number of white-collar office workers has grown significantly—from about 17 percent of the work force in 1900 to about 55 percent in the mid-1980s. According to the United States Bureau of Labor Statistics, about half of our service-oriented labor force is and will continue to be office workers. What is vital to understand is that the management of information does and will continue to depend on people—people who operate the computer equipment and people who use information to make essential decisions.

Managing Information and Change

As new and improved equipment continues to appear in offices, you may pause and wonder why. Why continue creating new ways to do things? What is wrong with the old and tried methods of doing business? These are the same questions many clerks and stenographers asked in the late 1800s, when typewriters were introduced to offices. Why, people asked, use typewriters when things are going along very well as they are? To answer these questions, it is necessary to look first at some of the problems facing business offices.

The ever-increasing needs of business for specialized ways of handling information demand even greater efficiency in office work. Businesses must have timely information to perform effectively. In the past, economic growth was based largely on industry and manufacturing. Now growth is coming from businesses that sell services rather than goods. Some of these businesses sell information directly to their customers; others use information to provide some other service more efficiently. Whatever service a company provides, its success depends on how well it manages information. For this reason, people will continue to be needed to do office work.

Even if you have never worked in an office yourself, you probably know someone who has. You know that most offices have a similar look to them: There are desks, chairs, telephones, and at least one typewriter or computer. But what do you know about the work all offices have in common?

Regardless of size, all business offices manage information of one kind or another. You have learned from reading about the stages in the information processing cycle that this usually involves originating, processing, storing, reproducing, and filing information. It also involves communicating and distributing information to people who need or want it.

That all business offices manage information is a fairly broad statement. An example of how businesses create and process information can help you understand the importance of this statement. Assume that you want to take a vacation trip. You might have some idea about where you want to go and how to get there. You send for travel brochures, maps, airline schedules, and rates. You get a list of hotels. You listen to weather forecasts. You figure out how much you have to spend. So far these items are separate, unrelated facts. It is up to you to organize them and give them some meaning. You have to convert the facts (process them) to information you can use to make an informed decision.

You might separate places at the seashore from those in the mountains, warm places from cold, or places you can drive to from those so far away you have to fly. Once you have sorted your facts, you probably will find that making a decision is easy. If you were a travel agent, your customers would pay you to do this for them. Part of your business activities as a travel agent would be managing travel information. Thus, in the business world, information is created and processed in ways so that it can be used by both employees and clients.

Productivity in an Information System

In the office, **productivity** refers to output per employee. A productive office is one in which people produce accurate, timely, concise, and complete information of a particular type in an appropriate form at the lowest possible cost and make it available to those who need it.

Productivity is greatly affected by the kinds of equipment and methods available to help employees accomplish their work. For this reason, managers look to automation as a way of increasing office productivity. Already you have seen examples of how machines can speed the processing of information. An inexpensive hand-held calculator can quickly perform calculations that would take a person using a paper and pencil much longer to complete; a computer can handle the work of an army of office clerks with astonishing speed.

As electronic equipment and automated methods make performing routine tasks easier and faster, office workers will take on more challenging and creative work that requires problem solving and decision making. This has important implications for your career. As an office worker today, you might use a typewriter only rarely. You will more likely use an electronic typewriter, word processor, microcomputer, or personal workstation for correspondence. This equipment will enable you to quickly key and revise a document. This will give you time for administrative responsibilities that no machine could do (interesting projects and tasks such as organizing meetings for your boss and correlating information from other departments).

The new equipment also has changed life in the office for many executives. A national sales director who used to spend endless hours creating a budget using a pencil, paper, and a calculator can now do the same thing faster and more simply on a desktop computer. The manager can key the numbers for the budget. After he or she enters the appropriate commands by depressing a few keys, the computer makes the calculations and instantly displays the results on the screen. With a few more keystrokes, the manager can send the results to others on the sales force—electronically. Data can be transferred from one computer to another without creating a paper document if the computers are networked in the proper manner. This gives the director opportunities to meet personally with members of the sales force and use critical thinking skills in developing marketing techniques for the company's products.

The Changing Office Environment

Office equipment has changed so much since the mid-nineteenth century that it has transformed the office environment. Offices are not the static workplaces they once were. Today's office is an exciting, changing place. Manufacturers now offer businesses such a wide array of equipment that you are bound to find differences from one office to the next. If you work in the same office for any length of time, you are almost certain to see continual changes in the systems you use and probably in your style of working, too. You might one day find that the job you have will permit you to do some of your work at home instead of in the office. For example, you may be able to write reports, process correspondence, and develop other communications at home.

New equipment has also changed office design, stimulating a concern for the relationship of employees to their working environment. New kinds of office equipment require new kinds of office furniture, different space needs, and new ways of organizing space so that the work can be done efficiently and comfortably. Office planners are carefully considering lighting, work area arrangement, machine location, and air quality in an effort to improve the interaction of people and their work environment. These and other environmental factors are discussed in Chapter 10.

In general, executives have begun to pay more attention to the office as an environment to be managed. They view it as a place where people, equipment, functions, and appropriate procedures can be organized to produce accurate, timely, complete, and concise information at low cost. They view it as an interconnected network of several components that must function effectively—an information system.

The Focus on People

The most vital role in an information system is played by the people who originate information and handle it as it goes through the stages of the information processing cycle. Although up-to-date equipment plays an important role in the information processing cycle, it is only a helping role. The office workers—knowledge workers who are information specialists—are the ones who de-

People play the most vital role in information systems.

cide the best way to arrange the information, the best way to have copies made, the best way to distribute information to the people who need it, and the best way to store it so it can be retrieved when needed.

In making these decisions, office workers must be aware of the need for productivity. They must understand how to carry out tasks in the most efficient and profitable way, regardless of the kind of equipment available. "Good people," as one writer put it, "are your most valuable resource." The new ideas they pump into an organization are its lifeblood. Their ability to put concepts to work is the substance of its success.

This book is designed to help you become one of those "good people"—to make you familiar with the concepts and applications associated with the processing of information within an information system. The more fully you understand the new and changing office environment, the better you will be at your job.

CHAPTER SUMMARY

- Everyone is affected by the rapidly increasing amount of information.
- Office workers must become knowledge workers, or information specialists, who can use the many components of technology.
- Many inventions and developments, including the typewriter, telephone, and computer, have radically changed the nature of office work.
- Office automation utilizes electronic equipment and new technologies to make office work faster and more efficient.
- An information system is made up of the components of a business that make it operate effectively.
- Information is most useful when it is accurate, timely, concise, and complete.

- Information processing, a vital part of an information system, involves organizing and managing information by using the combined efforts of people, equipment, and procedures.
- Word processing, text processing, and word/information processing are commonly referred to as information processing.
- The information processing cycle has five stages: input, processing, storage, output, and distribution.
- Information that has been processed and has reached the storage stage can be recycled to become an element in the creation of new information.
- The success of any business depends in large part on its ability to manage the information essential for decision making.
- A productive office is one in which people produce useful information in an appropriate form and at the lowest possible cost and make it available to those who need it.
- People are the most important element in an information system.

VOCABULARY

automation
data
data processing
distribution
format
information
information processing
information system
input
keyboarding
knowledge workers
microcomputer
miniaturizing
networking
office automation
output
processing
productivity
soft copy
software
standardization
storage
video display terminal (VDT)
word or text processing
work flow

CHAPTER QUESTIONS

1. With information growing rapidly and many people, especially white-collar workers, becoming information specialists, what suggestions do you have for preparing for an office career?
2. Think about some of the ways information and technology affect your daily life. How might your life be different without so much information and modern technology?
3. A complaint often heard about machines is that they put many people out of work. Since 1875, many work-saving machines have been introduced into offices; yet the number of workers has continued to increase. How do you explain this?
4. What were some of the advantages that machines brought to office work in the late 1800s and early 1900s?

5. Why might office workers be reluctant to welcome automated office machines? What advice would you give them?
6. Beginning in the 1870s, standardization became more and more important in offices. What advantages did it offer? Is standardization important today?
7. Why is productivity so necessary in the modern office? What are some of the factors that affect productivity?
8. Discuss the relationships between and among (1) data, (2) words/text, (3) graphics, (4) images, and (5) voice.
9. Automated equipment is important in today's offices, but people are even more important. Why is the physical and psychological well-being of workers important to office managers today?
10. How does the flow of information into and out of an office resemble a cycle?

CASE STUDY

Bradford Associates is a small company that develops advertising for department stores, hardware stores, and card shops. Its staff consists of a president, an account executive (who functions the way a sales representative does), a secretary, and a copywriter. The office has two electric typewriters and a small photocopier.

The president and the account executive spend much of their time outside the office, meeting with current and potential clients. After these meetings, they call the secretary and dictate correspondence, such as follow-up letters. The secretary often has to interrupt other work to take their calls, writing the information they give in shorthand. The secretary also performs administrative and recordkeeping duties for the company and draws up and keys contracts for new business. Each contract has many paragraphs, some of which are repeated from contract to contract.

Every new ad campaign begins with a meeting of the president, the account executive, and the copywriter. The secretary keys the new advertising copy, which may go through several drafts before it is mailed to the client. Copies are made and filed of all contracts, correspondence, and advertising copy.

Based on your understanding of the information processing cycle, identify the sources of information input and information output for Bradford Associates.

CHAPTER 2

Documents and Information Processing

Russell Harris reaches into his in-basket and pulls out two interoffice memos and two letters. As he expects, both memos relate to upcoming meetings. Mr. Harris knows that his secretary already has entered the meeting information into his computer calendar and message system. Turning his attention to the first letter, Mr. Harris sees that it is a short letter from a customer requesting information. He makes a few notes on the letter for his secretary to use in composing an answer to the customer. The second letter has a ten-page legal agreement attached to it. Mr. Harris realizes he does not have time to give the letter and agreement his attention until later. He sets these documents aside, picks up a file from his desk, and leaves his office for a sales meeting.

All businesses depend on information to operate. Office employees deal with a variety of communications daily—letters, memos, forms, reports, and so on. Those that convey information are called ***documents****. Some documents are simple and brief, and some are as complex as the lengthy legal agreement Mr. Harris will have to examine later.*

Efficient Information Management

Many kinds of written and oral communication are used in offices throughout the country, regardless of the size or nature of the business. Today's office must be an information management center where speed, efficiency, and accuracy are essential. The more quickly and efficiently a business can process, distribute, and act on incoming information, the more successful it is likely to be.

Consider, for example, the use of marketing information in product development and sales. Twist and Quest are two soft drink producers in direct competition. Both conduct periodic marketing surveys to learn more about consumer preferences. Twist's information system is far more efficient than Quest's, however. Survey information is channeled immediately into Twist's information system when it comes into the Marketing Department. The survey findings are handled and processed by secretaries using computer equipment. When Quest receives survey information, the documents are piled on top of a file cabinet until someone can get around to acting on them. At Quest, a team of people usually works together to tabulate the findings by hand.

At Twist, the printing of the survey findings is computerized; Quest uses hand-fed copying machines to process the information. Twist is able to compile and print its survey findings faster and more accurately than its competitor, which enables Twist's management to act quickly on this information. As a result of its greater efficiency, Twist discovered two months earlier than Quest that consumers do not want caffeine in their drinks. When Twist's first television and print ads appeared nationwide, Quest managers were only beginning to debate whether they should develop a way to produce their products without caffeine. By managing information more efficiently than its competitor, Twist is able to make decisions in a timely manner. This has allowed the company to increase its sales and profits.

Kinds of Business Documents

Documents are sometimes distinguished from simple correspondence by their greater length and complexity. In this book, however, a document is any business communication that contains information.

Documents can be divided into categories: letters, memos, reports, statistical tables, forms, envelopes, and labels. Letters and memos are the most common kinds of business documents. Sometimes these categories overlap. For example, a statistical table can appear within a memo or a report.

Letters

Business letters serve many purposes in the modern office. Depending on the nature of the firm, letters may be sent to customers and clients, suppliers, manufacturers, government agencies, contractors, other organizations and companies, or individuals. Some letters are intended to obtain information, others to provide it. Letters serve different purposes. They may express gratitude for or dissatisfaction with services rendered. They may urge customers to pay their bills. They may be written to generate new business or to "stay in touch" with customers and other companies. Sometimes a brief letter serves as a cover letter to accompany longer documents.

Nearly 75 percent of all business letters are only one page long, but some are two to three pages or even longer. The author of a letter may create a document by dictating it to a secretary skilled in shorthand, by writing it in longhand, by composing it at a keyboard (typewriter or computer), or by dictating it into a machine. In general, preparing a letter requires relatively few revisions, usually only minor wording changes or corrections.

Memos

Like a letter, a memo (memorandum) serves various purposes in an office. Letters are generally directed to people or organizations outside the company; memos normally are used for communication within a company. Interoffice memos may be sent from one floor to another, one office to another, or one branch of a company to another.

Memos usually are prepared in the same way as a letter. In many cases, they are shorter and less formal than letters, although this is not always true. Memos may announce a meeting, request information, confirm a decision, or announce a policy change. The amount of revision involved in preparing a memo usually is minor. Many companies use printed forms for memos, just as they use printed stationery for letters.

Reports

Many of the decisions made within a company are based on reports, which may be as short as a few pages or as long as 100 or more pages. They may be as technical as a pharmaceutical company's detailed analysis of a new drug or as simple as a sales representative's summary of a sales call.

Because the main purpose of reports is to present facts, accuracy is crucial. Reports also must be easily understood. Reports commonly go through several drafts to ensure both accuracy and clarity. In any of these drafts, the author may decide to revise content or language or even undertake a major reorganization. The longer and more complex the report, the more time usually is required to prepare a final copy.

The author of a report may dictate it to a secretary or into a machine, compose it at a keyboard, or write it in longhand. The author's own words are often combined with excerpts from other documents or sources. A government research report on urban crime, for example, might include a statistical table that appeared in a newspaper or magazine. A corporation's annual report to stockholders usually contains a chart showing the company's yearly figures and earnings growth.

A complex report may require considerable revision.

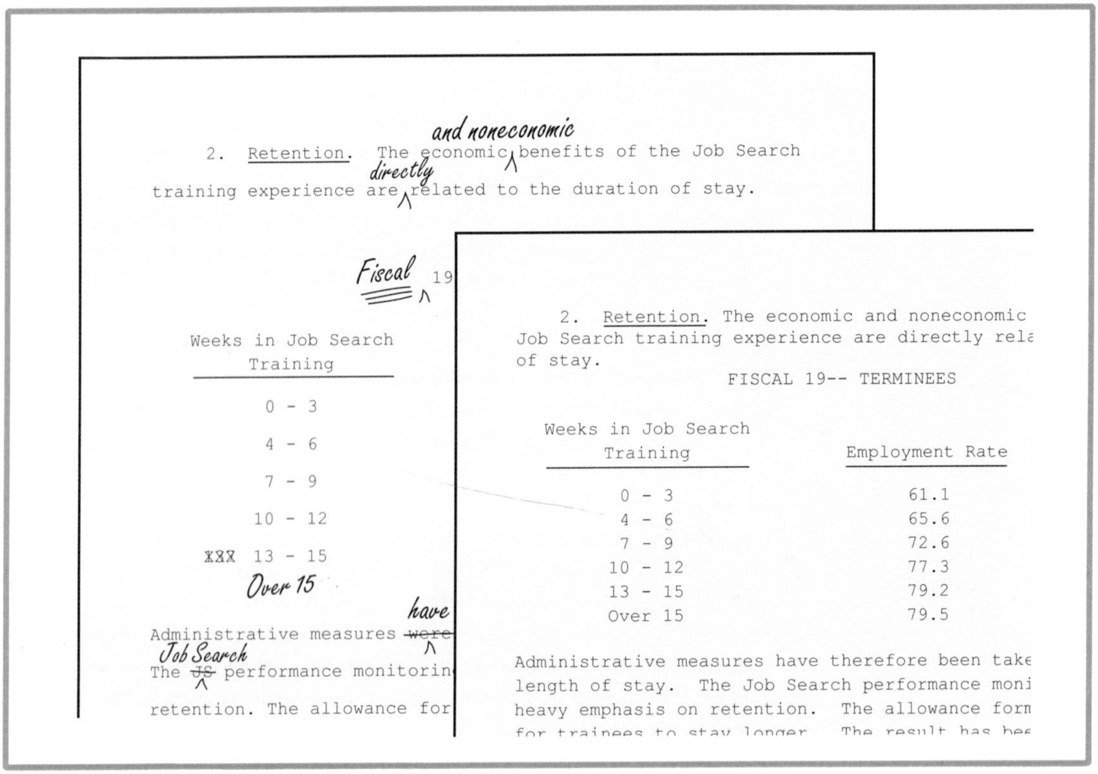

2. Retention. The economic [and noneconomic] benefits of the Job Search training experience are [directly] related to the duration of stay.

[Fiscal] 19

Weeks in Job Search Training

0 - 3

4 - 6

7 - 9

10 - 12

~~XXX~~ 13 - 15

[Over 15]

Administrative measures ~~were~~ [have]

The ~~JS~~ [Job Search] performance monitorin

retention. The allowance for

2. Retention. The economic and noneconomic Job Search training experience are directly rela of stay.

FISCAL 19-- TERMINEES

Weeks in Job Search Training	Employment Rate
0 - 3	61.1
4 - 6	65.6
7 - 9	72.6
10 - 12	77.3
13 - 15	79.2
Over 15	79.5

Administrative measures have therefore been take length of stay. The Job Search performance moni heavy emphasis on retention. The allowance form for trainees to stay longer. The result has bee

Statistical Tables

If you have ever had to key (type on a keyboard) a table with long columns of numbers, you know that the job can be difficult. Each statistical entry must be correctly placed on the page, decimals must be carefully aligned, and groups of figures must be precisely spaced.

Statistical tables are common in almost every field. Product sales reports, for example, show sales figures by region and date. Brokerage houses and other financial institutions compile statistics about stocks and bonds, earnings and dividends, interest and mortgage rates. Medical researchers prepare statistical reports on the results of laboratory experiments.

Some statistical documents are still prepared by hand, but computers have made it easier to create documents containing statistical copy. Computers can process and organize data many times faster than can be done by hand. The advantages of using computers to process and organize data have contributed to more and more authors using dictation and keyboarding to input and process data in producing statistical documents. Data entered into electronic equipment can be organized into tables merely by pressing a few keys. Although computerized equipment can help make some of those tasks easier, painstaking proofreading of statistical tables is still essential to ensure that the information in them is accurate.

Forms

Forms are part of everyone's daily life. You are probably familiar with application forms, insurance forms, bank forms, credit card forms, order forms, and tax forms. Sometimes it seems that almost everything people do these days requires a form. Indeed, in some offices, that is not too far from the truth because the paperwork handled by certain businesses consists mainly of forms.

Forms are most commonly used to standardize and simplify the processing of certain information. When filling out forms, accuracy and neatness are essential. Imagine, for example, the problems that can result when a purchase order processed by an agricultural machinery manufacturer is misinterpreted as calling for 100 tractors when 10 was the number actually intended.

Many forms are preprinted and packaged with carbon sheets or a carbon-backed paper. This kind of form allows users to make multiple copies while filling out the one on top. Many of these forms can be purchased in quantity from an office supply company; others must be specially created and printed for a particular business. Still other firms create their own forms by using a purchased software package with standard forms that appear on a computer screen and permit the operator to revise them to meet individual needs. The revised forms can be stored, printed, or photocopied for printing in large quantities.

Eagle Peak Mineral Water
999 Mountain Avenue
Santa Rosa, California 95401

INVOICE NO. 1099
Data November 13, 19--
Your No. 325
Terms 2/10, net 30

Sold To Gerry's General Store
454 Fourth Street
Santa Rosa, CA 95401

Ship To Same

Stock No.	Quantity	Description	Unit Price	Total
060-95	1	Case of 32oz. Mineral Water	$106.00	$106.00
		TOTAL		$106.00

Computer forms such as this one are standardized to simplify information processing.

Most businesses that use software packages of forms use them for completing the fill-ins on forms. In such cases, the form is stored in the computer. When it is shown on the screen, the operator fills in the form by keying the appropriate information in the right places on the form. The completed document is then printed. Many of the forms mentioned earlier have been produced this way. Forms used to simplify and standardize procedures must be carefully completed and proofread. A form is only as good as the information it contains.

Other Documents

Every office has a variety of other kinds of documents it must prepare. For example, envelopes must be addressed for distributing correspondence to customers. Accuracy is essential here because an incorrectly addressed letter will arrive late or not at all. For larger envelopes and packages, mailing labels must be prepared and attached.

Small index cards or file cards are another kind of document. Most libraries, for example, record the titles and authors of books on such cards. Many businesses keep a master card file of clients or specialized products or services. A reference book publisher may keep a card file of new technical terms and their meanings.

Envelopes, labels, and cards must all be carefully and neatly prepared. Alignment can be a problem with such documents, because smaller items tend to slip in a typewriter, and keying them may take longer than expected.

Computer technology has contributed to the ease of preparing most kinds of documents. Computer equipment also has many other advantages. Documents can be recorded and stored in a computer system. This permits quick and easy corrections and revisions without having to rekey the entire document. Computer equipment, including many word processors and electronic typewriters, makes it possible to align columns of words, numbers, and decimals in a fraction of the time it would take on a standard electric typewriter. Dozens of envelopes can be addressed flawlessly with just a few keystrokes. Forms, reports, and other documents can be created, formatted, revised, stored, and retrieved with remarkable speed and efficiency.

Categorizing Office Documents

Modern information processing equipment has brought about profound changes in handling office documents. However, the same kinds of documents are being produced in today's offices that were produced years ago. Letters, memos, and reports are still the most common types of business communications. Even so, it is helpful to classify these documents somewhat differently than was done in the past. The categories that follow are based not on the purpose of the documents, but on their manner of preparation.

Short Documents

Most of the correspondence produced in business offices is brief and straightforward and can be created quickly. For example, a short letter changing an appointment or a one-paragraph memo complimenting an employee on a job well done normally would require little revision, if any. Furthermore, such documents represent "one-time" correspondence. Unlike reports or statistical tables, these ordinarily would not be needed a second time. For this reason, they need not be stored in a computer or word processing system, although a file copy of the correspondence would be kept.

Repetitive Documents

Many documents that businesses distribute contain the same information **(repetitive** or **standard text).** For example, suppose the Brock & Lowry law firm plans to move its business to a new building across town. The company may send out hundreds of letters to its clients announcing the upcoming move and giving the new business address. Each would contain the same information but be addressed to a different person. Items that differ from letter to letter (name, address, and salutation) are called **variables.**

A letter such as the one announcing Brock & Lowry's move is said to have few variables and many **constants**—it is a **form letter.**

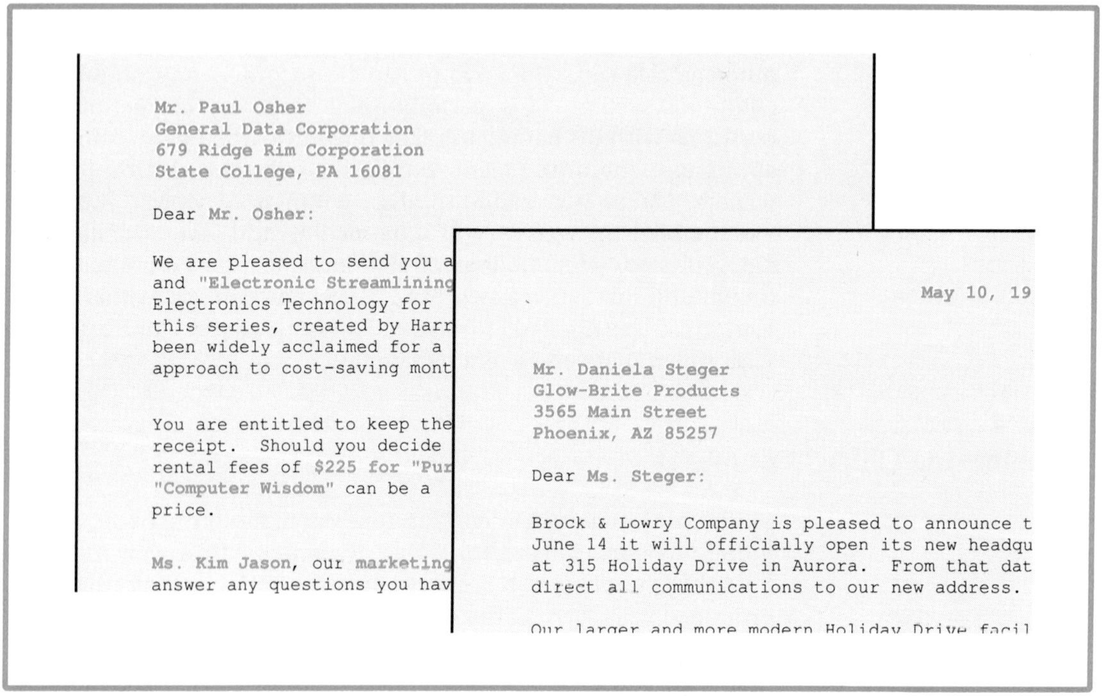

Mr. Paul Osher
General Data Corporation
679 Ridge Rim Corporation
State College, PA 16081

Dear Mr. Osher:

We are pleased to send you a
and "Electronic Streamlining
Electronics Technology for
this series, created by Harr
been widely acclaimed for a
approach to cost-saving mont

You are entitled to keep the
receipt. Should you decide
rental fees of $225 for "Pur
"Computer Wisdom" can be a
price.

Ms. Kim Jason, our marketing
answer any questions you hav

May 10, 19

Mr. Daniela Steger
Glow-Brite Products
3565 Main Street
Phoenix, AZ 85257

Dear Ms. Steger:

Brock & Lowry Company is pleased to announce t
June 14 it will officially open its new headqu
at 315 Holiday Drive in Aurora. From that dat
direct all communications to our new address.

Our larger and more modern Holiday Drive facil

Some kinds of correspondence require more variables than others.

The constants are the repetitive text, that is, those parts of the document that do not change. In this case, the entire body of the letter is a constant. The variables may be only the addressee's name and address and the salutation (as in the Brock & Lowry letter).

Other form letters with a great deal of standard or repetitive text include those from charitable organizations seeking contributions, sweepstake entries, and direct-mail advertising (such as from companies selling vacation packages or resort property). These kinds of form letters contain few variables.

Form letters with several variables usually are more personalized. A letter intended to collect payment for goods or services rendered, for instance, might list the exact amount the addressee owes. This would be a variable part of the document, as would the payment due date for each addressee. The rest of the body of the letter would remain constant.

The kinds of form or standard document used and the ratio of variables to constants in them vary. Some invoices, financial statements, and legal agreements contain many variables. Others might contain only a few. In every case, the automation of processing information has vastly simplified the production of repetitive documents. Preparing large quantities of individually keyed "form-type" documents once required hours of tedious and costly labor. Today, information processing systems can be used to generate virtually unlimited quantities of such documents. Each is an original—an original document automatically produced with only a few keystrokes.

Boilerplate Documents

The capability to produce repetitive documents on computerized equipment has improved the efficiency of many modern businesses. A "new" document can be created by combining standard text or stored paragraphs called **boilerplate text**. Even though new material is added sometimes, the process of combining the text is known in information processing as **document assembly** or **boilerplating**. A boilerplate document is a type of repetitive document because standard text, usually in the form of paragraphs, is used to create the "new" document. Also, any organization that uses

Boilerplate paragraphs are keyed for use in letters and other documents.

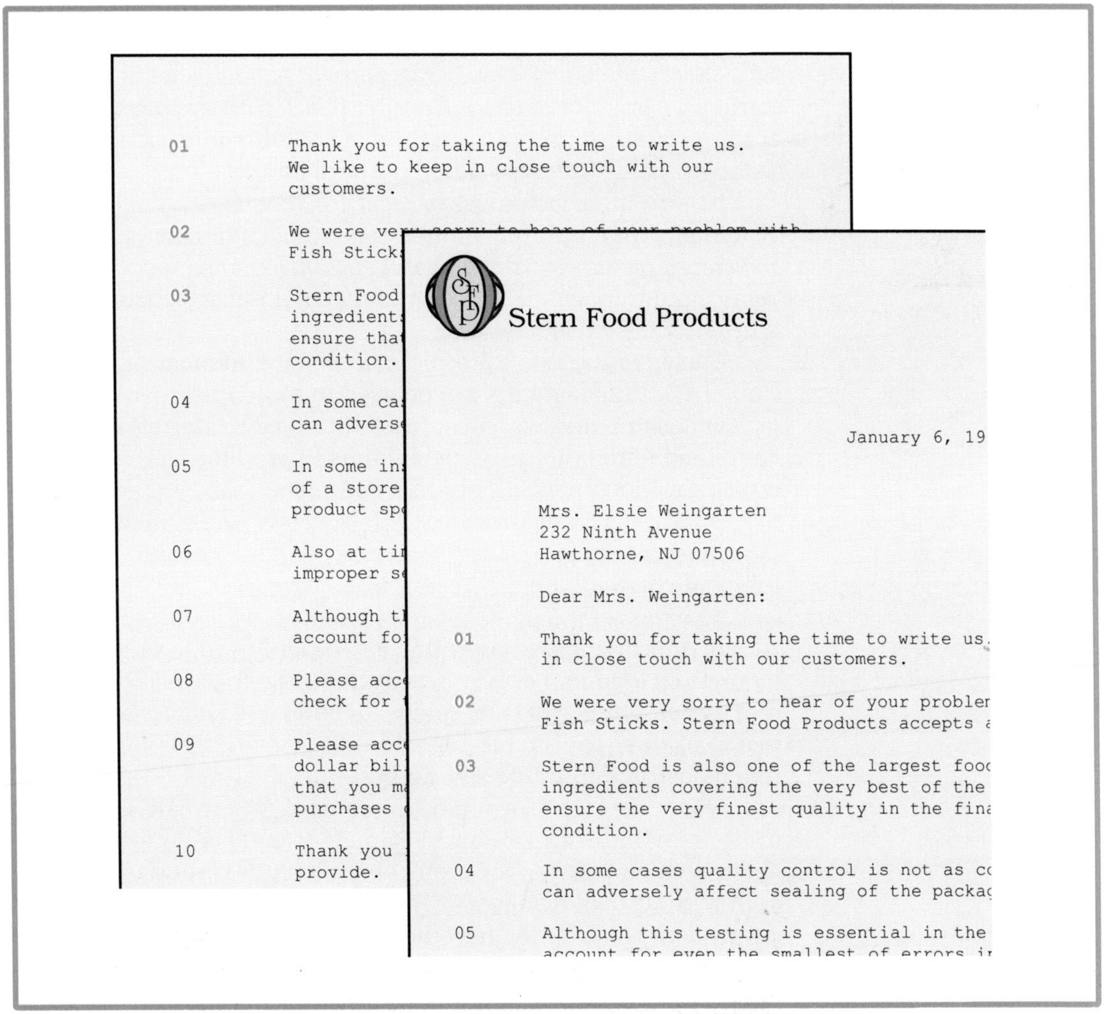

01 Thank you for taking the time to write us. We like to keep in close touch with our customers.

02 We were ve[...] Fish Stick[...]

03 Stern Food [...] ingredient[...] ensure tha[...] condition.

04 In some ca[...] can advers[...]

05 In some in[...] of a store [...] product sp[...]

06 Also at ti[...] improper s[...]

07 Although t[...] account fo[...]

08 Please acc[...] check for [...]

09 Please acc[...] dollar bil[...] that you m[...] purchases [...]

10 Thank you [...] provide.

Stern Food Products

January 6, 19

Mrs. Elsie Weingarten
232 Ninth Avenue
Hawthorne, NJ 07506

Dear Mrs. Weingarten:

01 Thank you for taking the time to write us[...] in close touch with our customers.

02 We were very sorry to hear of your proble[...] Fish Sticks. Stern Food Products accepts [...]

03 Stern Food is also one of the largest foo[...] ingredients covering the very best of the [...] ensure the very finest quality in the fin[...] condition.

04 In some cases quality control is not as c[...] can adversely affect sealing of the packa[...]

05 Although this testing is essential in the [...] account for even the smallest of errors i[...]

boilerplating probably sends the same, or nearly the same, document to several people. Thus, boilerplating is a method of creating repetitive documents.

Although the legal profession has been a leader in producing many legal documents in this manner, manufacturing also uses this process. For example, Tokeheim Electronics manufactures a wide range of products for use in industry. Every day, Tokeheim receives dozens of requests for information about its products. Some of these requests are for comprehensive technical data, some are for cost information, and some are for both. Many relate to several of Tokeheim's products.

The company's efficiency in handling all these requests has been improved significantly through the use of information processing equipment and procedures. Detailed information about each of the company's products has been written and stored in its computer system in the form of standard paragraphs, each stored by a short code name. One paragraph, for example, explains how a particular product is used. Another deals with its technical composition. A third presents cost and availability information. These standard paragraphs are called boilerplate text.

Answering a customer's letter at Tokeheim is easy using boilerplate text. An employee simply enters the code name for each of the stored paragraphs desired and specifies the sequence in which they should appear. The result is a custom-made document that answers a customer's request.

The advantage of boilerplate is that any number or combination of stored paragraphs can be used in a document, and they can be arranged in any sequence. In addition, new information can be combined with boilerplate paragraphs to produce an infinite variety of new documents, including contracts, wills, financial agreements, and customer service letters. Thus, boilerplate permits large amounts of tailor-made correspondence to be produced rapidly and efficiently.

Lengthy Edited Documents

At one time or another, most businesses will need to prepare long, factual documents varying greatly in content, format, and complexity, although sharing some common characteristics. Documents of this type include legal briefs, manuscripts for publication, construction proposals, and product analyses.

When Ramsey Corporation acquired two small consulting firms six months ago, Brian McKinney was asked to head up the newly created training division, which includes four departments, each with its own manager. It is now time to evaluate the progress and update plans for the new division. A document Mr. McKinney will need to prepare illustrates how many such reports are created. Mr. McKinney has asked each of his managers to prepare a section of the report.

Preparing the document for the Ramsey Corporation will require each of the four sections of the training report to be written by a different manager. They will want to work closely with Mr. McKinney in rewriting and processing the final document. They will need to decide what insertions, deletions, or rearrangements of paragraphs or pages are to be made. They also will find that one author's changes often trigger another's.

Each point outlined in the original training division plan must be addressed. Some data may need to be taken from the consulting firm's annual reports submitted before the takeover. Some of this material may be used in its original form; some may be updated or edited.

Mr. McKinney's report will include a breakdown, by department, of the types of training provided, the people to whom the training was given, the length of each training program, and a comparative evaluation of the training sessions. The final report probably will contain footnotes showing sources of information not included in the report but related to it. In general, many lengthy documents share the following characteristics:

- Several authors contribute to them.
- Reports and other such lengthy documents often use parts of other documents or previous reports.
- They contain charts, statistical tables, and the like.

Because information processing allows documents to be revised or reorganized without being completely rekeyed, Mr. McKinney's report can be prepared much more quickly and efficiently than it could have been some years ago. In fact, the more revision cycles the report has to go through and the more people who contribute to it, the greater the benefits of information processing to an organization.

The Impact of Information Processing in Business

Today, information processing technology is being used in almost every kind of business to improve efficiency and increase productivity. Microcomputers and other types of electronic equipment are popular tools for producing many specialized documents, including real estate agreements, case histories of patients, and forms for loans. The equipment can also electronically communicate the documents to put accurate and timely information in the hands of those who need it to make business decisions. Organiza-

Many law firms are using electronic equipment.

tions are using technology to process information more efficiently and effectively. Efficient and effective information handling usually contributes to a productive information system.

Law

Large and small laws firms alike have found that information processing can help attorneys save time in handling their paperwork. There are a number of reasons for this:

- Legal documents are often long and intricate.
- Legal documents must be error-free because they are binding on the parties who sign them.
- Legal documents frequently require substantial revision and several drafts before final approval.
- Legal documents frequently contain large sections of standardized text.

Attorneys, like many professionals, may use **online databases** (libraries of information that can be accessed by a computer) to help them gather information and prepare legal cases. A computer that has been networked, or connected by telephone to a central computer, is an efficient way for an attorney to search a database of court precedents and retrieve in a matter of minutes information that once would have taken a clerk months of researching to find.

Electronic equipment is popular in legal offices. For example, the medium-sized law offices of Adams, Rich, & Levitt use a microcomputer system. When a lengthy legal document needs processing and time is limited, several word processing specialists may work together on the same document. Each specialist keys and stores different parts of it. When the entire document is keyed, one specialist assembles it in proper order. With information processing, it is rarely necessary to rekey an entire document even when there are errors or revisions. Before the final document is printed, a proofreader reads it for accuracy.

Adams, Rich, & Levitt use standardized text in wills, contracts, and other legal documents. Their network of information processing equipment, software, and procedures is ideally suited to handle long, complex documents. Each specialist is able to process documents efficiently because each attorney asking for a document indicates beforehand what boilerplate information is wanted. The specialist recalls the text from a disk and inserts names, dates, and other variables.

Health Care

Information processing has many applications in the health care industry—from monitoring and administering drugs, to identifying and treating patient's illnesses—in addition to the many office applications. About four out of five documents prepared in a health organization are based on doctors' dictation. Thus, equipment for recording the voice is of definite significance to the health industry. Physicians dictate medical histories, examination findings, treatment recommendations, and discharge summaries for their patients' records. Most of these documents do not require revision and do not contain standardized text, although they can be easily stored and retrieved for updating and are readily accessible to the doctor who wishes to review a patient's records.

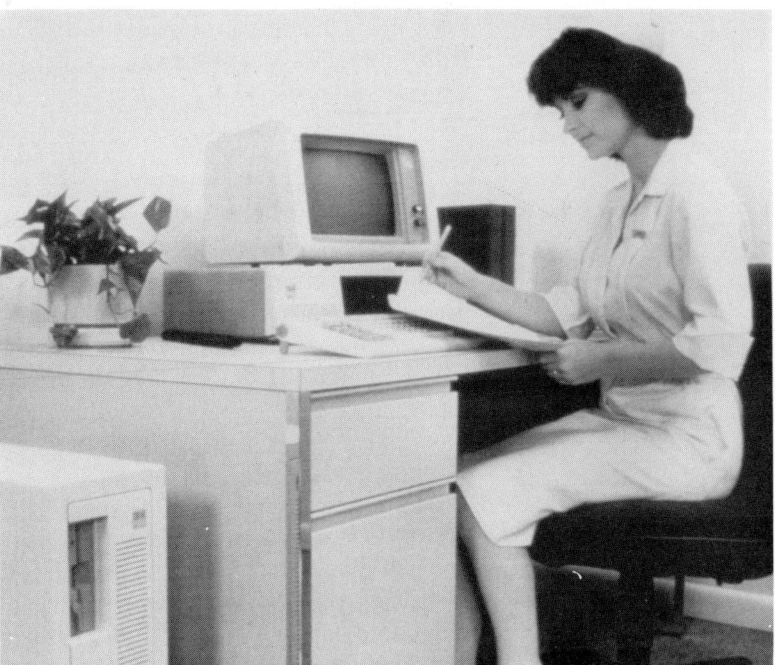

A medical office can benefit from information processing technology.

Doctors often report to a hospital only a few days a week. The hospital frequently needs to communicate patient information to doctors who are away from the hospital. Using telephone lines or other types of network technology, a hospital computer terminal or some other type of video display terminal can be connected to a terminal in the doctor's office. This gives doctors access to patients' updated medical records at any number of hospitals and clinics and in their private offices.

As with many technical fields, word processing operators in the medical field often maintain special lists of difficult medical terms, hard-to-spell names of drugs, and often used phrases. Each word or phrase has its own code name. To insert an entry from this list in a document, the operator enters the code with one or two keystrokes. Other computer aids that are valuable to the health profession (as well as to most businesses and individuals today) include the spell-checker, dictionary, thesaurus, and grammar checker. These help ensure that the document is correct before it is distributed or stored in its final form. They not only save time but reduce the possibility of error in a profession in which complete and accurate records are essential.

Just as using computerized equipment and information processing instead of hand methods makes it easier for attorneys to maintain a record of time spent on cases, it also helps doctors, nurses, and other medical personnel keep track of the time spent with each patient for billing purposes. Information processing equipment has made it easier to process medical information for reporting insurance claims and maintaining financial records in medical institutions.

Banking

Banks make intensive use of information processing because they must deal with a large amount of paperwork and handle a great deal of information. All financial transactions have to be confirmed by documentation of one kind or another. Letters and statements have to be sent out to depositors. Various statistical records must be originated and kept up to date.

Banks are offering customers more and more services, many of which require immediate processing. For example, you may have the convenience of having your bank make your mortgage payments, pay your utility bills, and complete similar transactions directly from your bank account, either automatically or by instructing an automated teller machine how much to pay to whom. When you access your bank account through such a machine, you are using an information processing method. For this electronic banking operation, you may use a card similar to a credit card, a **debit card.** This operation immediately debits your account rather than waiting until later, such as the end of the banking day or an accounting period. Certainly, this kind of convenience contributes to the increased amount of information a bank must process.

Another frequently produced document in banking is a one-page customer letter composed of boilerplate paragraphs combined with variables. These are commonly sent out in a mass mailing at the end of a fiscal period. The ability of information processing equipment to recall previously stored text and change it rapidly into original, but basically repetitive, correspondence has been of great benefit to bankers. The volume and variety of information that major banks handle make integrated and networked information processing systems essential to their efficient operation.

Insurance

Like banking, the insurance business uses documentation to record its many transactions. The result is a huge volume of paperwork that must be processed with speed and accuracy. In a large insurance company, information processing applications vary somewhat from department to department, as illustrated by Unitron Mutual. Unitron Mutual Insurance Company has three principal departments: marketing, legal, and claims. The Marketing Department uses information processing to produce standardized letters mass mailed to potential customers. The Marketing Department also processes various employee communications, produces announcements, and generates newsletters. To do these tasks, it uses

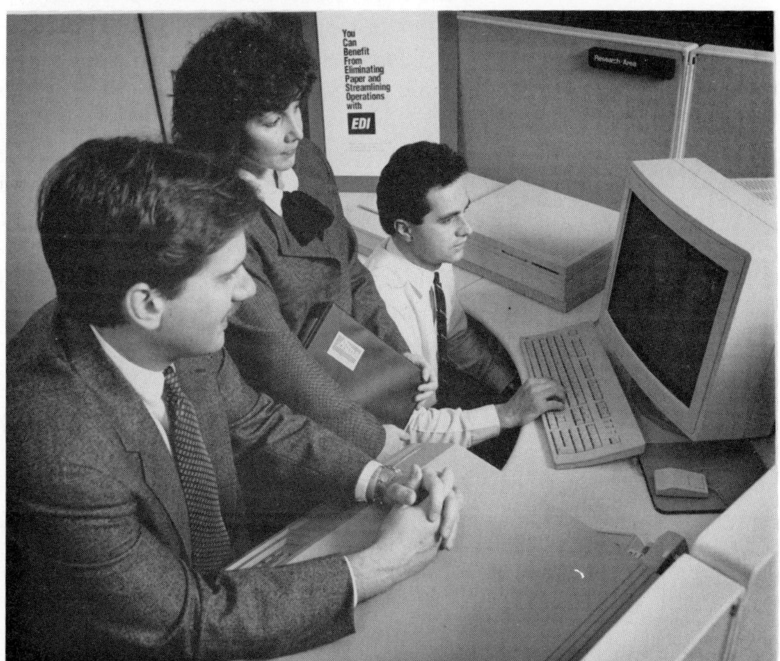

Word processing equipment is used widely in insurance companies.

several important information processing tools commonly referred to as **desktop publishing**—a combination of text, data, and/or graphics.

Unitron's Legal Department uses information processing in some of the same ways that the law firm of Adams, Rich, & Levitt uses it. The department also prepares reports for use by company employees. These documents, which often go through many drafts, make full use of the capabilities of information processing equipment.

The Claims Department at Unitron handles correspondence with policyholders. A typical letter received by the department will report an accident or ask for insurance coverage. Although variables may differ from one claim to another, the procedures usually are the same. Using microcomputers and information processing equipment, operators assemble paragraphs of boilerplate to answer these letters.

Retail

Most of your purchases in department stores, grocery stores, and other retail stores are processed with some type of information processing equipment. If you see a sweater you like in the window of a shop that is a branch of a nationwide chain of stores, you go in, try on the sweater, and decide to purchase it. The cashier uses a scanning device to scan the price tag, which indicates the cost of the sweater, and also records information that the business will find very useful—information that is saved in a computer's storage unit.

The data entered into a point-of-sale terminal is sent to a central computer for processing.

In some stores, the cashier uses a small keyboard on a **point-of-sale (POS) terminal** to key in the price of the sweater as well as additional coded data printed on the price tag. The POS terminal displays pertinent information about the transaction. The terminal may look like an updated cash register, but, like the scanning device, it is an important retail business tool. It gives retailers the timely, accurate information they need to make correct merchandising and business decisions. Along with the price on the price tag is coded data about key business indicators such as the following:

- What items are selling
- Which stores are doing the most business
- What kind of advertising works best
- Whether customers are responding to a particular coupon or discount offer
- What sizes, colors, and styles are running out of stock in the warehouse and need to be reordered

The data captured by a POS terminal may be transmitted to a central computer in the headquarters office for processing. Linked systems may be used to calculate and store financial information and produce the correspondence needed for purchasing and billing customers. By correctly analyzing the information they generate, retailers can use POS terminals to detect and evaluate shifts in consumer behavior and to anticipate future buying trends. The POS terminal has become an essential tool in competitively managing a retail business in today's environment.

Restaurants

Fast-food establishments and restaurants are using information processing in much the same ways that retail businesses use computers to make business operations more profitable. Have you ever walked into a restaurant, ordered a garden salad with Italian dressing and a pepperoni pizza, and instead received a spinach salad with blue cheese dressing and a mushroom pizza? How many times have you picked up your check at the end of a meal and found that you could not read it? Problems such as these will happen less often as more restaurants use computer terminals. Many fast-food chains have led the way in information processing by switching to computers.

The idea is simple. You give your order to the person behind the counter. Instead of quickly jotting down your order with a pencil on a pad or calling it into the kitchen, the person keys your order on a computer terminal. There is no need to spell out each word because every item on the menu has a key that corresponds to it on the keyboard. The person taking your order pushes one key for each item you order. There are extra keys for such things as "rare," "medium," "mayonnaise," and so on.

1 LAMB CHOPS
  BUTTERFLIED
  MEDIUM
  GREEK STYLE
1 BEEF LIVER
   RARE
BROIL
TO 10 05:30 PM
1699 01

A computer printout from a restaurant.

While the server is keying in your order, in the kitchen a machine connected to the computer prints the order out for the cook. A blinking light tells the server when your order is ready, and he or she simply picks it up at a serving window. To produce the check, the server presses the keys that tell the computer to add up the cost of every item you have ordered, calculate the tax (if any), and print out your check.

Manufacturing

Manufacturing is in a state of radical change. There has been a decline in manufacturing with the shift in our economy to a service-oriented society. However, manufacturing has also experienced rapidly expanding markets and marketing opportunities, rising costs, constant vendor and supply uncertainty, explosive new technologies, increasing government regulation, and foreign and domestic competition. Many manufacturers are using customized computer systems with sophisticated information processing. Not only is there a much greater wealth of information available to help businesses stay competitive, but automated equipment and electronic information transfer have significantly sped up many

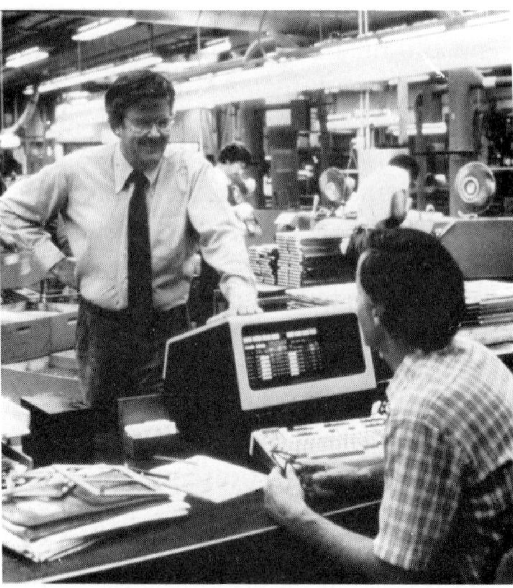

Computers are used in manufacturing environments.

manufacturing processes. Computerized systems provide companies with easily accessible, up-to-the-minute manufacturing information on products (such as part numbers, inventory availability, production schedules, and routing schedules), plants, work-in-progress schedules, finished goods location, quality control data, and shipping schedules. All the information that can be obtained, assessed, and used by management when making necessary business decisions means that most of our future work force will be information workers who can contribute to information systems.

Distribution

You do not usually walk into a factory, select a product off the assembly line, pay for it, and take it home. As a rule, manufacturers do not sell directly to customers. Instead, the product must first be shipped to a warehouse, often in a different part of the country or world. Today, it is no longer enough for a company to manufacture a superior product and then sit back and expect to make a profit. Distribution—getting the product from the factory to the store—is essential. The distribution process involves a number of factors that companies must consider and deal with successfully.

In a continually changing marketplace, managers need to know if material and labor costs are low enough to compete yet high enough to realize a profit. A plant manager has to know how a product is selling and precisely how much is in the warehouses. A retailer may call a production manager to ask if a shipment left the factory on time. A salesperson in the field may call headquarters to ask about a customer's credit rating. A product representative may need detailed specifications of a product to pass on to a customer. Without such information, the representative may risk losing the sale to a competitor. This kind of information must be available at a moment's notice.

In an automated distribution system, every department and office are linked to the system with a computerized terminal. For example, each time salespeople get an order, they key data about it into the system. When an order leaves the warehouse, an operator there keys and enters that information. The central computer instantly calculates the new inventory level and alerts managers, who may then adjust the production schedule. From this information, order entry and data reporting can be initiated and the information accessed from any location in the world.

Like POS terminals, automated distribution systems tell a company much more than just how many products have moved off the shelf. They provide valuable information about sales and profits by customer, supplier, product, product line, salesperson, and region. This information also can serve as the basis for directing sales efforts, developing promotional strategies, designing new products, and ultimately increasing company profits.

Other Fields

In addition to the businesses and industries already discussed, many other companies have put information processing equipment and various other office automation technologies and machinery to effective use. **Electronic publishing** can be used to handle lengthy edited documents such as book manuscripts and industry surveys. This type of information, as well as repetitive documents such as rejection letters, marketing-related correspondence, and sales literature, is being handled with increasing efficiency by publishers.

In government, information processing technology has been used to prepare proposals, regulations, specifications, budgets, and numerous other documents. Standardized information that will be used or revised later can be stored as boilerplate and retrieved as often as needed. In education, everything from dissertations to examinations, from student orientation information to computerized library access, and from registration to transcript storage falls within the province of information processing.

Professional, recreational, volunteer, and service organizations utilize office automation systems. Most of these use a variety of information sources and management functions to help with every phase of their operations. These include fund raising, membership drives, records management, accounting, seminar and convention management, and calendar planning to keep event agendas up to date.

There is virtually no industry that hasn't been touched by automation and computer technology in one way or another. Just think about the impact of such technology on your own life. A travel agent can help you plan your vacation or business trip in minutes by using a computer. You even leave the travel agent's office with the airline tickets in your hand. The hotel clerk can key in your name and instantaneously retrieve your home address, company affiliation, room number, length of stay, check-out plan, messages, and meeting commitments.

Office automation technologies have affected every industry. You can see these changes for yourself, not only in where and how people work, but also in the tools they use. As information continues to grow rapidly, more automation and computer technology will be available. The indications are that career opportunities in the office automation field will continue to expand for people who can manage information and change. You can be a part of this exciting field by preparing yourself with good information processing skills.

CHAPTER SUMMARY

- People in businesses and other organizations send and receive large amounts of information.
- The modern office is an information management center—an information system—where speed, efficiency, and accuracy are keys to success.
- The more quickly and efficiently information is processed, distributed, and acted on, the more profitable a business is likely to be.
- Businesses use many forms of communication, including letters, memos, preprinted forms, reports, charts, telephone calls, voice messages, newsletters, and brochures.
- Decisions made within a company often are based on reports—documents whose principal purpose is to present facts. Reports may be written by more than one person and may require several drafts.
- Forms are used in business to save time and to standardize the way in which certain information is processed.
- Automation has done much to improve the processing of correspondence, forms, statistical tables, contracts, and other business documents.
- The documents produced within an information system are classified into special groups—short documents, repetitive documents, boilerplate, and lengthy edited documents—based on the unique capabilities of information processing equipment.
- The more revisions a report or other document has to go through and the more people who contribute to its content, the greater will be the benefits derived from utilizing automated information processing.

- Office automation technology for information processing can be used in nearly every kind of business to increase efficiency and productivity. It is used widely in law, health care, banking, insurance, retailing, restaurants, manufacturing, publishing, government, and education.

VOCABULARY

- boilerplate text
- constant
- debit card
- document
- document assembly
- form letter
- point-of-sale (POS) terminal
- repetitive text
- standard text
- variable

CHAPTER QUESTIONS

1. How can speed and efficiency in information processing contribute to a company's profitability? Give a specific example.
2. Describe five purposes for which business letters may be written. Do you think information processing equipment can help accomplish these purposes efficiently? Why or why not?
3. Why are documents classified into special groups in information processing?
4. Which of the following documents would an information processing system be more helpful in producing: a one-paragraph memo setting up a departmental meeting or a monthly summary of regional sales figures? Explain the reasons for your answer.
5. What are three common examples of variable information in a form letter?
6. Why would the capability of an information processing system to automatically combine a stored document with a mailing list be a significant time saver?
7. In what ways can boilerplate be used to create "new" documents? Can you think of an example of a boilerplate document you have seen recently?
8. What characteristics do lengthy edited documents generally have in common?
9. Why is information processing particularly useful to law firms?
10. Compare the kinds of documents produced in the fields of banking, health care, and insurance. In what ways would information processing applications in these fields be the same? How would they differ?

CASE STUDY

McIlheney Publishing is a large company that specializes in publishing books on engineering and technology and in producing audiovisual materials. The company generates a wide range of documents. For example, its Marketing Division frequently purchases mailing lists and sends out advertising pieces to every name on the list. This same division also creates advertising copy, which must be approved by both the Editorial and Sales Divisions before it can be used.

McIlheney's Customer Service Division sends out correspondence in response to consumer inquiries and complaints. Much of this correspondence contains the same basic information. This department also sends brief memos to the company's department heads when a particular McIlheney publication draws an unusual amount of response. Of course, most of McIlheney's document preparation occurs in the Editorial Division, which handles the company's long, highly technical manuscripts. In addition to managing the development and revision of these manuscripts, McIlheney's editors correspond frequently with authors, freelancers, and experts in the field.

McIlheney is seriously considering installing a computer system for information processing. Do you think this is a sound idea? Why or why not? Which of the documents produced by McIlheney's various departments would fall into the special document groups in information processing (that is, short documents, repetitive documents, boilerplate, or lengthy edited documents)?

CHAPTER 3

Input

Dr. Vanessa Dubinsky exits a patient treatment room and walks into her own office. She begins dictating her findings from examining the patient, using a desktop dictation machine. She pauses to look at an X-ray and the facsimile copies of the patient's medical tests from an imaging clinic. She scribbles a note for her medical assistant to scan a couple of these documents to add to the patient's records. Then she rewinds and listens to a portion of her report and continues dictating. When Dr. Dubinsky finishes her report, she adds some instructions for her secretary. The secretary will later transcribe the dictation, key a memo, and electronically transfer both the memo and report to another physician's office.

The voice input method used by Dr. Dubinsky to create a patient report is a time saver in her medical practice. She likes the convenience dictation offers. She knows that her competent staff will transcribe the dictation for the patient's record and carry out the other instructions efficiently. However, Dr. Dubinsky also uses other methods of creating information. She knows that taking advantage of various input methods can increase the efficiency of her medical practice.

Creating Documents

In information processing, the person who creates a document—who in a sense "writes" it—is called the **author**, **word originator**, or **principal**. In this book, we refer to the document creator as the author. Because information processing is used in many kinds of work settings, the author may be a production supervisor writing an evaluation of a factory worker's performance, a scientist preparing a paper about the results of a research project, a personnel worker reporting on salary levels within a company, or a secretary composing a letter requesting information from an office supply company. Nearly everyone who works in the business world acts as an author from time to time.

There are five stages in the information processing cycle: input, processing, storage and retrieval, output, and distribution and communication. Document origination is the input stage. During this stage, the author must put his or her ideas into words so that they can be processed—usually by people and machines. The result, or output, usually is a document.

Dr. Dubinsky created her report with voice input, that is, by speaking directly into a dictation system. Her secretary can listen to her recorded voice and transcribe the information into a written document. Dr. Dubinsky could also have dictated her report to another person (for example, a stenographer). A stenographer could take the dictation in shorthand and transcribe it. Or the dictation could be keyed on a machine that produces a printed code for transcribing (which is common in court reporting).

Still other options for Dr. Dubinsky would have been to create her report with pencil and paper or by keying it on some type of keyboard—a computer or a typewriter. In the not too distant future, voice-to-text technology will enable her to speak into a machine and have her voice automatically converted into a written document. Dr. Dubinsky knows that by working together, she and her staff can utilize technology to create and process documents efficiently. Let's take a closer look at some common ways in which **document creation/origination** occurs in an office.

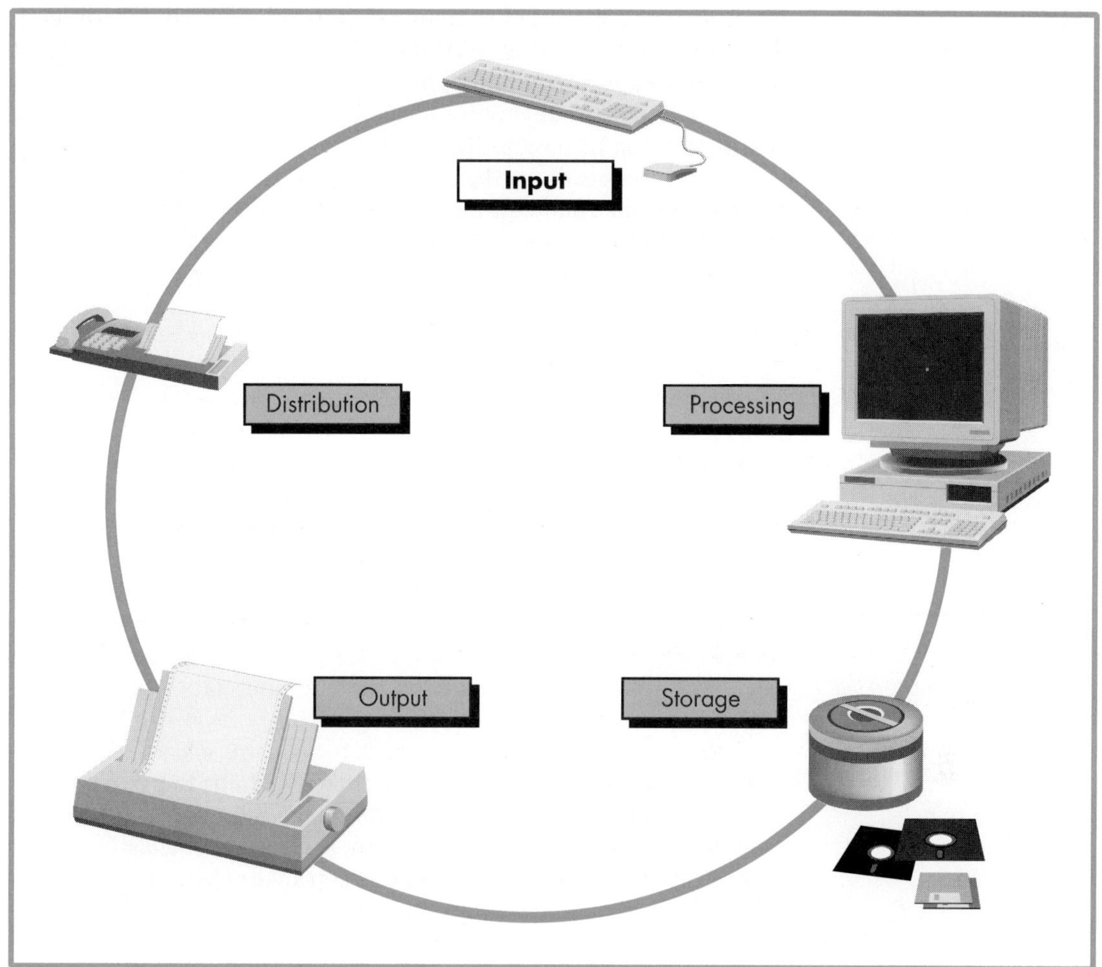

Input is one of five stages in the information processing cycle.

Longhand

For years, longhand was the most common type of **source document** or originating document. It also is the most unproductive way. Most people write in longhand at less than 30 words a minute. That is slow when compared to the rate of an average keyboarder (50 words a minute) and an average stenographer (100 words a minute). Longhand seems even slower when compared to the rate of **machine shorthand** (250 words a minute) and **voice-recognition** equipment, which can process words as a person speaks.

Longhand is not efficient if it is illegible, which it often is. But despite the inefficiency, many authors prefer to create source documents by hand rather than by using a keyboard, machine recording, or other means. Writing by hand seems more convenient and requires no special equipment. Some authors say they cannot organize their thoughts without seeing their words on paper. They dislike talking into recording devices or lack the skills needed to key even a rough draft. But none of these reasons for using longhand seems justifiable in light of the high cost and low productivity of this method of document origination.

Shorthand

Shorthand can involve manual or machine methods.

Manual Shorthand

Taking manual or handwritten dictation in a shortened or abbreviated form is referred to as **manual shorthand**. Some authors prefer to create documents by dictating their thoughts to another person, who transcribes them into a finished document. Take Caroline Gabor, for example. Ms. Gabor is the adult education director at Brooker Community College. She prefers dictating source documents such as letters to writing in longhand or composing at the keyboard. When she is ready to dictate, she calls her secretary, John Fredrick, who takes down her words in shorthand. If Ms. Gabor can't think of exactly the right words to use, she asks Mr. Fredrick, who can usually suggest wording that will help her express her thoughts. When Ms. Gabor has finished dictating, Mr. Fredrick reads back to her what he has written, sometimes suggesting a way to improve it. Once revisions have been made, Mr. Fredrick keys the final document and gives it to Ms. Gabor to sign.

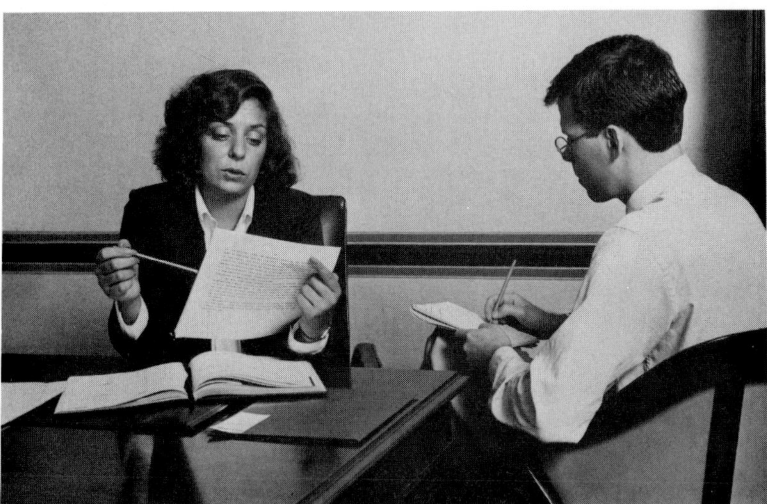

Face-to-face dictation is a common way of creating documents.

Ms. Gabor views face-to-face dictation as the ultimate in convenience. Like most people, she can dictate a letter about six times as fast as she can write it in longhand. Moreover, she knows that her handwriting is hard to read and that Mr. Fredrick can transcribe faster from his own shorthand notes than she can write. In addition, Ms. Gabor enjoys the feeling of security that comes from having her letters taken down by a private secretary who will keep information confidential. The give-and-take nature of dictation means the document usually can be finalized in one session between the secretary and the author, ensuring that the message the author wishes to send is clearly communicated in the first draft. Face-to-face dictation does take time. However, the time lost is not significant compared to the time saved by not having to traffic a document to and from a word processing center for keying and inputting corrections.

For the secretary, however, taking dictation face to face may not always be convenient. Sometimes when Ms. Gabor calls Mr. Fredrick in to take shorthand, he is in the middle of another task. While he is taking dictation, another secretary has to answer his telephone, which interrupts the other secretary's work. Frequently, Ms. Gabor's telephone rings while she is dictating, and Mr. Fredrick has to wait while she talks to a student or a faculty member. Then he has to read back the last sentence or two that she dictated to remind her of what she was saying when the call came in.

Not all keyboarders can read shorthand. Consequently, in an office, you cannot always ask a co-worker to transcribe a document for you if you have other work you must finish first. And once you have completed transcription, you have to spend a few minutes getting back into the work you were doing when you were asked to take dictation.

Machine Shorthand

Machine or electronic shorthand is a process of keying symbols and/or letters (and/or combinations of them) into a machine. A shorthand or stenographic machine is the most common type of equipment used; however, a computer with shorthand software also may be used.

Machine or electronic shorthand offers several advantages over manual shorthand. It is faster; a skilled shorthand machine operator can record shorthand at 250 words a minute or more on a shorthand machine. Because most shorthand machines are portable, they also are convenient. Machine shorthand operators frequently use shorthand in meetings where several people may be talking in rapid sequence, excitedly, or spontaneously. It is particularly suited to courtrooms, public hearings, and similar settings where an accurate record of the proceedings is required.

Stenograph transcribing machines are used to record testimony in courtrooms.

Shorthand machine input can be recorded and processed in different ways. As an operator keys symbols or letters into a shorthand machine, the keystrokes are recorded on paper tape or on magnetic media. An operator transcribing the shorthand in a traditional way would key the transcript on a typewriter from the paper tape. Newer technology in transcription machines permits the shorthand input to be saved in a computer's storage unit. When it is viewed on the screen, it is electronically converted to text that can be read by anyone. An operator can then read the words on the screen and use a keyboard to format the transcript. After all the corrections and revisions have been keyed, a few keystrokes can be entered to store and print copies. This process is a form of **computer-aided transcription**. The operator does not have to keyboard the entire document. Computer-aided transcription greatly reduces the time needed to produce final copies.

Keyboarding

Although handwriting will always be used for many purposes, keyboarding skill is vitally important to success in an office. Note how Jose Guzeman, a vice president at Texrite Fabric Mills, uses his keyboarding skill.

Mr. Guzeman occasionally writes articles about the latest textiles and designs for a decorating trade magazine. His articles tend

Computer-aided transcription equipment is useful for handling large volumes of work.

to be much longer than letters, and they sometimes contain sections of previously published documents. Mr. Guzeman finds that composing at a keyboard is more efficient than writing in longhand or dictating. His article still may be considered a "rough draft" because it needs editing, but it is much easier to read in **keyed rough draft** form than if he had handwritten it.

Before word processing equipment was installed at Texrite Fabric Mills, Mr. Guzeman would send the keyed rough draft of his article to the company's Public Relations Department, where an editor made handwritten revisions involving issues of accuracy, company policy, language, and grammar. Besides making corrections and adding editing symbols, the editor may have "cut and pasted" some of the pages to rearrange the information in the article. At this point, Mr. Guzeman's keyed rough draft copy usually is not even close to being "mailable." More often than not, it is nearly unintelligible to anyone not familiar with editing symbols. The effectiveness of keyed rough draft as a form of document origination, then, is directly related to each author's definition of the word *rough*.

Mr. Guzeman has his secretary, Gwyn Thomas, rekey the rough draft. Ms. Thomas must be able to understand the words and symbols the editor added as well as the rough draft Mr. Guzeman has keyed. Her task is to produce a neat, error-free document from the rough draft, just as she would do from her own shorthand. This will be easy if the editor's corrections are legible.

Workstation Document Transfer

Many times a document originates with another person or source (that is, information or an unformatted document may be trans-

This secretary is using a microcomputer to transcribe machine dictation.

ferred to your computer or workstation). The workstation transfer is an alternative way to input a document. Let's see how this input method works at Texrite Fabric Mills.

Now that word processing and other computer equipment has been installed at Texrite, Mr. Guzeman's rough drafts can be processed quickly and efficiently. He keys and stores a draft of his article on a word processor. Because his word processor is networked with Ms. Thomas's word processor and with equipment throughout the company, he does not have to make a hard copy of the article. He can send a **soft copy** (this usually refers to copy that is electronically stored) of his draft to the editor by electronic mail or **electronic transfer.**

With just a few keystrokes, Mr. Guzeman electronically sends his article from his word processor to equipment in the Public Relations Department. The editor who receives Mr. Guzeman's article can view the transferred input on a screen and key and store changes (rather than inputting them by hand on a hard copy). The revised document can be sent back (electronically) to Mr. Guzeman, who reviews it and, if he wishes, keys any final changes. Copy produced in this manner usually is called **clean copy** because it does not contain editor's marks, handwritten notes, or other marks that make the copy look edited. Mr. Guzeman's clean copy is no longer a draft. It is ready to be printed and sent to the magazine for publication. He asks Ms. Thomas to print a copy of the article and mail it to the publisher.

In Mr. Guzeman's case, input came mainly from keyboarding either before or after the electronic transfer of the document. Keyboarding has become an increasingly popular method of various phases of input, mainly because it capitalizes on the **first copy-final copy** principle. No hard copy is printed until all changes have been made; thus, the "first" copy is the "final" copy, as was the case with Mr. Guzeman's article.

Examples of How Keyboarding Often Is Combined with Other Methods of Input

- A printed work form (which originally was keyed) is completed in handwriting.
- A stored telephone message form (which originally was keyed) is viewed on a screen and completed by keying a telephone caller's message.
- A letter is dictated to a secretary, who takes it down in shorthand to transcribe later on a keyboard.
- A memo is dictated into a voice receiver (such as with dictation equipment) to be converted into text and viewed on a screen for a secretary to format.
- A report is electronically transferred from one computer to another, where a secretary will use a hand-held device such as a mouse or light pen to rearrange the text.
- A photograph is scanned and transferred to a computer for a keyboarder to input the text that will identify the various parts of the image.

Machine Dictation

Machine dictation is a fast and efficient means of creating a document. Several types of equipment enable the author to dictate a document when the secretary is not present. If the author is interrupted during dictation, the recording machine is simply turned off for a moment, and the secretary's time is not lost. Later the secretary transcribes the dictation while listening to a playback of it. The recording can be rewound to replay all or part of the dictation. If the telephone rings, the machine can be turned off for a few minutes and turned on again. On some dictation equipment, the author can add words to the middle of a document without starting over again.

With some machine-dictation systems, transcription can be handled by a word processing operator rather than by the author's secretary. However, some authors may be reluctant to give up the prestige of having their work done by private secretaries and may depend on the help and suggestions they get from them in face-to-face dictation sessions. Using dictation equipment requires skills some authors may not have. In addition to knowing how to operate the equipment and create a document without a secretary's help, they must be able to organize their thoughts and present them in a manner that will translate well into the written word. But many managers who have successfully integrated dictation machines into their office systems have found that they like the convenience of being able to dictate at any time, regardless of what their secretaries are doing.

Recording Media

Whether a dictation machine is a simple portable tape recorder or part of a large central processing system used by hundreds of authors and word processing employees, its purpose is to store words until a transcriptionist is ready to listen to them and then prepare the final document. One way machine-dictation systems differ from each other is in the **media,** or materials, they use for recording the author's voice. There are many kinds of **voice-storage media.** Some of them (for instance, cassette tapes) may be familiar, others may not.

Internal Storage Media In some dictation machines, the author's spoken words are captured on magnetic recording media that never leave the machine except when they wear out and are replaced. These are called **internal storage media** because they are kept inside the machine. One type is the **endless loop** (a long recording tape that has been joined at the ends into a continuous loop). It is housed in the tank of the machine and is never touched by the author or the transcriptionist. The tape travels around inside the tank, recording words as authors dictate and playing them back later for transcriptionists. An endless loop can store dictation for hundreds of documents. As new dictation comes in, the oldest transcribed documents on the tape are erased automatically to make room for the new. A single endless loop may be reserved for priority or confidential dictation or for a word originator with a great deal of dictation that requires very fast turnaround. Internal storage media are used most frequently with **central recording systems** (those that can record all the machine dictation originating within an organization from several authors).

External or Discrete Media Some dictation systems use recording media that can be easily detached from the machines and used on other dictation or transcription equipment. These are called **external** or **discrete media**. The most popular discrete media are cassettes similar to those used in a home tape player. One advantage of discrete media is that they can be saved in a file in case anyone needs to listen to them again later.

Because they can be detached and used on other machines, discrete media enable secretaries to handle rush transcription jobs with maximum speed. For example, one day each of three executives for whom a secretary works gives him a cassette of dictation that has to be transcribed immediately. If he works alone on them, one cassette at a time, he might not be able to finish all the documents soon enough. Distributing the cassettes to co-workers enables several secretaries to work simultaneously on transcribing the dictation and to finish the documents in less time than one person working alone could complete them.

Inscribed Media The oldest type of discrete media is called **inscribed media**. They are inscribed (usually cut or scratched) as the author's voice is recorded onto them. Because they cannot easily be erased or reused, inscribed media are not very popular today, even though some offices still use dictation machines that record the author's voice by etching an impression of it on some type of media (such as a flexible plastic belt).

Magnetic and Digital Media Today most dictation equipment uses **magnetic** rather than inscribed media. A main advantage of magnetic media is that they can be erased and reused. Erasable media usually are quite economical and convenient.

Voice can be recorded on magnetic media by means of electrical impulses (**analog signals** or continuous sound waves) and magnetism. Some magnetic media also may be **digital.** In this form of media, as the voice is recorded, sound is changed into **binary code** (on/off electrical signals) the machine can understand. The **digital audio tapes (DATs)** of your favorite recording artists are good examples of digital media. Digital media usually provide greater clarity, truer tone, and less background noise than analog recording media. (Although you will learn more about analog and digital signals later in this book, we emphasize digital because of its capabilities.) Dictation and transcription equipment manufacturers use several types of magnetic and digital media in their machines. Besides the endless loop, magnetic media may include belts, tape reels and loops, disks, disk cartridges, and cassettes.

Cassettes are a magnetic medium commonly used in office dictation systems. A cassette is a magnetic recording tape permanently encased in a small plastic container you can easily slip in and out of dictation and transcription machines. Cassettes have become increasingly popular because of their versatility and convenience. They come in several sizes: standard, mini-, micro-, and picocassettes.

Cassettes are available in several sizes.

On most **standard cassettes**, you can record as much as 180 minutes of dictation—90 minutes on each side. Usually, you can record up to 120 minutes on smaller cassettes **(minicassette** or **microcassette**). The smallest of cassettes, the **picocassette**, usually holds 60 minutes of dictation, weighs a fraction of an ounce, and can fit into a small matchbox.

The greatest advantage of cassettes, especially miniaturized cassettes, is that they can be used on small, portable dictation machines. They are frequently used by authors who spend a lot of time away from the office. They can record dictation anywhere and mail the cassette to the secretary for transcription. Another reason some authors and secretaries favor cassettes is that, unlike internally stored media, cassettes can be marked for easy identification and handling. As external or discrete media, cassettes can be filed if you think you might need to listen to them again later. If that is unlikely, you can easily erase and reuse them. However, because a cassette may be handled frequently, the chances of it being lost or damaged are greater than with internally stored media.

Media and Equipment Compatibility

One thing to consider in using dictation systems is **media compatibility**. For recorded dictation to be transcribed, it must be recorded on a medium that is compatible with, or matches, your transcription equipment. You cannot transcribe dictation recorded on a microcassette if your transcription equipment is a standard cassette unit, is part of an endless loop system, or if it accepts only inscribed belts. Partly because portable dictation machines with miniaturized cassettes have become so popular, some dictation equipment companies make adapters that can be used to play miniaturized cassettes on equipment intended for larger cassettes.

Dictation and Transcription Equipment

As the use of dictation machines has increased over the years, manufacturers have developed a variety of machines for dictating and transcribing.

Portable dictation units are small recording devices that are especially popular with sales representatives and executives who spend considerable time away from the office. The dictation is recorded on mini-, micro-, or picocassettes. The dictation units are self-contained (all in one unit), and some are small enough to fit in

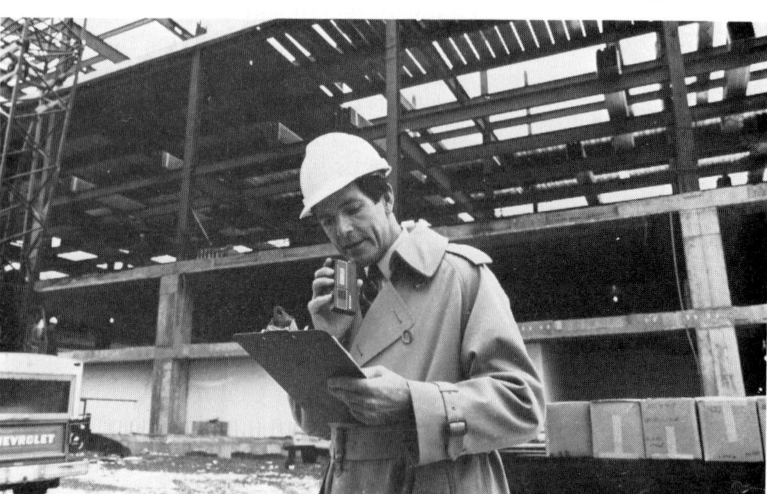

Portable dictation equipment allows people on the move to record information conveniently.

Desktop dictation units are in widespread use.

a pocket. Usually, they run on rechargeable batteries. Their microphones are built in and can be sensitive enough to record conferences without missing a whisper, even in a large room.

Desktop dictation machines can be a dictation unit, a transcription unit, or both. Desktop units that can be used for both dictation and transcription sometimes are called **combination units.** These are the most popular type of desktop unit.

Desktop units are used primarily by executives who do most of their dictating in the office and who dictate on a daily basis. Many desktop units are no bulkier or heavier than portable recorders. Some are small enough to store easily in desk drawers and may even double as portables. With advances in electronic technology, manufacturers of desktop units are constantly developing new features that can make the secretary's job—and the author's—easier.

In a **central recording system,** all the authors dictate their documents to a single, centralized device by calling the recording center on the telephone or by speaking into a microphone wired directly to the center. The recording device at the dictation center may be equipped with a feature called **voice-operated relay (VOR).** If the author stops talking for a few seconds on a VOR machine, the recording stops until dictation resumes. VOR makes transcription go faster because the secretary hears a continuous flow of dictation, without long pauses. Central recording systems usually are used in large offices with dozens or even hundreds of authors. They may be more economical than separate desktop units for each executive.

In some central recording systems, dictation is stored on an endless loop until it is transcribed. In central systems that don't use endless loops, dictation from a number of authors is recorded on a number of cassettes simultaneously. Like an endless loop, a

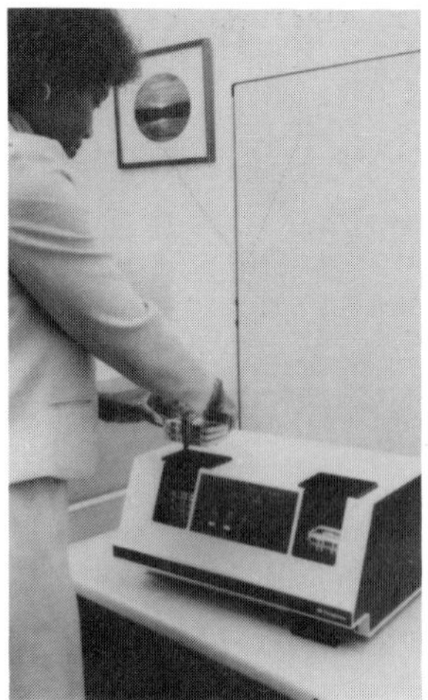

A multiple recording system like this one uses stacked cassettes.

multiple cassette system receives dictation from authors who gain access to it by telephone or special microphones and handsets. The cassettes are stacked on a machine that records them and plays them back for transcription. With a multiple cassette system, authors can dictate by telephone at any hour, whether or not the system supervisor is on duty. The recording device automatically arranges the cassettes in the order in which they are recorded. This means that those recorded earliest are the first to be transcribed unless another document has been designated as being more urgent.

A very large organization with a central recording system may have several transcription teams in different locations. Because cassettes are portable and easily distributed, transcriptionists do not all need to work in the recording center, as they do with endless loops.

The time it takes for dictation to be processed and returned to the author is called **turnaround time**. Whether a central dictation system uses an endless loop or cassettes, a supervisor is needed to keep track of the workload and turnaround time, assign the dictation to transcriptionists in sequence or by special priority, and check their work for accuracy.

In a modern word processing center, the supervisor often uses a computer to monitor and organize work. The computer's memory stores information about the workload—what work has been assigned to each transcriptionist, how much remains unassigned, how much already has been completed, turnaround times, and so forth. The supervisor can key this information into a computer (although some of it may go to the computer automatically from the recording equipment). The computer displays the information on a video display terminal or VDT (sometimes referred to as a video display or video screen). With the keyboard, the supervisor can instruct the computer to display any information in the computer's memory.

The supervisor can call for status reports on any documents processed by the dictation center. The video display can show if a document has been finished, is still being transcribed, or is awaiting the originator's revision or approval.

Voice Messaging

When you use the telephone, you are using voice messaging. The telephone transmits your voice so it can be heard by the person at the receiving end. As you speak, you input a voice message. When you finish your conversation, you hang up. If your conversation were stored by a **telephone answering machine,** it could be played back.

There are many advantages to having your voice stored by some type of **voice message system (VMS)**, especially in an office setting. For example, let's say you want to talk with Trisha Scott, a salesperson. Ms. Scott visits customers during much of her working day and spends little time in her office. At the end of each day, she usually has several calls to return. Ms. Scott realizes that many of the calls she receives are from customers who want to buy her products. If she waits too long to return the calls, she may lose a sale to her competition. Her VMS permits Ms. Scott to access her calls frequently so she can return them without having to return to her office. Ms. Scott can telephone her office several times during the day to listen to the **voice mail** (sometimes called **voice store-and-forward**) messages that have been recorded. She decides who must be called back immediately and who can wait. She does not have to interrupt her secretary to ask for her messages, which are as detailed as the caller wishes. No details are lost, as they might be when messages are taken by hand.

Voice messaging is a form of **electronic mail (E-mail),** defined broadly as distributing or communicating information using automated equipment. E-mail may originate as voice (as in voice messaging), by handwritten or keyed copy, and by images that may be scanned—to name a few. Voice messaging and other forms of electronic mail are discussed more fully in Chapter 7.

Voice Recognition

Voice recognition systems utilize speech as the method of input.

Voice recognition is probably one of the most exciting emerging technologies for the office of the future. As with voice messaging, speech is the input method. But unlike voice messaging, **voice** or **speech recognition** equipment actually "understands" human speech. **Voice-to-text** machines can recognize and change human speech into written words, which can be displayed on a screen just as if they had been keyed on a keyboard.

Although voice-to-text is available for commercial use, voice recognition technology is still in its early stages. Many obstacles remain. For example, the "vocabularies" of voice recognition equipment are being expanded from a few hundred to several thousand words. However, only a few hundred of these are "standard" or **speaker-independently recognized** to a wide range of speakers. Equipment can be "trained" to a particular person's voice patterns, but then fewer people can use it.

One of the biggest problems with voice recognition equipment is that voices are like fingerprints. No two people sound or speak alike. Not only do dialects vary from place to place, but even within one locality, each person has a very distinct style of expression, emphasis, and pronunciation. We also sound different at different times of the day, and when we have a cold or the flu.

Then there is the problem of grammar and punctuation. If a person says "whether or not to," the computer may hear "weather, or not too" or even "whether or not, two." Background noise also can throw a computer off. When you think about all these obstacles, it is remarkable that people are able to understand each other—let alone that machines can understand people. We still take for granted in our communication a lot of things that computers are not yet capable of handling.

However, the problems associated with voice recognition technology are being solved. Manufacturers are working to develop voice recognition into what could be the most productive office tool of the 1990s. Already, quite a few software products are being used, with varying degrees of success, to integrate voice and text. Here are some examples of how voice recognition can help distribute and communicate the increasing amount of information available to us.

A simulated airline reservation system (such as that developed by AT&T's Bell Labs) might work in the following way. You could call in and ask, "What flights leave for Chicago today?" A computerized voice would tell you the flight schedule for Chicago. You could make your reservation by computer or instruct your computer to switch you to an operator at the reservation desk.

The U.S. Postal Service also has experimented with a voice system. Voice recognition equipment could help route the ever-increasing volume of mail. For example, a postal worker reading the address on a package or a batch of mail might call out a ZIP Code, a city, or a mail route. A conveyer belt or other system could then direct the mail to the correct loading dock without a postal worker having to handle it.

For voice recognition systems to work, people will have to learn how to talk to a computer. They will need to know what the computer can and cannot understand. Speakers will need to identify themselves before they can begin communication—by voice or some other input method, such as use of a plastic card. The magnetic signals embedded in the card would **encode** (translate) the voice for the computer to identify it.

As with any input method, the key to voice recognition is people. It takes people making good decisions to instruct machines to help people complete work. Voice recognition promises an exciting future for the office—a future in which you and others like you will play major roles.

Scanning

Another way to input information is to scan it using a machine that "sees" and "reads" a document or image. **Scanning** is an optical, rather than keyed or voice, input that eliminates the need to rekey documents into a machine for processing. Scanning applications vary from text and data entry to **image scanning** and/or a combination of applications. A wide range of scanning equipment is available—hand-held units, desktop models, and floor consoles.

Optical Character Recognition

Scanning is most commonly done in offices today by **optical character recognition (OCR)**, an electronic method of scanning input. An OCR device, sometimes referred to as an **optical character reader,** is used to scan characters on a keyed or printed page. It recognizes the printed characters, which it converts into signals and records on magnetic or other media. The stored document may be "called" to the visual display of a computer. The soft copy on the screen can be edited and proofread by keying in changes. The finished copy can be stored or printed.

With OCR equipment, a printed document does not have to be rekeyed for processing. OCR equipment is popular in offices where a large volume of existing documents needs some type of processing. In such cases, scanning is a useful input tool for quick turnaround in producing a completed document.

Some of the older OCRs can scan only original documents that have very specific kinds of keyed characters. Other OCRs are **omnifont** readers and can scan almost any standard **font** (typestyle), including proportional type and dot matrix print. OCRs for text usually are referred to as **OCR page readers** because they recognize characters. Many newer OCR page readers are **intelligent OCRs,** meaning they have programming capabilities for such applications as communications and facsimile transfer.

Image Scanning

Images and graphics also can be scanned, stored, and edited. **Image** and **graphics scanning** have become popular because of desktop publishing. The image scanning process is somewhat different from the OCR process, so in general, image scanning has been viewed as a separate technology from OCR. Unlike OCR technology, image scanners do not recognize characters. Many image scanners capture a graphic image on a flat surface by **digitizing** it (changing the image into binary or on/off electrical impulses the computer understands). The image is stored in digital form but can be displayed on the screen as an image—just as it was viewed on the flat surface. An operator can manipulate the image by keystrokes, a light pen, a mouse, a joystick, and a digitizer (explained

Scanning devices make it possible to scan, digitize, and input documents into a computer without keying them.

in the next section). The image can be totally repositioned, or only certain portions of the picture may be moved. Other changes also can be made. For example, the size and color of some or all parts of the image may be changed.

Today OCR and image scanning as a combination technology is becoming popular. More and more OCR manufacturers are adding graphics capabilities to their equipment so that text and graphics can be integrated. Many OCR and image scanners can scan images, charts, illustrations, art, drawings, signatures, diagrams, and so on—even those that are colored. As a method of input, they scan documents accurately and quickly. Many OCR manufacturers claim their equipment can scan 300,000 characters with only one error. Depending on the type of document to be scanned, some OCRs can scan an entire page of text and images in five seconds or at over 700 pages an hour. Also, a document can be scanned directly to your VDT so you can start working on it before the OCR has finished recording it.

Whether you realize it or not, some type of scanning probably touches your life almost daily. For example, you may have had to fill out a form by marking your name on a grid. You made pencil marks in the alphabet positions representing your name. An **optical mark reader** can scan the marks you made and translate them into text—your name. When you write a check, the bank uses a **magnetic ink character reader (MICR)** to scan the code at the bottom of your check. The code identifies your bank, account number, and similar information so that the bank's computer system can properly adjust the amount in your account. When you go to the grocery store, a checker may scan the wrapper of a candy bar that you buy. The scanning machine reads the bar code or **universal product code (UPC)** label on the wrapper. The information on the bar code shows the price of the candy bar and provides the grocery store with a record of the sale and an accurate record of its current inventory.

Other Input Devices

Several types of input tools have been developed for use with microcomputers and other computer equipment. Many of these are designed to minimize the amount of keyboarding, often replacing function keys on a keyboard. However, these devices are generally used along with the function keys to help accomplish work tasks.

Joystick

One such device is the **joystick**, a hand-held instrument that lets the user control the cursor on the display screen. Joysticks are most frequently used with video games.

Mouse

With many computer systems, you can use a **mouse**, a small hand-sized device for manipulating the cursor on the screen and for performing other commands. Using a mouse connected to your computer, you can easily control the cursor movements, access files, edit and manipulate text, store and recall files, and print your work. One or more buttons to help you perform these operations may be on the top of the mouse. On the bottom is a wheel- or ball-type mechanism that allows you to easily move the mouse around on your desk. As you do so, the cursor on the screen moves because an electrical signal is transferred from the movement of the ball to your computer. The cursor movements on the screen mimic those of the mouse.

To operate a mouse, you need a small amount of space (about an eight-inch square) on your desk or some other flat surface. Some mouse users keep a "mouse pad" (an antistatic, semisoft piece of material) on top of their desks to help the ball or wheel on the bottom of the mouse roll evenly for smooth cursor movement. (A slick, hard surface sometimes causes uneven movement of the ball, which translates into choppy cursor movement.) A mouse pad also helps keep a clear space for using a mouse. The convenience of a mouse depends on each individual user's work habits. A word processing specialist, for example, may find it cumbersome to move back and forth from the mouse to the keyboard and still maintain a high level of keyboarding speed.

Light Pen

Another device for inputting information, especially good for graphics and image manipulation, is a **light pen**, which resembles

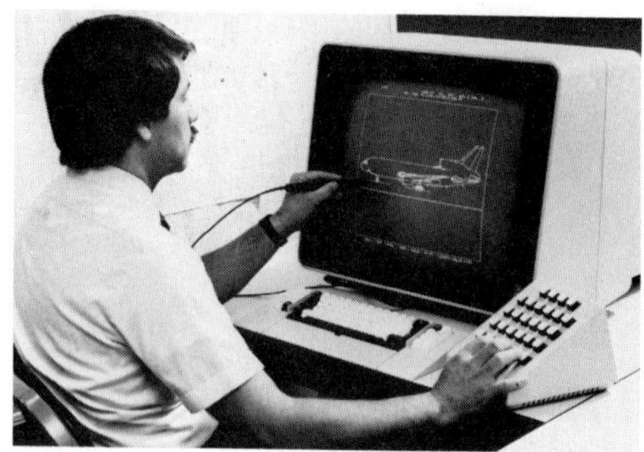

Computer-aided design equipment.

a standard writing pen with a light-sensitive cell on the end. When the pen tip comes in contact with the display terminal, a point on the display is identified, allowing information to be entered or "created" and modified.

Digitizer

A small hand-sized device called a **digitizer** also can be used to input images and graphics into a computer. Using a digitizer, you can trace art and convert lines and curves of a sketch or picture to reproduce the original. A digitizer "reads" each point of contact and translates the points into digital impulses that the computer can read. Digitizers frequently are used by individuals who do **computer-aided design (CAD),** which usually involves creating or manipulating detailed drawings on a computer screen. These drawings often are associated with manufacturing.

Graphics Tablet

Another input device useful for a CAD or graphics design system is a **graphics tablet**. It has a smooth, flat surface used for sketching figures, drawing designs, and tracing pictures. As you draw on the boardlike surface of a graphics tablet, your drawing appears on the computer screen. With some graphics tablets, you draw with a light pen to input and modify computer-generated art. Other types of graphics tablets require a special penlike device called a **stylus.** For some systems, a stylus may leave an "ink" trail on the tablet as you draw, allowing you to see your drawing both on the graphics tablet and on your computer screen.

Touch-Sensitive Screens

A **touch-sensitive screen** can be used as an input device. Possibly you have used a touch-sensitive display in a department store or shopping mall to get directions, place an order, or find out if a store stocks a certain item. Or maybe you have used an automated teller machine with a touch-sensitive screen for a banking transaction. These are easy to use. By touching a point or designated area on the screen with your finger, you select an action to be taken. Menus and questions may appear on the screen to assist you.

A touch-sensitive screen can be used as an input device.

When you touch the screen, the computer performs the action associated with the area or block touched. Thus, the computer responds much like it does to keystrokes, a light pen, mouse, or similar device.

Imaging and Graphics

Input is not necessarily accomplished by a single method. **Alphanumeric** information (letters and numbers), for example, can be inputted by several methods. Ways of inputting visual information, however, are more limited. Image scanning is an excellent way to input visual information such as pictures, charts, architect's blueprints, and maps. Other technological developments have provided several additional methods of inputting images, some of which combine various kinds of technology.

You are probably familiar with how video cameras and camcorders work. Although they may not be used for completing office tasks, they are used to record images. Similar devices are used in offices to input images. For example, by linking a camera to a computer, you can input images into a computer. These can be stored, edited, and printed; processed in much the same way written text and data are processed; sent over telephone lines to another office; transmitted by satellite to another location; or transferred electronically to another person's computer next door.

Inputting an image to send to another person or for processing may involve several methods. You may use a light pen, joystick, or mouse; a graphics tablet; or a touch-sensitive screen. Each presents advantages for inputting and processing information—

especially when images and graphics are involved. Image and graphic processing is currently becoming more integrated with text processing.

As you progress through this text, you will see how important input is in the information processing cycle. You will also learn how sophisticated equipment is making it easy for office employees to work with all types of inputs.

CHAPTER SUMMARY

- An author is any person who originates information that passes through an information processing system.
- In a business office, nearly everyone acts as an author from time to time.
- Word origination is the input stage of information processing. It is the means by which the author puts ideas into words.
- Documents can be originated by longhand, shorthand, keyboarding, workstation transfer, machine dictation, voice messaging, voice recognition, scanning, and imaging and graphics.
- Information processing with automated equipment has made keyboarding and workstation document transfer popular methods of document origination.
- In most situations, the fastest and most efficient means of document creation is by machine dictation.
- Machines for dictation use either internal storage media or discrete (external) media.
- Internal storage media, which are kept inside a machine, also are referred to as endless loops. An endless loop is a long recording tape that has been joined at the ends.
- Discrete media are recording media that can be detached from the machines and used on other equipment. They can be further classified as inscribed, magnetic, or digital media.
- Inscribed media usually cannot be erased or reused.
- Magnetic media are tapes that record the author's voice by means of electrical impulses and magnetism. Digital media change the voice into a binary code.
- A cassette is a magnetic recording tape that is permanently encased in a small plastic container. Cassettes come in standard and miniaturized sizes: mini-, micro-, and picocassettes.
- In order for recorded dictation to be transcribed, it must be recorded on a medium that is compatible with the transcription equipment.
- In a central recording system, all the authors dictate their documents to a recording device at a single, centralized location. An author gains access to such a system by calling it on the telephone or using a special microphone.

- A central recording system may use an endless loop or multiple cassettes.
- A major goal of any information processing system is to achieve fast turnaround from transcriptionist to author.
- In a modern information processing center, a supervisor keeps tabs on the workload and turnaround times, assigns dictation, and checks work for accuracy.
- Many input methods are used at various stages of processing information.

VOCABULARY

analog signals
binary code
central recording system
computer-aided design (CAD)
computer-aided transcription
digital audio tapes (DATs)
digital media
digitizer
discrete media
document creation/origination
electronic shorthand
endless loop
graphics tablet
image scanning
inscribed media
internal storage media
joystick
light pen
machine shorthand
magnetic media
manual shorthand
media compatibility
microcassette
minicassette
mouse
multiple cassette system
optical character recognition (OCR)
picocassette
source document
touch-sensitive screen
turnaround time
voice-operated relay (VOR)
voice message system (VMS)
voice recognition

CHAPTER QUESTIONS

1. What are some specific kinds of employees within a company who might act as authors?
2. There are a number of different methods of creating documents. Name five, and give some advantages of each.
3. What are some of the advantages of transferring documents between workstations?
4. How can machine dictation help managers as well as secretaries work more efficiently?
5. Why do some authors resist using dictation machines? Give at least three reasons. Which do you consider the most valid and the least valid reasons?
6. What kind of equipment should be used for transcribing dictation recorded on microcassettes? Why is your choice of transcription equipment limited?

7. What is turnaround time, and why is it a key factor in evaluating a word processing department?
8. What is the supervisor's role in tracing the progress of a document through a centralized word processing system? How can a computer help the supervisor?
9. How does voice messaging differ from voice recognition? What are the advantages and disadvantages of each?
10. What are three ways that images and graphics can be input for computer processing? Give at least one advantage of each.

CASE STUDY

Dundee Industries, an office supplies distributor, has grown dramatically in the last few years and is considering the purchase of information processing equipment. The company has two dozen executives and scores of other employees, but its methods of creating documents have changed little since it was a much smaller operation run entirely by two brothers and a sister. Dundee executives, who spend most of their working time in the company's headquarters, usually dictate documents to their secretaries, who take their bosses' words down in shorthand and later key the documents. Sometimes, however, the executives give the secretaries rough drafts of the documents that have been crudely keyed or written in longhand, and the secretaries transcribe them.

Dundee also employs about 25 sales representatives, each of whom is responsible for calling on office supply stores within a large territory. The representatives seldom visit the home office. When they are there, they generally spend most of their time writing follow-up letters to customers and prospects, using sketchy notes jotted down after calling on the stores.

The company's 12 secretaries key virtually all the documents the managers and salespeople generate. The top four executives have private secretaries. The other 8 secretaries each work for two or three lower-level managers. All 12 secretaries cooperate to process the sales representatives' work because these people do not have personal secretaries.

What kinds of equipment would you recommend Dundee purchase for its new information processing system? Explain your recommendations.

CHAPTER 4

Hardware

Loretta McBride noticed that more and more office employment ads stressed computer and word processing skills. To update her skills she enrolled in an information processing course offered by a local computer vendor. She found that her good reasoning and keyboarding skills were valuable in learning the concepts and basics of an information system. As she progressed through the course, she enjoyed learning new vocabulary and practicing on the equipment. She learned, too, how important it is to understand the concepts and basics, since there are many common features among equipment, software, and procedures. Transferring her knowledge to almost any office setting would be easy.

Automation has become commonplace in offices, and office workers who can operate electronic equipment efficiently are valued employees. Today, much of the automated equipment used in offices is computer-based. Fortunately, the many similarities in the equipment help office workers input, process, store, output, and distribute information.

No doubt you will acquire a new vocabulary as you learn about office automation and what it does. Just as the invention of high-fidelity recording and playback equipment added new terms to our language (such as woofer, tweeter, stereophonic, and cassette), computers also have added new words. Many of these terms are shortened word forms—CPU, ROM, RAM, WORM, and EPROM. Once you learn what each one means, you will find them useful for working in an information system. Let's explore some of the basics of computer technology that will be useful to you as an office worker in an office information system.

Hardware Categories

Office automation equipment frequently is referred to as **hardware**. Hardware differs from **software** in that hardware is the physical machine. It can be seen and touched. Software, on the other hand, is a set of instructions or a **program** to tell the hardware what to do. (Software will be discussed in Chapter 5.) The kinds of hardware in an office can vary widely. Hardware can be categorized in several ways—function, size, capabilities, and even cost. Frequently, the categories overlap, making it difficult to establish clear-cut divisions. As technology helps us produce more highly sophisticated equipment, the categories are becoming even more blurred.

In this text, hardware is grouped into two main categories: (1) word processors/electronic typewriters, and (2) computer systems. This distinction emphasizes how office automation has grown out of **manual** and **mechanical** (machine) methods into equipment using **electromechanical** (electronics and machines) and **electronic** methods. Although hardware might be grouped in many ways, you will find there are many basic characteristics among equipment used in an office information system.

Word Processors/ Electronic Typewriters

The concept of word processing has been around since 1918, the year the Hooven Company sold the first automated typewriting system. This noisy mechanical system used an Underwood typewriter as both the keyboard and the printer. The storage unit was an embossed cylinder, somewhat like the one in a music box.

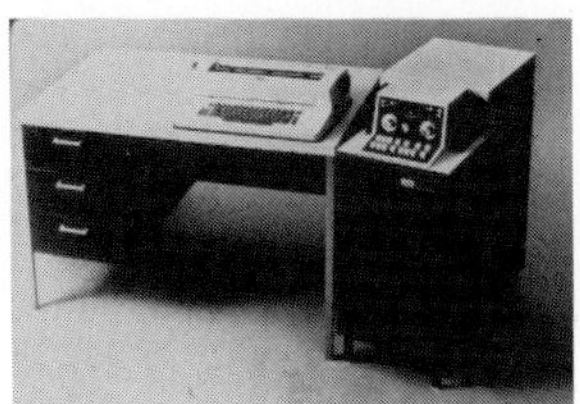

IBM's MT/ST (Magnetic Tape/Selectric Typewriter) was the first automated typing system to use a magnetic storage medium.

In the 1930s and 1940s, quieter automated typewriters were introduced. These machines recorded keystrokes by punching patterns of holes in paper sheets or strips. The principle was the same as that used in the old player pianos. When the punched paper was used to drive the typewriter, the machine automatically produced error-free typewritten copy.

Word processing as we know it today did not appear until the introduction of magnetic storage units—tapes that could be erased and corrected. Magnetic storage gave word processors the editing capabilities that made them useful for producing documents of all kinds. The MT/ST (Magnetic Tape/Selectric Typewriter) was the first automated typing system to record keystrokes on a magnetic storage medium. IBM introduced it in 1964, the same time they introduced the term "word processing." The MT/ST combines an IBM Selectric Typewriter with processing and storage components. The MT/ST stores up to 20 printed pages on a reel of magnetic tape and prints about 150 words a minute or about three times as fast as most typists can type.

In 1969 IBM introduced the MC/ST (Magnetic Card/ Selectric Typewriter), sometimes called the Mag Card. It stores keystrokes on a magnetic-coated card rather than on a tape, like the MT/ST. Each card can record one page of keyboarding—up to 75 lines, with 100 characters a line.

In 1972, CPT and Redactron introduced cassette tape text-editing machines. These store text on a tape cassette that holds up

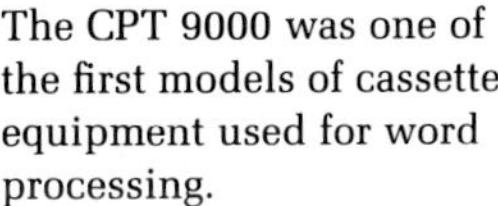

The CPT 9000 was one of the first models of cassette equipment used for word processing.

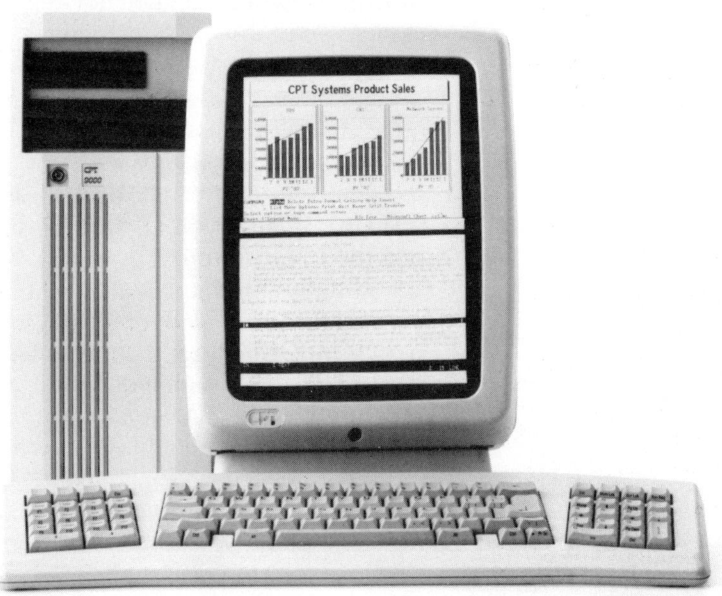

Display word processors display illuminated text during keyboarding.

to 60 pages of documents. The memory typewriter, introduced by IBM in 1974, has many of the same capabilities. However, unlike the earlier Mag Cards, all of its components (including storage) are internal to the typewriter. Its storage capacity is about 50 to 100 printed pages.

Equipment of the 1960s and 1970s is frequently referred to as **mechanical word processors**. These were **blind** units (lacking VDT screens that show the operator what is being keyed). Blind word processors are good for repetitive tasks such as automatic letters. They are not desirable when extensive text editing is required. Many of these machines also may be **dedicated word processors**, designed specifically for word processing functions rather than for other functions such as integrated word/data processing, automated filing, and electronic mail.

Lexitron introduced the first display word processor—a dedicated word processor—in 1971. By this time, word processing was the foundation of the entire office automation concept. The Lexitron had all the capabilities of earlier equipment—with one important addition. It had a video display terminal (VDT) that looked much like a TV screen. Essentially, it was an automated typewriter with a screen on which an operator could view the text being processed. Revisions, even extensive ones, could be easily made. The operator could see the changes being made. Hard copies no longer needed to be printed to show how the document would look in its final form.

Traditionally, word processors were classified as either standalones or clustered systems. A standalone unit is just what the name implies—self-contained. A **standalone** system depends only on its own components, operating without the help of other equip-

This IBM Wheelwriter 70 Series II typewriter has an add-on display.

ment. It is a single-user system. A standalone system usually includes a **central processing unit (CPU)**, keyboard, screen, storage unit, and sometimes even a printer. An operator who uses a standalone system can be independent and does not have to rely on other equipment or systems to input and process a document.

A **clustered** or **shared system** depends on equipment that several operators may use or network. For example, let's say you have your own keyboard and screen on which you process documents. Three of your co-workers also have the same hardware. However, none of this equipment has a CPU. You and your co-workers share the CPU through some type of cable or network that is attached to your equipment. When a CPU is shared, the shared system is called a **shared logic system**. Its brain (CPU) or "intelligence" is in one central place and is shared by several users.

One drawback of a shared logic system is that if the central processing unit breaks down, none of the operators who share it can continue working on the system until the CPU is operating again. A CPU failure can even erase documents from the **memory** or scramble them. A safeguard against this problem is for each operator's equipment to have some storage as well as its own CPU.

Such a system may be called a **smart terminal, intelligent workstation**, or **distributed logic system.** (Terminals not so equipped that are entirely dependent on a separate CPU for memory and operating instructions are sometimes called **dumb terminals**.)

If a shared system involves operators sharing types of resources other than a CPU, it is usually called a **shared resource system**. For example, several operators sharing a printer would be using a shared resource system. Sharing a printer is a common way for a company to save money. Because a printer usually is idle much of the time while an operator is busy with other tasks, sharing a printer makes sense.

Shared systems (both logic and resource) may also be referred to as **multiuser, multiterminal,** or **multistation configurations**. The **configuration**, or the way in which system components are shared, varies from office to office. For example, there may be 10 operators who work at 10 separate workstations but share storage, or the configuration might include 12 workstations and only 1 printer.

Other ways of sharing equipment might include **time-sharing** with each subscriber billed for time used. Time-sharing may be purchased through a tenant-sharing or a third-party maintenance service. Discussion of shared systems and services, multiuser systems, and characteristics of dedicated word processors, in contrast to other types of hardware, will follow later.

Today, **electronic typewriters (ETs)** are frequently called word processors. Electronic typewriters have gained popularity as more expensive dedicated word processors have faded from the

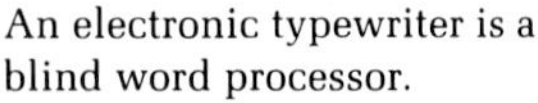

An electronic typewriter is a blind word processor.

A linear display, often called a "window into memory," is useful for verifying input.

market. When word processors became popular, few people would have guessed that electronic typewriters would become as prominent as they are in offices today. Electronics was the main factor for this trend. In the late 1970s, electronics made it cost-effective to introduce ETs. The early ETs were similar to automated typewriters, but many had greater storage capacity and capabilities for easier text editing—at a lower cost—than did automated typewriters.

Some ETs have detachable keyboards, but many look like a typewriter with a **linear display** just above the keyboard. (A linear display is usually a line display. It may also be a small liquid crystal or vacuum fluorescent screen. Some ETs show one, two, or more lines of 15 to 80 characters each.) The linear display is sometimes referred to as a **thin screen** or a "window into memory." A linear display helps the operator verify output, but it still falls short of being of real value for extensive text editing.

A wide range of electronic typewriters is available on the market today. They are popular because they can perform numerous word processing applications. Many of these applications are commonplace to word processors. Dedicated word processors usually are more expensive than ETs and are becoming obsolete because of the microcomputer industry.

Many of the popular electronic typewriters have a number of features in common. These features are built into the hardware of ETs and make the equipment **user-friendly** or easy to use. (Many of these features are common to software that can be used with numerous types of computer equipment.) These **text-editing** features represent some of the most common features built into ETs. (See Chapter 5 for more discussion of these and other features common

Features Common to Many Electronic Typewriters

- **block move/delete/copy**—extends add/delete/move/copy text-editing to "cutting and pasting" lines, pages, or other specified portions of text
- **carrier return**—like a typewriter, but faster and smoother; there is no paper "slippage," as with manual methods
- **centering**—centers text between margins
- **column layout**—sets up columns by longest line in column
- **column wrap**—added text does not disturb column order; column information "snakes" from one column to another and stays in order
- **correction**—covers or "lifts off" incorrect keystrokes
- **decimal tabulation**—aligns numbers in a column for adding
- **flush right margin**—aligns to right margin rather than left margin; good for dates and page numbers
- **forms mapping**—stored form appears on screen as a "map" to help operator fill in the blanks in the correct places
- **half spacing**—horizontal spacing of half rather than full spaces; good for forms and putting two characters in one space
- **hyphenation**—hyphenating words at the ends of lines
- **indent**—including temporary "margins" for indenting blocks of text
- **indexing**—moving up and down in text
- **international symbols**—foreign accent marks and Greek letters
- **line spacing**—allows .5 to 3 vertical lines
- **margins**—one or more sets of margins can be set/stored
- **pagination**—creates pages of a specified length and adds page numbers to the document
- **relocate**—return to keying location after correcting
- **right justification**—aligns copy so both right and left margins are perfect, as in textbook and newspaper copy
- **search/replace, global search/replace**—finds and changes each occurrence of specified text with a specified replacement
- **simultaneous input/output**—permits printing while editing
- **stop coding**—allows text to be inserted at "stop" points while printing a document
- **tabulation**—includes decimal stops for statistical copy
- **underscore**—underlines characters or large amounts of text
- **undo**—returns document to form before last editing change
- **word wrap**—word goes to next line if it extends beyond right margin

to more sophisticated ETs and many word processing software programs.)

One reason ETs have gained so much popularity is that they can be easily **upgraded** (enhanced or changed as improvements become available). Upgrading an ET is more economical than upgrading a dedicated word processor. Most ET vendors are providing add-ons and modular plug-in modules to give users of electronic typewriters more information processing capabilities. Add-ons might include screen displays, memory units, storage devices, or automatic sheet feeders. Many can be snapped on to ETs at a fraction of the cost of upgrading or purchasing a word processor that has similar features.

Many add-on vendors are equipping electronic typewriters with **interfaces** (devices for sending the pulses of the keystrokes to and from an add-on to enable processing to take place). These interfaces, called **KSR** (keystroke send and receive) devices, make it easy to install and use the add-ons.

Any type of add-on that is not essential to hardware operation may be called a **peripheral** (any device that extends equipment capabilities but is not necessary to its operation). Several types of peripherals, including storage devices and printers, are discussed later.

This electronic typewriter, the Sharp ZY-1000S, can also be used as a word processor.

Because many electronic typewriter manufacturers are making it possible to upgrade ETs with add-ons, these machines are looking more like word processors all the time. They are replacing electric and automated typewriters and rapidly gaining in popularity and sales in the word processing market. ETs that combine several functions and capabilities often are referred to as **secretarial workstations.** These are alternatives to the more powerful, multiple-function systems, such as those possible with microcomputers.

Computer Systems

In today's offices, most information processing is done with a computer system. While there is a wide range of computer systems, one of the most popular types of office computers is a **microcomputer**, the smallest of all the hardware in the computer family. This is also called a **micro, a personal computer (PC)**, or a **professional computer.** (This text uses PC, professional computer, and microcomputer interchangeably.) Just because microcomputers are small does not mean they are not fast and powerful.

Micros are relatively inexpensive and yet versatile enough for many applications in small, medium, and even large businesses. Micros can do what most large computers 10 to 20 years ago could do but they can do it better, faster, and cheaper. The popularity of microcomputers has given rise to a $200 billion-plus industry.

Because some micros are so powerful, they may be considered in the **workstation** category. As with many kinds of computer equipment, the definition of workstations has changed over the years—mainly because of their power and speed. Today a workstation is a computer with capabilities extending from networking to communications. A workstation usually is a multitasking (many functions), multiuser machine with large memory capability as well as mass (large) storage capability. Workstations may be as powerful and fast as some of the larger computers, yet cost less. The workstation, as a category of computer equipment, is growing faster than categories of larger computers. Workstations and PCs form the very core of many modern offices because they are designed for **end users** (operators or people who use computer equipment). But the workstation market has become somewhat blurred with the introduction of **supermicros** and **superminicomputers**, two categories of equipment that extend micro and mini capabilities even further.

Minicomputers or **minis** are medium-sized computers. Faster and more expensive than microcomputers, they can process larger amounts of information. Minis are designed for flexibility, which makes them attractive for many different kinds of users. Since 1988, the minicomputer market has had some difficulty keeping pace with the increasingly greater computing power and speed of micros. Also, the cost of minis has not decreased as significantly as that of micros. For these reasons, some vendors feel that minis and PCs may continue to compete with each other—especially in medium to large businesses. Microcomputers will probably continue to give minis some real competition.

Microcomputers are also providing competition for many **mainframes** (large computers). Mainframes are used primarily by large businesses today and probably will be for many years to come. They have a great deal of power and are used for large-scale information processing such as would be done by a marketing firm, a retail chain, a manufacturing plant, or even the U.S. Internal Revenue Service in processing income taxes. In addition to their being costly, mainframes are expensive both to buy and to maintain. They require highly trained operators and sophisticated programs to run efficiently.

At the very top or high end of the computer industry are **supercomputers**, the most powerful, fastest, expensive computers on the market. (Supercomputers are used for extensive calculations or "number crunching" such as performed by the U.S. government or by large financial institutions in compiling all types of labor and population statistics.) Supercomputers cost in the millions of dollars. Because their applications are not oriented for the office work of many businesses, let's turn our attention back to office-related hardware.

This Tandy 1400 FD laptop computer comes with its own carrying case.

Micros or PCs can be used by small, medium, and large companies in every type of industry. They also are used by all types of end users in government offices, other types of organizations and institutions, and even at home. Some people may use a **home computer** to complete office work. A home computer can be whatever type computer a person desires—from a simple keyboard attached to a TV screen to a sophisticated PC or workstation. Many home computers are used for computerized shopping, stock market access, banking, home financial accounting, video games, and even word processing.

Portable computers such as the Compaq 386 offer convenience and versatility.

Some PCs or microcomputers are **portable** or **laptop.** These vary in size. Some are so small they are considered pocket computers. Some are called laptops and have their own compact carrying case, while others fit into a briefcase. Larger portables, about the size of a tote bag you might take to the gym, are considered "luggable." Some portables weigh as little as three pounds and are as powerful as much larger micros. Many of the portables, especially laptops, are convenient for use on a plane, bus, or train. Small portables are popular for business people who have to be away from the office.

Of the many differences between microcomputers and electronic typewriters, the biggest is versatility. A micro is much more versatile, has more power, and is faster than an ET. Thus, a micro can do many more things than an ET. It is designed to use a variety of software programs that can change the micro from a terminal that does word processing, communications, image processing, or all of these and more. An ET basically is a dedicated word processor (although even this market is getting more blurred with so many features that can be added to ETs). Most ET features are built into the machine—they are considered part of the hardware.

Many businesses purchase micros because they wish to do more than just word processing, which is the main function of an ET. Word processing with a micro is software-based rather than "built in," as in many ET systems. Some of the following micro hardware characteristics and features allow their users to do several applications in addition to information processing:

- **central processing unit**—brain of the system
- **clock speed**—how fast the system runs
- **expandability**—system flexibility to do many applications, such as communications and image processing
- **I/O capability**—types of input and output devices it can use
- **memory and storage**—type and amount of internal memory and storage
- **operating system**—instructions for running the system
- **peripherals**—the capabilities of displays, printers, and other storage devices
- **software support**—types of applications the system can do

Having a general knowledge of these and other system characteristics will be valuable to you as you learn more about information processing.

Hardware Components

Microcomputers have the same components and the same operating steps as larger computers. Even though dedicated word processors and electronic typewriters are less powerful than micros, they also share many commonalities with micros. From what you have learned this far, you probably have a good idea of the purpose of each of the five major components of most systems:

- **central processing unit (CPU)**—the logic, intelligence, or brain of a computer or computer-like device, sometimes called an **internal processor**

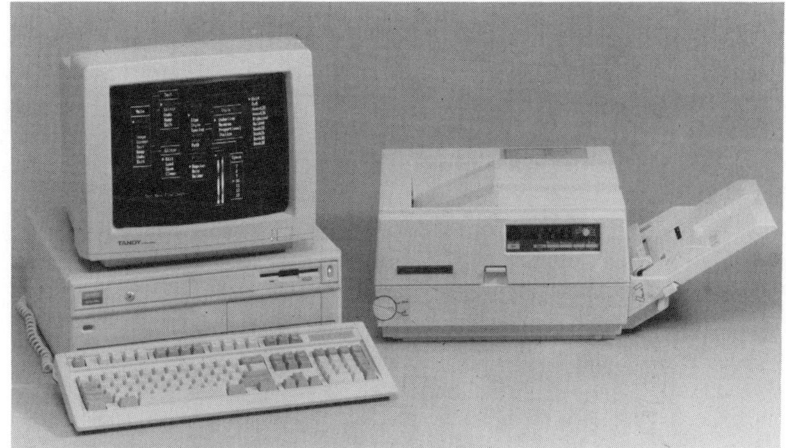

This microcomputer has the same operating components as a larger system: keyboard, display, CPU and storage unit (combined in this system), and printer.

- **keyboard**—much like a standard keyboard, but with additional keys for special functions
- **display**—a screen or monitor for viewing information, referred to as a *video* or *visual display terminal (VDT)*
- **storage unit**—where information is saved, stored, or housed; the storage media (for example, magnetic tape, floppy disk, and hard disk)
- **printer**—the device that produces a copy (for example, a paper hard copy)

Let's explore each component as it relates to processing information in an office information system.

Central Processing Unit

You can think of the CPU as the headquarters for all the computer's operations. It is where information is manipulated—data added and subtracted, text and images rearranged, and information sorted in logical ways. The software programs that give the computer the electronic instructions to do the work you want it to do also are executed (performed) in the CPU.

The CPU is a **microprocessor.** It may be a single **chip** or several **microchips**, usually wired together in an electronic circuit on a plastic board. Most chips are made of silicon and, in turn, contain their own electronic circuitry. Most chips are quite small, varying from a couple of inches to a fraction of an inch.

Computer circuitry works like a light bulb, except it is vastly more complex. You can see if an electric light is on or off. A computer can "understand" only on and off signals. Computer programmers use the number one to mean "on" and zero to mean "off." The number one thus means that the electricity can go through the circuit; zero means the circuit is closed, and electricity cannot get

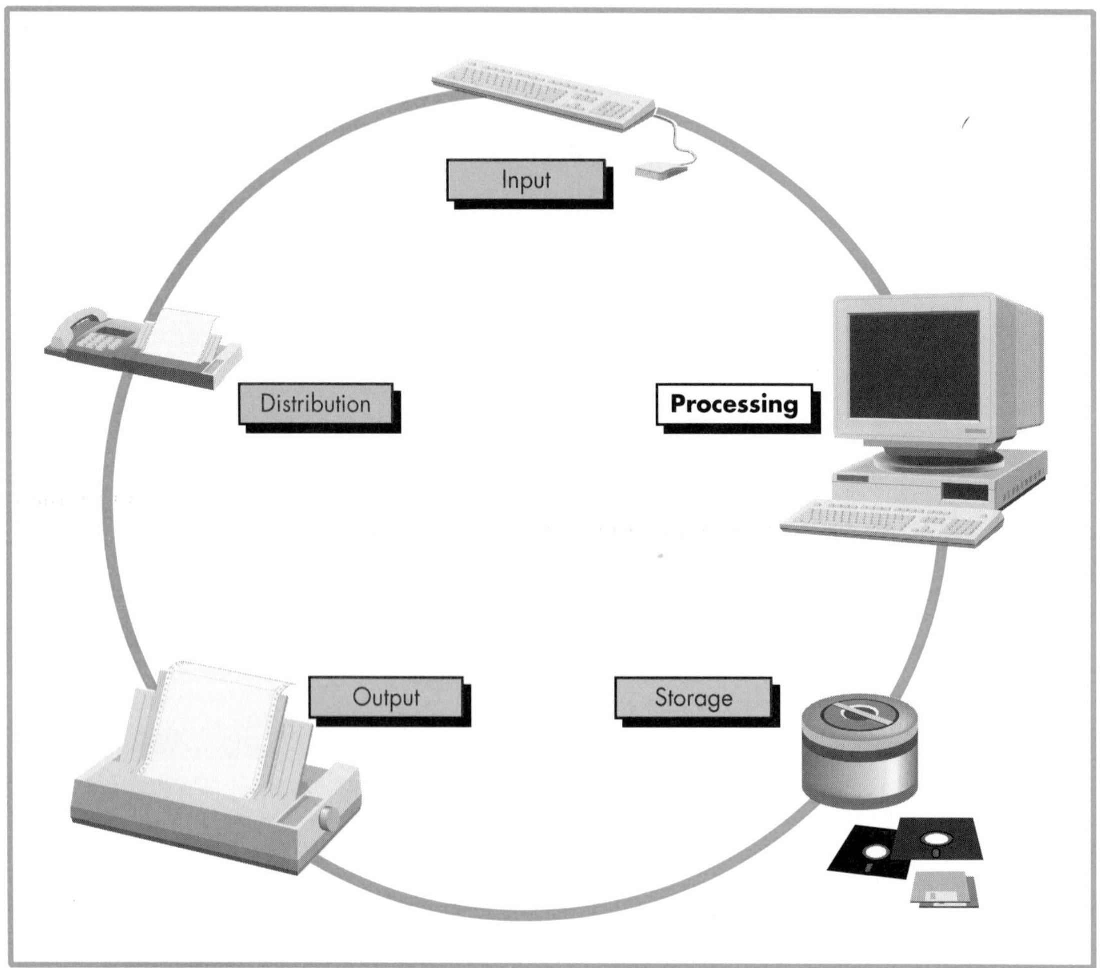

Processing is one of five stages in the information processing cycle.

past. Sending electricity through the computer's circuitry and then switching it on and off with great speed allows information to be processed.

A single one or a single zero represents the smallest unit of information a computer can understand: a **bit**. The word "bit" stands for binary digit (on/off electrical pulse). When these bits are grouped together, in a group of eight, it is called a **byte.** Computer memory capacity is referred to in bytes. The memory capacity of many office computers ranges from 64K (64 kilobytes or 64,000 bytes) to 1.5G (1.5 gigabytes or 1,500,000,000 bytes). The more memory a computer has, the more information it can process.

In addition to memory capacity, a computer's performance also is determined by its **cycle time** or **clock speed**—the time it takes to perform one instruction of an operation. The speed of a computer's CPU is considered the number of cycles performed in one second. CPU speed generally is given as **MIPS (millions of instructions per second)**. A **cycle per second (cps)** is called a **hertz (Hz).** A million hertz equal a **megahertz (MHz).** Cycle time, often referred to in megahertz, varies widely from computer to computer. Clock speed of early computers was around 2 MHz; a 33 MHz microcomputer was introduced in 1989. (Of course, supercomputers can process information many times faster than this.) Thus, you can see the enormous speed of modern computers. When you combine bit size, memory capacity, and cycle time, you can evaluate a computer's overall capacity or power.

The CPU has two types of memory: permanent and temporary. Let's compare them.

Permanent Memory The set of instructions (or the program) given to a computer by its manufacturer is kept in its **permanent memory** or **ROM (read-only memory).** Read-only memory is a set of instructions that enables the computer to act on the information entered from the keyboard. The larger the ROM capacity, the more functions it can be instructed (or programmed) to perform. Because ROM is permanent or **nonvolatile memory,** it only can be read; it cannot be changed. If the machine is turned off, the contents of ROM will still be there when it is turned on again.

In recent years, **PROM (programmable read-only memory)** and **EPROM (erasable or electronically programmable read-only memory)** chips were developed so program changes could be made easily and frequently. PROM allows the user to program the ROM for applications used frequently. EPROM allows the user to erase programs and program the system to be specific for the user. Until these developments were introduced, only the manufacturer could alter ROM.

Temporary Memory The CPU temporary memory is called **buffer** memory or **RAM (random-access memory)**. RAM is **volatile**; it is not permanent and is lost when the computer is turned off. As you input information into a computer, the CPU "writes" it into its temporary memory. The CPU can randomly add to, take from, or change information in its temporary memory.

Like permanent memories, RAM can vary in size. Some computers have large memories that may never be filled. Other systems have memories so small you may have to work on a long document in sections, keeping in storage all the sections except the one you are keyboarding or printing. Many electronic typewriters have limited ROM and RAM capabilities. Microcomputers usually have large ROM and RAM capabilities. Word processors fall somewhere in the middle.

Keyboard

Computer keyboards are similar to those on electronic typewriters, word processors, and manual typewriters. Most have a standard QWERTY arrangement of letters as well as number keys, a space bar, shift keys, and so forth. Some are dual keyboards, allowing the operator to switch or change to a Dvorak or other type of keyboard. (The Dvorak is an efficient keyboard that places the most commonly used letters on the "home row" or middle row of keys. The vowels and five of the most frequently used consonants are placed where keyboarders can reach them with the least amount of finger movement.)

The standard keyboard letters and numbers generally occupy the part of the keyboard closest to you, where you can reach them most easily. Keyboards also include a variety of **function keys**, such as cursor keys, operation keys, format keys, statistical keys, numeric keypad, and/or code keys. A 101-key keyboard has become quite standard, but there are many different configurations of keyboards on the market. Because there are some major differences in what the keys may do on different equipment, let's look at the various keys on an electronically controlled keyboard.

Function keys are for communicating instructions to the CPU. They help you perform automatically many tasks that would be tedious and time-consuming on an ordinary typewriter. For example, a function key on an electronic typewriter labeled "delete" tells the equipment to remove from your document the character, word, or amount of text you have indicated. Similarly, pressing a "HELP" function key may supply a definition or more information about a task you want to perform.

Cursor keys are function keys that help you move from one point to another within the document you are working on. A blinking spot of light on a display screen (a **cursor**) indicates the

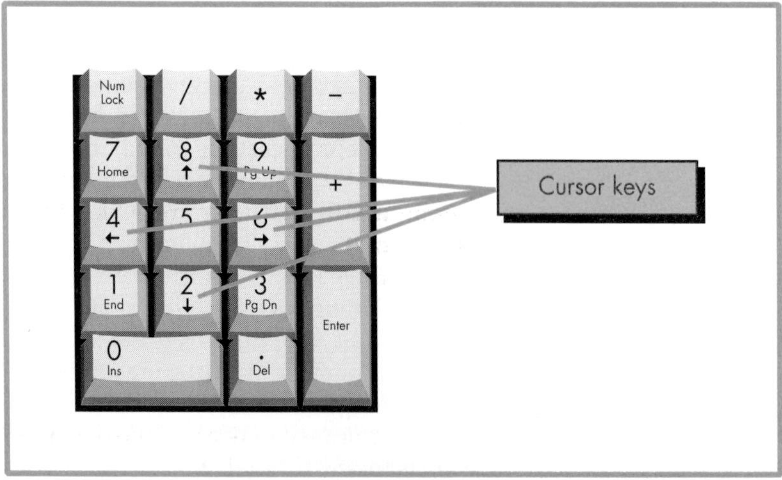

Cursor keys on keyboard.

position in the document where you may take your next action. If you do not wish to begin at that point, the cursor keys permit you to move the cursor around the screen.

Also, you cannot use the space bar to move to another place in your text as you would do on a typewriter. Using the space bar will create a space on the screen (and thus in the document). The space bar either inserts a space or creates one by replacing the character that was there before you pressed the space bar. Characters that have been replaced with blanks or with other characters cannot be retrieved; they have to be rekeyed.

Many keyboards have special keys that automatically send the cursor to the beginning or end of a document, page, paragraph, or line. Electronic typewriters (as well as dedicated word processors) are more apt to have more of these automatic function keys than are microcomputers.

The types of function keys vary widely from electronic typewriters and dedicated word processors to microcomputers. This is because microcomputers can perform many more functions than electronic typewriters or word processors—depending on the software program you are using. Let's say, for example, you are using word processing software on your microcomputer. By pressing an F4 function key, you may be able to center a line of text between margins. When you change your program to spreadsheet software, the same F4 key might be used to add a column of numbers. For this reason, microcomputer function keys may be labeled in a more general way (such as F1, F2, etc.) rather than as "ctr" or "center" for a center key function on an electronic typewriter. Because different functions can be assigned to these keys, they often are referred to as **soft keys.**

On a dedicated word processor or electronic typewriter, **operations keys** might be special function keys for storing documents ("stor"), sending the document to a printer ("print"), and similar operations. Keys on a microcomputer also may be defined by an operation the computer is instructed to perform. Usually, however, this is done with the software program rather than keys dedicated solely to certain operations. To help the operator remember what the keys do, many manufacturers provide key guides, called **templates** or function strips, that fit on or can be placed near the keyboard. Keyboard maps and operator instruction manuals are also useful references to keep close by.

Some keys and keyboards can be modified by manufacturers (or even by end users) to reflect the capabilities or the needs of a particular office. **Programmable** keys can be changed to do special applications. A communications function key, for example, may be programmed to instruct the machine to send documents to other word processors within the same system. Many microcomputer manufacturers have included a message window or "msg wdw" key to help the operator access the message system on a computer. Other function keys, such as **format keys,** may affect the placement of type on a page or establish the document layout. Format keys may include margins, tabs, line spacing, page breaks, centering, and underlining. Other function keys, such as **statistical keys,** may control decimal tabs, subscripts, superscripts, and other alignment or spacing adjustments often used in preparing tables or lists of figures. To enter numbers easily, a **ten-key numeric keypad** similar to a calculator's keys may be used along with the keyboard. The pad usually is positioned to the right of the keyboard.

Code keys are function keys common to many types of computer equipment. Some are designed to be used with other keys to expand keyboard functions. Code keys may operate in a manner similar to typewriter shift keys. If you hold down the shift key and press a letter, the letter is changed from lower to uppercase. In a similar manner, holding down a code key and pressing another key can change the keyboard. Code keys help an operator or end user perform a variety of operations from the keyboard.

Function keys usually have stored keystrokes to instruct the computer to execute specific operations. Some systems have the operation built into the keys; other functions become operational because of a software program. In either case, the functions have **default** settings that are preset by the manufacturer. Defaults are the standard settings (such as margins, tabs, and line spacing,) that the operator can change to customize formatting. Additional text-editing, formatting, and information processing functions are discussed in Chapter 5.

Even though you may become an expert on one system, you cannot expect to be an instant expert on another one. However, keyboards are more alike than they are different. Transferring from one kind of equipment to another will present little difficulty for you once you have become accustomed to electronic keyboarding in general.

Display

You have learned that a **visual display terminal (VDT)** is sometimes called by several other names, including **video display, display screen,** and **display terminal.** Sometimes it also is referred to simply as a **monitor, screen,** or **display.** Monitor technology ranges from **CRT (cathode-ray tube)** screens to **LED (light-emitting diode), LCD (liquid crystal display), vacuum fluorescent, gas plasma**, and **electroluminescent screens.** As information is input into the hardware, this television-like screen displays the characters in a pattern of closely spaced dots. The closer the dots, the easier it is to read the characters on the screen. The spacing or density of the dots is called **resolution**.

Video display terminals are designed to meet a variety of needs.

Screen resolution may be affected by the color combination of the characters and the screen background. Characters are displayed on the screen either in a light color against a dark background or vice versa. Screens may be green on black, amber on black, black on white (to resemble paper in a typewriter), and so on. Color monitors can have screens in nearly any combination of colors. In many cases, an operator can change the colors depending on a user's preference.

In the past, any equipment that provided automatic editing and keying of documents was considered a word processor. Today, information processing depends on equipment with a display. A display makes it possible to produce **soft copy** or images in light on a screen, and it is not always necessary to produce paper copies. As a result, the printer has become a separate machine or peripheral. One great advantage of this separation is that you can view an entire document before ordering the printer to produce a hard copy of it. With blind equipment (without a screen), it is necessary to make rough draft copies to see what has been done. The separation of keyboarding from printing means you can proofread and edit more thoroughly and efficiently than you can using hardware without a screen. Let's see how this is done in an office setting.

Mark Underwood, a manager at the engineering firm of Pitmann and Ross, studies the waste disposal problems of the firm's clients and writes reports on how to solve them. He is highly respected for his technical background and problem-solving skills, but he doesn't express himself very well. He admits that his reports tend to be wordy and difficult to understand.

In the past, his secretary, Jackie Dunn, would use an electronic typewriter to transcribe a report Mr. Underwood dictated and then review the keyed draft. She would often notice sentences and paragraphs that needed revision. But the limited capabilities of her machine made it impossible for Ms. Dunn to make changes without completely rekeying the report.

When Ms. Dunn's electronic typewriter was traded in for computer hardware with a display, it was quite a change for her. At first, Ms. Dunn was intimidated by her microcomputer, and it took her a few weeks to become accustomed to using it. The turning point came one morning as she was keyboarding a report. When she came to paragraphs on the display screen that she thought were awkward, she made changes in them. She moved words, sentences, and paragraphs around on the screen with just a few keystrokes.

When she had gone over the report thoroughly, Ms. Dunn directed the printer to prepare a printout. She gave the printout to Mr. Underwood with a note describing her changes. He welcomed her suggestions, made a few additional changes on the copy, and gave it back to Ms. Dunn. Ms. Dunn then went back to her microcomputer to work on the changes. It took only a few minutes to make the additional revisions Mr. Underwood had requested. The final printed copy of the report was on his desk before lunch.

Within a month, Ms. Dunn was so accustomed to her microcomputer that she could hardly imagine ever working on a typewriter again—even an electronic one. Her only complaint was that the screen was sometimes hard on her eyes, a concern voiced by many people who work with display equipment. (This issue is discussed in Chapter 10.)

Terminals sometimes need adjustments, just as you may have found with your television set. You can make some of these adjustments yourself. For example, you may adjust the image contrast and brightness. By turning a knob on the terminal, you can adjust the contrast of all highlighted text so the letters of the text do not run together. By turning up the brightness you can see some text that appears to fade away. You may not, however, be able to make adjustments to keep images from flickering, blurring, or ghosting. **Ghosting** (shadows or multiple images of the text) is most visible as you move from page to page in a document. Like many features on hardware, it is a characteristic that should be considered when selecting a monitor for your office applications.

Displays may be configured in different ways. Take Ms. Dunn's equipment, for example. On her microcomputer, the screen and the keyboard are housed in the same console (unit). However, most hardware has separate consoles for the storage, display, keyboard, and printing components of a system. Each console is connected by cables. When the components are in separate consoles, you can arrange them in ways that are comfortable and convenient for you. Consoles that contain more than one component may take up less space, but they don't allow as much flexibility.

Use vertical scrolling to see keyboarded text that precedes or follows a screenload.

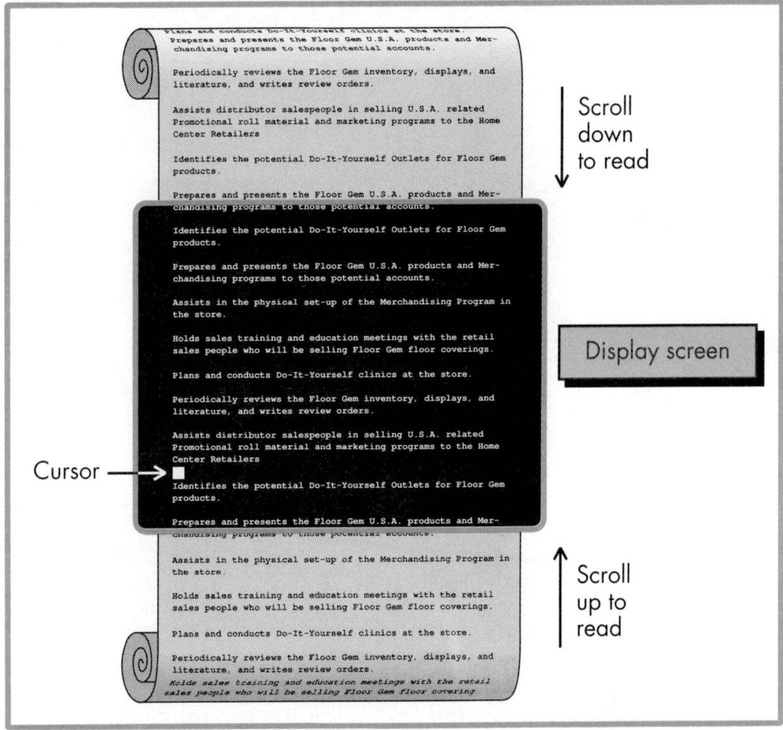

Screens also differ from one another in the size of their display areas. The amount of text that can be viewed on a terminal at one time is called a **screenload**. You see a document, one screenload at a time. When the screenload in front of you doesn't contain the part of the document you want to see, you use function keys to **scroll** the document. You might think of scrolling as the electronic way of turning the pages. With the function keys, you can move instantly to the screenload immediately before or after the one you are looking at. You can also scroll the document continuously backward or forward until you find the part of the document you need.

Some dedicated word processors became popular because of their **full-page** screens. A full-page monitor usually means the screen equals an $8\frac{1}{2}$- by 11-inch document or about 66 lines of 80 characters each. Large screens also have been popularized by desktop publishing. Many people prefer working on a monitor with a large screen because it enables them to see a page just as it will appear in print. A **large screen** is very helpful for people who spend most of their time working on documents that are usually one page long, such as letters and memos. Some monitors display two full pages and show the details of pages as large as a newspaper. **Two-page** screens are useful for page layouts of desktop publishing, such as newsletters and brochures.

Use horizontal scrolling to see keyboarded text alongside a screenload.

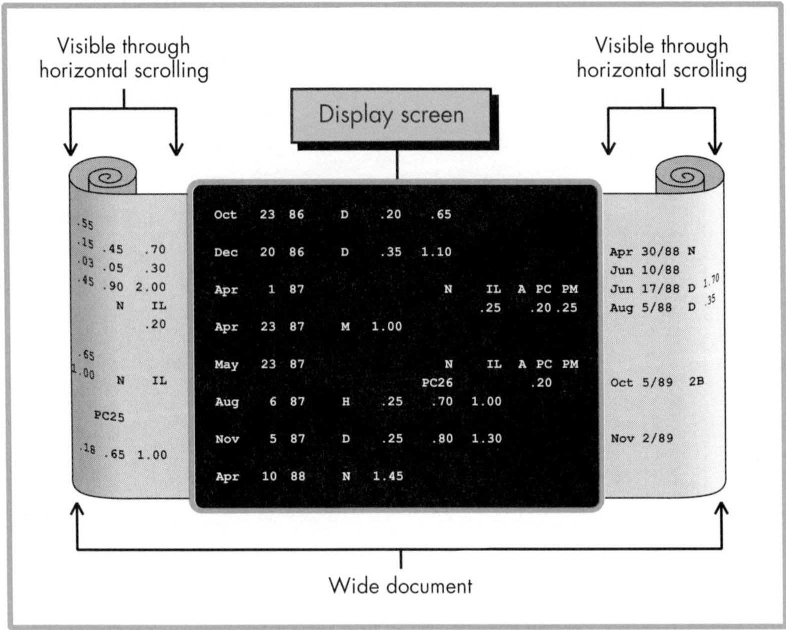

Most microcomputers have **partial-page** screens that display only part of a document page at one time. Although to work with partial pages may take some adjustment, partial-page display is not usually a big drawback. You can scroll to the rest of the page with just a keystroke. Some partial-page screens display about half a page; others hold only six or eight lines of text.

Generally, display screens are about as wide as a piece of ordinary typing paper, although some are narrower. Most systems also allow you to scroll horizontally, which is useful if you are working with tables or unusually wide documents. Horizontal scrolling allows you to move the displayed text from side to side on the screen so you can see the right or left side or the middle of the page as it will be printed. Most screens show about 80 characters per line at one time. Some show 132, 160, or more characters on a horizontal line. Software usually permits horizontal scrolling to enable you to work with documents that have as many as 256 characters on one line.

Most dedicated word processors and microcomputers have a single-screen display that shows one document at a time. Some systems have a **dual display,** so two documents can appear on the screen at the same time. You may hear this feature referred to as a **split screen.** Many office workers like split screens.

Saundra Roberts discovered the convenience of using a split screen when she compiled a new price list for Cicchini Tiles. She works in the company's Customer Service Department. Her man-

Dual display and partial-page display.

ager had given her an old brochure that had the new prices penciled in over the old ones, next to the descriptions and pictures of the company's merchandise. A few new items and their prices were written on the back of the old brochure. Ms. Roberts' job was to prepare a revised price list for the new brochure the company was developing.

Ms. Roberts had stored the previous year's list on the word processor. Rather than thumb back and forth through the printed ten-page list, she decided to work with it on the display screen. Using the dual-display feature, she was able to see her new list she had keyed on the left side of the screen while viewing the previous price list on the right side. Comparing the lists item for item was much easier than constantly looking back and forth between a single screen and the printed page.

Today, a video display is such an integral part of information processing that it is difficult to think of equipment without one. A monitor helps a user see what functions are being performed as they are entered into the machine. Thus, the operator knows what the equipment is doing with the inputted information. For example, a monitor may display at the top or bottom of the screen information that relates to document format, status, and functions such as these:

- **format line**—shows the settings of margins and tabs, the type style (pica, elite, and so on), line spacing (single, double, and so forth), and other page layout features

- **status line**—shows the name of the document that is recognized by the CPU, the page of the document where you are working, the line where the cursor is positioned, and other identifiers that help in formatting or editing the document
- **function line**—shows the function you have selected to perform, such as view, revise, print, or spell check

Displays can also be useful for other types of applications that may extend information processing. Some can be used with overhead projection units. The screen image is projected on a wall or reflective screen for large groups to see what is on the monitor. Although you might think this type of monitor would be used only in a classroom, offices utilize this technology for group meetings and conferences. The information can be altered and stored just as you might do in processing a document.

Storage

The storage component of an information system houses the document when you have finished keyboarding it and want to save it for future use. If the document is to be worked on again, you retrieve it from storage. You can send it back and forth as often and as many times as you wish. Any changes you make in the document are automatically included and recorded on the storage unit each time you send it to storage.

In some systems, each machine has its own storage unit or units. In others (shared resource systems), all equipment shares a storage unit at a central location. Equipment that shares a central storage unit may also have individual storage as a way of expanding the whole system's storage. An optional storage unit is one kind of peripheral. The additional storage extends equipment capabilities, but is not necessary to its operation.

The storage media most often used for information processing are **floppy disks** and **hard disks. Optical disks** and, more specifically, **compact disks (CDs)** are gaining in popularity. Some predict that CDs will be the next industry standard. (Other types of storage, such as **bubble memory, holography,** and **solid-state storage** are discussed in Chapter 8.)

Floppy disks and hard disks use magnetism to store information. Optical disks use light to store it. Although storage is discussed in more detail in Chapter 8, let's look briefly at floppy disk, hard disk, and optical disk storage media.

Floppy Disks For several years, **floppy disks** (frequently referred to as **diskettes** or **floppies**) have been the most common storage medium. They look like 45 rpm phonograph records in their protective jackets, although much thinner. They are flexible or floppy. Floppy disks come in three diameters: $3\frac{1}{2}$ inches **(microfloppy),**

Various sizes of disks serve different storage needs.

$5\frac{1}{4}$ inches **(minifloppy)**, and 8 inches. The 8-inch floppy has been used mainly with dedicated word processors. The decline in popularity of dedicated word processors and the introduction of the $3\frac{1}{2}$-inch disk have made the 8-inch disk nearly obsolete.

Disks are a magnetic storage medium. The delicate plastic material of a disk is coated with magnetic oxide and is permanently encased. A paper or plastic casing is used for $5\frac{1}{4}$-inch disks; a rigid plastic case is used for $3\frac{1}{2}$-inch disks. The casing not only protects the disk, but also makes it easier to handle. The casing has a few openings to permit the storage unit to "read" the contents of the disk in order to find the document you want. On $5\frac{1}{4}$-inch disks, you can see the magnetic media through these openings. You cannot see the magnetic media of a $3\frac{1}{2}$-inch disk. The $3\frac{1}{2}$-inch disk casing has a spring-loaded shutter or door to protect the medium. The door opens to expose the medium when the disk is inserted into the machine.

The plastic casings of disks help keep the media clean and prevent them from being damaged. For $3\frac{1}{2}$-inch disks, the plastic case also protects the media so well that no additional jacket is necessary. Manufacturers usually provide an additional envelope-type jacket with each $5\frac{1}{4}$-inch disk. The disk is taken out of the jacket when it is inserted into the machine.

Most magnetic media have a life span of two to five years. To make media more durable and prolong their life, some manufacturers coat their disks with Teflon. Teflon-coated disks are not affected by dust, water, smoke, and fingerprints, as most disks are. Some have antistatic liners to protect them from static charges. Some vendors are marketing their disks in colored casings for ease in filing. Others are preformatting the disks with instructions for use right out of the box. Disks need careful handling to prevent damage and thus to protect the information they contain. Careful handling will also prolong their life. There are some precautions to take in handling disks, especially the $5\frac{1}{4}$-inch type that does not have protective hard plastic casings.

Floppy disks can store much more information than can cards, cassettes, or tapes. Most floppy disks also offer random access, which means you need not go through the entire contents to find the document you want. Using function keys or a document directory displayed on the screen, you simply identify the document, and it is automatically retrieved from the disk and displayed on your screen.

A $5\frac{1}{4}$-inch disk can hold about 90 pages of single-spaced material. A $3\frac{1}{2}$-inch disk can hold about 200 pages. A disk's capacity depends on its density and whether both sides can be used. Single-density, single-sided disks have the least capacity. Double-density, double-sided disks can store the most material. Disks may also be

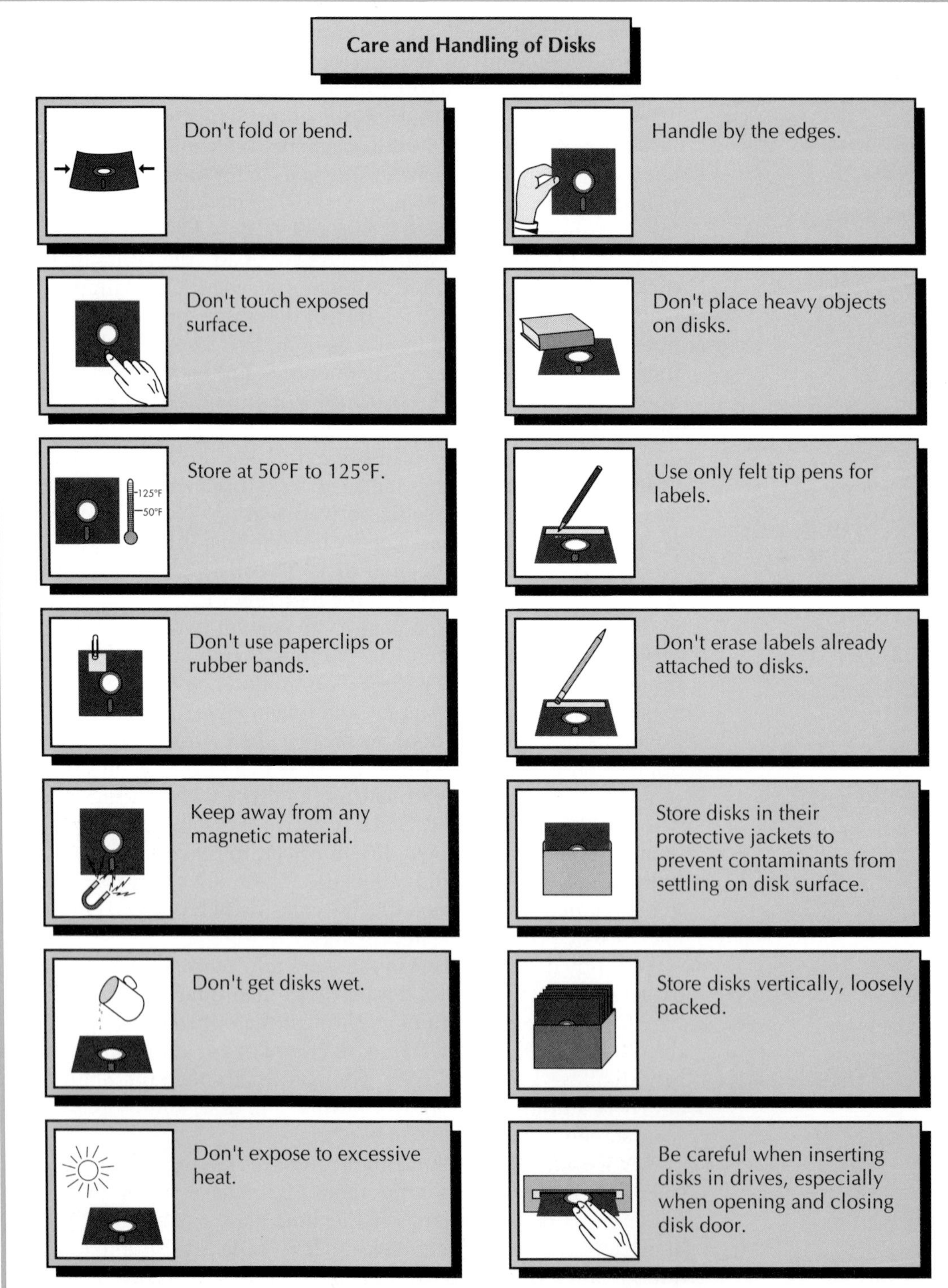
Care and Handling of Disks
Don't fold or bend.
Handle by the edges.
Don't touch exposed surface.
Don't place heavy objects on disks.
Store at 50°F to 125°F.
125°F
50°F
Use only felt tip pens for labels.
Don't use paperclips or rubber bands.
Don't erase labels already attached to disks.
Keep away from any magnetic material.
Store disks in their protective jackets to prevent contaminants from settling on disk surface.
Don't get disks wet.
Store disks vertically, loosely packed.
Don't expose to excessive heat.
Be careful when inserting disks in drives, especially when opening and closing disk door.

combinations of these two types. Some high-density $5\frac{1}{4}$-inch disks can hold about 320 pages of information. Newer high-density $3\frac{1}{2}$-inch disk storage capacity has surpassed that of $5\frac{1}{4}$-inch disks. Some $3\frac{1}{2}$-inch disks can store about 400 pages.

Diskette storage capacity varies, depending on the information processing equipment. Also, if both the disk and the information processing system in which it is used are maintained properly, the information stored on the disk can last several years.

Optical Disks If you have a compact disk player, you are probably familiar with one type of **optical disk** medium. You know that one compact disk plays for several hours—much longer than a cassette. The amount of information that can be stored on optical disks is a main reason they promise a great future for information processing. Optical disks may store up to a hundred times more information than can be stored on magnetic disks of the same size. Optical disk technology, first introduced in the 1970s, is laser-based.

The **CD-ROM (compact disk–read-only memory)** disk has been the most popular type of optical disk medium. A CD-ROM disk (usually 12 inches in diameter) contains information recorded in digital form. Lasers are used to create tiny pits in the reflective metal surface of a CD-ROM disk. The disk is "read" by passing light over the surface. The digital data is transformed into an understandable form that can be viewed on a monitor. The primary advantage of optical disk media is that they provide high-speed, random access to the contents.

The true storage potential of optical disk media may not be known until industry standards are established. Manufacturers estimate that the amount of information they can hold ranges anywhere from 150,000 to 200,000 pages. Although optical disks are gaining in popularity, only time will tell if this exciting technology will overtake other types of media in the information processing market.

Hard Disks Nearly any type of computer equipment you buy today can be furnished with a **hard disk**—even laptop computers. A hard disk is a magnetic medium that has a large capacity. Random access of a hard disk is much faster than random access of a floppy. Hard disks may be built into a computer system or housed in a separate case. You cannot touch the magnetic medium of a hard disk because it is vacuum-sealed in a rigid, dirt-free case.

Hard disks are no longer just for large companies. They are excellent whenever a great many documents need to be stored. Unlike with a floppy, you do not have to handle the media or worry about a hard disk being lost or misfiled. A hard disk is preferred

Half-height Winchester disk drive.

over a floppy because of its speed and large capacity. It can store upward of 75,000 pages of text. All hard disks are circular, like a stereo record, ranging from about 3 to 14 inches in diameter.

A common type of hard disk most often used with information processing systems is called a **Winchester disk.** These disks come in four sizes: 5¼, 8, 10½, and 14 inches. The magnetic storage is permanently sealed inside a casing, which makes the disks extremely reliable. Floppies can be affected by static electricity and dust, but Winchester disks cannot. They also have far greater capacity than floppies—in the millions of characters—allowing for storage of a large number of documents.

A disadvantage of early Winchester disks was that they were installed permanently in a computer. Once the disk had been filled, you had to erase (or purge) some copy to record more. Now manufacturers are making hard disks in sealed cartridges that can be removed from a computer when the disk is full. The total storage capacity of a system using removable hard disk cartridges is limited only by the number of cartridges available.

Disk Drives An information processing system that uses floppy disk storage has a component called a **disk drive.** It works something like a tape recorder. For example, you insert disks into the drive in much the same way that you insert cassettes into a recorder. Inside the drive, the floppy disk spins at a high speed under a device called a **head.** The head "reads" already recorded information to find the document or information you want. In recording new information, the head transfers the input through the CPU and "writes" it onto the disk. (The terms "read" and "write" as used here are derived from the read/write heads on cassette tape recorders. Hard disk drives also use reading/writing heads.)

A floppy disk drive may be housed in a CPU terminal, or it may be in a separate console. Dual drives are more popular than a single disk drive. Sometimes as many as three additional drives can be added to your equipment as peripherals. Frequently, a floppy disk drive and a hard disk form one unit. In other systems, a dual floppy drive may have one drive for a 3½-inch floppy and another drive for a 5¼-inch floppy—again, in one unit. The combination unit allows you to use both types of floppies in one system. Whatever configuration of disk drives you have, more drives enable you to work with more information at one time and/or access information more quickly.

Reading/writing head on a hard disk drive.

Multiple disk drives also allow you to copy your work onto separate floppies so that you have a **backup** in case one is damaged. ("Backup" is the term used to describe duplicate text that is magnetically stored.) The importance of making a backup copy is similar to having a copy of a report you give to your instructor. If

Fast and quiet, this laser printer offers high-quality printing capabilities for the office.

the original is lost (damaged or erased by mistake), you always have another. The backup disk becomes part of an **archive** (a collection of stored backup disks).

Printer

The printer is the device that produces the finished document after you keyboard, correct, and revise it. A paper copy of a document, which is the output of information processing, is referred to as either a **hard copy** or a **printout**. Printers are available in a variety of speeds and with different printing mechanisms to suit various office needs.

The most common types of printers used today include both **impact** and **nonimpact printers** of the following technologies:

dot matrix
electrostatic
ink jet
ion deposition
letter quality and near-letter quality
laser
thermal transfer

Printers, their characteristics and uses, as well as other output-related equipment (peripherals) that is frequently used with printers, are discussed in depth in Chapter 6.

As you can see from this overview of information processing equipment, there is a tremendous variety in how equipment can be arranged within an information system. The range of information processing capabilities is as vast as the types of hardware available. Each day brings greater knowledge and capabilities to process information in more efficient and economical ways. As technology makes new kinds of equipment available, new office procedures and arrangements will change how we do office work. The key to managing such an environment is people. People must become knowledgeable about managing information. Good decision makers will guide the direction of these developments in making offices effective information systems.

CHAPTER SUMMARY

- Hardware for information processing includes dedicated word processors, electronic typewriters, and a variety of computer systems.
- Modern word processing began with the introduction of magnetic storage media. These media record keystrokes, which can be easily erased and corrected.
- Many electronic typewriters have all their components in a single console. Because they have a number of automatic features to format documents, they frequently are referred to today as word processors.
- Some electronic typewriters are modular so that their features can be upgraded.
- Linear display electronic typewriters show as many as one or more lines of copy on a thin screen.
- On nondisplay electronic typewriters, the printer is part of a single machine. On many display models, it may be separate.
- A display screen shows what characters are inputted and allows the operator to review and revise them before producing printed copy.
- Display equipment for information processing permits extensive revisions and format changes before a document is printed. It offers more automatic features than blind equipment.
- Standalone information processing equipment consists of a self-contained, single-person system that does not share components.
- There are two kinds of shared or clustered systems: shared logic and shared resources. In a shared logic system, all terminals are linked to a central processing unit. In a shared resource system, operators may share peripherals or equipment that is not needed continuously.
- Today, more information processing is done in business offices with microcomputer systems than with any other type of hardware.
- Most computer-based information processing systems have five components: central processing unit, keyboard, display, storage device, and printer.

- The CPU acts as the intelligence or logic of an information processing system. It receives instructions from the keyboard or other input devices and conveys them to the other components of the system.
- In addition to the character keys and space bar found on a typewriter, information processing equipment has function keys, which are used to communicate instructions to the CPU.
- The storage unit houses magnetically recorded documents for future use.
- The printer produces the output of a word processing system.
- As computerized information processing becomes more sophisticated, information processing will become increasingly integrated to better utilize equipment, employees' abilities, and other resources.

VOCABULARY

archive
backup
bit
buffer
byte
central processing unit (CPU)
chip
clock speed
compact disk–read-only memory (CD-ROM)
configuration
cursor
default
disk drive
electronic typewriter (ET)
end user
erasable programmable read-only memory (EPROM)
floppy disk
function keys
ghosting
hard disk
hardware
linear display
mainframe
memory
microcomputer
minicomputer
optical disk
personal computer (PC)
peripheral
program
programmable read-only memory (PROM)
random-access memory (RAM)
read-only memory (ROM)
resolution
screenload
scroll
shared logic
shared resource
supercomputer
upgrade
user-friendly
workstation

CHAPTER QUESTIONS

1. How do dedicated word processors and electronic typewriters differ from microcomputers and other computer systems? Why are computer systems so popular for information processing?

2. What are ten features that commonly are built into electronic typewriters? Why aren't many of these features built into computer systems? What is needed for a computer system to be able to do information processing tasks?
3. What are some basic differences between the computer systems that can be used for information processing? Why would one business use one type and another use some other type?
4. What are the five components of an information processing system? Explain how the components are similar or different from some of the types of equipment you have used (or that is in your classroom).
5. People talk about the "logic" of a computer system. What is logic? What is the difference between temporary and permanent memory?
6. How do keyboards on automated information processing hardware differ from those on typewriters? What are the uses of some of the special keys?
7. What is a screenload? What is scrolling? Why is it helpful to be able to scroll?
8. Which component makes display information processing systems so much more versatile than blind systems? How does it do this?
9. What kinds of storage media are used in information processing today? Which kind is most appropriate when great storage capacity is required?
10. Where is the printer located on blind equipment? Where is it located on a display system? Which location is more advantageous? Why?

CASE STUDY

Neal McCartney is president of Reid & Associates, a small advertising and public relations firm. The company employs 20 people who produce advertising and market research reports for a number of clients. In addition, the company has a secretarial and photocopying service for local clients.

Mr. McCartney is seriously considering installing information processing equipment in his company. He has assigned his administrative assistant, Carla Maywald, to obtain information from several vendors about their equipment. Ms. Maywald is familiar with all operations of Reid & Associates and has obtained brochures on equipment from various manufacturers. She also has completed an evening course in word processing and information systems at the local college.

Ms. Maywald has organized the brochures into categories of equipment, such as electronic typewriters, microcomputers, displays, storage units, and printers. The next phase of her investigation will include meetings with sales representatives from the vendors.

Based on the information presented in this chapter about the types and equipment capabilities of information processing systems, make a list of questions that she might ask as she talks with the sales representatives. Keep in mind that Ms. Maywald will want to find out how easily and efficiently equipment can be installed at Reid, and how well it can do several kinds of tasks, such as reports, form letters, and proposals. Maintenance, service, and supplies will also be considered. Ms. Maywald will be interested in selecting equipment that will meet the company's current and future needs in providing customers with services they want.

CHAPTER 5

Software

Marlane Schilling, the new office manager of Nacagdoches Oil, Inc., asked her staff about the kinds of tasks they performed most frequently. She found that Ross Freedman was responsible for processing all the incoming and outgoing correspondence. Martha Lence handled budgets, department accounts, and cash flow analyses. Judi Ann Reagan designed and created charts, graphs, and other visuals. Ms. Schilling also found that information processed by one employee frequently was needed by another. Because the office tasks were becoming more sophisticated and integrated, she decided to update her knowledge of software applications programs to better utilize the firm's microcomputer equipment and its employees' talents.

The types of tasks performed in offices are getting more specialized and more sophisticated. Dedicated types of equipment, such as word processors and electronic typewriters, may not be able to do all the tasks a business demands. Although they are good at word processing, they may not be versatile enough to take care of the variety of office tasks in an information system. They usually are not capable of handling integrated and multiple tasks, let alone statistical and data analysis, communications, and even the large volumes of word processing required of offices today.

Software Capabilities

You have learned that some equipment has special capabilities that enable you to produce documents easily and quickly. The equipment can do this because its operation is based in part on **software** (instructions or programs) as well as hardware (the physical equipment of a system). On dedicated word processors and many electronic typewriters, the operating capabilities are built into the hardware. Sometimes these capabilities are referred to as **firmware** or **resident software**. Resident software is the set of permanently installed instructions that tell the hardware how to function. The only way to change equipment capabilities is to rebuild it.

The operating capabilities of computers are, in part, stored electronically in the central processing unit. Such capabilities are not permanent; they can be changed, sometimes as easily as by entering a few keystrokes. Because they are not part of the physical equipment, they are referred to as software rather than hardware.

Computers of all sizes, whether they process data or words, rely on **software** for their operating instructions. The software is the programmed instructions that tell the computer what to do. You do not need to know how a computer works to use one. But you do need to learn how to use the computer and the software.

The abundance of software on the market today is a result of increasing competition among vendors, predictable changes in technology, and the establishment of industry standards. Because of these factors, the computer industry has stabilized, even though more powerful equipment is being developed at lower and lower costs. The thousands of software programs on the market today are also more versatile and, in general, cost less than only a few years ago. Certainly, a user can find a software package for almost any purpose—professional, recreational, or personal. Several thousand software packages are available to meet the business needs of personal computer users. Expenditures for software already exceed those for hardware in many companies. The projected growth rate of software is about 20 percent per year from 1989 to 1994, which exceeds the projected growth rates for all types of computers combined. However, total personal computer expenditures also are expanding significantly each year. Some expect sales for both hardware and software to reach nearly $1 trillion by 1995.

Software can be divided into two categories: **system software** and **applications software.** Each works with and supports the other like building blocks.

System Software

If computer software were a building, its foundation would be the system software. It coordinates all the other software and manages computer operations. For most dedicated word processors, electronic typewriters, and all microcomputers, a collection of system software is called the **operating system (OS)**. Many systems rely on disk technology for their operation. They are called **disk operating systems (DOS),** pronounced "doss." Even though you frequently may hear a person refer to any type of operating system as DOS, technically this is incorrect. Although technology has provided us with alternatives to DOS, disk operating systems are still prevalent. The operating system or **system software** manages the resources of a computer system. It handles all the functions of the computer, including the keyboard and printer, transferring information from soft copy to storage. The operating system's function is to help all computer components **interface** (work together to perform operations).

Currently, there is no one standard operating system in the personal computer environment. There are many operating systems in use today. The most popular are MS-DOS (MicroSoft Disk Operating System, developed by Microsoft Corp.), PC-DOS (Personal Computer Disk Operating System, developed by IBM), UNIX (written in C language, developed by AT&T Bell Labs), Macintosh (developed by Apple Computers, Inc.), and OS/2 (Operating System/2, developed jointly by Microsoft and IBM). Many feel that OS/2 will become a standard in the years to come and will replace MS/PC-DOS.

Many microprocessors or CPUs of a computer usually are designed to operate with a specific operating system. In many types of computer equipment, the operating system is housed in the computer's permanent memory. Such an operating system is called **resident software** because it is permanently installed in the computer. The instructions of a resident program are built into its circuitry as ROM (read-only memory). The CPU is able to read and execute the instructions but cannot change them. In dedicated word processors and electronic typewriters, both the operating system program and the word processing program are resident to the system by being bundled together in ROM. **Bundled software** works automatically. When you turn on the machine or **boot** it, the resident program makes your machine ready for keyboarding. When you turn the machine off, the operating system and the word processing program remain in the ROM.

With a microcomputer, the operating system may be resident to the system. Or the operating system software and the word processing software may be stored on external media, such as a diskette. External media must be **loaded** or "written" into RAM, the computer's temporary memory, before the computer can "read" it. You do this by inserting the media that contain the program into the disk drive and keyboarding a few instructions. The computer processes the instructions to ready it for you to begin using your word processing software program.

Temporary memory is storage that is lost when you turn the machine off. Thus, where the operating system software is not resident in the system, you need to repeat the disk loading procedure (inserting a disk into the drive and loading a program) every time you use a microcomputer. You can eliminate the step of physically inserting the disk into the disk drive if you have stored your program on the computer's internal storage (usually a hard disk system). You merely need to make a few keystrokes to access the program to begin working at your terminal.

To describe how an operating system might work, let's compare it to a person working for a paper manufacturer. Carlos Bronsen makes deliveries for the paper products company of Yarwell and Klein. Upon checking his work orders one morning, he finds he must make a delivery to Ignatiev Printing, which is on the south side of town. He also has a delivery to the *Walla Walla Morning News,* which is located in the northwest part of the city. To be sure he delivers the right type of paper to the right customer, he follows a city street map. He determines what route he should take, then follows the map to make sure he gets to his delivery locations. Upon arriving at Ignatiev, he unloads the paper one box at a time using a handtruck. At the *Morning News*, a forklift picks up several rolls of paper that have been stacked together. Both companies now are ready to use the paper to produce the products they sell.

The comparisons might be as follows: Carlos Bronsen can be considered the computer—a person (hardware) with a brain (CPU). He "knows" the two companies cannot use the paper until he delivers it, but he needs a road map to help him get to the businesses. The map (operating system) provides instructions he will use to make sure he drives to the correct locations.

The paper Mr. Bronsen leaves at one business is different from the one he leaves at the other. Both businesses will use the paper in producing printed copy, but they will do it with different equipment in their own specific ways. Also, both companies will produce different products. Thus, the specific type of paper (software program, such as word processing or graphics) and the products (output, such as a letter or report) depend on the application.

Each company's operations depend on having the right paper at the right time—each relies on Mr. Bronsen following his map to make the deliveries to the correct location. This comparison should give you a general idea of how an operating system works. An operating system is vital for a computer to function properly. Its operating system software enables the computer to know how to use the applications software.

Every computer must have an operating system or system software to instruct it to perform its operations. Operating system software is written in **machine language**—the language that a computer "understands." It is written in a code that the computer can interpret as combinations of ones and zeros. It is a painstaking job to write or read row after row of machine code. It is easy to make errors and difficult to find them. Fortunately, this task was eliminated with the development of assembly language in the 1950s. **Assembly language** is a coded language similar to machine language except the codes are abbreviations of words. Assembly language is called **translating software** because it is used as an **assembler** to convert or translate other more "user-friendly" programming languages into machine language.

Computer programmers use many different **programming languages** for writing computer software programs that can be read by an operating system. There are hundreds of computer languages. Some are very tedious to use (like machine language). Others, considered "high-level" languages, closely resemble human language and thus are easy to use. Some of the most common programming languages include:

- **BASIC** (Beginner's All-purpose Symbolic Instruction Code)—the simplest of all computer languages, used for a wide variety of applications
- **COBOL** (Common Business-Oriented Language)—a popular language used mainly for business applications
- **Pascal**—a popular, more sophisticated language used for statistical and graphics applications

You may have heard about other computer languages, including FORTRAN, RPG, C, Ada, LOGO, and PROLOG. Most programs you are likely to work with already will have been compiled into

Use of Prepackaged Applications Programs

- Producing routine correspondence as well as more sophisticated reports
- Drawing up budgets, forecasting sales, and projecting labor and materials requirements
- Analyzing cash flows of prospective mergers and acquisitions, planning products, and developing performance requirements
- Determining the best sources and prices for raw materials and amounts needed
- Monitoring production processes and overseeing delivery of finished products
- Handling accounting and inventory control
- Transmitting electronic mail, voice mail, and other telecommunications

machine language. Unless you learn computer science or programming, you probably never will use a programming language.

Applications Software

Applications software, in reality, extends computer capabilities, providing the "knowledge" to perform many different functions. Applications programs are what give your personal computer personality. They are used for many purposes—business, personal, recreation, and education. The distinctness of these purposes, however, is becoming blurred. As applications software programs become more and more sophisticated, some of their features overlap. Thousands of prepackaged applications programs are available for personal computers to help office employees do a variety of tasks.

Because microcomputers can be used for so many purposes, they are increasingly being used for information processing in its broadest sense. That is, microcomputers extend "word processing" (or text editing, as traditional word processing has come to be known). Information processing, then, encompasses a wide range of applications that are necessary for an integrated information system to work efficiently.

The remainder of this chapter looks at a few of the applications software programs available for today's micros and personal computers. These applications are important because they are common to many offices. For convenience, they are grouped in the following sections:

- word processing applications
- spreadsheet applications
- database management applications
- graphics applications
- desktop publishing applications
- communications applications
- integrated applications

Discussion focuses on the main characteristics and functions of each type of applications software. Not all software packages that fall into a category may be able to do all the functions listed; some may do more. Some software programs may have features represented by one or more categories of applications software. Note the similarities and differences of the applications as well as how they overlap.

Word Processing Applications Software

Word processing is the most used application of all the software applications. There are hundreds of word processing packages available—from simple to complex in ease of use and functions. Today, only about 50 to 60 manufacturers produce all the word processing software, and the competition is becoming greater.

WordStar was the most popular word processing software package on the market for many years. It was powerful but cumbersome—especially for the occasional user. But WordStar's developers, MicroPro International, Inc., had little competition. A large number of early word processing operators became "sold" on it. In fact, many of these WordStar users have advanced into the newer updated WordStar versions rather than switching to other more popular word processing programs.

When a million copies of a record are sold in the music industry, the artist gets a gold record. If the same were true in the

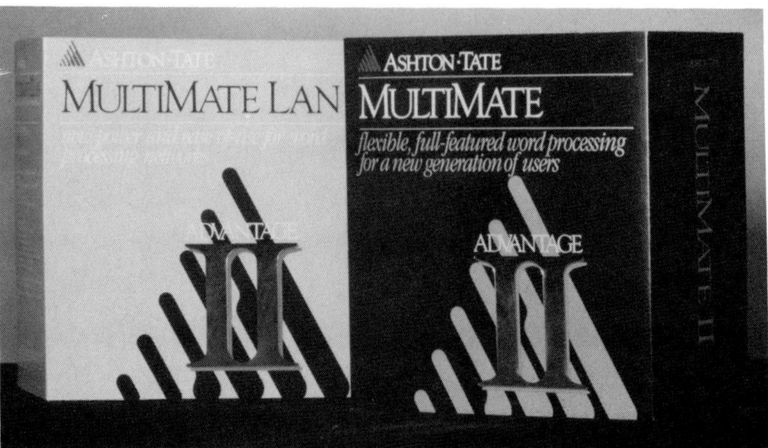

MultiMate® is one of several popular word processing programs.

Word processing programs can be either command-driven or menu-driven.

CM XyWrite
PRMPT
2 A:\XYWRITE P-L-10 C I

This is a screen from XyWrite.

XyWrite is an example of word processing software that is command-driven. All commands are entered at the CM (command) line at the top of the screen.

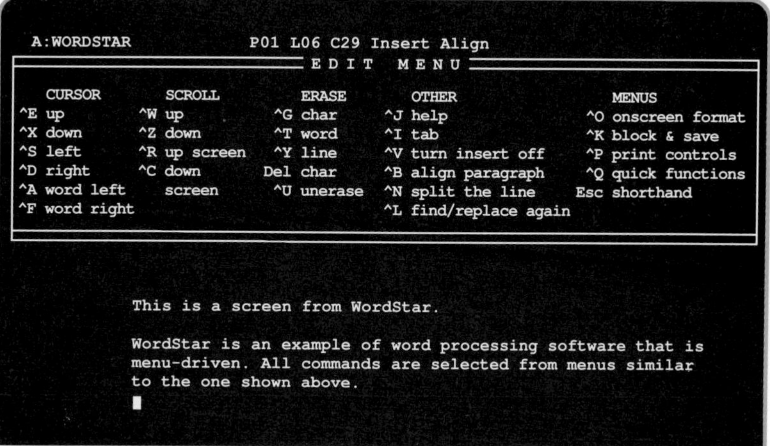

software industry, there would be several "gold record" awards for software—especially word processing software. WordPerfect would be at the top of the list. WordPerfect passed the millionth copy sold in 1988—less than six years after it was introduced. Developed by the WordPerfect Corp., this package is used in many businesses. Like many popular software packages, it has been **enhanced** (or improved) and marketed in several versions or updates (usually noted by new names and/or numbers, such as version 3.0, 4.0, 4.1, 5.0, and so on). WordPerfect 5.0, for example, is a very powerful program, is user-friendly, and is considered by many end users to be easier to use than WordStar.

Other popular word processing software includes versions of DisplayWrite (developed by IBM), Microsoft Word (developed by Microsoft Corp.), MultiMate (developed by Ashton-Tate), and PFS:Write (developed by Software Publishing Corp.).

The popularity of many word processing programs depends on what functions they do, how easily the functions can be executed, and how fast the functions can be carried out. Sophisticated packages such as WordPerfect, WordStar, Microsoft Word,

- Features -

Basic Word Processing Software Features

automatic basic text editing (add/delete/move/copy)
carrier return
centering
column layout
column wrap
correction
decimal tabulation
document assembly
flush right margin
forms mapping
half spacing
hyphenation
indent
indexing
international symbols
line framing
line spacing
margins
pagination
relocate
right justification
search/replace
simultaneous input/output
stop coding
tabulation
underscore
undo
word wrap

and Samna Ami have extended the capabilities of word processing into desktop publishing. In their enhanced versions, these programs are referred to as **rich text** or **word publishing** software.

Word processing programs are of two types: **menu-driven** and **command-driven.** Using menu-driven software is similar to reading a menu at a restaurant. You have multiple choices or several selections from which to choose. Once you make a selection, you may need to make additional ones from another menu **(submenu)** or respond to **screen prompts** that ask you questions about what you want to do. For example, you may choose the "print" function from a general menu. As soon as you have made your selection, a submenu or a screen prompt may appear asking you to be more specific about the printing function. You may be asked to pick the number of copies you wish to make, whether they are to be double or single spaced, and other specifics.

A menu-driven system helps reduce mistakes because you may have to make several selections before the operation actually is carried out. For an experienced operator, the process of going through several menus is cumbersome and slows down processing. Many vendors have responded to this problem by adding menu-driven **bypass** features to the software. These permit an operator to skip some of the "pop-up," "pull-down," or automatic multiple-choice menus to perform an operation more quickly. Manufacturers also are producing some software that combines both menu- and command-driven programs.

In a command-driven or coded program, each function can be completed with only a few keystrokes. The operator keys in codes

Computer Graphics

Computer graphics software programs have a wide range of applications. Some produce pictorial representations of data; others are used for drawing or drafting.

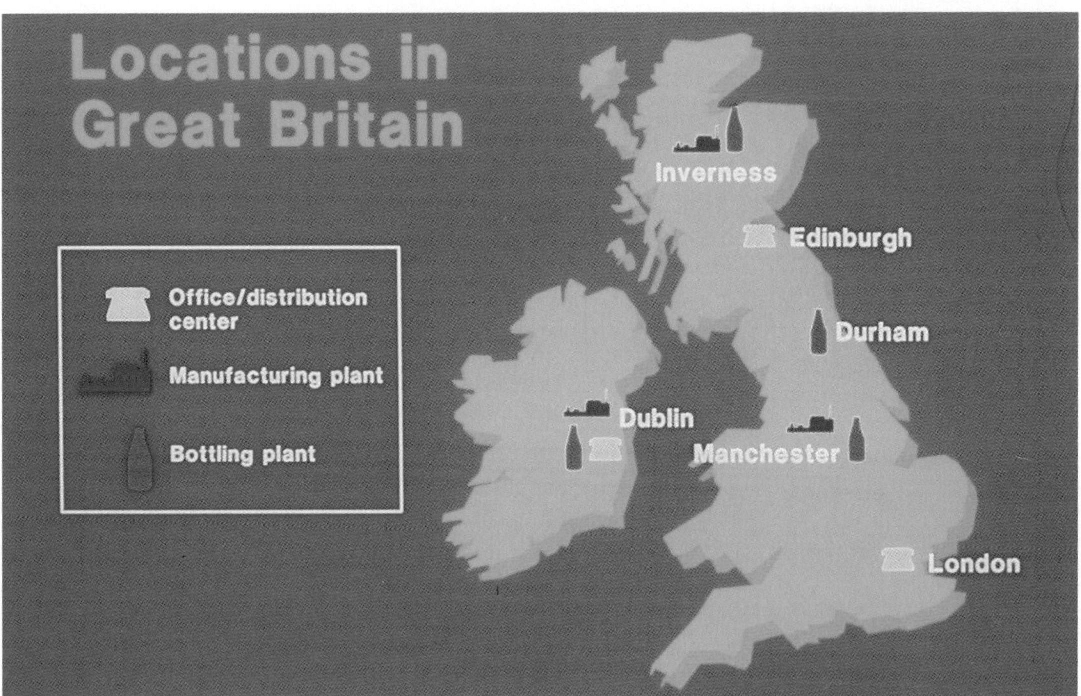

These screens illustrate how graphics programs can be used to convert various kinds of information into images: a map chart (shown above), a pie chart (shown below on the left), and a vertical bar chart (shown on the right).

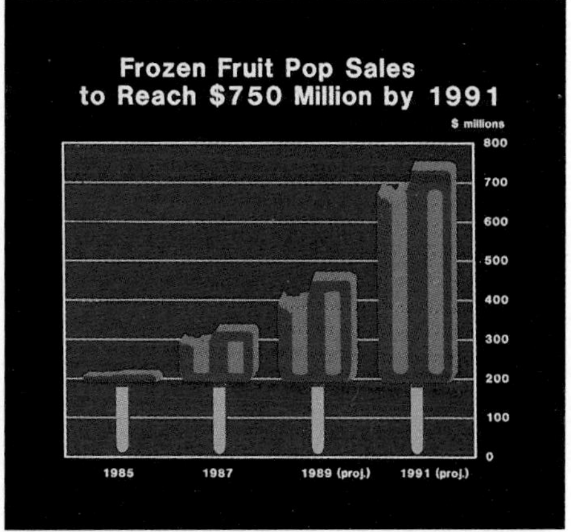

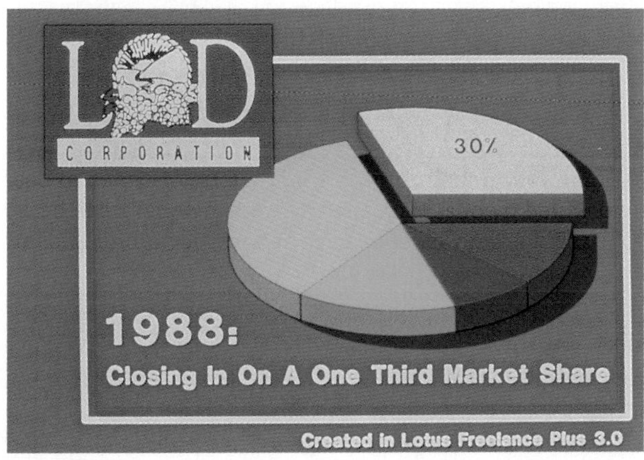

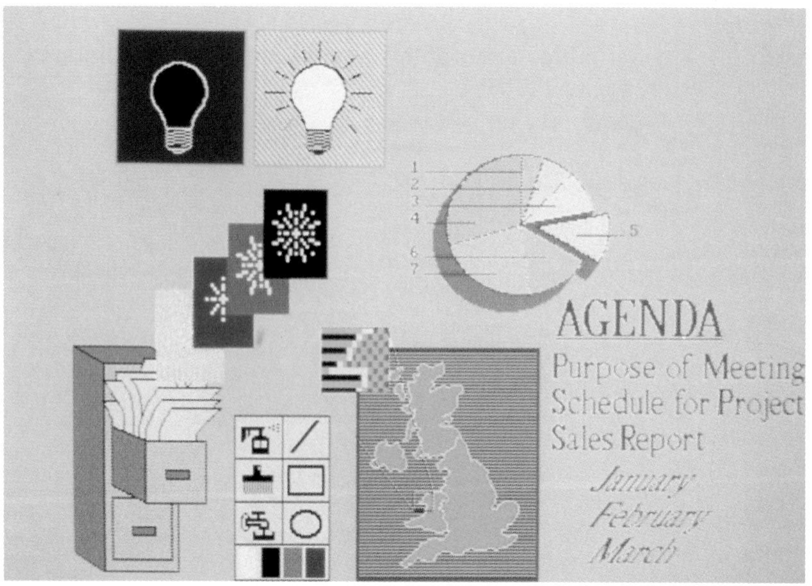

The graphic images shown on these screens can be output as hard copy and distributed.

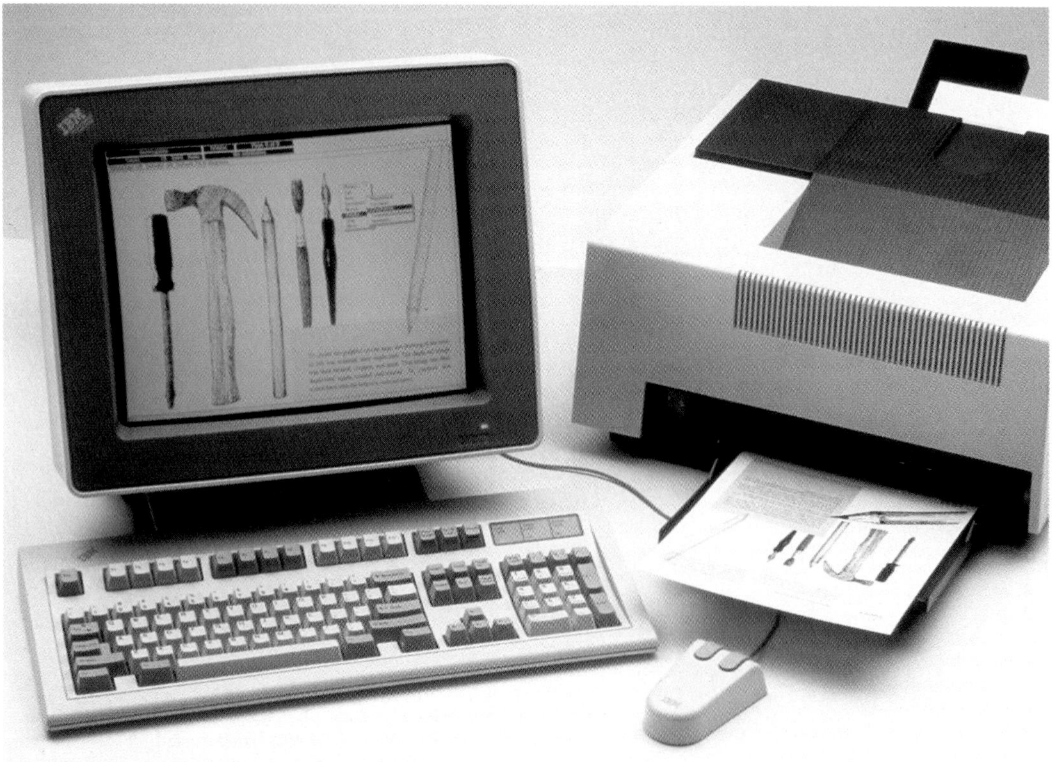

The workers in these pictures are using special equipment and software programs to create three-dimensional drawings.

Some graphics programs are designed to draw architectural plans.

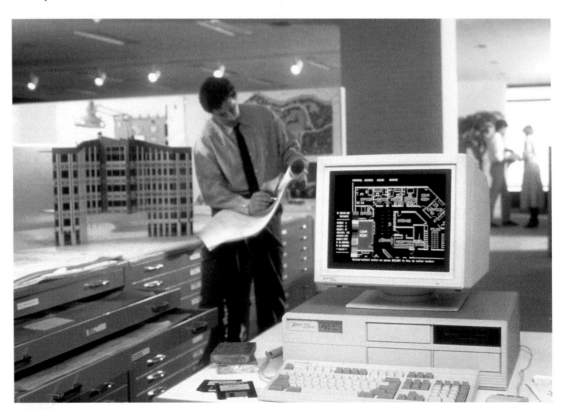

rather than referring to a menu to select functions. The codes in a command-driven program represent functional units. When the operator keys the codes into the text, the logical, sequential steps of the functional units are carried out automatically.

In general, command-driven software is not as popular as menu-driven software. Command-driven programs require learning the codes rather than relying on screen prompts of a menu. Most word processing beginners do not like command-driven software because they have to memorize the codes to avoid referring to the manual. Experienced operators like command-driven software because once they learn the codes, it is faster than having to make the selections required by menu-driven programs. Here's a case in point.

When Harry Marshall started his new job in an office that used coded software on microcomputers, he worried because his work went too slowly. The keyboard contained about the same number of function keys as the keyboard at his last job, but he had difficulty remembering which ones to use. The software did not have menus to guide him through even some of the basic operations.

Mr. Marshall frequently had to refer to the operating instructions to determine which function key he needed. Worse yet, text-editing functions such as copying a paragraph from one document to another required that he use special codes. Each time he performed one of those functions, he had to look up its code in the operating manual. At first, Mr. Marshall was afraid he would never be able to memorize the codes and key positions. He thought he would never be able to work as fast as he had at his old job.

He was wrong. He learned rapidly, and a few weeks later he had changed his mind about the coded system. By then he had become familiar with the function key positions. He found that he remembered most of the codes after he used them a few times. Already he was finding the coded program faster and easier to use than the menu system, mainly because each function required fewer steps.

Mr. Marshall learned there are many differences between software programs. He found that once he knew the basic concepts of the common functions, transferring from one system to another was not as difficult as he had thought.

Let's look at some of the common characteristics and functions of word processing applications software. Many basic word processing features common to many dedicated word processors and electronic typewriters also are common to word processing software.

In addition to the features presented in Chapter 4, several others can extend word processing capabilities. Some features are

Additional Features of Word Processing Software

- Moving text between documents and joining parts or all of multiple documents
- Automatic numbering of lines with selection of the location (right or left side, etc.) where vertical numbering is placed
- Macro creation ("programming" or storing keystrokes of frequently used multiple-step functions that can be accessed later with only one or two keystrokes to execute the entire operation)
- Inserting automatic headers and footers (and inserting them on alternating even and odd pages)
- File sorting, selecting, transporting, and printing functions
- Math functions (with four functions, percents, and other functions)
- Password protection, file locking, and file encryption (files coded to permit access by authorized persons only)
- Automatic envelope formatting and addressing
- Mail merge for merging addresses with form letters
- Spelling verification of up to and over 150,000 words (users may change or add to some word banks) and specialized legal, medical, and other dictionaries
- Thesaurus of up to 550,000 words and more
- Grammar and style checkers for checking construction of sentences, word usage, numerals and abbreviations, sexist language, cliches, and similar potential problem areas
- Glossary functions (storing of phrases to be recalled into the text with a few keystrokes)
- **Windowing** (Two or more functions may be viewed at the same time in windows on the screen, and tasks can be performed on any one of them by alternating between the functions.)
- Multiple column formatting where changes can be made in one column without affecting the other (Adding or deleting text in a column wraps or "snakes" text from the bottom of one column to the top of another.)
- **WYSIWYG** (what - you - see - is - what - you - get, pronounced "wissy wig") for screen viewing of all text and of underlining, bolding, font changes, scientific equations, and Greek symbols
- Automatic outlining, indexing, table of contents, and summary comments
- Automatic footnote relocation when moving footnoted text
- Text wrapping around "boxes" or spaces used for graphics
- File importing and integrating (creating compound documents by merging text with other formats and inputs, including databases, spreadsheets, graphics, voice, and video)

A spelling checker program.

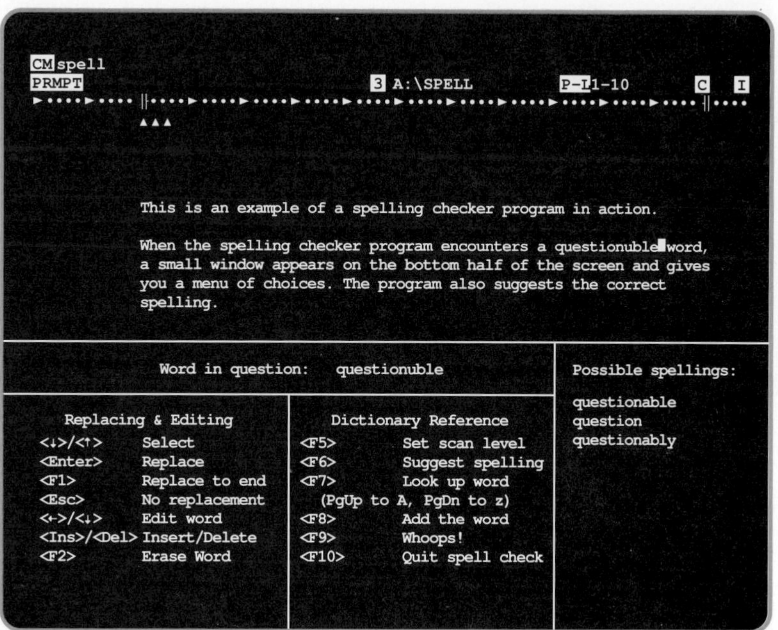

A thesaurus program.

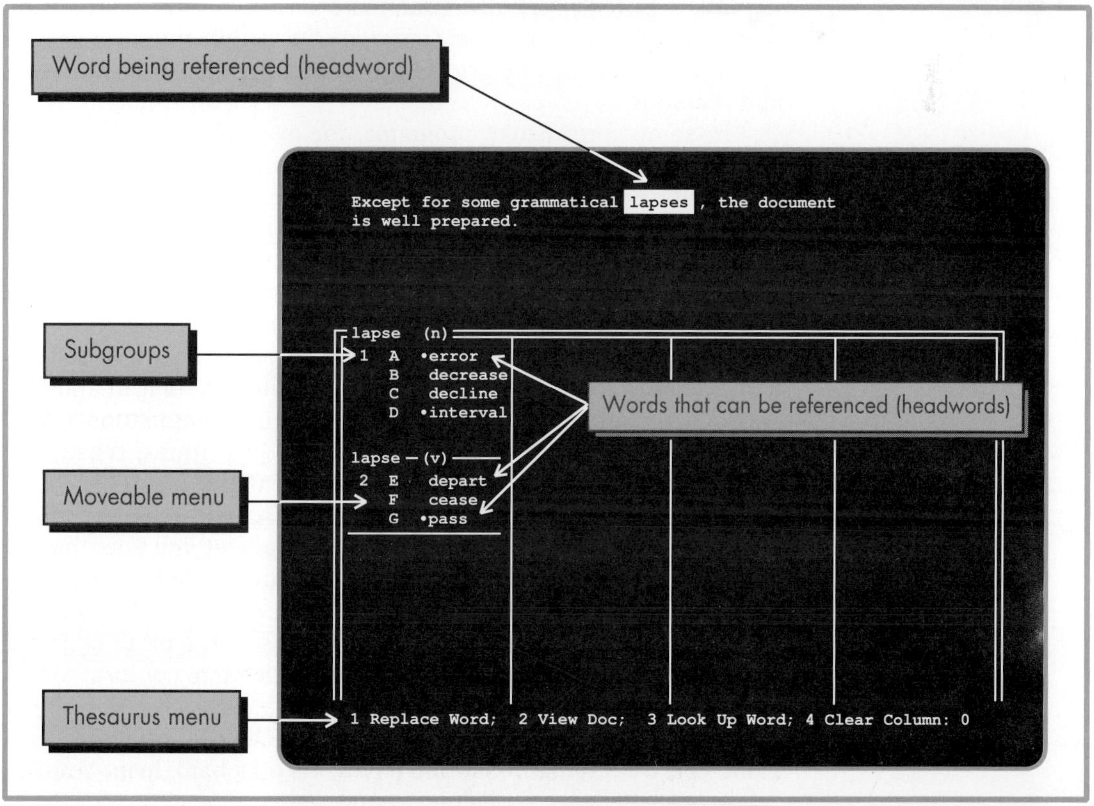

Word being referenced (headword)

Except for some grammatical lapses , the document is well prepared.

Subgroups

lapse (n)
1 A •error
B decrease
C decline
D •interval

Words that can be referenced (headwords)

Moveable menu

lapse — (v)
2 E depart
F cease
G •pass

Thesaurus menu

1 Replace Word; 2 View Doc; 3 Look Up Word; 4 Clear Column: 0

Word perfect
is command
driven

common to dedicated hardware (word processors and electronic typewriters), but more often will be found in word processing software. Also, more and more features are changing word processing into rich text or word publishing (referred to as **presentation features** because they are associated with electronic and desktop publishing).

This list should give you a general idea of the power and versatility of word processing software. Not all word processing software packages have all the features listed, and some have even more. Usually, there is a rather wide range between software packages as to the extent to which their features can be used. However, keep in mind that the more features the software has, the more powerful it usually is. More power does not necessarily mean it is easier to use, but it probably means the software may be used with other kinds of software. There are many advantages of being able to use different kinds of software in a connected or integrated way.

Spreadsheet Applications Software

Spreadsheet applications software is one of the most frequently used types of software with microcomputers. It also is one of the oldest. Spreadsheet software basically is a grid or model containing labels or text. The grid contains a series of **cells** made up of rows and columns. The user "programs" or enters numbers or values into the cells of the grid to give meaning to each of the rows and columns.

In some spreadsheet programs, for example, the cell where column A and row 36 intersect is cell A36 or its address. There can be thousands, even millions, of these cells. You can enter whatever alphanumeric information you want in a cell (such as your electric or phone bill). The numbers then can be edited and manipulated. Once you have made all your entries, you can keyboard instructions for the program to perform mathematical calculations with any numbers you have entered. That is, you can add up your bills and ask the program to put the total in another cell or perform any other calculation in any combination using simple arithmetic, trigonometry, algebra, or logarithms. When you finish creating a spreadsheet, you can print the results as hard copy or store them on a disk.

Your completed spreadsheet is a **worksheet** you can change automatically when you input new information. That is, once you have defined or programmed the meaning of each cell, you can change any number in any cell. The entries in the other cells related to that entry are automatically recalculated to conform to the new information.

Here is how **automatic** or **electronic recalculation** works. Assume you want to figure out the payments on a bank loan. You enter the amount of the loan, the interest rate, and the length of time you want to take to pay back the loan. The spreadsheet program will calculate the amount of each monthly payment. Now you can change the original amount of the loan, the interest rate, and the number of monthly payments. When you do, the program automatically will recalculate each amount.

One of the most popular spreadsheet applications programs on the market is Lotus 1-2-3. Introduced in 1982 by Lotus Development Corp., it has become an industry standard. Lotus 1-2-3 probably gained some of its popularity because users could add in functions and customize the program to meet their own needs. It also has database and graphics capabilities (discussed in later sections). It is not, however, as sophisticated as some of the other spreadsheet programs, even in its updated versions. Excel, developed by Microsoft Corp., and Quattro, developed by Borland International, have other enhancements that are providing competition for Lotus 1-2-3.

Spreadsheet applications software has many features and characteristics that also are common to word processing applica-

A spreadsheet program.

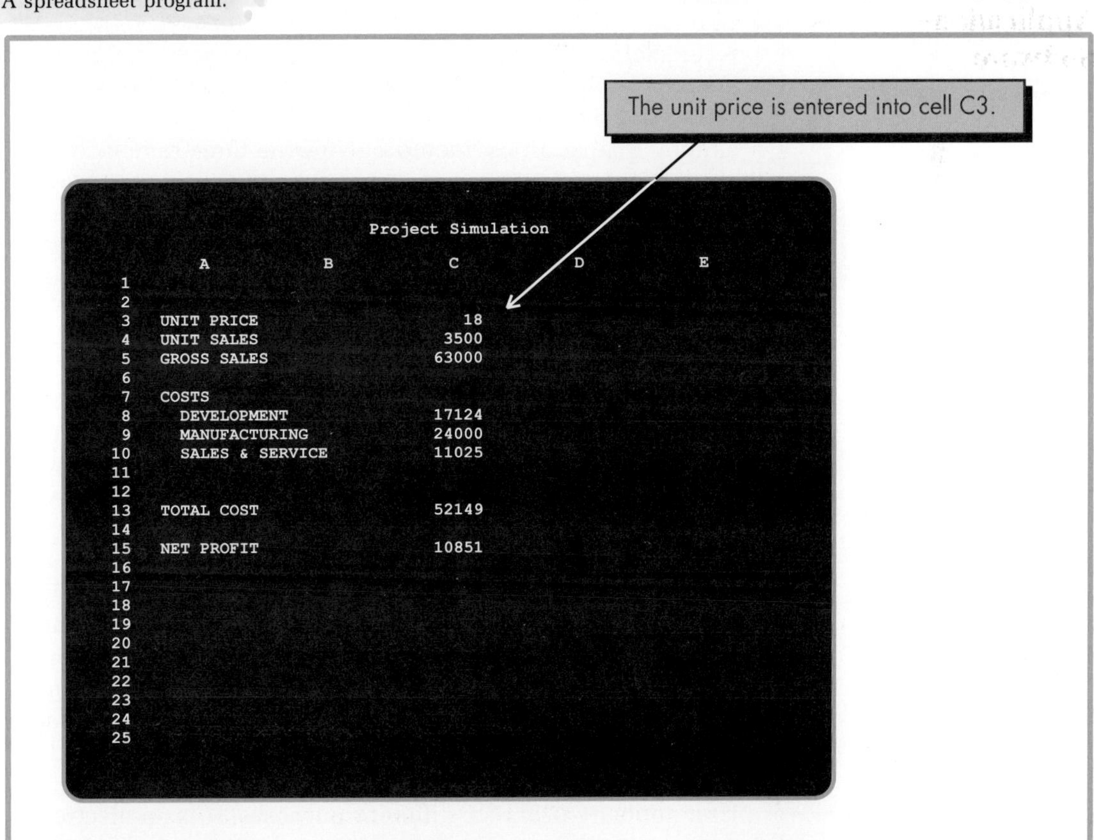

Features

Features of Spreadsheet Applications Software

- Help menus and formatting features
- Loading, combining, and saving files
- Moving, copying, deleting, and printing files
- Viewing spreadsheets by rows, columns, and pages
- Color, font, shading, and similar capabilities
- Date (day, month, and year) and time (seconds, minutes, and hours) functions
- Mathematics functions, including basic formulas
- Statistical functions, including frequency counts, averages, standard deviations, and variances
- Financial capabilities, including present and future value, interest rate, payment amount, and various depreciation methods
- Logic capabilities to check if a value in a cell is false, with options for evaluating and correcting it
- Macro library (stored keystrokes for one operation that are sent to a file for later retrieval and use)
- Linking of multiple spreadsheets without (or with minimal) recalculation in updating and consolidating worksheets
- Windowing to view and use several worksheets at once; resizing and reshaping
- Graphics capabilities, including viewing three-dimensional objects and adding more than one type of graphic to a page
- Exchanging and importing data to and from other spreadsheet packages as well as to and from other software, such as word processing, graphics, and database programs
- Built-in and add-in features
- Mouse and other input device support
- Printer, plotter, and other output device support

tions software. Later you will see how important integrated applications programs are in linking many business applications. And all these applications impact information processing.

Database Management Applications Software

Information is only as useful as the way it can be used by the right people at the right time. Fortunately, computers have contributed to quick access of vast amounts of information—with database applications programs. Data useful to people in an information processing system must be arranged and stored to give users fast and easy access. The concept of the database arose out of this need. A **database** is a collection of related information stored so that it is available to many users for different purposes. It is an electronic filing system with many individual **records** (the actual informa-

A database is organized to enable users to reorganize and retrieve data in many different ways.

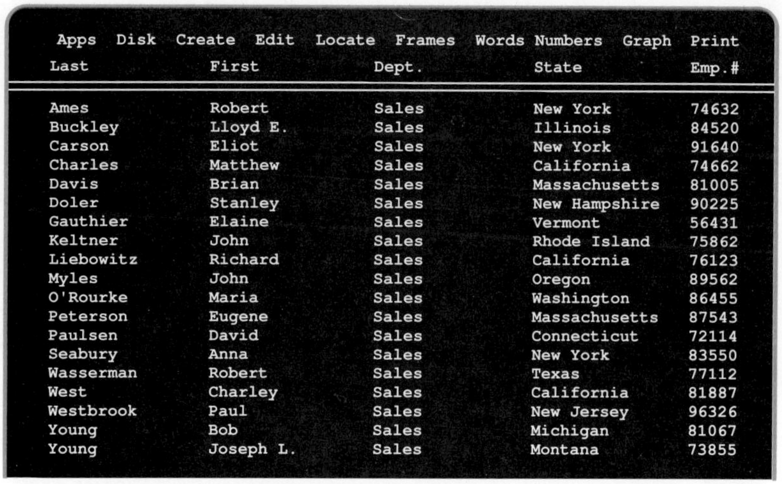

Apps Disk Create Edit Locate Frames Words Numbers Graph Print

Last	First	Dept.	State	Emp.#
Ames	Robert	Sales	New York	74632
Buckley	Lloyd E.	Sales	Illinois	84520
Carson	Eliot	Sales	New York	91640
Charles	Matthew	Sales	California	74662
Davis	Brian	Sales	Massachusetts	81005
Doler	Stanley	Sales	New Hampshire	90225
Gauthier	Elaine	Sales	Vermont	56431
Keltner	John	Sales	Rhode Island	75862
Liebowitz	Richard	Sales	California	76123
Myles	John	Sales	Oregon	89562
O'Rourke	Maria	Sales	Washington	86455
Peterson	Eugene	Sales	Massachusetts	87543
Paulsen	David	Sales	Connecticut	72114
Seabury	Anna	Sales	New York	83550
Wasserman	Robert	Sales	Texas	77112
West	Charley	Sales	California	81887
Westbrook	Paul	Sales	New Jersey	96326
Young	Bob	Sales	Michigan	81067
Young	Joseph L.	Sales	Montana	73855

tion contained in each file) and **fields** (the way the information is organized in each record).

A database offers many cross-references that give you a tremendous number of ways to reorganize and retrieve data. To be more precise, it is an electronic representation of a filing system such as you might find in any business. What is unique about a database is how it is organized to allow users to search for information. A database can represent the electronic equivalent of an ordinary Roladex file, a 3- by 5-inch index card file, or a business card file. Or it might contain every bit of information concerning a business or organization. It also can calculate "unknowns" from the data stored in the files. A database can handle all the details of a business inventory, such as accounting and filing. It can be used to prepare summaries, estimates, and reports drawing on the information in its files. It can store newspaper articles, magazines and books, games, and even digitized pictures (photographs). In fact, a database is whatever the last programmer to write one says it is.

Because information has many applications, **database management systems (DBMS)** have evolved. These are systems for organizing data for efficient handling and manipulation. Some DBMS are called **file managers** because they are easy to learn and use yet are quite powerful. Many DBMS are considered **relational databases** or databases that determine the relationship of the data when it is accessed. The real purpose of a relational database is automatic updating of all the data tables affected when you change one of the database records.

Imagine what a DBMS means to the Internal Revenue Service. Processing income tax records for every person in the United States is a tremendous task. Powerful computers can help with that task. The processing of your income tax return is aided by a

The data stored on these computer tapes represents approximately 1.8 million IRS tax returns and related documents of the nearly 200 million filed nationwide annually.

database management system. When you file your tax return, it is processed and stored. It is a complete "record"; yet several parts of it can be compared with any of your past tax returns. Normally, the IRS computers make several "checks" on tax returns, and these may alert the IRS to look at some returns more closely.

For example, the tax return you mailed to the IRS this year probably will be compared with your return from last year—if you filed one. The IRS routinely compares several years of returns for an individual. Comparisons result in trying to answer such questions as why there may be large dollar differences in some categories, why your overall income may have decreased or increased significantly, and so on. Such investigations require accessing and comparing records from several databases. Also, when letters regarding tax return audits are sent to individuals, the IRS uses its databases. Thus, information processing depends on databases and their management.

Individuals and businesses of all sizes have found that the more effectively they can collect, file, sort, and reproduce information, the more productive and successful they will be. In addition, with the proliferation of personal computers in offices around the country, database applications have become more popular than ever. The personal computer has brought information manipulation closer to the end user or person using the data. If the information is stored in a general-access database, it can probably be transferred into your personal computer and accessed at your convenience.

The growth of the database software industry has been rapid—about 25 to 30 percent a year. One program in particular, dBASE, has been extremely popular. This program has gone through several updates since it was introduced in 1981 by Ashton-Tate. Because Ashton-Tate has sold over three million copies of its dBASE

Features of Database Management Systems Applications Software

- Linking of multiple data or value files for access, consolidation, and updating of large, small, and varied files
- Math capabilities
- Macro and/or more extensive programming functions
- Data import/export support of various data formats
- Forms mapping and generation
- Query language capabilities for easily selecting data for viewing, constructing a report, etc., of a relational database; for example, Structured Query Language (SQL), a popular query language
- Report functions for viewing and scanning as well as capabilities for data manipulation, generation, and production
- Multiuser capabilities to permit simultaneous access by several users
- Security and password protection
- Help menus with interactive video and good documentation to assist the user

programs, it would have had a "gold record" award long before its dBASE V and even earlier updates, including dBASE IV (versions 1.0 and 1.1), were available to consumers. Several other competitors (and their software products) in the DBMS industry include Borland International, Inc. (Paradox), DataEase International, Inc. (DataEase), and Information Builders, Inc. (PC/FOCUS). These and other manufacturers are making a considerable impact in promoting sophisticated database management systems.

Many of the basic features of database programs are similar to those of word processing software programs. The importance of these features will depend on the sophistication of the database structure and the DBMS software used in a specific office setting. Database users can count on vendors to create better documentation and help functions to assist the user as competition in the database applications software market grows. Databases and DBMSs are discussed in more detail in Chapter 8.

Graphics Applications Software

Graphics applications software has become very popular with businesses. The competitive edge in business depends on communications. Presentation graphics make it possible to "present" data in many interesting ways. A shaded graph, for example, can picture information in a way that reveals more than countless tables with columns of statistical data. The use of computer graphics in presentation graphics helps people understand ideas and solve problems quickly and easily.

Computer graphics can range from simple bar graphs to very complex engineering drawings.

Today, computers can do more than just process words and numbers and chart the results. They can input, store, and transmit graphic information. They can integrate graphic material with text and help create many kinds of graphics. They can create and manipulate drawings and images on the screen to show three-dimensional quality. They can be enhanced (enlarged or changed in other ways) and rotated to allow users to look at all sides of an "object."

Presentation graphics are not limited to hard copy output. Many users create slide shows in much the same way you would develop and produce a presentation of slides with a slide projector. Some graphics applications software will make presentation outlines and notes of the graphics. Others can "organize" the graphics and integrate clip art, animation, voice, and music.

A very popular and powerful graphics software package is Harvard Graphics, which is marketed by Software Publishing Corp. It is easy to use and offers capabilities for creating text, charting, drawing, and spell checking. It has a large library of symbols and maps (about 300) as well as customizing features and screen show capabilities. Lotus Development Corporation's Freelance Plus is a strong competitor of Harvard Graphics. Freelance Plus is easy to use, supports nearly 1000 special symbols and templates, and can import files from several other software products.

Probably the most popular use of personal computer graphics has been in producing charts and graphs for business analyses and presentations. The ability to convert data from a spreadsheet or other report into an easily comprehensible chart lends more power to a presentation. Standalone business graphics packages compete to offer the widest variety of fonts (typefaces or styles), color options (gradations of up to many thousands of colors), scaling (size) options, and chart types.

Despite the increasing graphics power of software, computer graphics are only as good as the output devices that present them. There are several special kinds of printers that print in color and are used in computer graphics (see Chapter 6).

Romaro Lowe is administrative assistant to Othello Furnace's national marketing manager, Bernadette Thompson. Ms. Thompson likes to illustrate her quarterly reports with charts. Some of these show how sales compare with those of other periods, both for the company as a whole and for its individual products. Others show what percentage of the furnaces being sold throughout the country are Othello products. The charts clarify the information and illustrate the statistics in the reports.

In the past, Mr. Lowe has had to prepare rough drafts of these charts by hand, which required tedious formatting and drawing. With his microcomputer, he can use a software package that enables the system to translate tabular data into bar charts, pie charts, graphs, and other illustrations. He can display them on the screen and print them in color—all with a few keystrokes. It is easy to overlook a single figure in a sea of numbers, but you can hardly miss the orange wedge in a colorful pie chart—the wedge that shows what proportion of a department's budget is spent on salaries, for example.

Rather than list page after page of numbers, managers increasingly are using computer graphics to show important relationships between such numbers. This trend should also reduce the

Graphics Applications Software Features

- Conversion of data into a variety of charts and graphs, such as line, bar, pie, scatter, organizational, and flowcharts
- Creation, modification, and printing of three-dimensional charts and graphs in graduated shades and colors
- Automatic generation of titles and labels on charts/graphs
- Customizing, such as altering text sizes and fonts, chart scaling (sizing) and repositioning, and freehand drawing
- Spell checkers
- Math and statistical functions
- Data import/export features, including clip art, symbol and map libraries, and icons (images that show a function, such as a picture of a telephone to indicate a communications function)
- Multiple sets of data on one chart or graph and multiple charts/graphs on a page
- Outputs, such as slides, prints, and transparencies
- Film recorder, printer, and plotter support

amount of paper used for printing long, hard-to-read statistical reports.

Desktop Publishing Applications Software

"Word processing" has evolved into "information processing" because the capabilities of word processing are getting more diverse. You also can see this change in businesses, where increased emphasis is being placed on an information system. In an information system with interrelated components, knowledge workers are needed to process information (not just merely words). Although the term *word processing* may be with us for a long time, word processing software is expanding into other areas—including **electronic publishing** and **desktop publishing (DTP) applications**. **Desktop publishing** combines text and graphics to create an attractive presentation, frequently in a printed, publishable form.

Desktop publishing represents one result of the integration of graphics and text.

One of the most exciting aspects of the expansion of word processing software is its integration of graphics and words. Developments like this have led to electronic and desktop publishing—an industry that became popular in the late 1980s. As electronic and desktop publishing has continued to grow, the line between it

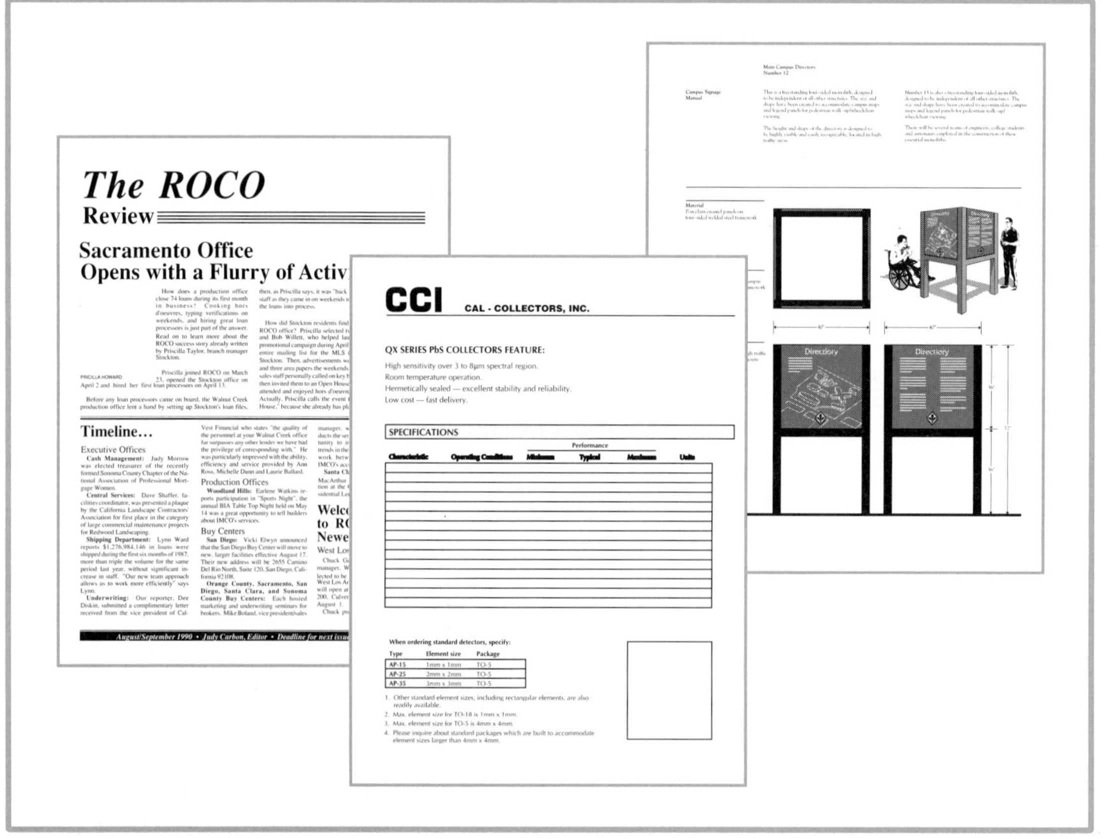

The ROCO **Review**

Sacramento Office Opens with a Flurry of Activ

How does a production office close 74 loans during its first month in business? Cooking hors d'oeuvres, typing verifications on weekends, and hiring great loan processors is just part of the answer. Read on to learn more about the ROCO success story already written by Priscilla Taylor, branch manager Stockton.

PRICILLA HOWARD

Priscilla joined ROCO on March 23, opened the Stockton office on April 2 and hired her first loan processors on April 13.

Before any loan processors came on board, the Walnut Creek production office lent a hand by setting up Stockton's loan files.

Timeline...

Executive Offices

Cash Management: Judy Morrow was elected treasurer of the recently formed Sonoma County Chapter of the National Association of Professional Mortgage Women.

Central Services: Dave Shaffer, facilities coordinator, was presented a plaque by the California Landscape Contractors' Association for first place in the category of large commercial maintenance projects for Redwood Landscaping.

Shipping Department: Lynn Ward reports $1,276,984,146 in loans were shipped during the first six months of 1987, more than triple the volume for the same period last year, without significant increase in staff. "Our new team approach allows us to work more efficiently" says Lynn.

Underwriting: Our reporter, Dee Diskin, submitted a complimentary letter received from the vice president of Cal-Vest Financial who states "the quality of the personnel at your Walnut Creek office far surpasses any other lender we have had the privilege of corresponding with." He was particularly impressed with the ability, efficiency and service provided by Ann Ross, Michelle Dunn and Laurie Ballard.

Production Offices

Woodland Hills: Earlene Watkins reports participation in "Sports Night", the annual BIA Table Top Night held on May 14 was a great opportunity to tell builders about IMCO's services.

Buy Centers

San Diego: Vicki Elwyn announced that the San Diego Buy Center will move to new, larger facilities effective August 17. Their new address will be 2655 Camino Del Rio North, Suite 120, San Diego, California 92108.

Orange County, Sacramento, San Diego, Santa Clara, and Sonoma County Buy Centers: Each hosted marketing and underwriting seminars for brokers. Mike Boland, vice president/sales

August/September 1990 • Judy Carbon, Editor • Deadline for next issu

CCI CAL - COLLECTORS, INC.

QX SERIES PbS COLLECTORS FEATURE:

High sensitivity over 3 to 8µm spectral region.
Room temperature operation.
Hermetically sealed — excellent stability and reliability.
Low cost — fast delivery.

SPECIFICATIONS

Characteristic	Operating Conditions	Performance: Minimum	Performance: Typical	Performance: Maximum	Units

When ordering standard detectors, specify:

Type	Element size	Package
AP-15	1mm x 1mm	TO-5
AP-25	2mm x 2mm	TO-5
AP-35	3mm x 3mm	TO-5

1. Other standard element sizes, including rectangular elements, are also readily available.
2. Max. element size for TO-18 is 1mm x 1mm.
3. Max. element size for TO-5 is 4mm x 4mm.
4. Please inquire about standard packages which are built to accommodate element sizes larger than 4mm x 4mm.

Features of Desktop Publishing Applications Software

- Full-featured capabilities (combining page and document features) to permit a wide range of applications and their management
- Style sheets (formats for pages and varied sizes of paper), and other layout and makeup features
- Right/left page formatting, which includes separate headers, footers, and page starts (for example, formats for front/back printed documents to be bound or placed in a three-ring binder)
- Multicolumn layout of variable widths; multiple fonts
- Importation of varied files and formats from other software—especially from word processing and graphics software
- Text wraparound variable-shaped graphics (in addition to wraparound defined boxes)
- Kerning (adjustment of spaces between letters) and other text features
- Graphics features for scanning, enlarging/reduction, cropping (make smaller by trimming—frequently by zooming in on part of a picture or image and cutting it to size), scaling, rotating (both vertical and horizontal), shading, and toning
- Page Description Language (PDL) support (page composition "language" for sending a document to be printed)
- Mouse (and other pointing devices), scanner, and high-quality laser (light) printer support

and word processing has become finer. Thus, "information processing" has taken on even more significance.

PageMaker (developed by Aldus Corp.) and Ventura (developed by Xerox Corp.) are two popular types of desktop publishing software. PageMaker began as a **page-oriented** system—where attending to the details of each page was most important, and each page could be a distinct file. Ventura began as a **document-oriented** or **code-oriented** system—concerned more with layout and formatting of the entire document (similar to word processing) than with page-by-page details. More recent versions of both of these trend-setting packages combine page and document features.

Some features will be more useful than others, depending upon the type of text/graphics editing needed. Some offices use desktop publishing features to eliminate or reduce the amount of work sent out for phototypesetting. Other offices use DTP software to make routine documents more attractive. Whatever the use, desktop publishing adds yet another dimension for users to develop good decision-making skills—and a new vocabulary.

Communications Applications Software

There are many different types of communications applications software packages on the market. They help make equipment compatible or capable of receiving information from each other. **Compatibility** not only is a main part of communications, but it also is vitally important for any technology to work with another.

For example, on October 19, 1987, the New York Stock Exchange crashed, and millions of shares of stock were sold at a record rate—so fast that stockbroker communications lines were jammed for hours. Several hundred million shares changed hands that day, and stock prices plummeted from record highs. Many factors were responsible for the stock market crash, but one of the most significant was the increased use of data communications that permit computerized trading. Now that stockbrokers and investors can receive the latest market information using sophisticated communications systems, they can analyze stock information quickly and respond instantly to tips and trends. So much information and the chance to act on it so fast can, in itself, turn a snowball into a devastating avalanche in a single day.

Stock trading is only one communications application (and involves the use of databases). You can use a computer to send information to, and receive it from, someone using a computer at another location. You can also work with a computer that has no operator but is programmed for communication.

You can use a microcomputer to search large libraries, shop through electronic catalogs, pay bills, play games, contact special interest groups, and exchange information on bulletin board services. An electronic **bulletin board service (BBS)** permits a subscriber to use a micro to access and view the same kind of information that you would expect to find tacked up on a community or school bulletin board. Communications and office applications are discussed in depth in Chapter 7.

Integrated Applications Software

Some software programs support several kinds of applications. Some also can be used with other software. Even though more and more software packages on the market today have multiple applications, many of them can and do run independently of one another. That is, you may use a word processing software program to keyboard text or a spreadsheet program to prepare a budget.

Sometimes with separate applications software programs, transferring information from one program to another (for example, from a spreadsheet to a word processing document) can be tedious and time-consuming because you must load each program each time you want to change applications. Loading and reloading programs is a slow process, even on fast machines. The process is slowed further in transferring information. That is, if you cannot "transport" (import/export) the information from one program to another, you must rekey or reenter the information you wish to transfer.

Integrated applications software eliminates these problems. The main goal of **integrated software** is to link or interface applications to enable the user to do multiple applications within an all-in-one software program. With integrated software, you can perform a variety of tasks uniformly and simultaneously. You can also pass information freely and easily between tasks. With many integrated programs, you will use the same commands to perform all tasks in a similar way (referred to as a **unified command structure**).

With integrated software, it is possible to store the program in the temporary memory of a microcomputer. For example, if you are using an integrated software program that contains spreadsheet, database, and graphics applications, once you load the software, you can move freely from one function to the next (retrieve data from a database, calculate it on a spreadsheet, and graph the results) without changing programs. You can change operations in integrated software with a few keystrokes. And you don't have to reenter data.

A general characteristic of integrated software packages is **windowing**—so you can see multiple functions simultaneously. Each window is a separate area or box on the screen that can display a different aspect of your work. (Windowing is a feature of some of the types of applications software discussed earlier.) Win-

Windowing is a common characteristic of integrated software packages.

dowing has become a popular **multitasking** software feature. It permits you to view, move between, and work on several functions merely by selecting and accessing a window on your screen.

Let's say, for example, you are preparing this year's financial report. You can display a word processing window to prepare the text, a spreadsheet window for your year-end balance sheet, and a graphics window for a pie chart depicting the year's expenses. The windowing system makes it easy to refer to the spreadsheet for statistics while writing the report, to create the pie chart by transferring figures from the spreadsheet, and to move the graph into the word processing document. Windowing tasks are made even simpler with systems that perform these functions with a mouse or similar device instead of keyboard commands.

Many integrated programs allow the user to overlap several windows on the screen, similar to the way you might overlap sheets of paper on your desk. The task or window you are working on is always on top. Each of the other windows is partially covered. You can uncover each with a mouse or with keystrokes as easily as if each window were a sheet of paper. This concept may be referred to as a **multitasking environment.**

Some software permits you to separate the windows and place them side by side and/or top to bottom as you would lay tile (called **tiling**). Tiling limits the size of each overlapping window in proportion to the total number of windows on the screen—the more screens, the smaller each window is, and the less of its contents you can see. If you delete a window, the remaining windows may expand to fill up the screen. Other software permits you to place the windows where you want them on the screen, to reduce or enlarge their sizes, and so forth. Some software supports 50 or more windows on the screen and in the temporary memory of your micro. Usually, four or five windows are all you need.

Integrated packages have varying capabilities, including combinations of word processing, spreadsheet, graphics, database and project management, voice messaging and other communications, appointment scheduling, and dialing of phone numbers using cross-indexed electronic files. The most popular integrated programs include word processing, spreadsheet, database, graphics, and communications applications. Although integrated packages have advantages, there are some disadvantages, too. They frequently are not as powerful as individual or separate applications. One application usually is better than another (or others). Integrated packages usually are more expensive than separate applications and may not be the best choice for persons who use one application (such as word processing) most of the time.

The first integrated software program on the market, a recent version of Lotus 1-2-3, combines three functions: spreadsheet, database, and graphics. Lotus 1-2-3 is a popular spreadsheet program, which was originally its main function. Similar examples of blurred integrated/specific applications programs include those in the desktop publishing category.

If there are "true" integrated programs, the most popular ones marketed today include Microsoft Works (developed by Microsoft Corp.) and PSF:First Choice (marketed by Software Publishing, Inc.). Both are relatively inexpensive and easy to use. More expensive, powerful, and complicated integrated software programs include versions of Symphony (developed by Lotus Corp.) and Framework (developed by Ashton-Tate). All these software packages are popular for integrating word processing, spreadsheet, database and/or file management, graphics, and communications.

Information and Software

Executives and secretaries are working with greater volumes of information in preparing spreadsheet budgets, financial plans, company personnel records, and a variety of reports. The increased information flow has placed greater demands on office systems, software, and people for processing the information. Many of today's businesses use **horizontal applications software**, software such as word processing, accounting, and spreadsheets. These may be used by any type of business. Businesses, organizations, or professions with specialized needs use **vertical applications software**, designed to meet the specific requirements of a particular business or specialized industry. Good examples are software used in real estate, medical diagnosis, and weather forecasting.

There are many types of applications software that can be used with computer hardware to help office employees complete their work. This is probably the single most important reason many businesses are shying away from dedicated equipment. (It is also a major reason more and more manufacturers are producing add-ons and add-ins to make equipment more versatile.)

The tools used with the numerous and varied applications software programs have contributed to the automation of many office functions. More and more of these functions will depend on multiuser and multitasking environments. New and better tools will be developed for successfully integrating and interrelating office functions. **Hypermedia** (the linking of related information by association from all types of media) will be one of these "tools" to bring related information together for better information access and decision making. Such developments should increase productivity and efficiency, contributing significantly to the operations of effective office information systems throughout the world.

CHAPTER SUMMARY

- There are two categories of software: system and applications.
- System software is essential to the ability of a computer to know how to access applications software programs.
- Software programs are written in special computer languages. Some of the better known are BASIC, COBOL, and Pascal.
- Bundled software means that both the disk operating instructions and the word processing functions are built into the hardware and begin working automatically whenever you turn on the computer.
- Software-based equipment can be given additional capabilities because internal processing is based on software (programs) rather than on hardware (the machine itself).
- Applications software is what gives a microcomputer personality and is created to solve a particular problem, whether it be business, recreational, personal, or educational.
- Some of the applications software packages include word processing, spreadsheet, database management, graphics, desktop publishing, communications, and integrated programs.
- Word processing software is one of the most popular kinds of applications software. Because it is becoming more versatile, it continues to be an important information processing tool.
- Rich text or word publishing is one example of expanded word processing.
- Menu-driven and command-driven programs offer advantages and disadvantages to both beginners and experienced users.
- Automatic recalculation of data is an important characteristic of spreadsheet programs.
- Database management systems software helps organize related information into databases so many users can retrieve it from the system's storage for a variety of purposes.
- Some software programs let computers convert numeric and other data into graphic form, making the information easier to comprehend.
- As desktop publishing and word processing continue to mesh, information processing will take on new meaning.
- Compatibility is one of the most important factors in an information system and relates to every part of office automation and electronic information transfer.
- Some integrated software programs use a feature called windowing, which displays various functions on the screen at the same time.
- As companies seek new ways to pool their information, we can expect technological advances in multiuser and multitasking applications.

VOCABULARY

applications software
assembly language
automatic recalculation
boot
bundled software
command-driven
compatibility
database management system (DBMS)
desktop publishing (DTP)
disk operating system (DOS)
document-oriented
firmware
hypermedia
integrated software
loaded
machine language
menu-driven
multitasking
operating system
page-oriented
presentation graphics
programming languages
resident software
rich text
software
system software
spreadsheet
windowing
WYSIWYG

CHAPTER QUESTIONS

1. Define software. What are the two types of software?
2. What is the purpose of operating system software?
3. Name at least three different software applications packages and some of the characteristics of each.
4. What is machine language? How does it differ from other programming languages?
5. What is the difference between a menu-driven and a command-driven program? Name some of the advantages and disadvantages of each.
6. Suggest a possible database and discuss two ways in which it might be used.
7. What are the advantages of using a computer to illustrate information in a report?
8. Why is "compatibility" so important to communications? Name some areas in office automation where compatibility is essential.
9. Define automatic recalculation, boot, end user, icon, multitasking, version, and windowing.
10. What are the advantages of integrated software?

CASE STUDY

Trapper Fox & Sons is a Portland, Maine, mail-order house that markets camping goods—everything from tweed shirts to fishing lures to corduroy knickers. Trapper Fox attributes much of its success to the microcomputer systems it installed two years ago. Many of the operations that once took days, if not weeks, are now completed within a matter of hours. For each application listed below, identify which software program (package) would be required. Explain your reasons for selecting that specific program.

1. Automatically keyed response letters to customers
2. An up-to-the-minute inventory list that allows the company to control its inventory rather than overstock merchandise
3. A quarterly report of itemized income and expenses
4. A pie chart, created in conjunction with the quarterly report, depicting each expense area
5. The sending of internal documents to the branch office in Seattle, Washington
6. The company newsletter
7. The catalog customers' file, which enables the company to track customers (includes ZIP Codes for establishing target markets)
8. Individual customer accounts indicating dates of purchases; items ordered, including catalog number, quantity, and a brief description; amounts received and outstanding; and balance due
9. The company's annual report to be sent to all stockholders (includes the president's annual message, reports from department managers, financial statements, and multicolor charts and graphs)
10. A printout of a customer's final order, including a mailing label and the amount of postage required

CHAPTER 6

Output

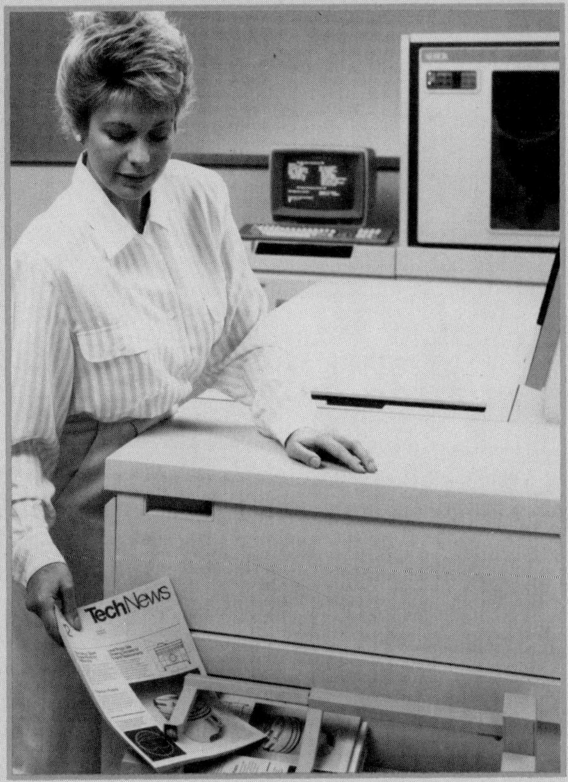

Jason Samuel manages the Reprographics Department of Hartford Trust Corporation, a large bank. Whenever a document requires more than ten copies, it is sent to Mr. Samuel's department for reproduction. On a typical day, he may receive a 1-page letter to be sent out as an original to 15 new customers, a 2-page memo to be distributed to the bank's 3000 employees, and a 100-page report to be typeset, copied, and bound in 20 copies for the bank's top executives. Each job has a deadline. Mr. Samuel decides on the best way to get each job done based on the number, format, and distribution of copies requested.

As the amount of information has grown, output methods have also expanded. Before high-speed output equipment was developed, a job like Mr. Samuel's probably would not have existed. Hartford Trust would have used outside companies to handle its high-volume reprographics needs. In recent years, however, many companies have purchased printing and reprographics equipment for greater production and cost-efficiency. The new equipment is capable of handling a wide variety of projects. In today's office, you will need to be aware of the rapidly expanding capabilities of this output equipment and its relationship to information processing.

Soft Copy Output

Video display terminals brought with them an important advance in output—soft copy. Information displayed on a screen does not require paper, printing, or **reprographics** (producing copies). In offices where every person who needs a terminal has one, many letters and memos are never printed in hard copy. Let's look at how the firm of Manville & Associates, interior design consultants, uses soft copy output as a means of "reproducing" information.

Ms. Manville, president of the company, creates most of her correspondence at the keyboard of her personal computer. At 9:15 one morning, she keys a memo informing her associates of an important bid meeting scheduled for tomorrow at 2:30 P.M. at the world headquarters of Lynhoff-Rothka, a manufacturer of robotics materials. Manville & Associates will be bidding for the contract to design the reception and office areas of Lynhoff-Rothka's new building. In her memo, she requests that each of the associates respond, saying whether or not they will be able to meet today at 3 P.M. to form a strategic plan for the bidding session.

Having proofread the final memo, Ms. Manville then accesses the communications capability of her computer and sends the document electronically to each associate. Flashing lights on each associate's terminal indicate that a message is waiting. They access the electronic message system on their computer, read the memo displayed on the screen, and respond electronically to Ms. Manville's memo. In this instance, Ms. Manville sent a "copy" of the memo to each associate without a hard copy having been made (printed). By creating at the keyboard and using the communications capability of her PC rather than a more traditional method, she saves time—time she can't afford to waste.

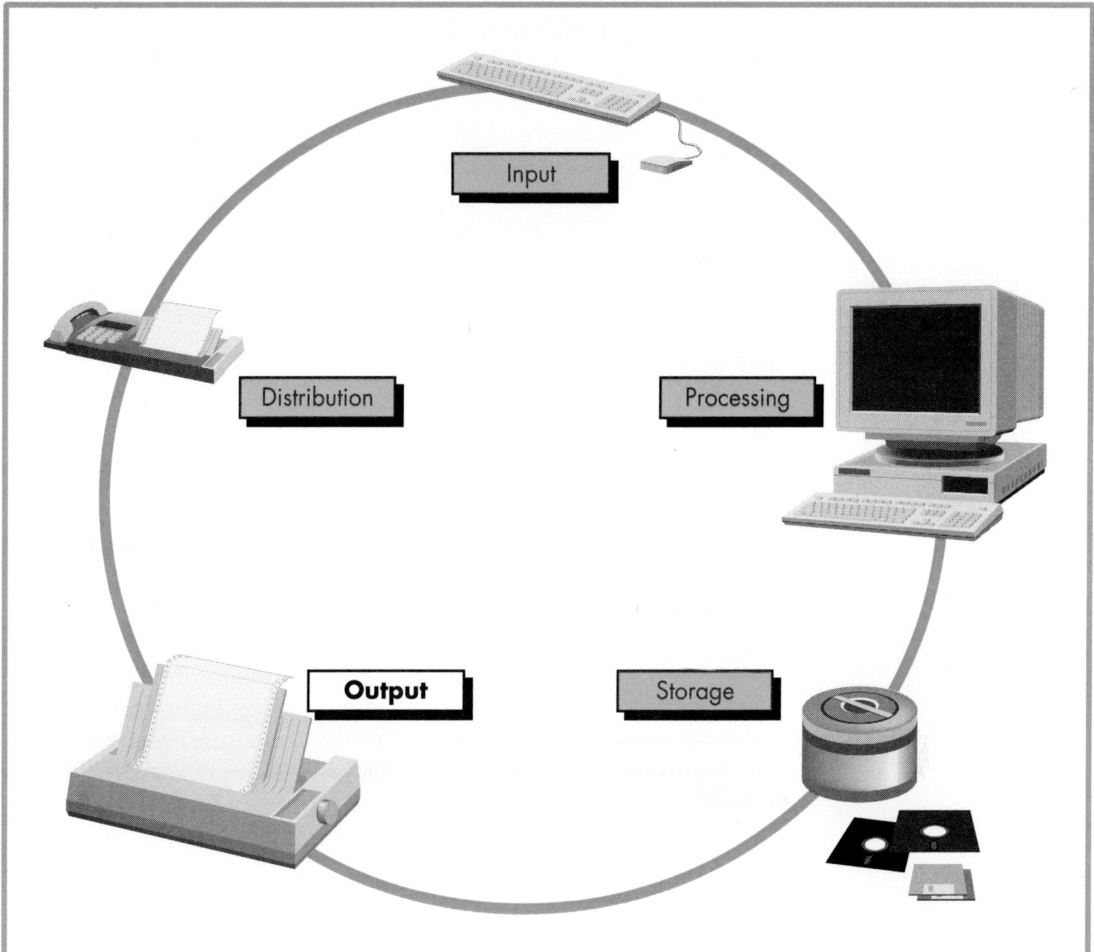

Output is one of five stages in the information processing cycle.

Printed Output

Although the concept of a paperless office did not gain the popularity it might have, soft copy has changed the office dramatically. It has also contributed to fewer printed drafts, but the printed output is still irreplaceable. Printing documents is essential; and printing speed, flexibility, and convenience mean more to office workers than ever before.

Most electronic typewriters combine keyboarding and printing in the same unit and print between 20 and 40 **cps (characters**

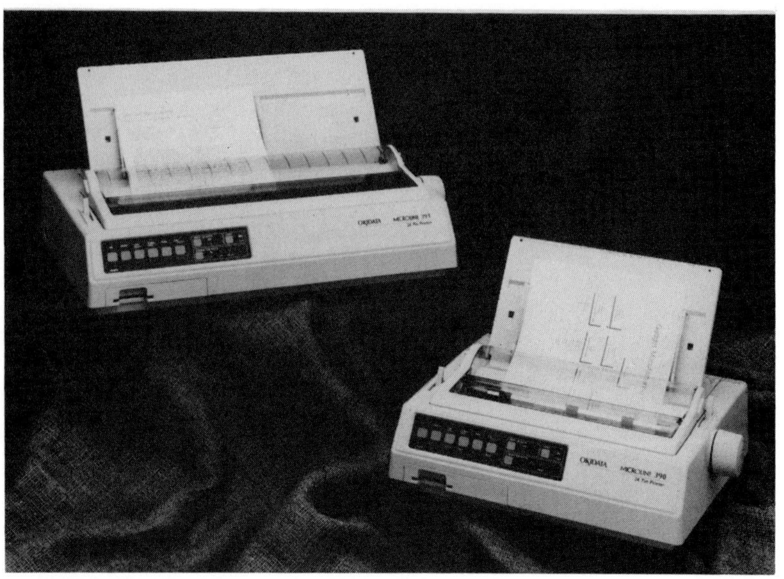

Impact printers such as these strike the type against the ribbon and paper to produce output.

per second). Electronic typewriters with expanded functions (especially because of add-ons) may interface with a separate printer—and usually can print faster. Microcomputers and other computer equipment rely on printers as separate components. Many systems permit you to keyboard, edit, or revise one document while another is being printed, a feature called **background printing.** This flexibility makes your work go faster and enhances your efficiency.

There are many types of printers on the market today with a wide range of printing quality, speed, and capabilities. Printers may be described in two basic categories: impact and nonimpact.

Impact Printers

Typewriters and **impact printers** are similar in that they both print by striking the type against a ribbon and the paper to produce output as an original hard copy of a document. Unlike typewriters, however, many impact printers are **bidirectional** (print in both directions). The print mechanism prints first from left to right and then from right to left. It can do this because the text has already been keyed and stored.

Impact printers that print one character at a time are called **character printers.** These may or may not be bidirectional, and are used for letters and other kinds of output that must be of high quality.

Element, Daisy Wheel, and Thimble Printers Character printers may use an **element** or "ball" to print letters in uppercase and lowercase. Elements are available in many **fonts** (typefaces) and

The daisy wheel and thimble type elements take their names from their shapes.

sizes. Because one element usually contains a complete set of characters of one typeface and one size, they are called single-element fonts. You can change a printer element just as you change the ball on any element typewriter.

Most character printers use a **daisy wheel**–type element, which gets its name from its shape. Its "petals" are straight bars of type, with the characters at the ends. The type wheels may be plastic or metal—metal is more durable. The wheel spins at high speeds, and when the correct character is positioned over the ribbon and paper, a tiny hammer strikes it. In comparison with other types of printers, element and daisy wheel printers are not very fast. Some may print around 100 cps, but most print in the range of 20 to 50 cps or 240 to 600 words a minute.

Character printers may use another ball-type print mechanism known as a **thimble.** A thimble element also has bars arranged in a circle and extending from a center, with alphanumeric characters at the tips. It is similar to a daisy wheel, but the bars are shaped to resemble a thimble. Thimbles are made of plastic, and the quality of their output is not as high as that of a metal daisy wheel. A thimble spins constantly as it travels back and forth across the page, similar to the ball element.

Character element printers, including the daisy wheel and thimble, are **letter quality (LQ)** printers because they print whole or entire, full-formed characters. That is, each character (a letter, number, or symbol) is uniformly dark when it is printed because each character is a preformed shape similar to a cookie cutter. The characters are printed one after another, one at a time. For this reason, character printers are usually referred to as **serial printers.**

The quality of character printers usually is excellent, and as impact printers, they can produce carbon copies. Character printers, however, can be noisy and inflexible—especially for printing graphics.

Chain and Band Printers **Chain printers** and **band printers** are extremely fast impact printers. Both produce output in similar ways, and both are **line printers** because they print a line at a time. They may have several sets of characters on a continuous loop made of steel (chain) or plastic or metal (band). The chain or band rotates at a high rate of speed during printing. Hammers strike the chain or band as it moves around a gear mechanism. At each "strike," the character that is hit is forced against a ribbon, which prints the character onto the paper.

Chain and band printers may be referred to as **parallel printers** (versus serial printers) because they process and print several characters at one time—in this case, an entire line. Both chain and band printers are reliable. Chain printers are not quite as fast as band printers, which can print up to 4000 lines a minute. As impact printers, band printers can make up to six carbon copies at one time. Chain and band printing usually is less than letter quality; however, print quality is improved if printing can be slowed down. Many organizations use chain and band line printers for internal documents, particularly if volume and speed are major concerns.

Dot Matrix Printers The main advantages of dot matrix printers are speed and flexibility. A **dot matrix** printer is an impact printer. It prints a series of closely spaced dots in a matrix (pattern or grid) to form each letter, number, symbol, etc.—a technology particularly adapted to printing graphics. A dot matrix printer has a printhead with a matrix of tiny pins or wire bristles. As the printhead shuttles back and forth, the wires change position and form the characters before they strike the ribbon and paper.

There can be wide variations in the quality and readability of dot matrix printing. High-quality dot matrix printers are referred to as **near-letter quality (NLQ)** printers because they produce clear, dark, continuous print. Near-letter quality print may be produced if the **dots per inch (dpi)** are increased. When the number of dots per inch is increased, better resolution (clearer images) results. The number of wires on a printhead usually determines how close dots can be printed to each other. The closer the dots, the higher the resolution and the more difficult it is to see the printing as "dots." Some dot matrix printers create sharper characters by making several "passes" of printing with the dots in a slightly different position each time. Other, more sophisticated printers "calculate" where extra dots are needed and print single dots in the right places to make the print look uniform.

Dot matrix printers are relatively inexpensive compared with other kinds of impact printers. They are typically much faster than character printers and are widely used in offices. They can be versatile in the quality of type for internal documents, rough drafts, and graphics (including color) yet produce professional-looking type for other correspondence. The speed of a dot matrix printer is usually related to print quality. That is, the higher the print quality, the slower the printing speed. The range of speed for dot matrix printers varies widely, from 20 to 30 cps at the low end to draft quality of 1400 cps, or over 300 times faster than an average keyboarder could produce it.

Nonimpact Printers

Other types of printers are classified as **nonimpact printers.** Because the printhead does not actually hit or embed print on the paper, nonimpact printers cannot produce multiple or carbon copies. Nonimpact printers produce one copy at a time (an original); some require special paper. Nonimpact printers can produce even higher quality output than character printers with no loss in speed.

Several types of nonimpact printers are **page printers** because they "assemble" and print entire pages at a time—a feature especially suited for printing multiple fonts along with graphics. Page printers are of three basic types:

1. **electrophotography**—static charges on a light-sensitive surface, which includes laser (focused light), LED (light-emitting diode), and LCS (liquid crystal shutter) technologies
2. **electrography**—negative ion charges, as in ion deposition printers
3. **magnetography**—magnetic charges, as in magnetographic printers

These technologies are explained as each type of printer is discussed in the following sections. Page printers use page description languages (PDLs), which permit the user to create sophisticated layouts. PostScript, software developed by Adobe Systems, Inc., is one of the most popular PDLs. PDLs such as PostScript allow you to combine several fonts of different sizes, rotate and angle text, overlap and shade graphics, and so on. Many page printers print 10 to 30 pages per minute (ppm). Some of the more expensive models can print about 90 to 100 ppm.

Ink-Jet Printers One type of nonimpact printer, the **ink-jet printer,** sprays electrically charged ink onto paper. Ink-jet printers can shape characters in a variety of type styles and sizes. They

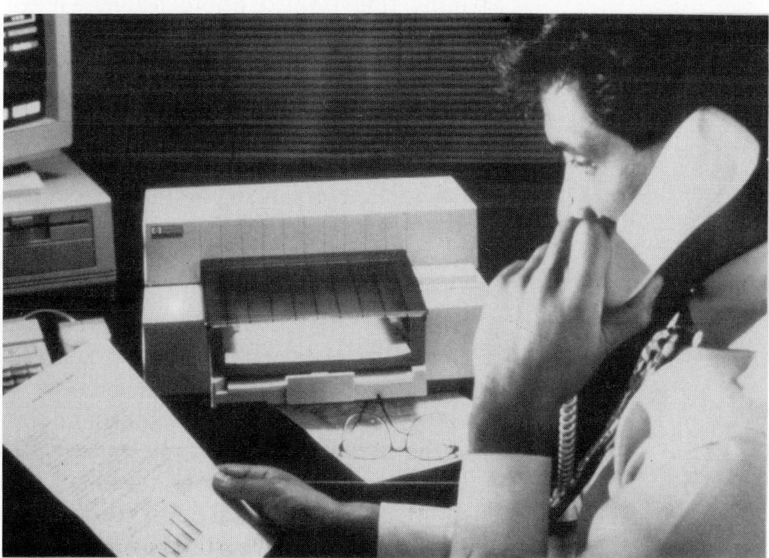

Printers such as this Hewlett-Packard Deskjet are designed for desktop use.

have several advantages over impact printers (they are practically noiseless, need little or no maintenance, may print several colors on a page, and are very fast).

Some ink-jet printers require special paper to get true letter quality print. In these cases, "bleeding" or smearing of the ink may occur if special paper is not used (few printers are currently being designed this way). Many high-quality ink-jet printers cost more because they produce very clear, sharp images even on rough paper. Such printers are said to have high resolution or a high density of dpi. The speed of many ink-jet printers is comparable to that of dot matrix printers. Some vendors feel that ink-jet technology will challenge that of page printers.

Thermal Transfer Printers Several methods of thermal printing use ink and heat and/or electricity in a matrix technique. The oldest of these methods, **thermal printing**, uses a special heat-sensitive paper. As the heated printheads move across the paper, images are produced. **Thermal transfer** is a newer process that transfers heat-sensitive ink to paper. In thermal transfer, the printhead is heated and passed over a waxy inked ribbon (or transfer sheet) to melt the ink onto the paper. A similar type of thermal transfer is resistive transfer, which uses electricity to heat and melt the ink off the special ribbon onto the paper.

Thermal transfer is a quiet and clean nonimpact printing method. It also is fast; some thermal printers can print about 600 lines per minute (lpm). However, most thermal printers print about 30 to 130 cps and give very good resolution. The output from a thermal transfer printer is clear and sharp, closely resembling that from a photocopier. Thermal printer operating costs may be high if special paper is required. Also, many thermal ribbons do not last long. If you print a lot of detailed graphics, you may have to replace a colored ribbon about every 20 pages and a black ribbon about every 100 pages.

Laser Printers A popular type of nonimpact printer, **laser printers** vary in size from desktop to large floor models. Using focused light instead of ink and ribbon to create images on paper, lasers print high-quality characters extremely fast. Laser printing equipment has become cost-effective for individuals, small businesses, and large corporations.

Laser printing uses a laser—a narrow beam of pure red light—that can carry millions of characters at once. It is a type of electrophotography that converts text and images into a matrix or grid of dots with static electrical charges. With high-speed photography, the light is shaped into characters and beamed onto light-sensitive paper. Laser printing makes it possible to print whole

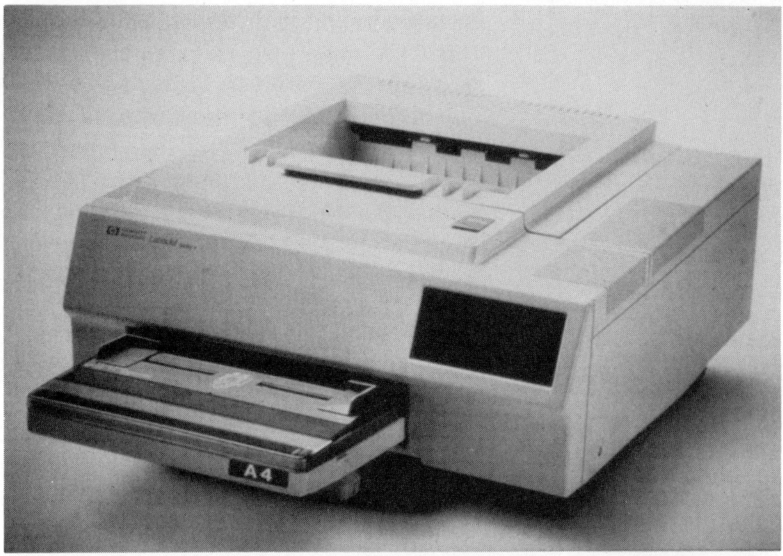

Fast, cost-effective, high-quality printing is available in desktop laser printers.

This Xerox Laser Printing System has the capability to produce publications complete with covers and section dividers.

pages at once at speeds of more than 100 ppm using several fonts of varying sizes. Laser printing quality is so good that it can be used to print company logos and letterheads. A laser printer can print facsimiles of signatures that are virtually indistinguishable from the originals.

Ion Deposition and Magnetographic Printers The process of printing with ion deposition printers and magnetographic printers is similar. The basic difference is how images are fixed to the paper. **Ion deposition printers** use an electrography process of negatively charged ions to attract dry ink particles to a drum. As the drum rotates over the paper, the ink is pressed onto it. **Magnetographic printers** use magnetic charges with pressure and/or heat to bind the images to the paper. The heads of magnetographic printers are similar to those of tape recorders. Both ion deposition and magnetographic printers are extremely fast page printers (upwards of 100 ppm). Because they are expensive, it may be some time before they seriously challenge other, more popular types of printers.

Plotters

Sometimes text and/or graphic illustrations require sophisticated equipment for printing. **Plotters** are useful in illustrating text and statistical data as well as in producing high-quality drawings, detailed maps, engineering plans, weather forecasts, and many other types of artwork. Pen plotters are impact plotters that apply color to paper by touching the ends of colored pens to it. As the pens and/or paper move (both back and forth and sideways), detailed images can be drawn. At the same time, they can be partially or completely shaded and colored, or made finer and broader. Nonimpact plotters may use many of the previously discussed printer technologies (ink-jet, thermal, laser, and electrostatic methods) for plotting text and images on various sizes of paper.

Printer Peripherals and Other Output-Handling Devices

Several manufacturers offer devices that help printers perform at their maximum speed and efficiency. These peripherals include automatic sheet and envelope feeders, tractors, and bursters. Another peripheral, usually separate from a printer but vitally important to many offices, is a paper shredder.

Sheet feeder.

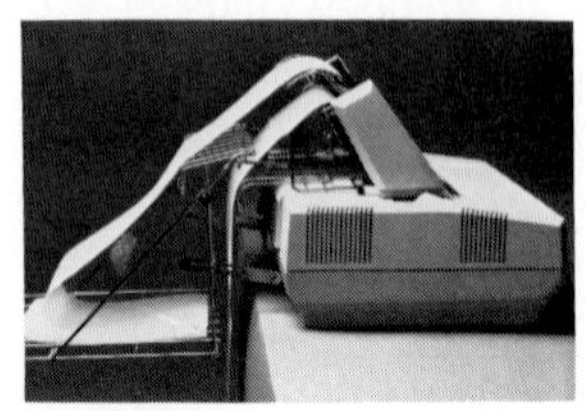

Tractor.

Automatic Sheet Feeders

Automatic sheet feeders are available in several models that can be attached to both electronic typewriters and a variety of separate printers. Most of these **cut-sheet feeders** hold between 50 and 250 sheets of paper in a **bin,** align them, and insert them one at a time into a printer. Printed pages are moved to a receiving tray for pickup as blank sheets are fed into the printer. This process, which takes only a few seconds, is known as the feeder's **cycle time.**

Sheet feeders are controlled by built-in microprocessors that can be commanded from the keyboard or set independently from the feeder itself. Feeder controls can also be used to feed single or unusually shaped pages manually into the printer. The feeder automatically signals the operator when paper has run out, is misaligned, or is jammed.

Sheet feeders that hold two or more separate stacks of paper in separate bins are available. **Dual** (two trays of paper) and **multiple** (three to four trays of paper) feeders are useful for printing large batches of single-sheet or multiple-page documents. For example, one bin could hold letterhead stationery, another plain bond paper, and so on.

Envelope Feeders Envelope feeders may be separate units similar to a sheet feeder or may be part of a sheet feeder. An envelope feeder can hold up to 200 envelopes. Depending on the feeder's cycle time, it can feed up to 1600 envelopes an hour into a printer.

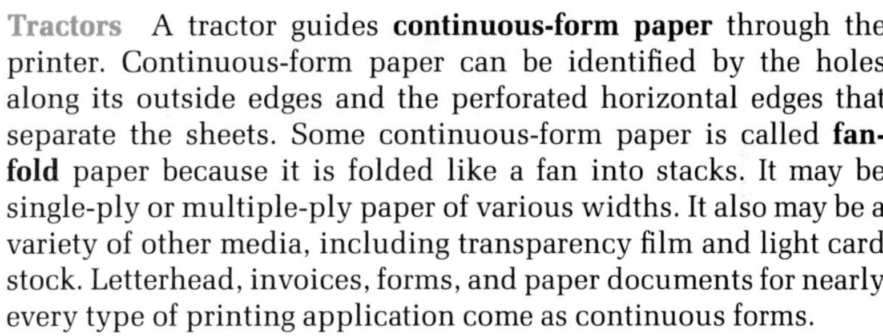

This machine automatically signs, slits, and bursts up to 18,000 continuous-form documents per hour.

Tractors A tractor guides **continuous-form paper** through the printer. Continuous-form paper can be identified by the holes along its outside edges and the perforated horizontal edges that separate the sheets. Some continuous-form paper is called **fanfold** paper because it is folded like a fan into stacks. It may be single-ply or multiple-ply paper of various widths. It also may be a variety of other media, including transparency film and light card stock. Letterhead, invoices, forms, and paper documents for nearly every type of printing application come as continuous forms.

The tractor mechanically moves the paper forward and sometimes backward through the printer by a **pinfeed platen** or a series of sprockets that stick into the holes along the outside edges of the continuous form, ensuring a steady movement of paper through the printer. Tractors that move the paper in two directions (bidirectional tractors) make it possible to print charts, graphs, subscripts and superscripts. A tractor can handle multiple-ply forms up to six sheets thick as long as they are attached at the corners and are not fastened by staples, glue, or tape, which might jam the machine. If a stacker (shelf or bin for catching paper from a printer) is attached to the printer, the printed paper can be neatly stacked.

Bursters Continuous-form paper is convenient and efficient for high-speed printing of large amounts of text or data. However, it is usually necessary to separate the continuous forms into individual sheets for distribution. A stacker is helpful for keeping the sheets in a neat stack, but without a burster separating the sheets can be a time-consuming task. A burster cuts continuous-form paper into individual sheets at the perforated lines. The pin-feed mechanism on a burster fits into the holes along the sides of the continuous-form paper and draws the pages into the burster. As the paper moves through the burster, it is separated horizontally along the perforations between the sheets. Most bursters also cut off the holes along the sides of the paper; some have a trimmer that trims off the perforated edges as well as the holes along the sides of the paper; others stack the sheets in order after they are separated or cut.

A burster is helpful for separating continuous-form paper into individual sheets.

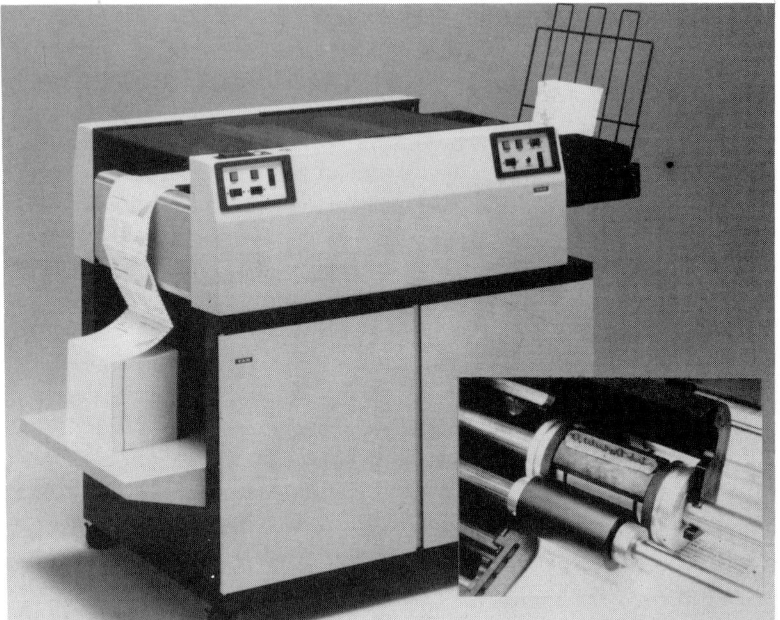

Paper Shredders As offices continue to generate paper, there will be an ongoing need to destroy printed information. Information to be destroyed must often be kept confidential. Paper shredders are a convenient and foolproof way of destroying paper so that the security or confidentiality of information is protected. Several different models of shredders are available, from large to small units. Some are so small they are considered desktop units. Others have a built-in funnel that accommodates large documents such as blueprints and engineering drawings. More and more organizations are using shredders. The U.S. government and corporations that engage in research and development of a highly technical or sensitive nature usually have large-scale units.

Reprographics

Have you ever thought about how much of the printed information you see every day has been copied? Books, magazines, newspapers, announcements, bills—all are copies of one kind or another. They are reproduced. Even your telephone bill is a reproduced form that has been individualized by adding your name, address, phone number, and charges for the month.

Reprographics is the term given to the process of producing one or more copies of graphic or written material. The word covers several different technologies, including photocopying, phototypesetting, offset printing, and duplicating. Strictly speaking, reprographics does not include processes that are related only to the assembly of copies, such as collating, binding, folding, and inserting. However, because these processes complete the total job, it makes sense to examine them as part of the general subject of reprographics.

Reprographics should not be taken for granted because output must be managed. Within an information system, there may be a variety of outputs—letters, memos, forms, reports, manuals, booklets, newsletters, announcements, instructions, cards, charts, and so on. The volume of output or the number of copies to be made depends on the purpose of the document and how many people are to receive it. Determining the number of copies means investigating the most efficient and economical way to produce them and choosing the most appropriate kind of equipment to use.

Reprographics Methods

Just as there are several types of output, offices may use several methods to produce copies of documents. Some methods use equipment such as typewriters or printers. Others use equipment that has the sole function of producing multiple copies, such as duplicators, offset printers, and photocopying machines.

Repetitive Printing A common method of reprographics, repetitive printing simply means printing more than one original hard copy. If you are using a typewriter, you will have to key the original document over and over to generate several original copies. With automated equipment such as an electronic typewriter or a microcomputer, you simply command the printer to print as many hard copy originals as you need. Because original letters have more personal appeal than duplicated form letters, repetitive printing is ideal for sending originals of the same letter to several people.

Carbons and NCR Paper Carbon paper was introduced soon after the typewriter was invented. It is still used, but in different ways. Today, with high-speed impact printers, you can produce an error-free original and five or six copies with carbon paper quickly and economically. (Of course, error-free copy does depend on you and your proofreading ability.)

Several types of carbon paper are available today. **Carbon packs** or **copysets** are commercially prepared sets of up to five sheets of carbon paper interleaved between plain paper (sometimes tissuelike) sheets. Instead of carbon, some copysets have a chemically treated paper called **NCR (no carbon required).** With NCR packs, the characters printed on the original carry through to the copies. Single-carbon packs may be bound at the top, bottom,

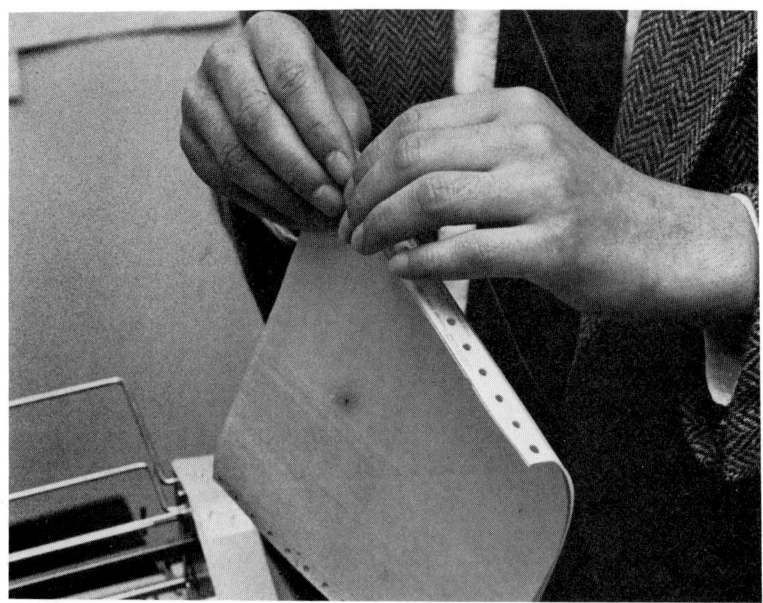
NCR ("no carbon required") packs produce multiple copies.

or sides. Continuous-form packs have holes and perforations on the sides so the continuous copysets can be fed through a pinfeed printer. When the pack is removed from the printer after printing, the carbon sheets are thrown away, and the copies are distributed.

Duplicating and Offset Printing Repetitive printing and carbon copies are reprographics methods suitable for a small number of copies. A **duplicator** is used with a **master** (usually prepared on a typewriter or impact printer) to make a few hundred to several thousand copies. The number of copies generally depends on the duplicating method—spirit, stencil, or offset—which also determines how the master is made. In some cases, a master may be photographed, etched on a plate, and inked to produce as many as 50,000 copies. (Today, some copier/printers produce masters by photography. After only a few seconds, the operator can select the number of copies desired and produce 120 or more per minute.)

Spirit and stencil duplicators have all but disappeared from most offices, but **offset printing** is still prevalent in businesses with reproduction centers. Copies produced by offset printing **(direct lithography)** can be extremely clear, even in color. Good offset copies can look like an original.

XEROXING

Photocopying The most common method of reprographics used in offices today is **photocopying.** For about 30 years, photocopiers have been used to produce millions of copies every day. Photocopiers do not require a master to be prepared or an operator to be specially trained. They are available in a variety of models, each designed to serve certain reprographics needs ranging from making an occasional copy or two of an original document to making a few hundred copies of a multipage report.

The prototype copier, based on a patent granted to Chester Carlson in 1937, reproduced documents on either plain or coated paper using an **electrostatic process,** originally called electrophotography, later changed to xerography—or Xerox, for short. "Xerox," although a brand name, is almost synonymous with photocopying, and the company bearing this name is one of the largest producers of photocopying equipment. Photocopies made on today's machines are of excellent quality, often better than those made by offset duplicating or printing. There are several types of copiers—electrostatic, laser, thermal, and plain-paper.

Plain-paper copiers use a two-part process that combines the ink particles (toner) and developer before heat and pressure bind the image to the paper. This process produces high-quality images that are clear and uniform and does not alter the background. Most plain-paper copiers do not require special paper for making copies, which makes them versatile in an office. Letterhead, memo paper, colored stock (paper), and even card stock can be used in many plain-paper copiers. Cost per copy varies, but some plain-paper copiers produce copies at a fraction of a penny. For these reasons, plain-paper copiers are extremely popular in all types of businesses.

Copiers have many features. Some models print on both sides of the paper, a process known as **duplexing.** Some can reduce or enlarge the image of the original document. Others automatically vary the size of the output paper and provide copies in color or on colored stock. Some copiers can copy onto card stock and have

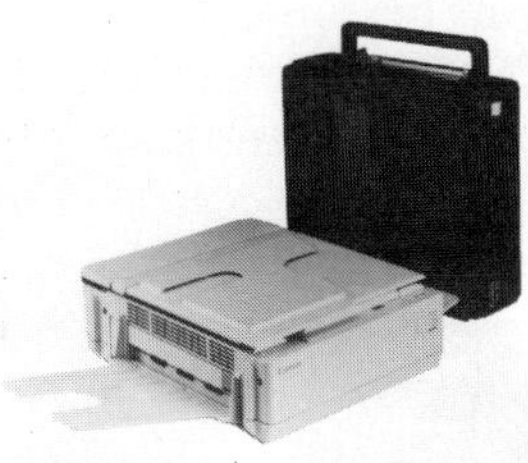

Different sizes and models of copiers serve specific reprographics needs.

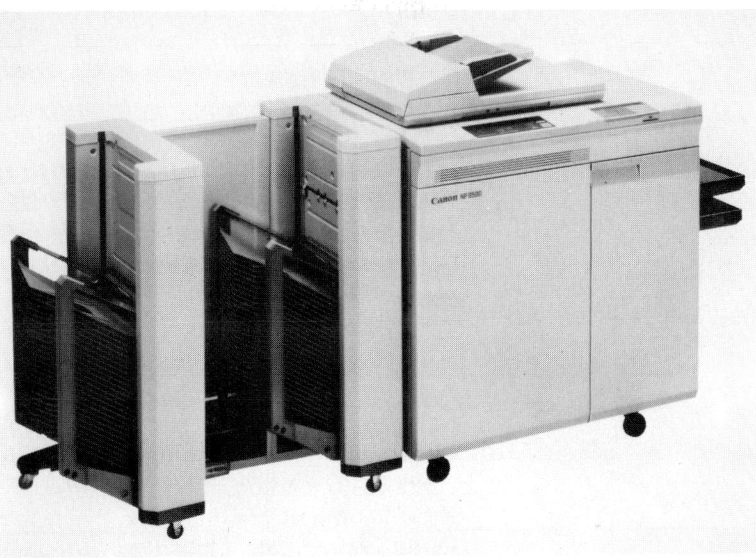

such options as sheet bypass (for feeding single sheets) and document and continuous-form feeders. Many have two cassettes (holders) for paper, and some have multiple paper cassettes (usually from two to five, each holding 100 to 500 single sheets—a few can hold up to 2500 single or cut sheets).

Some copiers have automatic sensors to select the right light exposure, depending on the lightness or darkness of each original. Some also have finishing functions, such as collating, stapling, and stacking copied documents. (These and other features are discussed later in this chapter.) Some copiers, especially large volume machines, have **sorters** (up to 50 bins) for assembling sets of documents, security lock systems to prevent unauthorized use of the system, and automatic standby and shutoffs for saving energy. Small desktop copiers can produce about 6 to 12 **copies per minute (cpm).** A majority of photocopiers can produce copies at rates of 12 to 50 cpm; some large machines can produce 100 or more cpm. Color copiers are considerably slower, from 5 or 6 cpm to about 25 cpm.

As the copier industry continues to add innovative technological enhancements to equipment, you will see some drastic changes in the way work is performed. For example, you might create a first-quarter income statement spreadsheet on your personal computer, extract information from it to produce a graphic illustration (such as a bar chart), and send it directly to the phototypesetter or even a photocopier for printing in color. In this instance, you would completely bypass your personal computer printer for printing the graph. The entire operation would provide you with a much clearer graph produced in less time than your dot matrix printer would require.

Facsimile The word **facsimile** means an exact reproduction or copy of something. To this extent, all photocopies are **fax** or facsimile copies. However, in reprographics, facsimile refers to a special process by which a copy of a document or graphic illustration is sent electronically from one machine to another via telephone lines or other electronic means of communication. Fax machines may be in the same building, or they may be separated by great distances.

Fax technology involves all stages of the information processing cycle—input, processing, output, distribution, and storage. Also, fax has much in common with printer and copying technologies, including thermal, laser, and electrostatic recording techniques. Fax technology is probably one of the few in which vendors have taken standards seriously. As a result, a fax device is a good communications link. Because most fax machines are compatible with each other, they can communicate with each other.

A facsimile machine can be used to transmit electronically a copy of a document or illustration.

News agencies have used facsimile transmission for many years to send Wirephotos between distant locations. Technological advances since the 1960s have made facsimile useful for most businesses, such as those needing to transmit information between branch offices, and even for individuals.

Facsimile technology involves changing the visual image of a document into electronic signals, which are transmitted and reconverted into an exact copy of the original document. Fax machines are known either as analog or digital, depending on the method by which they create the copy of the document.

Analog facsimile is not widely used, mainly because it is not extremely fast. In analog facsimile, a scanner moves across the document, reading every part of it—characters, spaces between characters, spaces between lines, margins, and other blank spaces. The analog facsimile converts each scanned element into an electrical signal, which it transmits over telephone lines to another facsimile machine. The receiving facsimile processes the signal and reverses the scanning process. The transmitted document is reproduced line by line. These devices produce very good copies at the rate of one every three to six minutes. Transmission can be speeded up if an analog machine can communicate with a digital machine and vice versa.

Digital facsimile is much faster than analog. In digital fac-

Advantages and Features of Fax

- Fax machines are easy to use.
- Fax is a fast reproduction method.
- Fax is a low-cost transmission method.
- Fax machines can scan text, photos, signatures, images, etc.
- Fax machines have automatic feeding, dialing, and receiving features.
- Some fax machines can store 60 or more documents; documents can be stored for forwarding at a later time.
- Automatic error-checking fax machines can alert the receiver of missing information and retransmit the document. For example, errors might result from a poor telephone line connection.
- Fax machines "handshake"—that is, a copy is sent only if it can be accepted by a receiver.

simile, a scanner "reads" only the part of the document that contains actual information. It does not read blank spaces or margins, as an analog facsimile does. The digital scanner converts images to short binary signals (a series of ones and zeros) that can be easily and quickly transmitted over communications lines. Digital facsimiles transmit copies at a much faster rate than analog facsimiles—10 to 50 seconds for a one-page document. But copies produced by digital facsimiles may not be as clear as those produced by analog machines.

Fax transmission is becoming more and more attractive to businesses looking for an alternative to the postal system. Facsimile copies, after all, cannot be lost or damaged in the mail. Original documents of at least a page can be transmitted faster than you can read or describe the document. And what can be more accurate than an exact copy, especially if it has a signature or other graphic information on it? Fax has other advantages, too, such as ease of operation of the machines. No special skill is required to operate a fax machine. Copies can be sent to a receiver even when there is no one in the office, making it possible to send copies cheaply at hours when phone rates are lower.

Fax machines are becoming smaller, more sophisticated, and less expensive. Desktop and personal fax machines are becoming popular at home as well as in the office. Lightweight, portable fax machines may have important significance to many traveling executives. Personal computer users can install a fax board and, with applications software, send a document in minutes. Sending documents in a group (**batch fax**) at off-peak hours, such as during the evening or at night, can save costs of several separate transmissions during the day. Fax machines are classified into four groups according to transmission speed of a document and CCITT standards (see Chapter 7):

Group 1: 4 to 6 minutes

Group 2: 2 to 3 minutes

Group 3: up to 1 minute

Group 4: further subdivided into classes according to capabilities to transmit and/or receive images, characters, and mixed mode (images and characters)

Fax is not limited to use between two persons or offices. It may also be used to send output to several receivers (**broadcasting**) or from several transmitters to one receiver (**polling**). Some predict that fax will continue to grow at extremely fast rates, possibly over 30 percent a year for the next several years. Such a trend may be possible because fax has many applications for networking, video and teleconferencing, and merging with copiers for copier/facsimile plain paper copying and transmission.

Electronic Copier/Printers An important kind of reprographics equipment, **electronic copier/printers** combine the technologies of an information processing printer, an office copier, and a facsimile machine. The basic difference between electronic copier/printers and other kinds of copiers is their ability to accept input from information processing equipment and convert it into high-quality hard copies.

Some electronic copier/printers are considered **intelligent copier/printers** because they can accept many kinds of informa-

Electronic copiers/printers operate online with the computer.

tion, manipulate it, and convert it to output in another form. For example, they can combine graphics and text in the same report. Intelligent copiers can also transmit information over telephone and other communications lines in much the same way as facsimile machines.

Optional features and connections with other equipment may permit an intelligent copier/printer to assemble, print, collate, staple, and address documents. It may be able to store information on tape or disks, reprint reports from tape or disks, and receive, store, or transmit information from microcomputers and/or other intelligent copiers. In short, an intelligent copier/printer has a "mind of its own," which, of course, the user controls. **Dumb copier/printers** merely carry out your instructions for printing. They don't have electronic memories and they lack many of the capabilities of intelligent copier/printers.

Electronic copier/printers, whether intelligent or dumb, are nonimpact printing devices. They usually use laser or other electrophotographic processes for printing. Information transmitted to an intelligent copier/printer is stored in its memory until you command the machine to print. At that point, it converts the data into matrix patterns, which are printed as characters in the style of type and format you have chosen. The printing device creates lines of characters, which are scanned and transmitted to a photosensitive device, where a copy of the entire document is developed and printed at speeds of up to 120 ppm.

Intelligent copier/printers also can store formats and text for all kinds of documents, such as booklets, reports, and files. If you are working in an office where an intelligent copier/printer is connected to your microcomputer, you can make corrections, giving the copier/printer the appropriate instructions, and never see the document until it is printed in final form. Later, you can reprint it just by pushing a few buttons on the copier/printer. You can even change the format size, reducing or enlarging it, without having to rekey it.

Electronic copier/printers are best suited to large offices where a great many copies are produced. These machines can be expensive and are often leased or rented. In general, their purchase can be justified if production needs are around 20,000 or more total copies a month. Linking them to mainframe computers helps justify their cost.

Phototypesetting or Photocomposition Typeset output is quite common. A good example is the type in this book. Typeset copy is different from that produced by a typewriter. The most noticeable difference is the spacing between characters. The space around keyed characters is uniform. In typesetting, less space is allowed

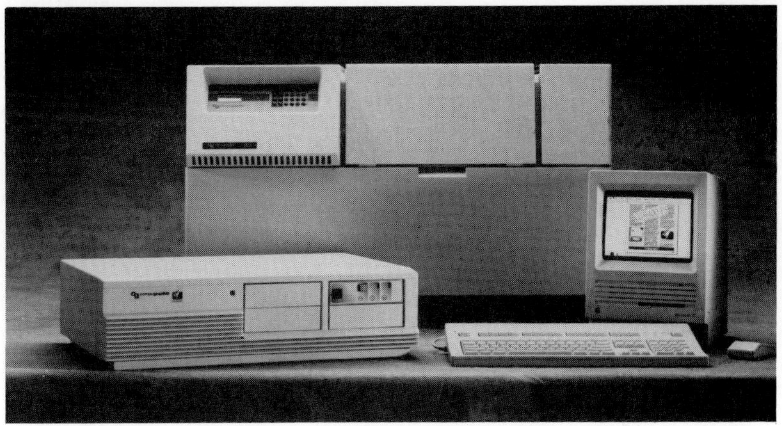

Phototypsetting can be a worthwhile investment for businesses that have a large volume of printing.

for characters that take up less space (i, l, and t) and more space for letters that take up more space (M and W). Most typewriters give the same amount of space to each letter, whatever its width, so spacing between letters varies. Because of the spacing, one typeset page is equal to about two pages from a typewriter.

The most common method of typesetting is **photocomposition** or **phototypesetting.** In photocomposition, a light source exposes an image of a character on film, producing a photographic positive. The film positive can then be proofread, corrected, and converted to a master that is reproduced, usually by offset printing.

Phototypesetters have two basic parts—a keyboard unit and a photographic unit. The speed, storage capacity, and the quality of the output of phototypesetting systems make them an ideal choice for producing various kinds of books, including catalogs, directories, dictionaries, and indexes.

Phototypesetting offers large offices several advantages, one of which is saving paper. When set by photocomposition, two or more pages of typewritten text will fit on a single printed page. Still another advantage is the quality of reproduced material. The wide range of type styles and formats available makes it possible for an office to produce documents that appear to be professionally printed.

Many businesses use phototypesetting in conjunction with information processing. Take Klipler Books, Inc., a direct-mail advertiser of discount books and records. Klipler distributes thousands of catalogs throughout the country.

Today, Klipler keyboards its catalog on a microcomputer, stores it on hard disk, and updates it continually. Several times a year the copy from the hard disk is transferred directly to the company's own phototypesetting equipment, which can translate the text into clear, distinctive, professional-looking print. No errors can creep in once the soft copy is correct, and the savings in time and money are impressive.

Although not all microcomputers and phototypesetting machines work together that way, phototypesetting is becoming affordable for more and more businesses. Desktop publishing software is also helping businesses become more interested in phototypesetting. As time passes and equipment becomes more compatible, many offices will be able to handle their own printing jobs, both large and small, including reports, newsletters, and office forms. And they will have more choices in the way they process and output documents. This means word processing secretaries and operators will have more control over document production, from initial keyboarding to printed copies.

Voice Output

Soft and hard copy and their reproductions are output—visual output. Your voice can also be output. You can store your voice in a computer that digitizes it. When you access the disk, your voice is translated from the digital data back into voice. You can hear the words you spoke into the microphone of the computer voice output.

Another type of voice output is created by software and a computer **voice synthesizer**. Words or characters of words are assigned sounds as the software program translates the stored words. The computer voice synthesizer applies certain rules to the stored words, characters, letter combinations, and patterns—in much the same way we learn to speak unfamiliar words by applying the various rules of speech. Tones, sounds, and patterns are assigned to the single letters and combinations of letters to form the "speech." When the speech is played back over speakers in the computer, you are hearing **synthesized speech.** You can probably think of several applications of synthesized speech, such as at the checkout counter of a grocery store, automobile warning devices, mail-order offices, telephone survey "callers," and many kinds of vending machines.

Other Output

Other types of output include producing images on tape, film, and other media. Some include sending information via **Electronic Data Interchange (EDI),** and transmitting voice via **Voice Message Systems (VMS)** and similar means of communication. Other outputs, such as **Computer Output Microfilm (COM),** relate to storage. These and other types of outputs are discussed in Chapter 8.

Assembling Output

Once hard copies are produced, several additional processes may be needed to complete the job. These include collating, binding, and folding copies. There are several methods for accomplishing these tasks.

Collating and Sorting

You have probably had to hand-collate several copies of a short document at one time or another. For instance, you may have laid out ten pages of a document on a table, with five copies of each page in a stack. Then you gathered the pages one at a time in sequence to make five completed ten-page documents.

Collating means gathering the separate sheets of a multipage document. Collators function independently of copiers. Copies of each document page must be hand-loaded into them. There are three kinds of collators: manual, mechanical, and automatic.

Manual collators are available in desktop or floor models with capacities from 4 to over 100 bins (also referred to as **stations, pockets,** or **hoppers**). The number of bins determines the number of document pages that can be collated at one time. With a manual collator, you push a lever that activates a feeder arm on each bin. The arm moves the top copy forward so that it can be gathered by hand and combined with copies of consecutive pages.

Mechanical and semiautomatic collators have motor-driven feeder arms that push top copies forward at regular intervals. **Automatic collators** push top copies forward out of the bins, gather the pages, and deposit completed documents in a receiving tray. Automatic collators may include finishing units that fold, trim, stitch, and staple copies.

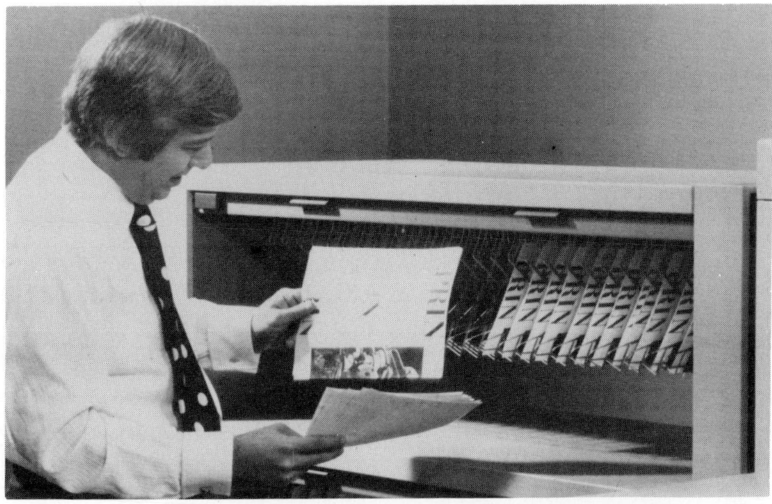

An automatic collator can save time in assembling pages.

Sorters are usually attached to copiers. As copies of one page of a document come off the copier, they are routed to bins. Each sheet goes to its own separate bin. Copies of other pages of the document are routed in the same way until the entire document has been copied. Each bin then contains a complete copy set of the document. You can make as many copy sets as there are bins. A sorter usually does not have the kind of finishing equipment that a collator has. However, some large copiers have built-in sorters that staple and stack sets of copied documents.

Binding

Documents containing several pages often are bound in some way to prevent the pages from getting lost and to make the document easier to read. You have probably seen documents with several different kinds of **binding,** including stapling, plastic "comb" binding, and gluing.

Stapling is the most common form of binding. Staples are generally used for documents having up to 50 pages. Documents may be stapled along one side or in the center of folded pages. Staples can be inserted manually with an ordinary or heavy-duty office stapler; some copiers automatically staple documents.

Spiral comb binding is a popular way of binding documents; the spiral comb binding is similar to a three-ring notebook. A spiral plastic comb is inserted into a series of rectangular holes punched along one side of each sheet. The spiral comb can be removed to insert additional sheets or to remove old ones.

Sturdy and somewhat more permanent than spiral comb binding, **flat comb binding** uses a two-part plastic comb strip threaded through a series of round or square holes along the left side of the document. The plastic comb and punched sheets are then heat-sealed.

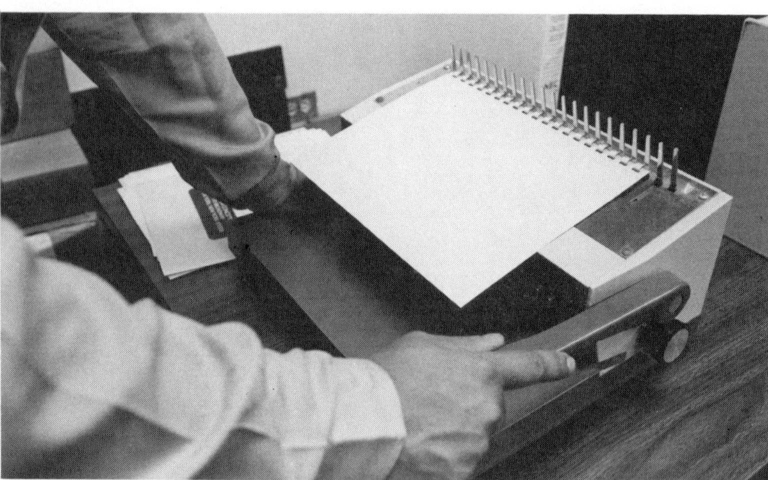

Comb binding is one method of fastening pages together.

In the VeloBind process, a strip of plastic pins is inserted into prepunched holes in the document, cut, and sealed to produce a secure binding.

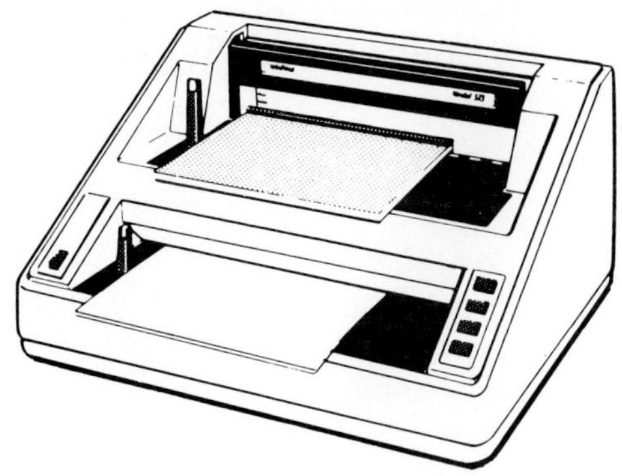

Two other binding methods use heat. In the **hotmelt glue method,** small pellets of glue are inserted into the binding equipment and heated until they melt. Then the spine (the part of the document that receives the binding) is inserted into the machine and spread with glue. A flat cover may be added when the document is glued.

A second heat method uses **thermal tape** to bind document pages. In this method, a fabric strip and glue are applied to the spine and then heated under pressure.

Folding and Inserting

Suppose your boss handed you a stack of 500 envelopes and 500 one-page letters and gave you the task of folding the letters by hand and inserting them in the envelopes so they could be mailed. You not only would be busy for an hour, you also would be quite bored. However, if your office had an automatic folding and inserting machine, you could do the same job in ten minutes.

Folding and inserting machines are able to insert many kinds of documents into regular business or window envelopes. They can be instructed to fold bills, letters, notices, flyers, leaflets, booklets, lists, bulletins, and other short documents into any of several shapes. More sophisticated machines will also insert, seal, and stamp documents.

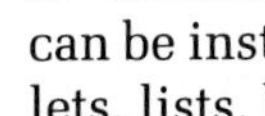

Automatic folding machine.

Reprographics Office Systems

Reprographics is an important aspect of every information system. Office reprographics systems may be responsible for 90 percent or more of the output of many organizations. The quality of the output may be determined by the equipment, but it is still up to people to use the equipment in a productive way. Efficiency may depend on where the equipment is located.

Printing and reprographics operations should be placed in the best location for the equipment to be used. The decision is affected by office size, frequency of equipment usage, number of people using the equipment, amount of space the equipment takes up, and volume of work the equipment generates.

In general, sophisticated and heavy laser and phototypesetting equipment or machines usually are placed in a central area. Smaller, less expensive equipment may be placed at strategic locations in an office. Many microcomputer users may have their own printers at their desks; however, it is common to share printers. Also, there may be different kinds of printers to fill different needs. For example, a micro may be linked to both a desktop printer and an electronic copier/printer in a central area.

Centralized Reprographics Centers

In large offices where a heavy volume of copies is produced, a **centralized reprographics** area may be most appropriate. The centralized operation—sometimes called the "copy center"—serves the entire company or office and may even serve branch offices in other buildings. A heavy volume of copies requires large-size copiers or duplicators, which in turn require a large amount of space. At Midland Oil and Gas, for example, 13 people operate a copy center serving this large oil company. The center handles 400 to 500 jobs every week, producing about 25 million copies a year.

Ideally, in a centralized system, original documents, masters, and requests for copies are picked up and delivered to the repro-

A modern reprographics center.

graphics area through the company's internal mail system. Copies of documents are distributed by the same means. This method results in higher productivity because employees do not have to interrupt their work to go to the reprographics area. Another advantage of this system is that equipment usage is controlled. The amount of paper used can be easily monitored, requests for copies can be scheduled in order of priority, and a number of copying jobs may be done at once, depending on equipment capabilities.

An alternative to a centralized system is a system of minicenters in which a few reprographics areas serve a large office. Copies may be picked up and delivered by the office mail system, or employees may have access to the equipment even though they may have to walk a distance to reach it.

Decentralized Reprographics Centers

With copies becoming less expensive and equipment more sophisticated, many companies are purchasing more copiers. In a **decentralized reprographics** system, copiers are conveniently located throughout the company. Employees do not have to walk far to reach the machines and can make copies whenever they need them. This kind of system works well in smaller offices where the volume of copies does not justify a centralized system.

The biggest advantage to decentralization is convenience. Its major disadvantage is lack of control. Employees may use machines to make copies unrelated to office work. Some offices take preventive measures, such as equipping copiers with locks so that only authorized persons may use them or give permission to others to make copies. In some offices, employees are required to log the number of copies they make at one time.

For some companies, a combined centralized and decentralized system may be practical. For example, if an office routinely produces a large volume of copies, but employees in certain divisions also need a small number of copies, the company may have one centralized copy area and one or more conveniently located machines for producing output.

CHAPTER SUMMARY

- One form of output not requiring external reprographics equipment is soft copy—text displayed on the screen of a display terminal.
- A printer for automated equipment, such as a microcomputer, produces characters on paper by impact or nonimpact methods. Only impact methods can produce carbon copies; nonimpact printers have the advantage of extremely high speed.
- Most printed information is some form of reproduced copy.
- Reprographics refers to several methods and kinds of equipment by which copies of written or graphic materials are made.

- The choice of reprographics method depends on the number of copies to be made, the desired quality of the output, and the cost involved.
- Repetitive printing with a microcomputer and printer may be an efficient method of producing original hard copies of a document.
- Impact printers include element, daisy wheel, thimble, chain and band, and dot matrix printers.
- Nonimpact printers include ink-jet, thermal transfer, laser, ion deposition, and magnetographic printers.
- Line and page printers are faster than character printers.
- Plotters are excellent output devices for detailed graphics.
- Automatic sheet and envelope feeders, tractors, bursters, and paper shredders are useful in the office as printer-related and paper-handling devices.
- Offset duplicating is an efficient means of reprographics when a large number of high-quality copies is desired.
- Photocopying is the most common method of reprographics used in offices today.
- Photocopiers produce copies of uniform quality and offer such capabilities as duplexing, reducing or enlarging the image of an original document, copying in color or on colored stock, sorting, and stapling.
- Facsimile machines transmit and receive copies of documents by means of electronic signals that travel over telephone lines or through other electronic means of communication.
- Electronic copier/printers can receive data from information processing equipment and produce multiple copies.
- Intelligent copier/printers can store and manipulate information in various ways before it is printed.
- Phototypesetting creates text by means of a light source that projects character images onto film, which is then developed.
- Voice-synthesized speech is computer speech output.
- Collating, sorting, binding, and folding are often needed to complete a copying job.
- Collating machines are separate from copying machines and assemble copies of documents page by page.
- Sorters are attached to copiers. They arrange copies of document pages into complete sets.
- Commonly used methods for binding documents include stapling, plastic (spiral or flat) "comb" binding, and gluing.
- Reprographics systems may be either centralized or decentralized. A centralized area serves the needs of an entire company or building. Decentralized areas serve the needs of groups of employees throughout the office.

VOCABULARY

background printing
band printer
bidirectional
burster
centralized reprographics
chain printer
character printer
collating
continuous-form paper
daisy wheel
decentralized reprographics
dot matrix
electronic copier/printer
facsimile
font
impact printer
ink-jet printer
intelligent copier/printer
ion deposition printer
laser printer
letter quality (LQ)
line printer
nonimpact printer
offset printing
page printer
parallel printer
photocomposition
photocopying
phototypesetting
plotter
repetitive printing
reprographics
serial printers
sorter
thermal transfer
thimble
tractor
voice synthesizer
xerography

CHAPTER QUESTIONS

1. What advantages do printers for microcomputers offer over standard typewriters for jobs that require repetitive printing?
2. What are the differences between impact and nonimpact printers? Name some of the different types of printers in each category, along with their advantages and disadvantages.
3. What are some of the advantages and disadvantages of dot matrix printers? Explain letter quality and near-letter quality printing.
4. How has the photocopier changed office practices? Would life be more difficult without it? Explain.
5. What is a facsimile? Describe some of its advantages as a method of reproduction.
6. To what extent does an intelligent copier/printer have a "mind of its own"? What makes it different from a dumb copier/printer?
7. What kinds of printing projects lend themselves to photocomposition? Name three advantages of phototypesetting for large businesses.
8. What is synthesized speech? Name several ways it is used as output in businesses.
9. Why might you choose a form of plastic comb binding over staples if you were binding a 50-page document?

10. Would you recommend centralized or decentralized copying facilities for a small company with a fairly light copying load? Why?

CASE STUDY

The Franklin Electric Company provides power services and engineering equipment to a small community in central Indiana. The company has a central reprographics area, which in a one-week period handled the requests listed below. Choose an appropriate method of reprographics for each request from the following options: soft copy, repetitive printing, carbon paper, offset duplicating, photocopier, facsimile (analog or digital), Electronic Data Interchange (EDI), electronic copier/printer, and photocomposition. Explain your reasons for choosing a specific method. If binding is required, specify the type you would choose—staples, spiral comb or flat comb, hotmelt glue, or thermal tape. The requests are as follows:

1. A two-page memo to be distributed in the office to three people
2. A 40-page sales report to be distributed to ten key executives
3. A one-page letter advising clients of an increase in company rates to be distributed to 30,000 clients
4. A 30-page company brochure describing the company pension plan to be distributed to 1200 employees
5. A reprinting of three copies of a ten-page proposal for the development of new equipment stored on a floppy diskette
6. One copy of a purchase order to be sent as quickly as possible from the central office to a branch office in St. Louis
7. Six thousand copies of a 200-page catalog of electrical engineering equipment to be sold to various engineering firms around the country

CHAPTER 7

Communication and Distribution

Tricia Miles is in the middle of a busy day at the executive offices of Rearden's, a nationwide mail-order firm. Ms. Miles has spent most of the morning planning the buying strategy for next year's catalog. Before going to lunch, she checks her computer message system. A blinking light indicates that she has a message. She keys in her identification code and requests the machine to identify the caller. The machine responds by printing "Jan Trout." Ms. Miles keys in a command to view the message from Ms. Trout, her boss, who is visiting a plant in Cove, Oregon. Ms. Trout's message reads, "Cancel order from Focus Fashions. Manufacturer unable to deliver on time." Ms. Miles acts immediately on the instruction.

Never before have we had so many options in ways to communicate information. For example, to stay in touch with a friend, you can send a card through the mail or pick up a phone and talk. In business, you have additional alternatives for communicating—from computer to computer as well as between copier/printers, facsimile machines, voice mail, and electronic networks. ***Telecommunications*** *is the common term used to describe the transmission and reception of communications, usually electronically, over distance. Telecommunications has been a big contributor to the feeling that the world is shrinking. Our communications can be so instantaneous and the options for distributing information are so broad that nearly everyone in the world is within easy "reach."*

An information system's effectiveness frequently is measured by how well information reaches the right people at the right time for informed decision making to take place. Thus, distribution and communications make up an extremely important phase of the information processing cycle.

Traditional Distribution Methods . . . and Beyond

U.S. Postal Service

Probably the oldest and most widespread method of distributing information outside the office is the U.S. Postal Service. Each year it handles about 180 billion pieces of mail, enough to fill the Empire State Building. More than 40,000 post offices with 800,000 civilian employees handle 500 million pieces of mail every day, six days a week. To handle this volume of mail, the postal system prints enough stamps each year (about 20 billion) to encircle the globe.

Trained postal workers can sort mail at about 600 to 800 pieces an hour. Automated scanning equipment, such as optical character readers (OCRs), can speed up mail sorting to 30,000 to 45,000 pieces an hour—about 50 times faster than by hand. Automation of mail sorting is one reason the postal service would like customers, especially businesses, to follow their guidelines for using the nine-digit ZIP Code system. Bar coding will be added to this system in 1995 to automate mail sorting even more.

The U.S. Postal Service is the cheapest means of distributing information, even though the cost of postage has increased considerably over the past few years and continues to go up. Paper, too, has become increasingly expensive. Nevertheless, the post office is an established, inexpensive way of distributing large volumes of information on paper over a wide geographic area. To help its customers, the postal service has an information line about its services and rates. This automated voice message system is available in most cities nationwide. To access it, you call a local telephone

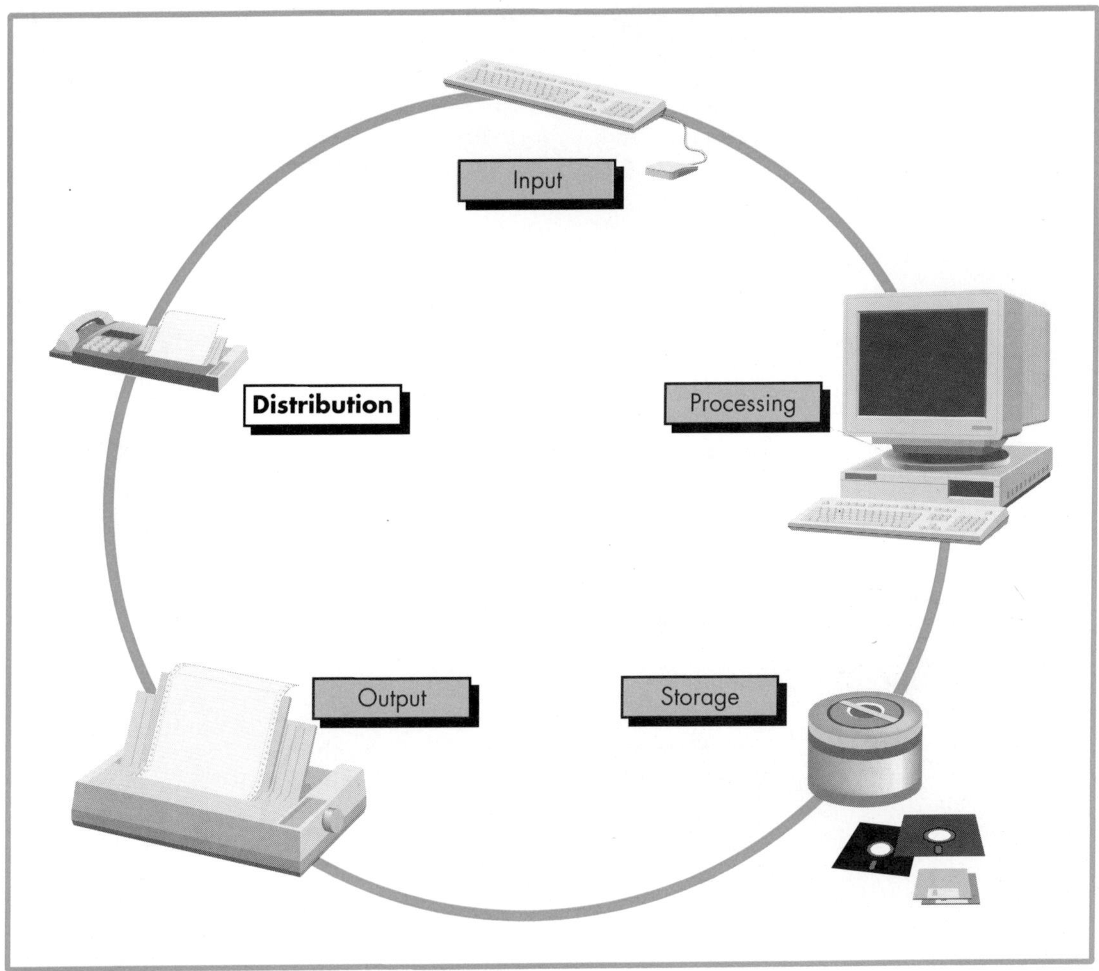

Distribution is one of five stages in the information processing cycle.

number (check your local telephone directory for availability in your city).

Another service of the U.S. Postal Service is **INTELPOST,** an acronym for **International Electronic Postal Service.** It is a high-speed facsimile transmission of information between post offices anywhere in the world. Almost any kind of document can be transmitted, including photographs, graphs, charts, and text.

Express Mail was the postal service's answer to the increasing demand for speedier mail service. Several types of Express Mail postal services are available, including same-day airport service between airport locations, insured two- to three-day international service, custom design service, and next-day or overnight delivery of mail to many cities within the continental United States. Over 100,000 Express Mail pieces are mailed every day through the

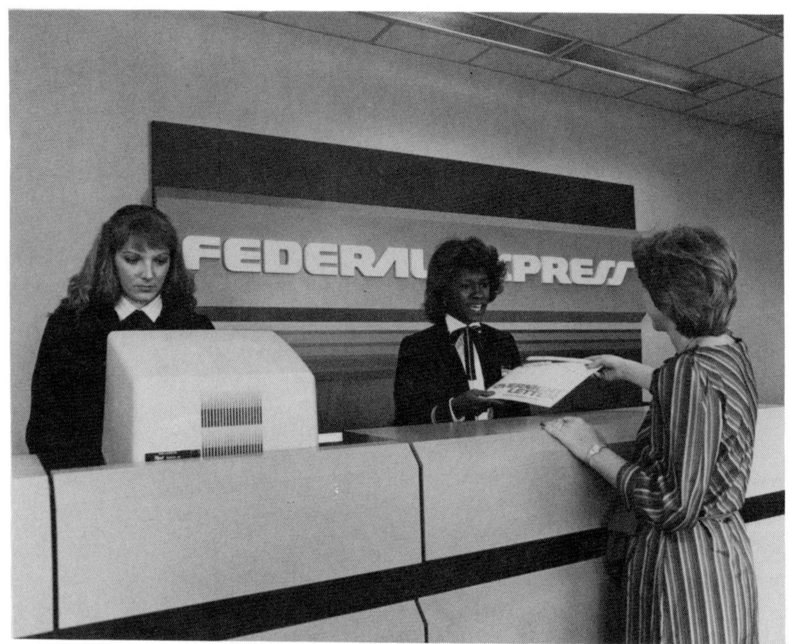

Federal Express is among several couriers offering express and overnight service.

postal system, even though the service can be quite expensive (sometimes 10 to 40 times more than regular mail). In some cases, heavier documents can be mailed by the postal service's Express Mail at nearly the same cost as by regular mail.

Since the U.S. Postal Service began Express Mail in 1971, several couriers have entered the express overnight letter and package business. Federal Express handles more than ten times the volume of the U.S. Post Office Express Mail service on a daily basis. Some couriers, like Federal Express, offer pickup and delivery, convenient drop boxes and drive-up locations, airport and other service centers, and free packaging. With many of these delivery services, you can establish a charge account and receive a statement of your account each month. Other overnight air and speedy express mail services include United Parcel Service, Airborne Express, Burlington Air Express, and DHL Worldwide Express.

Western Union

It was nearly 100 years after Samual F. B. Morse's first long-distance data communication over telegraph wire on May 24, 1844, that Congress authorized Western Union as the domestic message carrier. By that time, Western Union already had offices in Germany and was growing throughout Europe and the world. Western Union **telegrams** (although nearly a thing of the past), **cablegrams,** and **Mailgrams** have become legends in communications. Mailgrams and **computer letters** are still quite popular.

Mailgram and Computer Letters A Western Union Mailgram is a text message that utilizes the postal service network, takes advantage of the speed of electronic equipment, and minimizes the movement of paper from one place to another. You can fax a Mailgram message to a Western Union office; dictate a message by calling a Western Union operator, who keys it into a terminal; or key your message into a computer or Western Union Telex terminal and send it electronically to Western Union. When Western Union receives your message, they transmit it via electronic equipment to a major U.S. post office near its intended destination. Your Mailgram is delivered the next day through the regular mail service.

Computer letters are similar to Mailgrams except that they do not utilize the postal system. They are transmitted directly to the receiver's computer, fax, or Telex equipment.

Telex I and II A very old, fast, and widely used distribution system of text is the teletex message system—originally Western Union's Telex and AT&T's **TWX (Teletypewriter Exchange Service).** Since Telex and TWX merged under Western Union, the systems are compatible with each other. They are known as **Telex I** and **Telex II.** In this system, information is transmitted over telecommunications lines between two terminals. The terminals have keyboards, like typewriters, with rows of keys, and are called **teletypewriters.** The message is sent over telephone or telegraph lines to the receiving teletypewriter, which prints it out automatically. Thus, Telex terminals communicate with each other. With Telex **emulation** (imitation of one system to permit it to act like another system), some electronic typewriters and word processors can communicate with a teletype system.

Small amounts of information usually are transmitted via a Telex system because the relatively slow transmission speed (66–100 wpm) makes the system inefficient for sending large quantities of information. However, the Telex system has a store-and-forward feature that allows messages sent to a busy terminal to be held until the receiving terminal is free. At that point, the message is automatically printed on the receiver equipment unless the receiving operator chooses to delay it further to carry out a task of higher priority.

There are about two million subscribers to Western Union's system worldwide. Many lease Telex terminals; however, Western Union provides many services that make it attractive for customers to use computers for transmitting messages rather than the more costly method of renting a Telex terminal. For example, EasyLink is a messaging and data communications network management system for exchanging electronic messages such as Telex,

This terminal communicates information to and from other terminals in an electronic message system.

facsimile, and data within a company, between branch offices, or internationally. **Connectivity** is the underlying principle of EasyLink. This system permits different kinds of equipment to communicate with each other on public or private networks. One of the services available with EasyLink is InfoMaster, a collection of nearly 1000 **information services** or **electronic databases** you can access with your computer. An InfoMaster subscriber may browse through an airline schedule, obtain stock market quotes, identify current research on a technical subject, check financial data and credit reports, access world news services, or even keep up on the daily horoscopes.

Telephone

The telephone is the most convenient and quickest traditional method of communications. Since its development in 1876, the types of services available to the average person and businesses have grown. Telephone systems no longer are simple devices for incoming and outgoing communications. We have become accustomed to services such as **Wide Area Telephone Service (WATS)** for making frequent "800" and other long-distance calls at reduced rates. For a flat monthly fee and assigned numbers, many businesses use a foreign exchange (FX) service for calling remote areas. Both WATS and FX have lowered the costs of long-distance service for many people. **Tie lines** (used for linking remote sites to telephone switching centers) also are used by businesses as private communications channels. These and many more services are available from common carriers—licensed, government-regulated businesses such as a telephone or telegraph company.

Cellular phones have become a multibillion dollar business because people like the convenience of calling from a car, hotel, or remote vacation spot. Another mobile service, **Telepoint** (or CT2), is a cordless phone system that is less costly and more compact than the cellular phone. In Britain alone, the Telepoint system is predicted to become a $1.4 billion business by 1994. The future of Telepoint in the United States depends on its success in Britain. Several U.S. companies have entered the CT2 market and are making large-scale plans for its use in this country.

Private Branch Exchanges A **private branch exchange (PBX)** is a telephone system that "manages" and transmits incoming and outgoing calls both inside and outside an organization in an efficient and economical manner. Probably the most familiar use of a PBX, used interchangeably with **PABX (private automatic branch exchange),** and **EPABX (electronic private automatic branch exchange**) is to route telephone calls to the phone extensions within an organization. A PBX also can be used to transmit text and data by telephone line from a terminal to any other equipment in the same way that the phone system is used for voice communications. The greatest appeal of PBXs for information processing is that the telephone lines they rely on are already in place.

Modern PBX systems convert analog signals (voice) to digital signals (electrical pulses), which are carried over transmission lines and reconverted into analog signals at the receiving end. The receiver takes advantage of this digital control, switching, and transmission technology by receiving a clear, nondistorted message. This type of digital system makes it possible to connect many other products used for telephone data transmission with **local area networks (LANs)** and other networks. The trend is clearly toward simultaneous transmission of voice and text, called **voice/data integration**. Combining the telephone with the data terminal and transmitting voice and data at the same time (**multiplexing**) have great potential for high-speed, cost-effective communications.

More and more features are making PBX systems compatible with computers. Vendors use the term **seamless integration** to refer to adding on features that easily and smoothly extend system capabilities and applications. For example, with **Open Applications Interface (OAI)**, certain PBX applications can be **interfaced** with (connected to) a computer system. If you call your credit card company using OAI to get information about your account, the vital information about your account may be brought up on the computer screen of the representative receiving your call. The system both routes your call to the right person to answer your questions and provides pertinent information about your account to speed up your communications.

Like all technology, PBXs have certain drawbacks. Many small offices still can't afford them even though they are getting less expensive and more sophisticated. System failure is another concern. If a PBX is centralized and fails, the information processing network that depends on it fails too. In a decentralized system, each group of users has its own control processing unit, which eliminates total system failure. Although there is less chance of having the entire company "down" in a decentralized system, there is also less control over all the system resources. There are many resources that can be purchased to safeguard against some of these hazards; however, each one will add to the cost of the system.

Teleconferencing You may have had the opportunity to participate in a **telephone conference call** in which the operator connected three or more people over telephone lines. (Or you may subscribe to a similar service in your home.) Several people can talk simultaneously. This is a simple form of **teleconferencing** using only audio communication. If you have done this, you know that the more people there are on the line, the more difficult it is to immediately identify who is talking. In fact, you may have missed some important information during the conversation just because you were trying to identify the speaker. With the addition of a variety of electronic equipment for teleconferencing, this problem can be eliminated.

For example, at some point in your office career, you may find yourself present in a conference equipped with several kinds of audiovisual equipment, including a video camera, microphones, large television monitors, and a facsimile machine. Your boss may have several charts, graphs, and documents ready for a meeting with a number of other people. In preparing for the meeting, no one has had to make plane reservations, pack baggage, race to the airport, rent a car, get lost on a strange highway, or stay in an expensive hotel. The other people attending the meeting are not physically present. They are at similar studios or conference rooms in different parts of the city, state, or country.

When the meeting begins, your boss can see, hear, and respond to any of the people almost as if they were in the same room. And the facsimile machine is useful in sharing documents, charts, and graphs. This kind of meeting is called a **teleconference**—sometimes also called a **videoconference**—a meeting of people who are geographically separated but connected by a telecommunications system that uses two-way voice, text, or video communication. A teleconference permits interaction between two or more people at different locations. The back-and-forth communication makes it a teleconference. Something close to telecon-

Teleconferencing permits communication among meeting participants who are geographically separated from one another.

ferencing occurs in television news shows, where a newscaster converses with a person at a distant location. Both speakers can be seen on the television screen.

A service for distributing information quickly to a large number of people which has some of the same features of teleconferencing is called **point-multipoint communication**. Offered by some video studios and hotels, point-multipoint communication allows a person at one location to interact with people at several different locations. A sales manager in a central office, for instance, may communicate audiovisually with several sales representatives in different parts of the country. Point-multipoint communication is useful, but it is one-way only. People on the receiving end cannot join in and respond to each other or to the person giving the presentation.

Teleconferencing, more than telephone conference calls or point-multipoint communication, is likely to increase in the years ahead. Teleconferencing has the great advantage of permitting personal interaction, complete with sight and sound, without requiring the time and expense of travel.

Electronic Data Communications

Traditional message, delivery, and communication services have come a long way. Technology has provided the U.S. Postal Service,

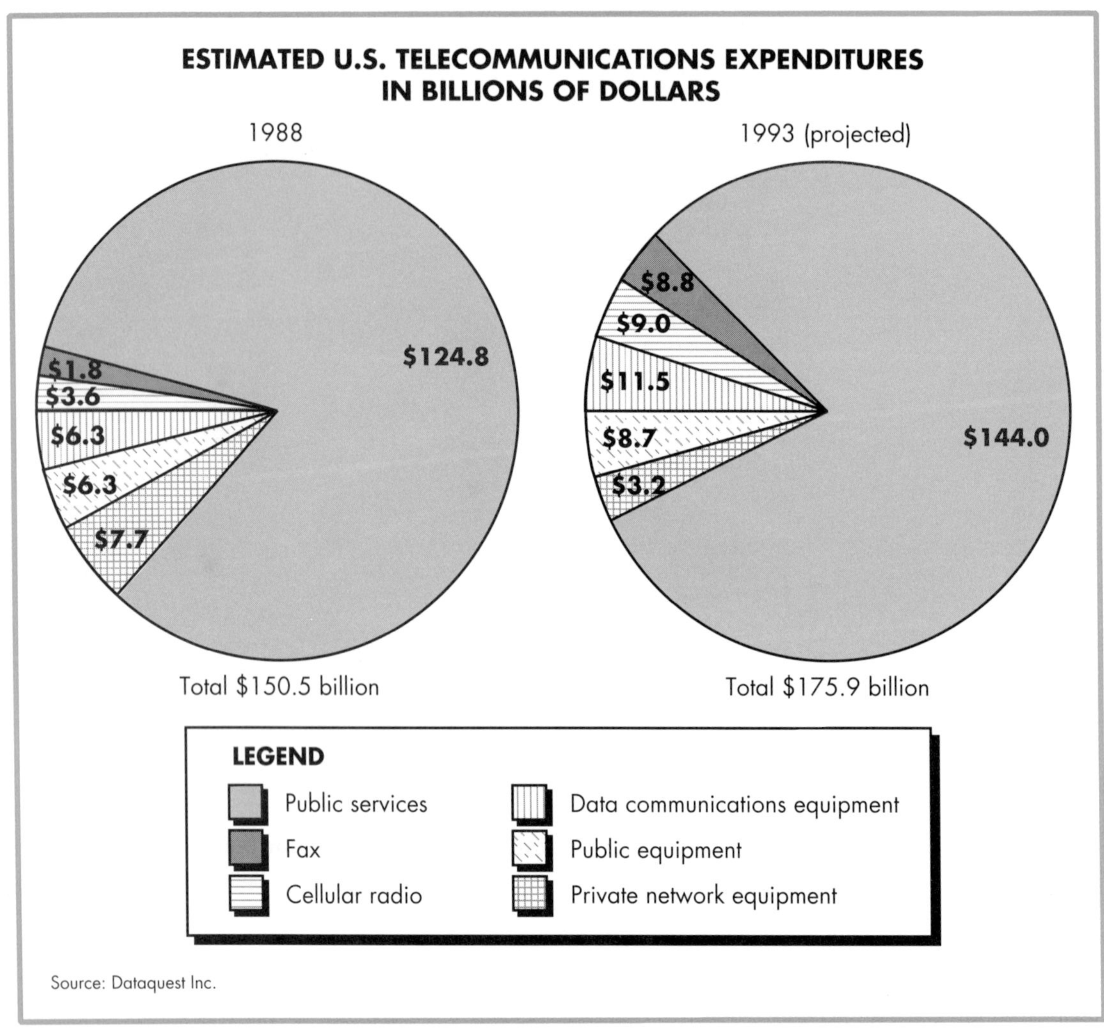

Western Union, and telephone companies capabilities for fast worldwide delivery of many kinds of communications. Technology and electronics are continually improving, allowing large quantities of information to be sent nearly instantaneously over communications lines and other transmission media. Transmitting information in this manner sometimes is referred to as **electronic data communications** ("data comm" for short) or **electronic mail (E-mail)**.

Electronic mail in its broadest sense refers to any text or graphic information to be transmitted electronically. E-mail technology generally has included all types of electronic messaging, including facsimile transmissions, Telex, Mailgrams and telegrams, bulletin boards, videotex and online databases, electronic data interchange (EDI), and voice mail (VM). With the sophisticated technologies and communications of recent years, E-mail usually is associated with some type of **linked** or **networked** system. Because computers can input and output vast quantities of information, E-mail is becoming an increasingly important tool for businesses that need to distribute large amounts of information quickly.

Two main factors are significant to the importance of E-mail: (1) Electronic data communications allow different pieces of electronic equipment to communicate with each other. (2) Information between communicating machines is in the form of electronic signals rather than paper. Communications may be accomplished via telecommunication lines (such as telephone and telegraph lines, **coaxial cable,** and **fiber optics**), **microwaves**, and **satellites.** E-mail has the following advantages over other more traditional methods:

- Speed of transmission is fast, even for large amounts of information.
- Fast turnaround can be expected for replies.
- Telephone tag is eliminated. (Telephone tag refers to having to initiate or return calls several times because you and your caller have difficulty reaching each other.)
- Information can be stored until it can be received.
- An audit trail is made.
- Paper transfer is not necessary, but a hard copy can be printed.
- Transmission is cost-effective, efficient, and economical.
- E-mail is more convenient than courier services.

Of course, the advantages vary with each type of E-mail transmission method, the type and volume of documents to be transferred, and the frequency of transmission.

Computer-Based Message Systems

A computer-based message system (CBMS) transfers information electronically, permitting electronic equipment to communicate or to transfer information from one terminal to another. CBMS has become one of the most important developments in information processing. Now that communications software has become so sophisticated, nearly all types of electronic equipment can be linked or networked. Networking has contributed to improved communications and connectivity of equipment including word processors, microcomputers (as well as mainframes and all types of other computers), Telex terminals, intelligent copier/printers, OCRs, and phototypesetters.

Messages keyed to be transferred in a CBMS while the communications link is "on" are considered **online** communications. Usually, to save money, an operator will key and edit a message **offline** (while there is no communications connection). When the message is ready to be sent, the communications link is made (by

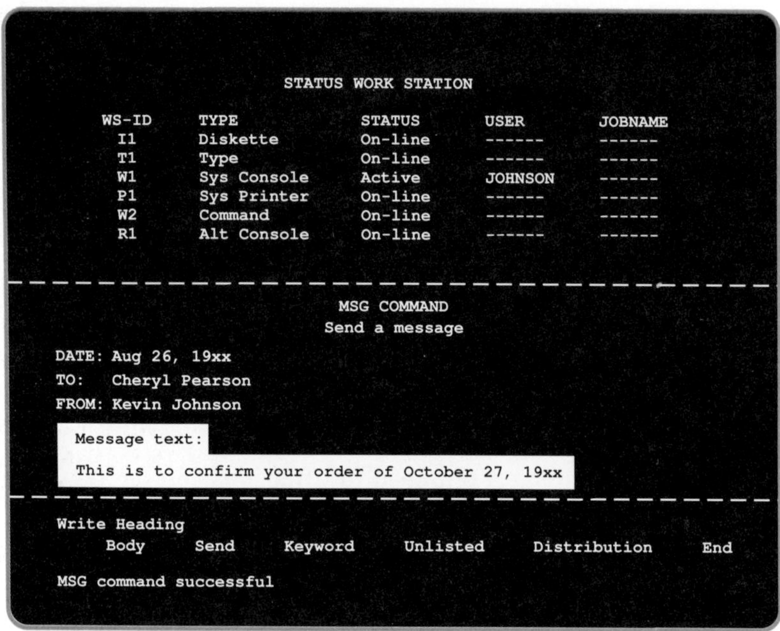

Computer-based message systems have a message blank on the screen that the user can fill in, as shown.

making a few keystrokes), and the communications software permits the communications to be transferred from one terminal to another—almost instantly. Communicating machines may be located across the aisle in the same building, separated by many miles, or around the world.

When a company already has a computer system and many employees have display terminals at their workstations, a message system is easy to implement. Basically, it consists of a simple data-processing program that introduces a message blank on the terminal screen. To send a message to another terminal, you simply fill in the blank on your display terminal, using the keyboard; insert the recipient's address in the appropriate blank; and the computer instantly routes the message.

You can categorize messages according to priority and privacy. For example, a message labeled "urgent" is positioned ahead of all others. Messages labeled "private" require the recipient to use a special password code to access them. If you send a registered message, you will be notified when it is accepted. You also can designate a message to be delivered at a specific time of day—a useful advantage when sending messages across time zones.

Computer-Based Voice Message Systems

Many businesses are using software that "personalizes" their CBMSs with voice capabilities. **Electronic audio communications** (voice mail or voice message system) may permit outgoing as well as incoming calls to be recorded, stored, played back for editing or revising, and forwarded at designated times to one or more specified receivers. A caller to a voice message system (VMS) or **computer-based voice message system (CBVMS)** is greeted by the voice of the intended receiver. Upon being invited to leave a message, the caller speaks into the telephone (or into a computer with a microphone) to leave a voice message.

The voice storage device records the caller's voice and stores it in the recipient's "mailbox" for access at a time convenient to the receiver. Many CBVMSs have recorded voice messages for the caller to listen to when the person being called is not available. Such a CBVMS works very much like a telephone answering machine, on which your voice usually is recorded on magnetic tape as an analog or continuous signal. If the person being called is not available, a **message switching system** activates so the caller can hear the intended receiver's recorded message. The caller can leave a message that the intended receiver can access later. If the system is a **digital voice exchange (DVX)** type, the voice messages are converted to digital form, stored, and ready for playback by anyone having the correct access code to the computer-stored message device or **audio mailbox** (voice mailbox).

Facsimile Transmission

You have learned from Chapter 6 that facsimile equipment has become a useful means of fast transmission of all types of documents. Facsimile equipment, used to transmit INTELPOST messages, can also be employed in many office communication situations. It is especially useful to send exact copies of reports, diagrams, and charts in manufacturing operations, where such changes are frequent. Other applications include transmitting shipping and receiving orders to improve inventory handling; price quotations and order confirmations for purchasing departments; and delivery schedules, specification sheets, drawings, and proposals for sales and marketing.

The user need not be present at the receiving unit when a document is being transmitted. Automatic answering devices and document feeders have made facsimiles almost completely self-operating. If the transmitting machines use telephone lines, documents can be sent at night when phone rates may be lower.

Portable facsimile units that can fit into an attaché case are available. A traveling executive or sales representative can transmit documents from any location simply by hooking the machine up to the nearest telephone receiver and dialing the number of a receiving facsimile machine.

Electronic Data Interchange

In **electronic data interchange (EDI),** documents are transferred from one point to another in their original form. EDI is similar to facsimile, except it exchanges or transfers the information in

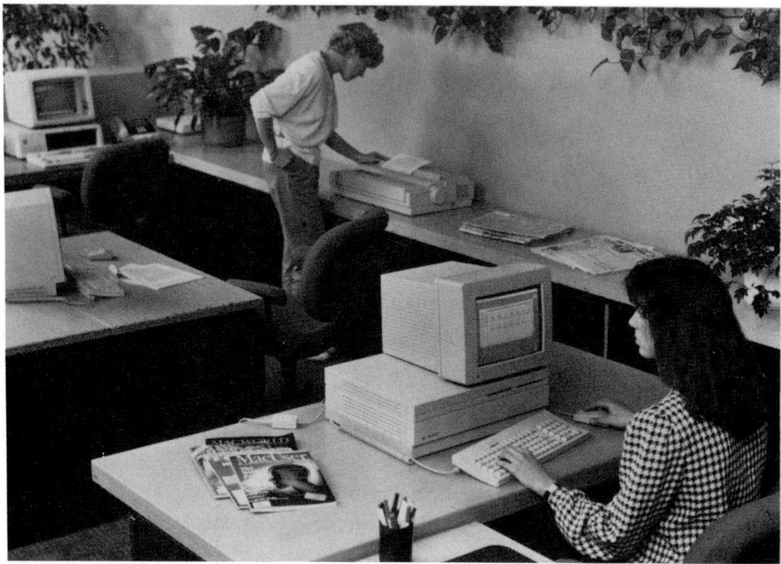

Electronic Data Interchange (EDI) permits documents to be transferred from one point to another in their original form.

computer-readable form. For example, say you frequently place orders with several suppliers, each of whom requires that you send a purchase order. If a supplier is an EDI user, you would enter the information on the purchase order into your computer—in a standard way. The information would be transferred to the supplier by a network. As soon as the information exchange occurs, you and the supplier have the information in exactly the same form. The supplier may either print a hard copy of the purchase order or use the soft copy to fill your order.

Although EDI has been around for more than 20 years, it has only recently become popular. Like facsimile, its popularity has been due to the establishment of industry standards. Thus, connectivity and compatibility have become important issues in making EDI a good communications method.

Communicating Workstations

A common characteristic of many computers is the ability to communicate or link with other computers. Many electronic typewriters and word processors also can communicate. In a shared logic system, for example, documents can be sent electronically from one word processing terminal to another (communicating word processors). Using **communicating workstations,** two or more people can exchange a vast amount of information in a few minutes.

If a company does not have its own computers or does not wish to use them to relay messages, it can establish a message system by buying services of a **public data (computer) network.** Public data networks, frequently called **value-added networks (VANs)**, offer many services that enhance the features of a common carrier such as the telephone or telegraph system.

Many of these services use **packet switching,** a network that groups data into packets. Packets do not necessarily contain the complete message because the purpose of packet switching is to send the various parts of your message in the most efficient path to the receiver. Because messages are "divided" into packets, codes are needed to reassemble the message at its intended destination. Some companies subscribe to a timesharing system or a shared-tenant system for many types of services. Subscribers may pay fees for using time accessed from equipment owned by another organization. (Several of these services are explained in more detail in Chapter 9.)

Networks

Networks utilizing technology expand the possibilities for processing and managing information. As a result, networks enable people and equipment to communicate and interact more effectively.

Public Network Services

You have learned about several public network services already. For example, a **bulletin board service (BBS)** is an information service that provides announcements, messages, schedules, notices, and similar types of news. The information in it can be read by **downloading** the information. (Downloading is a common communications term that means transferring information from a communications network to a computer; **uploading** is transferring information in the opposite direction—from your computer to a communications link.) In many cases, you can save and store the bulletin board information in your computer for later access.

You also have learned that a database is an organized collection of related information. Many online databases have become popular because they provide in-depth and current information about many topics. There are thousands of online databases that can be accessed (downloaded) from such networks as Western Union's EasyLink and the U.S. Videotel Network. Individuals and businesses can subscribe to these services and view on their computer screens stock market reports, bibliographies, weather, sports, news, and other kinds of information.

One type of public computer network system is **videotex,** a type of electronic mail that provides a wide range of visual database information to individuals and businesses. For example, videotex is used in airport terminals, so you can view airline arrivals and departures. The video or TV screen helps you locate a flight gate. Another videotex information service gaining popularity is Prodigy, an online IBM–Sears Roebuck information service for shopping and hundreds of other consumer services. Online service also permits you to compute your income tax return using a computer.

An example of a public computer network for electronic mail is Telenet Communications Corp.'s Telemail service, an electronic messaging and document transfer service that has over 250,000 subscribers. Telemail lets you send a message from a display terminal in one office to a terminal in the same office or to one across the country. All the messages, regardless of where they originate and where they are sent, are processed by Telenet's central computer in Virginia. Most offices use the system as an electronic memo service for short communications between sales representatives and the home office. Similar services are offered by AT&T's AT&T Mail, Compuserve Inc.'s EasyPlex and InfoPlex, Digital Equipment Corp.'s DECmail, MCI International's MCI Mail, and Western Union's EasyLink. The features of each of the services vary.

Wide Area Networks

Few things in life seem simpler than picking up the phone and making a call. Yet for the phone company, it is not quite that simple. Even a local call requires a complex network of electronic equipment that understands the number you dial, makes the connection, transmits your voice, knows how long you talk, adds up your calls, and bills you at the end of the month.

It is even more difficult for computers to communicate. The telephone system does not care what language you speak; it simply transmits the sound of your voice. Computers not only must send and receive signals so that they know when to make connections, when to disconnect, and when one message has priority over another; they must also perform many other functions.

A system for computer communication over long distances is called a **wide area network (WAN).** Telex and telephone services are good examples of WANs. A variety of communications services and networks may be provided by several common carriers for the transfer of information over several wide area networks. For example, a company with offices in several parts of the country might use various common carriers and transmission media (public and private leased telephone and cable lines, fiber optics, satellites, etc.) to transfer information from one point to another. The actual connections for transferring information from station to station in a WAN are referred to as **switching matrices.**

An effective communications system, especially over a WAN, must have some common ways for users to exchange communications. A set of standards for communications that has been re-

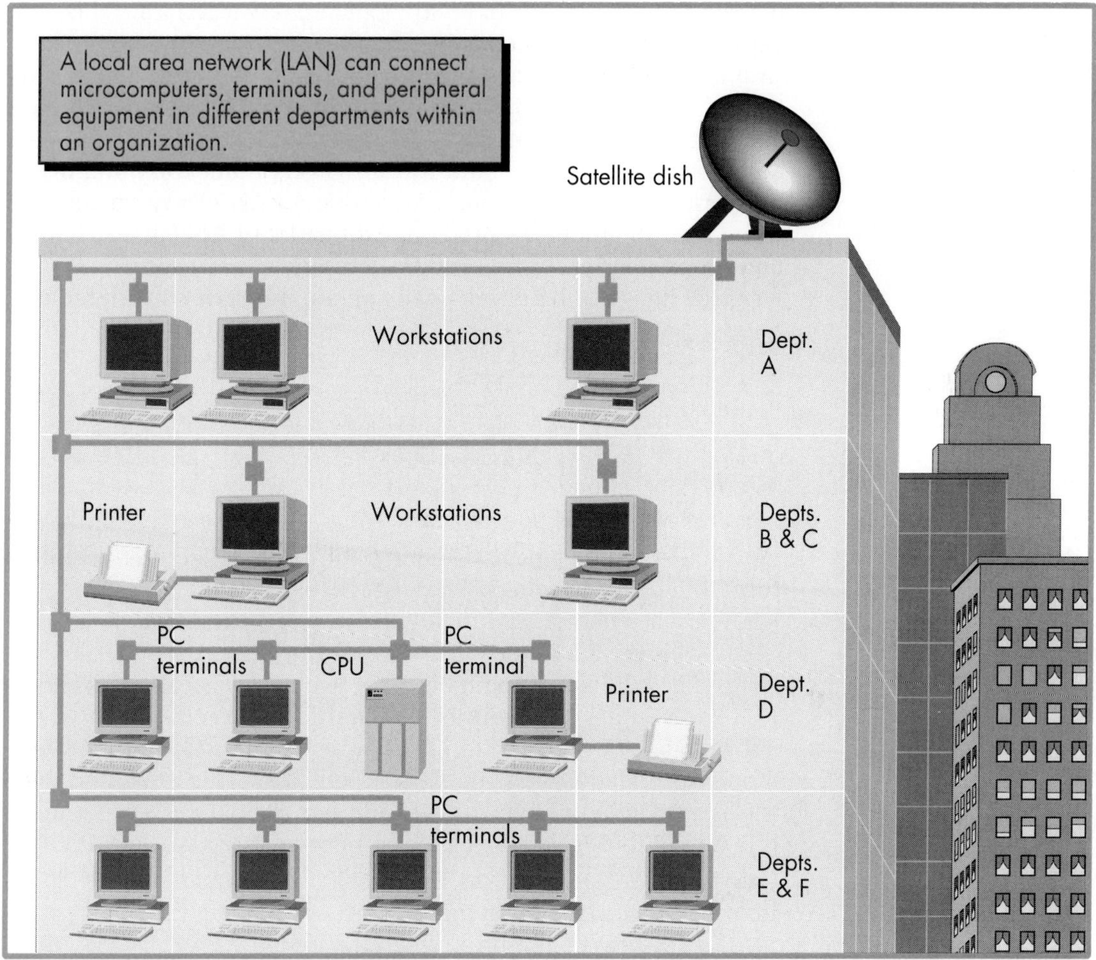

commended by the Consultative Committee for International Telephone and Telegraph (CCITT) is the **Integrated Services Digital Network (ISDN).** With ISDN, information (text, data, graphics, voice, and video) is transmitted in digital form through a standardized digital communications network. The purpose of ISDN is to permit communications between dissimilar equipment. With so many kinds of hardware, software, media, and methods promoted by manufacturers, the ISDN standard has real merit for compatibility of services.

Local Area Networks

A system for computer communications over a short distance—between offices on several floors or with a building not too far away—is called a **local area network (LAN)**. A LAN can link computers, a telephone system (a PBX is a good example), or a combination of other types of equipment. The distance a LAN covers usually is no more than about 50 miles.

There are many ways a LAN is like a telephone system. Just as you can use your telephone to talk to anyone else who has a phone connected to the system, a LAN is designed so that each computer connected to it can communicate with every other computer in the network. Sometimes a company builds a LAN solely for its own use. Other businesses lease connections to a LAN (shared-tenant and timeshared systems) to share computer information.

How you use a LAN depends on a number of considerations:

- the type of equipment connected
- the transmission distance
- the kind of communication used
- the geographic or geometric arrangement of the computers and their peripherals

Basic Network Topologies

Equipment arrangement or configuration is called the **architecture** or network **topology.** There are several basic LAN topologies. Each place where a terminal, printer, or peripheral is located is called a **node.** Each node is connected to the LAN by a separate cable. The connecting path between two nodes is called a **link.**

The simplest network is a shared logic system linking three nodes to one CPU. An example of a simple network might be your terminal and a terminal in the next office sharing a printer, with each peripheral connected to a CPU across the hall. Even though this configuration is not typically referred to as a LAN, it illustrates how each node must be connected to the CPU by a separate link.

The terminals in this simple network do not need to communicate with each other. If they did, a cable would be needed to link each terminal. When too many people try to communicate at the same time in a larger network, messages can collide and cause traffic problems.

A star network solves the problems of too many cables and too much traffic. In a **star network,** a central switching device plays the role of telephone operator. The central controlling node is called a **hub** or **central controller.** Instead of people communicating with each other directly, messages go first to the hub, which routes them to the receiving node.

The star network has its drawbacks. In many of them, the CPU handles hub functions. This can mean that, when traffic is heavy, the CPU is so busy switching calls it has no time to handle other tasks. Moreover, a star network depends on one piece of equipment: the central controller. If it fails, the LAN fails.

A star network.

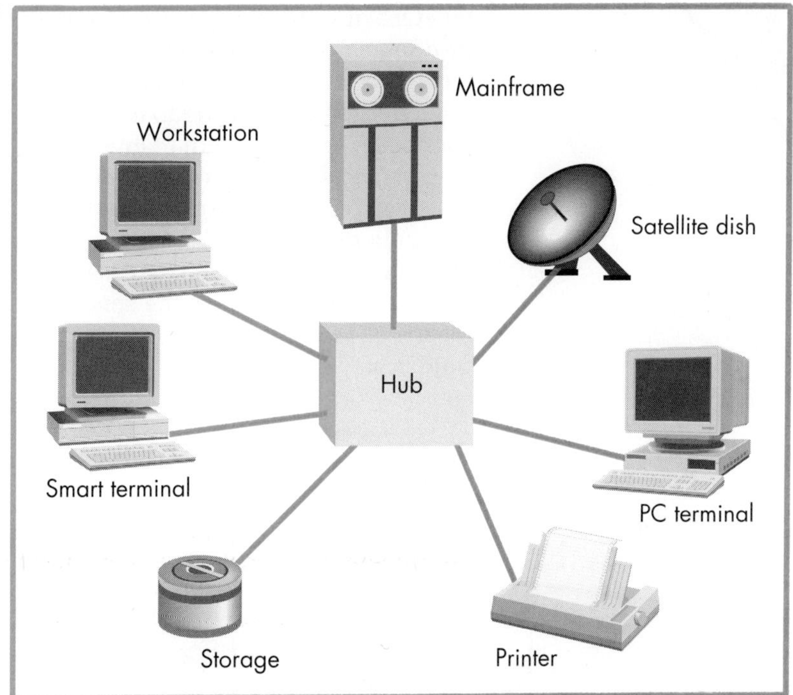

A ring network.

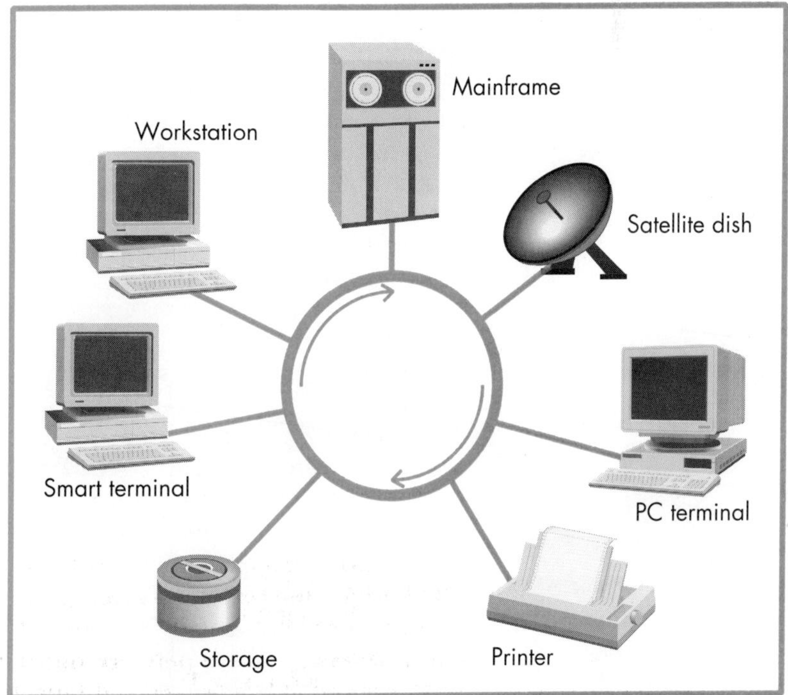

One way to eliminate the problem of relying too heavily on the hub is to link the nodes in a configuration something like a ring. In a **ring network**, messages are communicated from one node to the next, similar to a group of people passing a note from one to the next at a round table.

The design of some ring networks permits a node to receive a message, read it, and send it on to the next node. On other LANs, the node reads the address first. If the message is intended for another node, it is ignored and passed on. Some ring networks let the addressee add a note to the sender to show that the message was received. Many ring networks use a hub, or controller, to direct traffic; but the controller is not connected centrally, as it is in a star network. It is simply another node in the ring.

The main disadvantage to a ring network is that, like a chain, it is only as strong as its weakest link. A ring network is, in a sense, even more vulnerable than a star network. If even one node

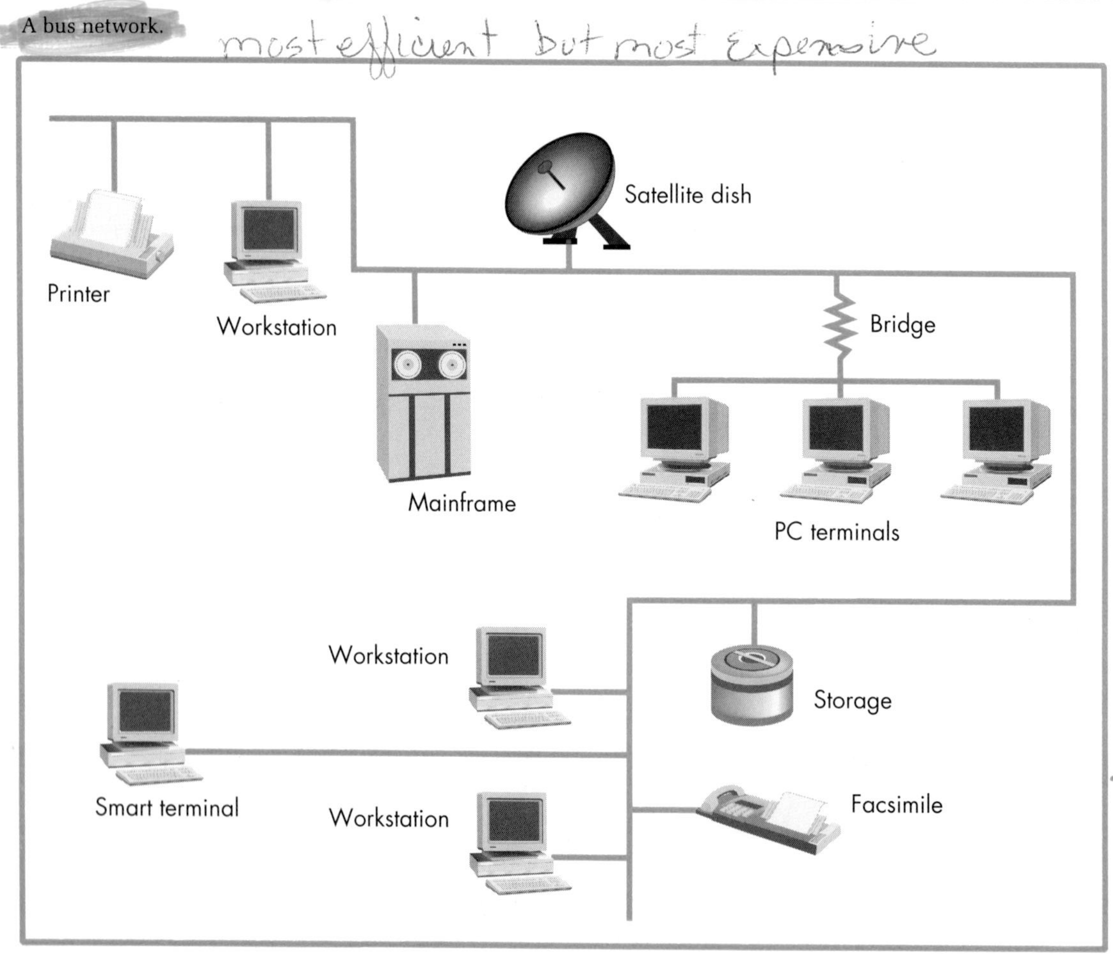

A bus network.

breaks down, no matter which one, the entire LAN will **crash** or go down. People who work with computers frequently say the system crashed or the system is down when the system is not working. Failure in either the computer hardware or software or in the electrical power supply can cause a system to crash.

One of the ways to get around the problem of a total ring network breaking down is to combine the star and ring topologies. In a **star-shaped ring network,** a hub reroutes or switches calls if any of the nodes should fail. Thus, the LAN can continue functioning. A popular adaptation of this design is IBM's **token ring network.**

The most flexible topology is the bus or **tree network.** This has only one cable, and any number of nodes can be plugged into it anywhere along its length. Individual nodes can be removed without affecting the LAN's operation. The bus/tree will not fail if any of its nodes fails.

Xerox's Ethernet is probably one of the best known bus/tree networks. There is no central CPU or hub in a bus/tree network. The function of the hub is performed by a special software program that routes and exchanges messages. Each node in a bus/tree network has its own CPU; therefore, it can function independently of the other nodes. The messaging software can be stored in the disk system of any node. More than one node usually stores a copy of the messaging software, thus serving as a backup. If the CPU that is acting as the controller should fail, another CPU that is storing the messaging software can take over, and the system continues running. Any user on a bus/tree network can send a file to any other user.

Other Topologies and LAN Devices

Several other configurations or topologies, such as honeycomb, orchestra, and diamond, are used in offices. Many are adaptations of star, ring, or bus networks.

Because all networks are prone to traffic congestion, "traffic lights" are needed, just as in a highway system. In communications, a method for multiple access is called **contention.** A contention scheme permits each user to access the network by taking turns and responding to changing traffic patterns. A common contention scheme is called **carrier-sense multiple access with collision detection (CSMA/CD)** or merely CSMA if the network does not have (or need) collision detection. CSMA is an efficient technique we take for granted—just as we do not think of "traffic jams" on a telephone when we reach our party on the first try.

LANs make it possible for people to use computers to communicate with each other from one office to another or one building to another, whether in a plant, a corporate headquarters, a campus, or any other locally-based organization. For communications at greater distances, a LAN can be connected by phone lines

Devices and Interfaces Used With LANs to Permit Transmission Between Equipment

- **gateway**—connects LAN to a main computer or to another communications network not in the LAN.
- **bridge**—connects two similar LANs so they can communicate.
- **file server**—frequently referred to as a workgroup computer; may act as a file or software depository and a hub for E-mail. Provides mass storage services to LAN users, controls the use of files when they are accessible to several users to avoid any loss of information in a file.
- **printer server**—directs output of computer to the correct printer when there are several printers in the network.
- **utility server**—used for accessing special devices (such as a modem) that cannot be handled by other servers on a LAN.

to other LANs. Communications by satellite enable one computer terminal to communicate with another terminal virtually anywhere in the world. LANs have taken on new significance as connectivity issues are being addressed.

Data Transmission System Components

Our ability to access an enormous and growing amount of information requires us to find the best possible ways to transmit that information—to get it from one piece of equipment to another, from one place to another, and from the person who has it to the person who needs it. Whether the machines are next to one another, tied together by a LAN, or thousands of miles apart, moving the information back and forth between them requires some type of **transmission system.**

Transmission systems are vital to creating integrated information systems that link different computer-based functions and equipment such as word processors, computers, Telex terminals, copier/printers, facsimiles, and laser printers. Office automation means that machines involved in generating, processing, distributing, and storing information are part of one system.

Unlike people, computers are not flexible in overlooking errors and forgiving mistakes in communicating information. When computers transfer data back and forth, they must talk the same language and at the same speed. Other signals they exchange must also be identical. Because manufacturers are competitive, they discourage standardization and try to make their equipment different and unique. However, manufacturers know that if there is not sufficient compatibility in the transmission system, there may be problems in the communication—or worse yet, no communication. Several elements of transmission systems are essential for linking data communications terminals and networks.

Interfaces and Transmission Protocols

Data communications require special rules and procedures. Because communicating systems are not always compatible, special equipment must be designed to ensure that all codes, formats, instructions, speeds, and languages are recognized by both the sending and receiving systems. Manufacturers have agreed on standardized **interfaces** (standard "connections") to make equipment compatible with each other. An interface can be hardware, such as the plug used to connect equipment by cable, or software.

The type of transmission lines, how the information is sent, and transmission procedures are extremely important for compatibility, which is important for communications to be sent and received. A technique or procedure for transmitting data that is agreed on by both the sender and receiver is called a **protocol.**

Manufacturers have created software programs for communications between otherwise incompatible equipment. These supply the necessary translation from the logic of one machine to that of another. In addition to software conversions, some equipment may need the help of devices known as **protocol converters,** which translate the sending machine's instructions into commands the

Types of Protocols

SIMPLEX MODE

→

sender *receiver*

- **simplex**—transmits data in only one direction. An example is a computer that monitors the temperature in an office. Such a computer needs only to receive data from a temperature sensor. It does not need to send information back to the sensor.

HALF-DUPLEX MODE

⇄

receiver *sender*

- **half-duplex**—allows data communications between both the sender and receiver, but only in one direction at a time. One computer must "listen" as the other computer "transmits" the message, and vice versa.

FULL-DUPLEX MODE

↔

receiver *sender*

- **duplex or full-duplex**—allows data to go in both directions at the same time. Simultaneous computer-to-computer transmissions can occur just as two people can talk at the same time on a telephone and still hear each other. The receiving terminal can return or "echo" the communication back to the sending terminal.

receiving equipment can understand. A value-added communications network can also be used for making computers compatible.

Modems

The human voice has a wide range of varying frequencies that form a pattern called an **analog wave**. Telephone lines are designed to carry analog waves or signals. Computers send information using only the binary language of **on** and **off.** Binary pulses are called **digital signals.** In order for a computer to send data by telephone, you need to convert its signal from digital to analog. When the message is received, the analog signal has to be converted back to a digital signal so the receiving computer can process the transmitted data. A **modem** (short for **modulator/demodulator**) is the device that converts analog signals to digital signals and vice versa. A modem is used whenever the telephone or some other analog device transmits information.

A modem converts electrical signals for transmission over telephone lines.

The modem links the computer and the telephone in either of two ways. A modem installed inside the CPU is called an **internal modem.** Usually you cannot see an internal modem. Most computers on the market today are equipped with internal modem capabilities. A modem that is a separate unit is called an **external modem.** An external modem is usually placed on the desk between the phone and the PC. It may look like a box about the size of a videocassette tape. External modems are connected to the phone and CPU with cables and jacks.

Some external modems are called **acoustic couplers**. Instead of cable or jack connections to the phone, an external modem has a cradle for a phone receiver. The cradle fits tightly around the phone receiver so that room noise is not picked up. The computer's digital signals are changed to an audible sound signal and transmitted the same way your voice is transmitted when you make a phone call. Acoustic couplers are not as popular as they used to be; however, several kinds of office equipment, such as facsimile and copying machines, may be linked to a type of acoustic coupler in an integrated information processing system. Many manufacturers are combining a telephone and an adaptation of an acoustic coupler into equipment used for transmitting information.

Baud Rate and Transmission Modes

The smallest piece of information a computer can recognize is a bit, represented by either a one or a zero. A one lets the electric current pass through; a zero shuts it off. A byte is a group of eight bits that together represent one alphanumeric character. These bits are sent from one computer to another in data communication.

The speed at which you send data can vary with the transmission method, equipment used, and cost. How fast data travels over communications lines is measured in **bits per second (bps),** frequently referred to as **baud rate.** Common baud rates for PCs to exchange data are 300, 1200, 2400, 4800, 9600, 19.2K (1000 bytes) bps, and even higher. When CPUs communicate data to each other without a modem, the transmission rate can be as fast as several million bps. The two basic types, or modes, of data communications are asynchronous and bisynchronous.

With **asynchronous transmission,** characters are sent one at a time at uneven intervals rather than in a steady stream. Microcomputers generally exchange data asynchronously.

With **bisynchronous** (or **synchronous**) **transmission,** characters are sent all at once. Only after the entire message is sent does the receiving computer check for transmission errors.

Control Characters and Control Codes

Two computers cannot communicate without instructions for transmitting the actual message. For example, it is not enough simply to send the text of a document or file in the form you see displayed on the screen after keyboarding it on your microcomputer. If the message is to be printed when it is received, your formatting keystrokes must also be sent to the printer at the receiving computer. These codes and instructions (and others like this) are sent before, during, and after the message itself is transmitted. They are called **control characters** or **control codes.**

In the same way the Morse Code was needed to send telegraph messages, codes are needed for today's data communications. In 1967, the **American Standard Code for Information Interchange (ASCII)** (often pronounced "ask-ee") was devised for data communications exchange. There is an ASCII character for each alphanumeric character, all the punctuation marks, and the various control codes. Two other common codes that have become standard in transmitting communications are **EBCDIC (Extended Binary Coded Decimal Interchange Code)** and **Baudot** (devised by IBM).

A **parity bit** is one of the control codes almost always used in data communications. Parity bits are sent along with the groups of alphanumeric bits. They give the receiving computer a way of checking whether the data received is identical to that sent or if an error occurred during transmission.

Several other control codes are transmitted to establish the pattern of information flow from sender to receiver. They communicate such things as the following:

- determining if the two systems are synchronized to send or receive data simultaneously
- the start of the message
- the end of a block of data
- a request for identification or "who are you?"
- canceling the transmission or "disregard the data sent"

- a request for human attention during a computer-to-computer transmission
- the end of the transmission

Transmission Media

Communications channels or pathways are used to transmit data from one place to another. The data transmitted on one or more of these channels may be in the form of electricity, sound, light, or radio waves. If the data is transmitted by telephone, either by voice or with an acoustic coupler, then sound also is used.

When the data leaves one computer on its way to another, it begins as an electrical impulse. Like any form of electricity, it needs a medium, or **conductor,** to get from one place to the next. Conductors vary according to how much information they can carry and the extent to which they are susceptible to interference. Interference or **crosstalk** is not uncommon with telephone communication. Telephone wire may be a **twisted pair cable,** (two insulated copper wires wound together). With **coaxial cable** media, a mesh shield surrounds the insulated copper wire. The insulating layer (air or plastic) around each coaxial cable wire minimizes crosstalk.

Fiber optics, a glass-fiber media, transmits data using light pulses. Thousands of signals or communications can be transmitted—

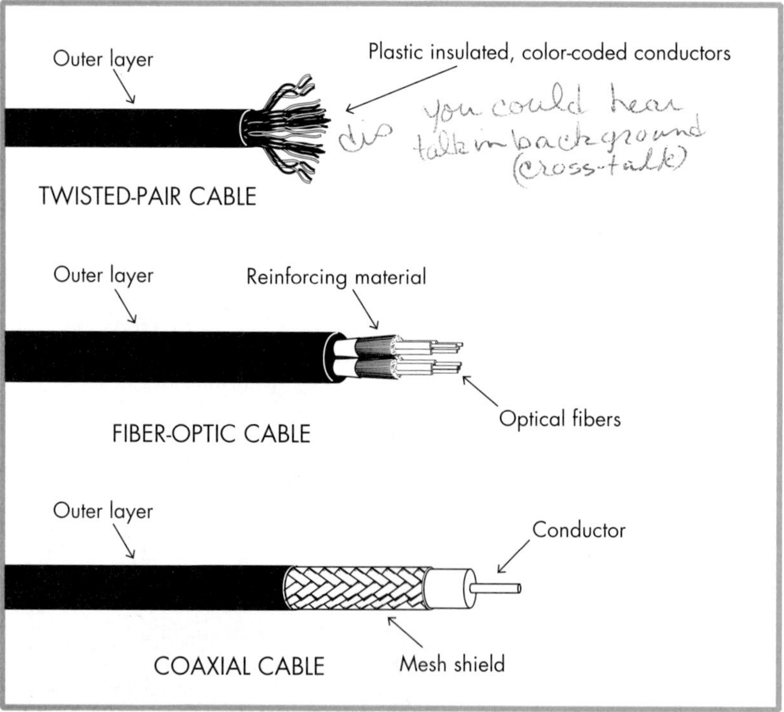

The three basic types of communications wiring: twisted pair, fiber-optic, and coaxial cable.

This microwave relay station transmits high-frequency radio waves.

at the same time and at the speed of light—over a single hair-like fiber-optic cable. Another fast transmission medium is **microwaves** or high-frequency radio waves that travel through the air. Relay stations, usually up to 30 miles apart, are used to send microwaves. Over longer distances, signals can be beamed via **satellites** as a very fast means of communications.

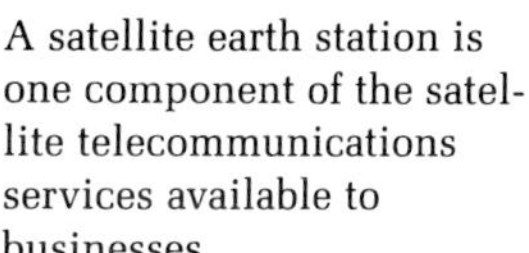

A satellite earth station is one component of the satellite telecommunications services available to businesses.

When a signal is transmitted to a satellite, it is called an **uplink**; when it is received, it is called a **downlink**. A number of organizations provide satellite telecommunications services to businesses. When you get news of an earthquake in a remote area of the country, it is probably because of these services. Trucks with portable disklike antennas can be driven (or sent by air) to remote areas of the world so you can follow the news of the world and special sports events on your home TV set via satellite.

The speed of communications is determined by transmission **bandwidth** (the number of signals that can be carried at the same time). When only one communication at a time is carried, it is called a **baseband** signal. A **broadband** network can carry thousands of communications simultaneously.

Standards for Connectivity

Connectivity of equipment for communications is possible because of standards that permit communications links. Standards set up by various organizations such as the **International Standards Organization (ISO)** have contributed to our ability to communicate more effectively—with an individual in a nearby office as well as among large business organizations throughout the world. For example, **Open Systems Interconnection (OSI)** is a seven-layered model to standardize information transmission for global communications and internetworking. **CCITT X.400** standards, defined by the Consultative Committee for International Telephone and Telegraph, are being used around the world to interconnect various types of electronic message-handling systems as well as other OSI-based applications. Standards are necessary for integrating the parts of the communications industry so information can be accessed and exchanged quickly and easily.

Many factors contribute to connectivity so senders and receivers can communicate. We depend on information every day—information that can be communicated quickly, efficiently, and cost-effectively. No doubt we will see many significant developments that will make the future of communications promising for every one of us.

CHAPTER SUMMARY

- The U.S. Postal Service is the least expensive method of distributing information outside the office.
- The U.S. Postal Service's Express Mail is a speedy delivery mail service that now competes with many private courier services.
- A Western Union Mailgram uses capabilities of the telephone, telegraph, and U.S. Postal Service.

- Western Union's Telex I and Telex II (TWX) use telephone or telegraph lines as a means of communication.
- Private branch exchanges (PBXs) route calls within an organization and are used to transmit computer data by telephone.
- Teleconferencing involves the simultaneous back-and-forth exchange of information utilizing two-way voice, video, or text equipment.
- Electronic mail is the method by which information is transmitted over telecommunications lines without requiring the physical movement of paper.
- The key to electronic mail is the ability of pieces of electronic equipment to communicate with each other via telecommunications lines or satellites.
- Electronic mail makes it possible to send large amounts of information at high speed.
- Information transmitted by electronic mail can be stored at a receiving location until it is required.
- Types of equipment used in telecommunications include word processors, Telex, facsimile machines, and computers.
- A computer-based message system allows soft copy messages to be initiated, forwarded, and stored by means of a computer program and computer terminals.
- A computer-based voice message system or voice mail transfers audio communications similar to soft copy messages in a CBMS.
- Voice mail or electronic audio communications uses a company's phone system to initiate, forward, and store voice messages via a computer system.
- Facsimile equipment transmits an image electronically over telephone lines to a receiving unit that can print it in hard copy. Portable fax units are convenient for traveling because you can use them from any telephone location.
- Electronic data interchange (EDI) is becoming a popular method of soft copy document exchange between computers.
- Communicating workstations are being used increasingly to exchange information in the same building as well as between offices in distant locations.
- A wide area network (WAN) is a system allowing communications over long distances. A WAN frequently involves several network systems.
- Public data networks lease their communications channels to private companies, which use them to send messages from one terminal to another in the same office or across the country.
- Local area networks (LANs) link computer equipment for data communications up to 50 miles. One LAN can communicate with another at a different geographic location over telephone and other transmission lines.

- In a star network, several terminals are connected to a central controller that switches calls.
- A ring network connects each terminal to the next in a circle.
- A bus network is the most flexible in both topology and function. Any number of nodes can be connected or disconnected without affecting its operation.
- Other LAN devices (such as gateways, bridges, and servers) are used to connect equipment.
- A modem converts a computer signal from digital to analog so it can travel over a telephone line. At the receiving end, a second modem changes the analog signal back to a digital signal for the receiving computer.
- Bits per second (bps) and baud rate are used to measure how fast data is transmitted.
- For communication to take place, both computers exchange control codes in addition to the actual message being transmitted.
- A parity bit checks to see that the data is correctly received.
- In asynchronous transmission, data is sent at uneven intervals; in bisynchronous transmission, the entire message is sent at one time.
- A half-duplex protocol can transmit data back and forth from sender to receiver, but only in one direction at a time.
- With full-duplex protocol, data can travel in both directions at the same time.
- Transmission media include twisted pair and coaxial cables, fiber optics, ground-relayed microwaves, and satellite signals.
- Compatibility and connectivity in the communications industry depend on standards for the exchange of information.

VOCABULARY

acoustic coupler
American Standard Code for Information Interchange (ASCII)
architecture
asynchronous transmission
baud rate
bisynchronous or synchronous transmission
bridge
bus or tree network
central controller
coaxial cable
computer-based message system (CBMS)
computer-based voice message system (CBVMS)
connectivity
control code
crash
data communications
digital voice exchange (DVX)
downlink
downloading
duplex or full-duplex
electronic data interchange (EDI)
E-mail or electronic mail
Express Mail
fiber optics

file server
gateway
half-duplex
hub
interface
Integrated Systems Digital Network (ISDN)
link
local area network (LAN)
Mailgram
microwave
modem
node
online or electronic database
point-multipoint communication
private branch exchange (PBX)
protocol
ring network
satellite
star network
telecommunications
teleconference
teletypewriter
Telex I and II
topology
twisted-pair cable
uplink
uploading
value-added network (VAN)
videotex
voice mail
voice/data integration
wide area network (WAN)

CHAPTER QUESTIONS

1. Why is distribution/communications an important phase of the information processing cycle?
2. In relation to speed and quantity of information, what are the differences between distribution by electronic equipment and distribution by Express Mail and similar courier mail services?
3. How might teleconferencing be advantageous to a large corporation with branch offices throughout the country?
4. Explain how a private branch exchange (PBX) works.
5. What are the similarities between a computer-based message system (CBMS) and a voice system (CBVMS)? What are the differences?
6. How does facsimile differ from electronic data interchange (EDI)? Name some of the other ways electronic mail is distributed.
7. Why do you think the use of communicating workstations is rapidly increasing? List and describe some of their uses.
8. How are LANs used? List some of the similarities and differences between the star, ring, and bus local area networks.
9. Why are so many components necessary for data transmission? Define interface, protocol, modem, control code, and types of communications channel media (twisted-pair, coaxial cable, fiber optics, microwaves, and satellites).
10. Why are standards so important in the communications industry?

CASE STUDY

Lenigrade-Bargé is a large national electronics manufacturing firm headquartered in Arlington, Virginia, with branch offices in 20 major cities around the country. The company also has offices in Europe (the Netherlands), Asia, Australia, and North Africa. Lenigrade-Bargé sells a wide range of electronic equipment including computers, word processors, and fax machines. The company services machines purchased or leased by its customers and also provides data and word processing services for companies that do not wish to buy or lease their own equipment or that need to supplement their own equipment by having processing done at another site.

Lenigrade-Bargé has a large in-house staff, a large sales staff, and employees at its branch locations. Service and leasing customers are billed monthly.

Describe at least four methods of electronic communications that Lenigrade-Bargé might use and the advantages of each.

CHAPTER 8

Storage and Retrieval

Carmen Kurz, one of several attorneys in the Legal Department of Petroski, Inc., needs to refer to a great many company records. Quick access to Petroski's records is possible because the company uses a computerized records system. All documents at Petroski are stored in reduced form in the company's central files. As Ms. Kurz prepares a defense against a price-fixing charge aimed at Petroski, she uses her computer to access and view such company documents as orders, contracts, and letters. Ms. Kurz enters the correct codes into her computer terminal to retrieve the files she needs and views each document on her screen.

It might have taken Ms. Kurz hours to obtain the records she needed if Petroski, Inc., did not have a computerized system for keeping records. She would probably have written a request, indicating the file number or name of the client, and handed it to a records clerk. The clerk would have had to search for the document among volumes of paper files. If the last person to access the files returned them to their proper place, the requested documents would be where they were supposed to be on the shelf. However, in paper file systems, documents are sometimes misfiled, pages are missing from files, or files are missing altogether. These problems introduce additional delays into records retrieval.

Although we have made great advances in storing and communicating information electronically, probably nothing will ever completely replace paper-based filing systems, at least not for decades to come. Nevertheless, new technology is changing dramatically the way businesses manage their records.

Storage Media

In an information-saturated society, being able to find and access information is vital. Whatever the business, records retrieval is a matter of great importance. A major task of business is managing information, and an essential aspect of managing information is the ability to store and later find specific documents, such as purchase orders, payroll records, customer files, production and inventory records, manuscripts, contracts, and financial statements. Reasons for care in storing information include the need to keep it safe from damage by fire and other hazards, and to comply with federal regulations. Reasons for ease of retrieving information include updating and checking information and providing information to clients, customers, or employees—in a timely fashion.

Advances in information storage and retrieval have been necessary to keep pace with the amount of information available. Some of the advances stem from the form of storage used. At one time, paper was the only medium available for storing information. Film and magnetic media significantly changed the way we manage records. Several other technological advances in electronic records management have been developed for even better information management. Optical or (laser) disks, image processing, microimage transmission, and computer systems for database management are being used by many organizations.

Paper Storage

Over 80 percent of all the information that exists in the world was created in the last 25 years. Most of this overwhelming amount of information is available on paper—in books, documents, news-

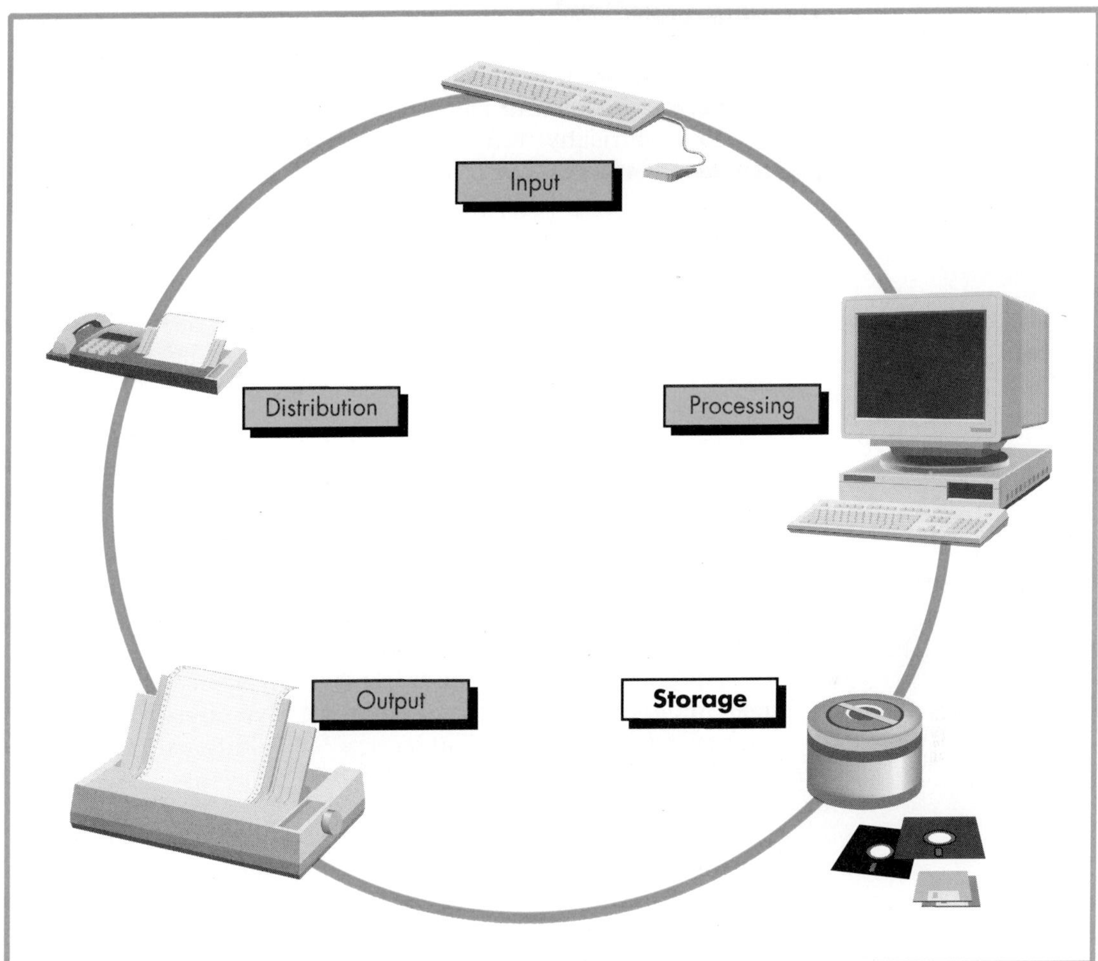

Storage is one of the five stages in the information processing cycle.

papers, magazines, computer copy, punched cards, index cards, and so on. If each of the 50 or so million office workers has eight file drawers of information (a conservative estimate), a packed filing cabinet drawer might hold about 3000 pages, making each office worker responsible for about 24,000 paper documents. That works out to a total of 1.2 trillion pages—a figure that is growing by about 3000 pages for each employee every year. In short, modern business creates a lot of paper that needs to be organized, stored, and made accessible.

There are four common methods of storing paper:

1. **Vertical filing** is the most common system for storing paper records. Vertical files are upright file cabinets with drawers stacked one on top of the other. Papers are stored facing the front of the drawer.

2. In a **lateral file** cabinet, papers are arranged so that they face the sides of the cabinet. When a drawer is pulled out, all documents in that drawer are accessible at once.
3. **Open-shelf storage** is just what the name implies: open shelves, stacked vertically. You can see everything on the shelf.
4. **Rotary file** storage can be either a "lazy-Susan" arrangement, or it can encircle a desk. Rotary and open-shelf storage require somewhat less space than vertical or lateral files.

Of the four methods of storing paper, open-shelf files are the most cost-efficient and provide the most storage space per filing inch. In addition, they provide easy access and are suitable for color-coded systems, which are quite popular. Nevertheless, any kind of paper filing system takes up a great deal of space and is thus a costly means of storing information. Companies are therefore interested in using other methods.

Magnetic Storage

Magnetic media—such as magnetic cards, magnetic reel-to-reel and cartridge tape, floppy disks, and hard disks—lend themselves to many of the same kinds of storage systems used for paper. Similar cabinets and shelving arrangements can be used. However, magnetic media systems require far less office space to store the same amount of information. While we have already examined these magnetic media in Chapter 4, a few additional points bear mention.

Plastic **magnetic cards**, often called **mag cards**, can hold about 10,000 characters. They became popular in the 1960s when word processing was introduced. Magnetic tape, available in cassettes, reels, or cartridges, has greater storage capacity than mag cards, but the information may take longer to retrieve. Many cartridge tape systems are particularly popular for both "original" storage and backing up documents. Some computers use 14-inch reels of magnetic tape, although magnetic disks are a more common form of storage with microcomputers.

Magnetic **disks** (floppy disks and diskettes), are popular today in $5\frac{1}{4}$- and $3\frac{1}{2}$-inch sizes. Because the disk medium is sensitive, it is encased in a protective cover. Some disks can hold about 400 pages of information. In terms of storage space, this means that a file drawer of paper is equal to about six floppies—a smaller amount of space than the space taken up by one or two paperback books.

Magnetic **hard disk** storage is a popular storage medium for computer data. A hard disk is sometimes called a **fixed disk** because it is permanently encased in its drive to avoid exposure to dust and other particles that might affect the medium. More than 75,000 pages of information, or about 33 file drawers of paper documents, can be stored on a single hard disk. The amount of storage and the sizes of hard disks vary among computer systems. Some hard disks may be smaller than a Tupperware sandwich container.

Because you can store vast amounts of information on a hard disk, it is wise to organize your files on the disk. Files can be organized by creating **directories** and **subdirectories** where files are to be stored. For example, a directory might be similar to one drawer in a filing cabinet where you file pertinent company documents. Within that drawer or directory, you have one, two, or a few file dividers to separate groups of similar files. Directories and subdirectories are given names the same way you label your files in a cabinet by your desk.

There are several types of hard disks, including Winchesters (discussed in Chapter 4) and the **Bernoulli Box** (a removable fixed disk housed in a cartridge). This type of hard disk is extremely reliable and has a high storage capacity—many millions of characters. Unlike many other hard disks, a Bernoulli Box is not susceptible to **head crash** (the head or the read/write mechanism drops down on the medium because of a power interruption, an unusual vibration, or a similar problem). Head crashes can damage the disk and destroy the data it contains.

You will recall that because of the great sensitivity of magnetic storage media, especially floppy disks with exposed media, you must take certain precautions when handling them. Never write directly on a disk label with a ball point pen or a pencil. Write on the label with a felt-tipped pen. Keep magnetic disks, tape, and cards free of dirt and dust by storing them properly. (See Chapter 4 for care guidelines.)

Equipment and methods of storing magnetic media are similar to those for storing paper. Because tapes, cards, and disks can store much more information than paper, they require considerably less space. In a small office, desktop trays, binders, boxes, or tubs may be sufficient for storage. These are portable and can be locked in desk drawers for security.

In small offices, desktop storage is often appropriate for floppy disks. Plastic file boxes or three-ring binders that have plastic pages with pockets are typically used. The disks slip into the pockets. The file boxes have suspension inserts or index tabs so disks can be easily identified and retrieved. The boxes also have covers that protect disks from dust, smoke, and other potentially harmful substances.

In large offices and in situations where many floppy disks are produced, rotary files offer easy access and may be the best equipment for storage. They can be stacked one on top of the other to allow for more storage capacity in a limited space.

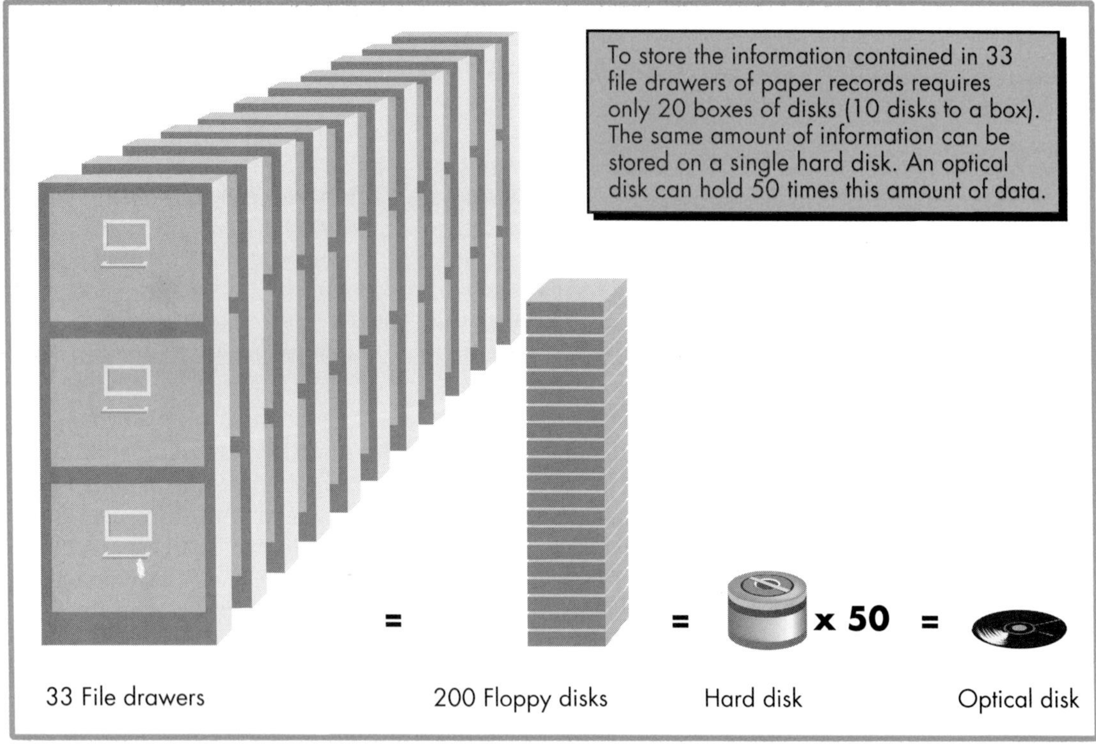

To store the information contained in 33 file drawers of paper records requires only 20 boxes of disks (10 disks to a box). The same amount of information can be stored on a single hard disk. An optical disk can hold 50 times this amount of data.
=
=
x 50
=
33 File drawers
200 Floppy disks
Hard disk
Optical disk

Large reels of computer tape and computer hard disks are too bulky and too sensitive to be stored in desktop equipment. Several manufacturers offer cabinets with internal partitions that hold computer reel tapes, large folders of computer printouts, and hard disk containers. Cabinet doors open vertically or horizontally and protect against extreme variations of temperature and humidity. They also can be locked.

Some large organizations maintain computer tapes in open-shelf file systems within a controlled area such as an air-conditioned storage room. In these open-shelf files, tapes are kept in their protective cases and are easily retrieved.

Solid-State Storage

A **solid-state storage** device is rigid and has no moving parts. It is similar to a hard disk drive, except it has electronic circuits and can be accessed much faster than many conventional disk drives.

RAM Chips

One type of solid-state storage device is made up of a series of **RAM (random-access memory) chips** organized into rows on a board. The **RAM chip board** is plugged into the computer CPU. A RAM chip storage device is very fast but also quite costly.

Bubble Memory Another type of solid-state storage is called **bubble memory**. This is a permanent (nonvolatile) memory that frequently has internal storage. It may be of the removable cartridge type. Bubble memory is not affected by extreme temperatures or power outages. Because it is expensive, it has not been used extensively except by the military. Although some vendors say it is much faster than more traditional types of memory, it is still a relatively slow medium to access.

Laser (Light) Storage

Optical Disk **Optical disks** use light in the form of laser beams to write and read data. The laser records information by focusing heat that creates a small bubble on the disk surface. When the disk is read—that is, when you retrieve a document—light is bounced off the disk. If the disk has information stored on it, the angle of the reflected light changes in such a way as to transfer the data recorded on the disk to your display.

Optical disk storage has made great strides and is quite impressive. It is fast, quiet, and does not need a controlled temperature. One 14-inch optical disk can hold about 6.8G (gigabytes or 1000 megabytes) of information, an amount equal to one complete set of the *Encyclopaedia Britannica*. Another example is Kodak's library system of 150 14-inch optical disks, which holds about a terabyte (Tb or 1000 gigabytes) of information.

A single 14-inch optical disk can store as much information as is contained in an encyclopedia.

The three different types of optical disks are CD-ROM, WORM, and erasable disks. With a **CD-ROM** or **compact disk–read only memory disk,** the user cannot write on the disk. Readers can write on the second type of optical disk, a **WORM** or **write once–read many times disk**. Usually you cannot erase anything you have written to a WORM disk. There are several methods of writing to a WORM disk **(ablative, bubble forming, bimetallic alloy, dye polymer,** and **phase change).** All these methods apply digital binary information to the disk. The third type of optical disks is erasable. **Erasable optical disks** can be used for recording, erasing, and reading data. **Magneto-optical disks** combine laser/optical and magnetic technology.

Mass storage or library systems are common for optical disk storage as well as for several other types of storage media. Some manufacturers have developed "jukebox-type" storage devices for this media. Such devices may hold hundreds of optical disks, making it possible to store volumes of documents inexpensively and access them quickly. Combined in a local area network with an electronic filing system, optical disk mass storage places staggering amounts of information within easy access of any terminal.

Holography Holography is a laser light photographic technology that produces images in what appears to the viewer as lifelike three-dimensional forms. An image or photograph subjected to this process is sometimes called a **hologram**. A series of holograms may be so real that they appear to be solid and touchable—just as objects appear in real life. The lifelike forms that can be produced by holography hold great promise for many applications involving viewing objects in three dimensions. This low-cost, high-capacity storage medium has fast access capabilities.

Electronic Imaging Storage

Image scanning, **electronic imaging,** or image processing is a form of input that also can be a method of storage and retrieval. For example, material such as handwritten applications, books and magazines, original artwork, pictures, charts, mechanical drawings, and graphic images often need to be entered into a computer. It is not efficient or possible in many instances to keyboard the information. However, electronic imaging makes it possible to enter this material into a computer without keyboarding.

Equipment for electronic imaging consists of a personal computer, image processing software, a scanner, and a laser or thermal printer. A photo, illustration, or text is copied by placing the image under the scanner. The image is converted into digitized bits for the computer. Once the image is copied and you have enlarged or reduced it to the size you want, you can edit it. You can use the image as an illustration in a page of text, merge it with another document, store it on a disk, or transmit it to another microcomputer.

For example, insurance companies have many forms clients must fill out. Until recently, they were all kept as paper files. Now, with electronic imaging, each form can be scanned and stored in the computer under the client's name.

Photographic/Film Storage

Photographing or **filming** documents is an extremely popular method of storage, especially in reduced form. Records reduction dates back to an 1839 experiment by John B. Dancer. He found he could use camera lenses to reduce an image. Although Dancer did little with his findings, his experiment was remarkable. Because he was able to reduce a document significantly (by 160 percent), his experiment was an important step in the evolution of modern-day storage methods. Thus, film has become a popular means of records storage.

Micrographics

A fast-growing field of information storage in which documents are reduced and filmed is called **micrographics**. Micrographics involves photographically reducing images of text and graphic information and recording them as tiny (micro) images on film. The products that result from this process are generally referred to as microforms.

Micrographics is an excellent way to store large quantities of information in a limited amount of space. Companies can save between 95 and 98 percent of the space needed for storing paper records by putting them on microforms. But these savings can be achieved only on records that have to be maintained for a fairly long time—five years or more. Otherwise, the cost of converting records to microforms will probably outweigh the advantage of saving space.

Microform Types

A **microform** is a miniaturized image of a document. Information can be stored and retrieved on several kinds of microforms: microfilm, microfilm jackets, aperture cards, microfiche, micro-opaques, or ultrafiche. To be fully retrieved, microform images must be magnified so they can be read by the naked eye. **Microform readers** or viewers, which you may have seen in libraries, are special machines that perform this function.

Microfilm The oldest type of microform, **microfilm,** is a continuous roll of film containing reduced images of graphic or textual material. The first microphotograph developed in 1839 had to be viewed under a microscope because it was a 1/8-inch-long image

Microfilm can be used to store old documents.

of a 20-inch-long document. During the Franco-Prussian War, microfilm strips were attached to carrier pigeons, which carried several million documents from one destination to another as a means of communication. In the 1920s, businesses started using microfilm. Since the 1940s, it has been possible to use microfilm as evidence in court cases. Microfilm records usually are photographed with either 16- or 35-mm film. For documents on $8\frac{1}{2}$- by 11-inch paper, such as correspondence, invoices, and reports, 16-mm film often is used. Larger documents and graphic images—including newspapers, X rays, and blueprints—usually are photographed on 35-mm film.

Microfilming can be expensive and time-consuming. Before converting to microfilm, a company will often conduct a feasibility study to determine how and if it can gain in efficiency and cost savings by transferring its records to film. A **feasibility study** for records management is a detailed analysis of a company's records management system to determine how information reorganization or equipment can be used to increase efficiency and productivity. Such studies are an excellent first step, and if microfilming is recommended, they will also show which information should be converted.

Document pages are photographed in sequence. The number of pages that can be recorded on a standard 100-foot **roll** or **reel** of 16- or 35-mm microfilm depends on the degree to which the pages are reduced. At a ratio of 24 to 1, about 600 $8\frac{1}{2}$- by 11-inch pages can be photographed on one reel of 16-mm film. Nearly 3000 pages can be recorded on 35-mm film reduced in this manner. The basic medium of all microforms is black-and-white film. Therefore, some kind of camera is involved in their creation. Microfilm can be produced by means of a **rotary camera** that photographs documents as they are fed onto a mechanical conveyor. The term *rotary* refers to the fact that a belt rotates the documents into the machine, past the camera lens, and out of the machine.

A **planetary camera** is usually used for microfilming large documents, such as engineering drawings and newspapers. A planetary camera looks very much like an ordinary photographic enlarger with copying lights attached to each side. With this kind of camera, the documents to be photographed remain stationary. Because the pictures are taken one by one, the process is considerably slower than rotary camera filming. The planetary camera is capable of producing images with great precision at reductions up to a ratio of 30 to 1. Further reduction is possible if required.

Microfilm can be stored on reels, cassettes, or cartridge magazines. It is often stored in desktop files or carousels that hold 100 to 300 storage units. A microfilm **cartridge** or **cassette** is not only a convenient package, but it protects a roll of film. Cartridges also

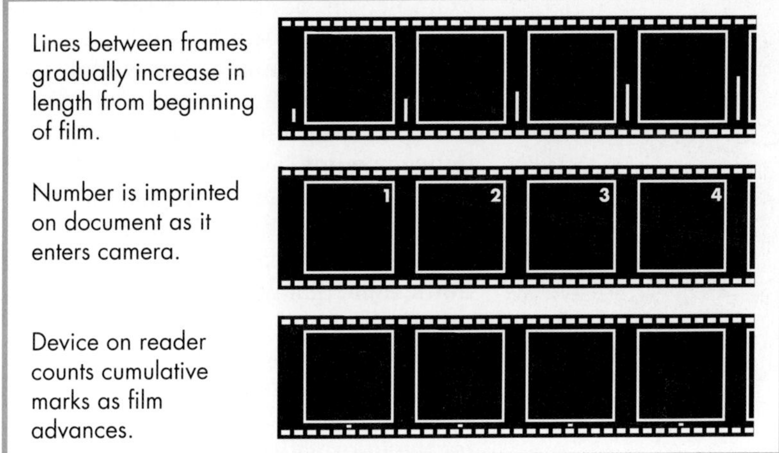

Lines between frames gradually increase in length from beginning of film.
Number is imprinted on document as it enters camera.
1
2
3
4
Device on reader counts cumulative marks as film advances.

Indexing microfilm: top—line coding; middle—sequential numbering; bottom—image counting.

simplify threading, storing, and handling film rolls. Microfilm reels, cassettes, and cartridges have been standardized so that any microfilm reader that accepts a storage unit from one manufacturer will accept similar units from other manufacturers.

It is easy to find a specific document on a roll of microfilm if an **index code** is added when documents are photographed. The images can be coded in several ways, including line coding, sequential numbering, and image counting.

A horizontal line separates each frame if the microfilm has been **line coded**. At the beginning of the film, the lines are short, but they gradually increase in length until the end of the film is reached. These lines are indexed numerically. Numbers on the side of the microfilm reader screen identify the increasing length of the lines as the film is run through the reader—almost like a horizontal speedometer. When a certain number is reached, the user can slow down the film.

The **sequential numbering** method of coding microfilm consists of photographing numbers along with each document page. A separate keypunch card can be made at the same time. **Keypunch cards** are a form of record in which holes have been punched to record data. The card indicates the number of each document page as well as the number of the microfilm roll. Such cards are used as an index, making it possible to quickly locate specific images on a microfilm roll.

Another method of coding is called **image counting**. With the image count procedure, small rectangular marks or **blips** are imposed on each frame of microfilm. A separate index shows the cumulative image count for each document. The marks are then counted by a device in the reader (odometer) so that images can be located rapidly as the film advances (called **film pulldown**). For example, the odometer would locate the ninety-first frame—the indexed one you want to find—by totaling up the square marks as the film is run, making it easy for you to stop the machine at or near the ninety-first frame.

A more recent method of microform coding is called **photo-optical coding** or **binary coding**. With photo-optical coding, a coding pattern mark is registered below each frame as the document is filmed. The code refers to one or more terms that describe the frame. A microform reader of photo-optical coding has electronic logic that permits a person to access the correct page by entering topic and subject information. The concept is similar to automating the way you would manually refer to an index in a book. First you look up the topic in the index to find the page on which it is found. Once you know that, you can turn to the page for the information you want.

Probably the biggest advantage of microfilm is the amount of space it saves as a storage medium. As office storage space becomes increasingly expensive, microfilming provides a way to store more for less. Microfilm, as a form of storage, is also well suited to recording long documents that do not need to be accessed frequently, such as old newspapers, other dated periodicals, and old books. For example, when books at the Library of Congress begin to deteriorate, they are microfilmed.

Another advantage of microfilm is that pages of a microfilmed document cannot be lost or misplaced easily. Microfilm therefore offers an aspect of protection against document loss that regular paper files cannot provide. And microfilm is admissible in courts of law if it has been filmed properly, with a certificate of authenticity.

Although the advantages of microfilm have added to its widespread use, a few drawbacks are noteworthy. Rewinding problems are fairly common; users sometimes experience eyestrain; and an occasional poor copy will make a document illegible. Also, users cannot make notes on the film as they could on a paper document.

Film jacket.

Updating microfilm records involves splicing film, which can be cumbersome. New sections of film can be spliced into the continuous roll. The film also can be cut into smaller segments, from one frame to a strip of several frames, producing **unitized microform.** Unitized microforms can be stored like index cards. They are a useful way to record and store one short document or a few drawings. Microfilm jackets, aperture cards, microfiche, microopaques, and ultrafiche are all forms of unitized microforms.

Film Jackets **Microfilm jackets** are simply two sheets of acetate or plastic sealed at the top and bottom. The film jackets are divided into horizontal sections that hold the strips of microfilm. They come in several rectangular sizes, but 4 by 6 inches is the most common. Some jackets hold only 16-mm film, some hold only 35-mm film, and some can accept two sizes of film. The top of each jacket has a strip of tape on which labeling information can be typed or written.

Aperture Cards Aperture means an opening or hole. An **aperture card** is a type of keypunch card with a rectangular hole that holds one or more frames of microfilm. Information about the contents can be printed at the top. One advantage of the aperture card is that it is a convenient storage form for one-page documents and drawings, such as microfilm reductions of engineering drawings. Also, aperture cards can be arranged and rearranged easily in different sequences, either manually or by keypunch equipment.

Microfiche Fiche (pronounced "fish") is a French word that means *small card*. A **microfiche** (or **fiche**) is a small sheet of film, sometimes about the size of a 4- by 6-inch index card. The film contains reduced images of documents—anywhere from 50 to more than 420 $8\frac{1}{2}$- by 11-inch pages, depending on the degree to which the original documents are reduced. The reduced images are arranged in rows and columns. The columns are numbered across the top, and the rows are lettered along the side. In this way, specific images can be located in the same way that you locate places on a map.

Fiche has a tremendous storage capacity; yet it takes up less space than microfilm rolls. It can be filed as easily as index cards and can be sent through the mail—a convenient and inexpensive way of sending a great deal of information to another location.

Microfiche forms are easy to handle and retrieve. To facilitate fast retrieval, microfiche is indexed in a number of ways. A tape strip across the top of the card holds information such as names,

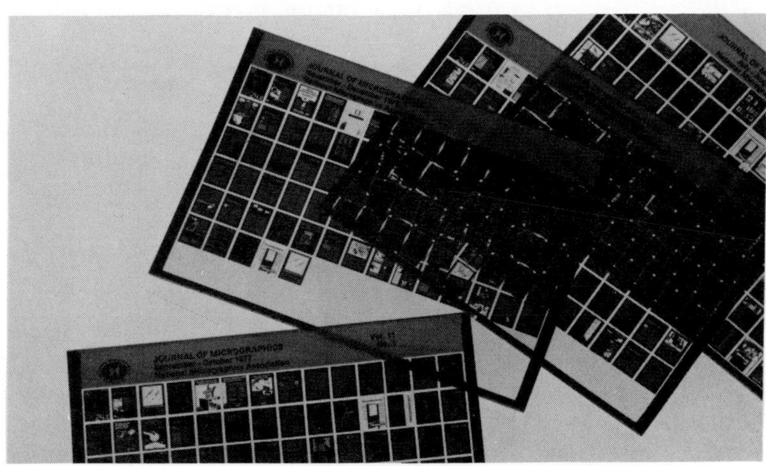

Each microfiche shown here can contain as many as 98 pages of information.

dates, and key words relating to the subject. In addition, one frame in the lower right corner of the card contains indexing information about the other frames on the microfiche. This frame may include the row letters and column numbers of the other images on the card.

Indexing information also can be put on keypunch cards, which can be used to create an index somewhat like a telephone directory. The directory identifies each document by its grid pattern frame, such as F-8. The index can provide a short description of each document, relevant dates, author's name, and so on.

Microfiche offers the same advantages as microfilm for recording lengthy publications, such as research papers, newspapers, and books. However, because fiche can be filed and retrieved more easily than microfilm, it is well suited for documents that are used frequently. The cards can be labeled on the top for easy identification.

Production and storage of fiche provide savings in other ways, too. These include ease of updating and duplicating files and the ability to transmit information by electronic means or mail. You can easily see the savings in duplicating documents: Photocopying 2500 pages at six cents a copy would cost $150. Microfiche images cost about one-tenth of a cent per image to produce, a total of $2.50 for 2500 pages. Although machines for producing microfiche are expensive, their cost is offset by the volume of records that can be stored in a short time and by savings in retrieval time and storage space.

Micro-Opaques **Micro-opaques** have many similarities to microfiche. The basic difference is that micro-opaque images are stored on photographic paper stock rather than on film. Images can be printed on each side of the paper. Because light does not pass through a micro-opaque, a special type of reader with high-intensity illumination is necessary to read this medium.

Ultrafiche Anything that is "ultra" is extreme. **Ultrafiche** and ultrastrips are the most extreme form of image reduction. A 4- by 6-inch ultrafiche can contain as many as 4000 pages of information. The length of a continuous film or ultrastrip is limited only by the way it is to be stored. (In one experiment, the entire King James Bible was reduced to an ultrafiche only 2 inches square.) The reduction process is so exact and delicate that it can be done only in a laboratory. It is very expensive as well. Nevertheless, ultrafiche and ultrastrips are practical for storing large publications such as catalogs, indexes, dictionaries, and encyclopedias.

Computer Output Microfilm In addition to being created by means of a planetary camera, microfiche and other microforms can be produced using **computer output microfilm (COM).** As the name implies, COM represents an integration of computer and microfilm technologies. Both involve the processing of information.

In many computer operations, output is produced on paper by means of a printer attached to the computer. With COM, instead of a paper printout, you get microforms—usually in a microfiche format. The advantage of this method over the camera method of producing microfiche is that COM units can produce many microfiche at an extremely fast rate (200 to 300 full-page documents a minute). The COM recorder can accept data directly from the computer or from computer tapes or disks. The COM recorder thus becomes an alternative to paper printers as a way of producing computer output.

Retrieval of Microforms

For microforms to be useful, retrieval involves two parts: First, you must get the microforms from the files. Second, you need to find specific documents on them. Two important considerations in this process are the kind of microform being retrieved and the system of indexing used.

Microfilm rolls, reels, cassettes, and cartridges may be retrieved manually from their storage shelves or cabinets. If they are part of an electronic library system, automated retrieval may be possible. Both microfiche and microfilm jackets can be filed like index cards in desktop or floor units, depending on how many there are. In most situations, they are retrieved by hand from their file locations. In automated filing systems, microfiche can be retrieved by a machine in seconds. Aperture cards, like microfiche,

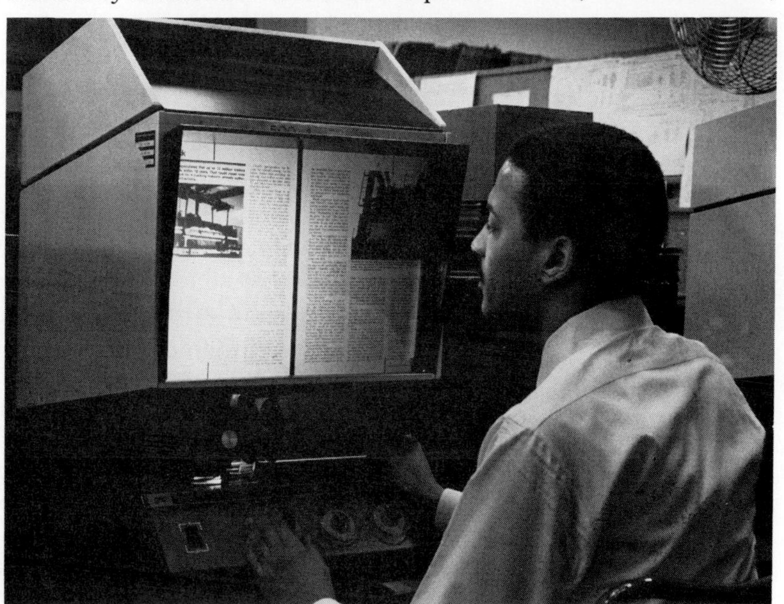

Microfilm readers enlarge and project the tiny filmed images.

can be filed like index cards. They can also be filed, sorted, and retrieved by keypunch equipment.

Microform Readers To find a specific document on microfilm, you need a **microfilm** or **roll film reader**. This is a machine that enlarges and projects the microfilm image onto a screen for easy reading. Specific pages can be located using one of the coding or indexing methods already discussed—line coding, sequential numbering, image counting, and photo-optical coding.

Each type of microform has its own type of reader because the microform media must be compatible with the machine. If a microform reader also can print copies of miniaturized documents, it is called a **reader/printer**. Methods of producing copies vary in the same way that duplicating and photocopying processes differ, depending in some cases on the manufacturer and on the kind of microfilm medium.

Computer-Assisted Retrieval (CAR) Computers play an important role not only in producing microforms but also in retrieving them. Microforms can be retrieved at high speeds with a **computer-assisted retrieval (CAR)** system. Other types of media, such as magnetic and paper storage, can be accessed by a CAR system. Thus, a CAR system can be quite efficient in managing and accessing information.

Imagine yourself in a large modern library, sitting at a computer terminal equipped with a video screen. You are doing a research paper on Ulysses S. Grant, and the library has a copy of his diary for the month of November 1863. Using an index similar to a phone directory, you find the entry "Grant, Ulysses S., Diary, November 1863" and an alphanumeric symbol such as "CWUSG1163, A-1." You enter this code into the computer, and in five seconds or less, the first page of Grant's diary for November 1863 appears on your screen. To view subsequent pages, you merely press appropriate numbers or letters on the keyboard.

The code you entered on the terminal was sent to the central filing system of the library. This central file may be in the same building, in another building, in another part of town, or even in another state. The code was converted to a signal that rapidly scanned filed microfiche until it found the card with the matching code. That card was conveyed to an automatic microfiche reader, and the image was transmitted back to your terminal. Using the same method, doctors can retrieve a patient's X rays and other medical records from a hospital's central filing system almost instantly.

Computer-assisted retrieval systems are extremely important to many businesses. Documents can be retrieved and viewed at

Computer-assisted retrieval (CAR) gives instant access to files.

terminals at almost any location as long as the terminals are electronically linked to the central file system. A CAR system can locate your files that may be stored in several formats—hard copies, microforms, magnetic, or other media—because it uses the same filing system for all types of media.

The key to a CAR system is organization. Thus, once you have your files organized and each location is coded—whether it is a frame on a roll of microfilm or a manila folder in a box in a warehouse—the computer simply searches for the code that represents the location for the document you want.

A CAR system is based on the computer's ability to search through and manipulate great quantities of information in a fraction of the time it would take to do it by hand. This makes it possible to access and update files instantaneously, and it reduces filing time and cost. In some instances, this may mean that you can change your filing system in ways that previously might have been too costly and time-consuming to make it worth the trouble. You could use CAR, for example, to take advantage of the search and replace function in word processing.

Media Compatibility and Accessibility

Media conversion (changing one medium into another) makes it possible for many types of media to be easily accessed. Because information stored on most computer media is in digital form, conversion is becoming less of a problem than it has been in the past. Together, digitized records and image scanning technology have made it possible to transmit all types of records, even microfilm, from one computer to another.

The market for micrographics storage currently appears to have stabilized and is not expected to show significant gains in the near future. Not so with optical disk storage. Advances in optical disk technology are expected to boost sales of optical disk storage by 50 percent or more in the next few years. One of the drawbacks of optical disk storage is that it is still quite expensive. Also, the standards are not as well defined for optical disks as they are for micrographics.

Because of the advantages of micrographics and optical disk storage, it is possible that both technologies will continue to have important roles in helping businesses manage information. How information is managed will depend on the compatibility of various media and storage systems. If people are expected to access and use the wealth of information available, the conversion and transmission of media must be relatively easy, efficient, and cost-effective.

Database Management Systems

Information is now stored in greater quantities than ever before. Computers and mass storage have contributed to the storage—and fortunately, the retrieval—of information. The usefulness of information depends on how well it is organized so that it is quickly and easily accessible to anyone who needs it. The concept of a database arose out of this need. A **database** is a collection of related information stored so that it is available to many users for different purposes.

Computer databases use electronic filing systems with many cross-references that give you a tremendous number of ways to organize and retrieve data. A database is often designed to operate with a software program that can calculate "unknowns" from data that is already stored. For example, a program could determine the company's income tax payments using a database that contains its sales figures. A database can handle business inventory, accounting, and filing and use the information in its files to prepare summaries, estimates, and other reports. It can store newspaper articles, magazines, books, and games. There are computer databases that provide specialized information for highly select groups of users on almost any subject. In fact, a database may contain any information that can be keyboarded or inputted into a system.

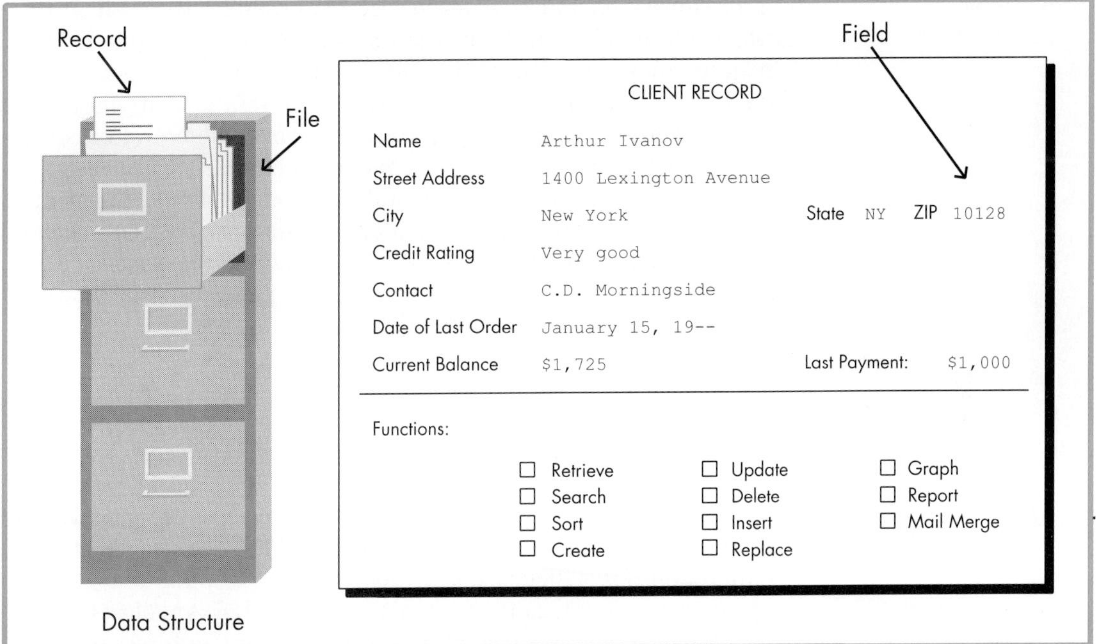

Record
File
Field
Data Structure
CLIENT RECORD
Name Arthur Ivanov
Street Address 1400 Lexington Avenue
City New York State NY ZIP 10128
Credit Rating Very good
Contact C.D. Morningside
Date of Last Order January 15, 19--
Current Balance $1,725 Last Payment: $1,000
Functions:
Retrieve
Search
Sort
Create
Update
Delete
Insert
Replace
Graph
Report
Mail Merge

The client record (right) is one record that makes up the file that is part of the database.

Of course, the key to accessing and using information is in the way a database is managed. A **database management system (DBMS)** is a combination of hardware and software that helps set up and maintain a database and manage access to and retrieval of information stored in it. You are already familiar with databases and some of their characteristics from the discussion about database software in Chapter 5. However, because databases, and especially DBMSs, are so important to the efficiency of an office, we will examine this area a little more closely here.

If you consider the way files are organized in a file cabinet, you have a good idea of a DBMS concept. For example, picture the common four-drawer office file cabinet. The cabinet itself is like a personal computer. What's inside is a database. Your videocassette tape collection is also a database. A **file** is a group of related pieces of information that are stored together. The cassette tapes in your videotape collection are your individual files. A **record**, a collection of information, would be the information contained on each tape in your collection by individual recording stars. A **field** is a single item of information, such as the song selection, orchestral arrangement, composer, accompanist, or catalog number. If you are familiar with manual filing, you can think of a field as a single filing unit.

Database Characteristics

Many database features involve ease of use. Businesses sometimes avoid setting up computer databases because of the time it takes initially to enter information into them. However, information needed on a continuing basis and/or in different formats should be entered into a database that can be accessed with computer equipment. The process of accessing records and transferring data by hand is not efficient. It is slow and thus can be costly. Creating a document by manual transfer of data is more susceptible to errors than generating a report by computer. When the same data is needed by several people for different purposes, the most timely and efficient access to that information is probably through a database.

Online Databases and Database Information Services

Most businesses have several databases, each set up for a specific purpose. Many of these are created by a business for its own use. Businesses also may get information from commercial databases created by database publishers. (These databases are entirely different from the applications software for managing a database with a microcomputer discussed in Chapter 5.)

According to Cuadra Associates, Inc., of Los Angeles, California (database specialists), about 2000 database publishers create and produce databases that can be used by others, usually on a fee basis. Some of these databases are accessed through one of the nearly 600 companies that provide database services. An **online database** or **information service** is a provider or supplier of access to one or more databases. Some information services create their own databases in addition to providing access services. Businesses or individuals who subscribe to such services can access these commercial online databases through a modem that connects a computer terminal via a telephone line to the specific database.

Some commercial databases are considered statistical and consist of information such as economic statistics, stock market prices, and population figures. Others have complete document, text-based files (sometimes called **full-text** databases) and contain such information as newspaper articles, court decisions, patents, or other documents that are indexed and cross-referenced according to key words.

Most databases are structured with a similar purpose—to make information easily accessible to as many users as possible. Just about any kind of information you can think of is stored in a database somewhere. Gaining access to it by a modem can save you hours of searching in a library of printed documents—if, indeed, it even exists in a conventional library. In fact, you might think of commercial online databases as libraries at your fingertips.

The *Directory of Online Databases*, a Cuadra/Elsevier publication of databases, is updated quarterly. Over the past several

Database Characteristics

A good database management system will have several common features or characteristics which make the system useful to the people accessing it. Some of these basic features include:

1. Once files are created, selected data (information) may be added, modified, or deleted. Entire files also may be created, added, or modified.
2. Any of the information in the database may be retrieved at will, either selectively or collectively.
3. Records may be sorted or indexed at the user's direction and discretion.
4. Reports may be produced in formats that are predetermined (standard) and/or user-defined.
5. Forms may be modified and developed by the user without having to program the commands for using the form.
6. Mathematical functions can be performed, and data can be moved and manipulated.
7. Files can be rearranged without affecting the existing data.
8. Macros (saving or programming several keystrokes as a single keystroke) may be used in customizing a database to the user's needs.
9. Security measures may be set up to limit only authorized users to access part or all of a database.
10. Good manuals, on-screen help features and tutorials, and menus for selecting database operations may contribute to the system's user-friendliness and to its usefulness.

years there has been steady growth in the number and type of online databases, services, and publishers available for business and individual use. For example, in 1979, there were about 400 computer databases, 59 of which were online. By 1995, it is estimated that nearly 5000 online databases will exist. Here are brief descriptions of the leading current online services and/or databases:

- Dialog. For sheer quantity, Dialog has more text and information of all types available than any other database service in the world. It has more than 500 databases containing information ranging from art history to zoology.
- NewsNet Inc. NewsNet Inc. provides over 300 databases of full text newsletters. While the newsletters are mainly business oriented, the databases serve all types of people. Some of the newsletter databases include Nation's Schools Report, Air/Water Pollution Report, and Telecommunications Week.
- Data Resources Inc. (DRI). DRI is the largest computer-accessible database of numeric and statistical information. The vast

store of worldwide demographic, industrial, scientific, and economic information that it provides is used by many analysts in industry, government, and finance.

- Dow Jones News/Retrieval. Dow Jones provides business and financial news and statistics from databases compiled by Dow Jones's news services and publications, including *The Wall Street Journal*. It also offers price quotations on more than 6000 stocks and other securities.
- Lexis and Westlaw. These are the two leading databases for legal information. They help lawyers find court rulings that support their arguments. Their databases store the full text of many court opinions and decisions, statutes, regulations, legal documents, and other government administrative materials. Westlaw also provides legal analysis of court decisions.
- Medline. Physicians use Medline to diagnose rare diseases and develop treatments. Medical researchers also rely on this database for published research providing a wide range of medical information. Medline contains articles published since 1966 in over 3400 medical journals.
- Nexis. This Mead Data Central, Inc., database service has a medical information database service similar to Medline. It also stores the complete text of *The New York Times*. It offers other newspaper articles and magazine articles, the *Encyclopaedia Britannica*, government records, Federal Reserve regulations, and presidential documents. Financial, political, and scientific data also are available, including a patent library.
- Knowledge Index. This online service is a modest and less expensive version of Dialog. Knowledge Index is designed for smaller businesses and home use. Available only nights and weekends (non–prime-time hours), when telephone rates are the lowest, it offers current news through *Standard & Poor's*. Its magazine index contains about 450 popular periodicals.
- Bibliographic Retrieval Service (BRS). This database service is popular even though it has less stored information than the Dialog/Knowledge Index databases. It has many other advantages, especially its After Dark service, which capitalizes on evening telephone rates. BRS is designed for use by businesses that do not maintain computer databases or a library.

The databases and database services described in the preceding section originally were designed for use by companies, professional organizations, and libraries with heavy research needs. With CD-ROM technology, the push for database services is slowing down and the expensive online databases are becoming more accessible to the general public.

Online information services can give you keyboard access to business, educational, recreational, and personal information at a moderate cost. Two leading online services are CompuServe and The Source. The fees for subscribing to each are low enough to make them practical for home use.

Both CompuServe and The Source offer the leading news services (Associated and United Press International); *The Washington Post*; quick updates on news, weather, and sports; and numerous electronic libraries of articles on major topics of interest. CompuServe stores ten years of daily stock market data. You can check historic and current stock prices; with links to participating databases, you can even invest right from the keyboard. These services also offer other kinds of data, including hobby-oriented information ranging from hot air ballooning to quiltmaking. In some cases, a **conference board** or a "computer chat" is available for exchanging information with someone about a specific topic.

You can make travel arrangements through CompuServe and The Source by accessing the *Official Airlines Guide* (OAG). Several other databases provide many other types of information to help you plan a trip to nearly any destination. Because both services offer CompuStore, you can shop at your keyboard, too, ordering from thousands of products 24 hours a day, 7 days a week.

Databases and services such as BRS are ideal for college students and others doing research. For example, you might want to search a database such as ERIC (Educational Resources Information Center) for information on a term paper topic. The wide range of BRS databases includes business/financial, science and medicine, reference, education, social sciences, and humanities. BRS also has the complete list of *Books in Print*.

Bulletin Board Services

A **bulletin board service (BBS),** like any local or community bulletin board, is used for everything from announcements, schedules, and notices to local chatter. Many companies have their own computer bulletin boards, which list descriptions and prices of products and services. Computer hardware and software companies run bulletin boards that sometimes, as an incentive for you to continue calling, offer free software that you can download. You may contribute to a BBS as well as be a part of a conference board or forum—all from your desktop personal computer.

Managing Information in an Information System

Information storage and retrieval is a vital stage in the total information processing cycle. It is not enough just to generate useful

Considerations in Setting Up an Efficient Records System

1. What volume of records does the office generate?
2. Which records have only a temporary use?
3. Which records are permanent?
4. Which records must be updated frequently?
5. What type of security system is needed for records access?
6. What government regulatory standards apply to the office (such as the IRS or Federal Communications Commission)?
7. What backup and disaster recovery methods need to be considered?
8. How often are certain records needed by employees or customers?
9. Do the records lend themselves to a specific form of storage medium (paper, microfilm, magnetic tape, or hard, floppy, and optical disks)?
10. How much space is available for storing records?
11. In view of how frequently or how quickly people need access to the records, what system of retrieval seems best—manual, mechanical, electronic?

information. It must be easily accessible, or valuable time is lost. An efficient records management system can result in more efficient and more productive employees.

An effective **Management Information System (MIS)** depends on organized management of personnel, equipment, and other resources as well as records. As part of an MIS, an efficient records system cuts down on the amount of time it takes to get necessary information. This time can be used for other office tasks and more creative activities.

An efficient records system does not just happen. To create one, you need to take a careful look at the kinds of records an office has and how they are used.

There is more to records management than keeping related information together, in alphabetical order, by category. If more than one medium is used for storage, there are other considerations. The most important of these is how to keep useful information available to the people who need it. With office space continually rising in cost, it often pays to separate timely and temporary from permanent information.

Centralized Records Management

Company records that are stored in one place are referred to as a **centralized records management system**. Frequently, the central location of records is referred to as the file room or the records section. A central system is usually managed by a small staff of employees who control access to records, file and update records, handle requests for records, and keep track of the flow of records in and out of the centralized area. Usually there is a system for retrieving files that may involve filling out forms and going to a special document viewing area.

The central records area in large companies often has automated or electronic equipment to speed storing, updating, and retrieving information. Such equipment may include cameras, mechanical filing systems, COM recorders, readers, reader/printers, photocopiers, and even microcomputers.

To assure that all records are where they belong when an office employee needs them, the original document never leaves the records area in most centralized systems. A clerk may make a copy of a document to be sent to a person who requests it. Or an image of the document may be sent electronically to a terminal of the person requesting the information. A centralized records system creates career positions in the field of records management. The staff needed in such a center is composed of people who specialize in records management and micrographics.

Decentralized Records Management

Records may be maintained in several areas throughout the company in a **decentralized records management system**. Every company department, for example, may have its own filing system. A decentralized system can be as simple as a plastic box of floppy disks or a carousel of microfilm cassettes on someone's desk.

Most companies use some combination of centralized and decentralized storage. Many businesses store duplicate sets of all but the most current files at more than one location as a form of disaster insurance.

Records Inventory and Retention

Periodically, every business should conduct a **records inventory** to determine what kinds of records are being retained. That is, it is useful to know what records are currently being used and which ones are infrequently accessed from storage. A records inventory does not mean that every document needs to be counted. It is a general inventory to determine if changes are needed in the **records management system**. A records inventory can be helpful in determining **records retention** and **destruction schedules** for controlling the length of time records are stored.

Records have to be stored for as long as they are needed. Most companies have a records retention schedule that specifies how long certain documents should be held. The length of time a document is stored may be entirely a management decision, or it may depend on government regulations. When there is no further use for files stored on magnetic and other types of media, they can be erased.

Usually, some documents should be **archived** or stored permanently. Archived records include historical records, company charters and legal papers, fiscal and general accounting records, and documents that are truly vital to the organization. Archived documents are frequently stored away from the general company files. Some businesses archive records in vaults in another city or state.

A **records disaster recovery plan** is important in case vital business records are destroyed or accessed without authorization. Security and archiving methods depend on how important the records are to the survival of an organization.

People and Electronic Records Management

Although generating and storing information are easy with computerized equipment, retrieving documents can be a nightmare, especially if we expect automated office equipment to work magic with a poor filing system. Businesses and organizations of every size are generating documents with all types of computer equipment. Without an orderly filing system, documents are not updated on a timely basis or are unavailable when you need them. If only one person knows where a document is filed and that person is not in the office when a document is needed, the information is not retrievable. When information cannot be retrieved, business, customers, and goodwill are lost. For these reasons, companies need to develop filing systems to match their increased information processing capabilities.

With the amount of equipment available to businesses, most organizations cannot be without even a simple **electronic filing system**. In such a system, documents can be cross-referenced in a number of ways so they can be easily retrieved by many people who use the system. In the most basic electronic filing system, records should be coded or classified with such identifying information as document name or number, author, creation date, retention date, and location. More sophisticated **decision support systems (DSS)** or information management systems for managing spreadsheets and databases are becoming popular with businesses. Businesses are finding DSS software an excellent tool to standardize their procedures in an organized way.

Standardizing procedures for filing documents is essential regardless of how documents are created. If you are using a word processor or a computer to create and store documents, you will find that following a standardized system is a good way to create, maintain, and store your records. Certainly, accessing your files and databases will be much easier if you have a set of standards for the entire information processing cycle.

The Future of Management Information Systems

Technology has provided advanced equipment for everyone in the office to participate in the information processing cycle at optimum efficiency. Fully integrated information management will continue to speed up and simplify the passage of information from one step in the information processing cycle to another. The most useful equipment will be designed to accept information in any form from any user and transmit it instantly to any user in a compatible medium. Compatibility and connectivity will become less important issues as ways are found to access information that now may be inaccessible.

Managing information has become a science. Management Information Systems (MISs) have evolved into complicated and intertwined combinations of planning, organizing, and controlling automated equipment, resources, and records. As more and more people need to access greater amounts of information for decision making, networks will take on new meaning. Local area networks will link electronic filing systems and computer-assisted retrieval. The optical disk and other media will emerge in the years ahead to make sophisticated database management a reality even for small businesses. Online information services will give us easy access to greater amounts of information.

People who choose a career in any one of these areas will find it a challenge to create innovative capabilities to efficiently manage vast amounts of information. The advances in all areas of technology promise a great future for information systems. Coordinating the fully integrated electronic office into a system for information management is a goal that is both realistic and reachable.

CHAPTER SUMMARY

- Information is a business resource to be managed and protected.
- A good storage and retrieval system can result in more efficient and more productive employees.
- Information can be stored on paper, magnetic media, laser disk, or film.
- Magnetic media require considerably less storage space than paper for the same amount of information.
- Solid-state storage is a fixed storage device that includes RAM chip boards and bubble memory.
- Optical disks and holography are two types of laser or light storage.
- Optical disks use laser technology to store a tremendous amount of data in a fraction of the space used by magnetic media.
- You can convert a picture or other graphic information into digitized bits with image processing equipment and then store or print the image on a computer.
- Mass storage is a collection or a library of storage media.

- Micrographics is the process of photographically reducing text and graphic images and recording them on film. Most of the space (95 to 98 percent) needed for storing paper records can be saved by putting the records on microforms.
- Microforms include microfilm, microfilm jackets, aperture cards, microfiche, micro-opaques, and ultrafiche.
- Microfilm can be stored on rolls or reels, cassettes, or cartridge magazines. Microforms can be coded in various ways to make storage and retrieval efficient.
- Microfiche can contain more than 420 pages of documents on a 4-by-6-inch card. Microfiche can be made directly from computer data by a process known as computer output microfilm (COM).
- A microform reader converts microimages to the size of the original document or larger by means of lenses and mirrors. Hard copies of microforms can be produced by means of a reader/printer.
- No matter how a document is stored—on paper, microform, or a magnetic medium—it can be retrieved electronically with computer-assisted retrieval (CAR).
- A computer database uses an electronic cross-referenced filing system to give users many ways to access information.
- The hardware and software for setting up and maintaining a database is called a database management system (DBMS).
- Database services make database information available to subscribers for a fee. Access to an online database is through a modem connected to a computer and a telephone.
- An online database or information service provides access to one or more databases. Many online database services are inexpensive enough for private individuals and smaller businesses to use.
- Subscribers pay for the time they are connected to an online information service. Online database services offer a virtual supermarket of business, professional, recreational, and personal information and services.
- An online service to exchange current and useful information by modem communication is called a bulletin board service (BBS).
- In a centralized office records system, company records are stored in one area. In a decentralized system, they are stored in several different areas.
- There are many advantages to using an electronic filing system or decision support system (DSS). Documents can be cross-referenced in a number of ways by name or number, author, creation date, retention date, and storage location.

- Easy document access and retrieval can be accomplished by following standard filing procedures.
- Conducting a records inventory can help a business develop records retention and disaster recovery plans that may be crucial to its survival.
- Using electronic equipment for records storage and transmission can contribute to an integrated, efficient, and cost-effective system for information management.

VOCABULARY

aperture card
archived
Bernoulli Box
bubble memory
bulletin board service (BBS)
compact disk–read only memory (CD-ROM)
computer-assisted retrieval (CAR)
computer output microfilm (COM)
database
database management system (DBMS)
decision support system (DSS)
electronic filing system
electronic imaging
erasable optical disks
field
file
film jacket
fixed disk
head crash
holography
magneto-optical disks
Management Information System (MIS)
mass storage
media conversion
microfiche
microfilm
microform
micrographics
micro-opaque
online database or information service
optical (laser) disk
RAM chips board
reader/printer
record
records disaster recovery plan
records inventory
records management system
records retention schedule
solid-state storage
ultrafiche
unitized microform
WORM disks

CHAPTER QUESTIONS

1. Why is paper sometimes less desirable than other storage media? Why would magnetic or film media be a more likely choice than paper for a storage and retrieval system?
2. What are some of the advantages of desktop storage units for magnetic and film media?
3. What are the advantages of optical disk storage? How might the use of optical disks for filing help a company that is pressed for office space?

4. How can microforms increase the information-handling capability of most offices?
5. What function is performed by a microfilm or microfiche reader? Under what conditions might an office manager choose just a reader for the office microforms instead of a reader/printer?
6. Why should microforms be indexed and labeled?
7. What advantage does COM have over other forms of producing microfilm or microfiche?
8. What are two types of databases? Give an example of a type of related information that could be grouped in a database, and describe how you would organize a database management system for this information. Give an example of how commercial databases may add to a company's own database resources.
9. What advantages does a centralized records system offer? What advantages does a decentralized records system offer?
10. Describe the importance of a good records management system. List some essential characteristics for efficient information storage and retrieval.

CASE STUDY

Southern Washington State University has an enrollment of 25,000 students on four separate campuses. Each campus has its own administration office that keeps records on all students on such matters as financial aid, academic achievement, entrance exam scores, grades transferred from other colleges and universities, and extracurricular activities. The offices also keep records on faculty members, including such information as health insurance, tenure status, and publications.

When students transfer to other schools or apply to graduate schools, the university provides copies of their records to the other schools.

SWSU maintains an alumni association of 10,000 graduates, to whom it mails a monthly newsletter. The newsletter is compiled from information provided by faculty and alumni. Some of this information is included in faculty and alumni records once it is printed in the newsletter.

SWSU also has a large library system with a central branch on the main campus and small branches at the other three campuses. The library has copies of scholarly publications, including master's and doctoral theses, which are sometimes requested by journal editors and researchers for reference or publication. The library subscribes to many publications and to several newspapers. Recently, it was given a private collection of old books and letters from a famous alumnus. The library would like to make these books and letters available to students and faculty but is concerned about damage.

The university has been suffering from staff cutbacks and increasing demands for information from various sources. Most of its documents are paper, stored in vertical files and boxes. The campuses are running out of storage space. Despite budgetary problems, school officials are exploring the possibility of an electronic storage and retrieval system.

From what you have learned in this chapter, what kinds of equipment and what systems of records management would you recommend?

CHAPTER 9

Integrated Information Systems

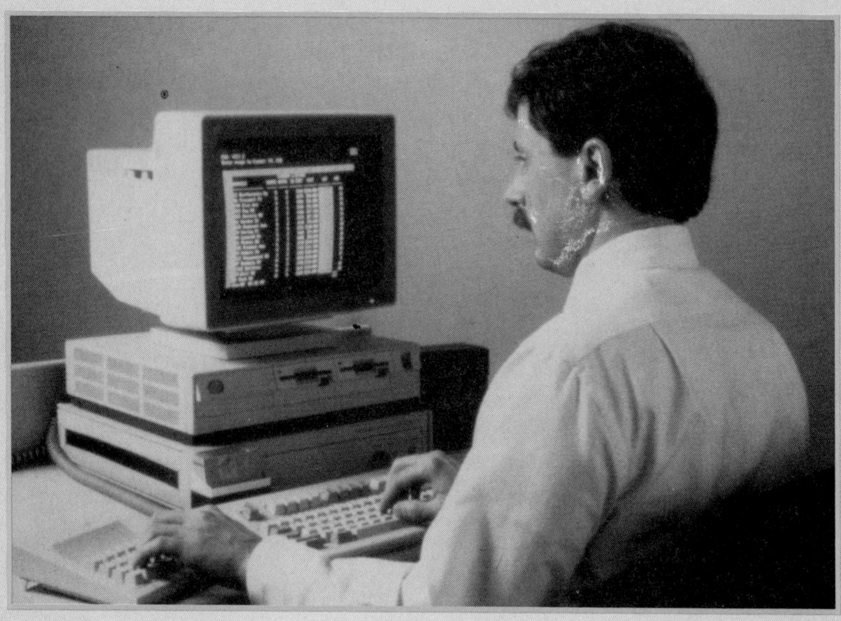

Peter Nugent's workstation is part of a shared logic system in the information processing center at Marvell Associates. Marvell also has a computer system used for payroll and other financial functions in its Accounting Department. Presently, if Mr. Nugent needs information about a financial aspect of the company for a report, he requests a computer printout from Accounting, scans it for the figures he needs, then keys them into his report. Marvell is considering integrating the data and word processing systems. If the company had an integrated system, Mr. Nugent could obtain financial data as easily as he accesses the databases for word processing. Mr. Nugent realizes that, to be productive, he needs to learn more about integrated systems.

For an information system to be effective, all its parts must be integrated. That is, all elements involved in daily business operations must work together or interact for a company to produce a product or service. Although this sounds simple, it frequently involves teamwork and networking, which can be complex. Accomplishing the organization's goal depends on the flow of the information processing cycle.

A breakdown in any phase of the information processing cycle (inputting, processing, storing and retrieving, outputting, and distributing and communicating) can have negative results. An information system depends on an effective integrated network of people, procedures, and equipment.

A Systems Approach

Computer technology has provided a tremendous challenge for many businesses to choose the right office systems, products, and services to automate their offices. For example, a few years ago, manufacturers introduced personal computers without giving businesses enough of an idea of what they were for or how to use them. In addition, corporations that already had word processing in one department and data processing in another found it difficult to justify the added cost of replacing their equipment with an office system that would integrate both. Because of automation, vast amounts of information became accessible; how to access it was a growing concern. Today any business that is competitive needs an integrated information system and can benefit from a systems approach to accomplish its work.

When offices are automated, many types of equipment, each performing a different function, may be joined electronically. An individual user at one terminal can have access to information from, and communicate with, any other user at a terminal connected to the system anywhere in the world. Office equipment connected in this way is called an **integrated information system** (or **integrated office system**). An effective information system is an integrated information system. (See Chapter 1 for definitions of information systems and information processing.) Looking at the office as a whole—the sum of all the parts integrated as a system—is called a **systems approach**.

The Importance of Systems Integration

Within an information system, the systems approach looks at individual tasks and how they fit with other related tasks. In word processing, for example, keying a document is only one step in the information processing cycle. The document also is stored; and it may be copied, mailed, or communicated electronically. The systems approach helps us look at how employees and equipment interrelate so that a company can make the best use of both resources—personnel and equipment.

Office managers sometimes refer to a systems approach as **systems integration**, **information resource management**, **networking**, or **office automation**. Systems integration does not mean just installing some advanced equipment. The equipment must be interconnected so that people working in the office can work with it and share information efficiently.

Interconnecting equipment into a system is not always easy. The computer industry still has some major hurdles with compatibility. In general, standards usually restrict and define limits; however, the limits usually increase accessibility for more users. For example, can you imagine what might happen if we didn't have standards for floppy disk sizes? How useful would the most sophisticated software be if its operating system were not accepted by the hardware? What if a facsimile machine in one office were not compatible with that in another? Standards are not only useful; they are necessary. The development of industry standards helps ensure compatibility.

Why Businesses Need Integrated Systems to Stay Effective

- Competition from other developed nations is putting pressure on U.S. companies to raise productivity.
- Office automation has become commonly accepted and is being utilized by top executives and decision makers at all levels.
- Integrating computer technology into everyday business operations is vitally important to most businesses.
- Growing numbers of office workers are using electronic equipment to accomplish everyday work tasks.
- People in general are becoming more and more computer literate and as a result are demanding more services.
- Businesses are demanding technology-related products and services that meet real business needs; they are not satisfied with whatever vendors provide or supply.
- Industry standards are being developed for office systems to be compatible among different manufacturers.
- The cost of automation is decreasing as the technology becomes more available.
- Information access is prompting the integration of office operations; thus, separate departments such as data processing, word processing, telecommunications, and even reprographics are being combined into a total system.

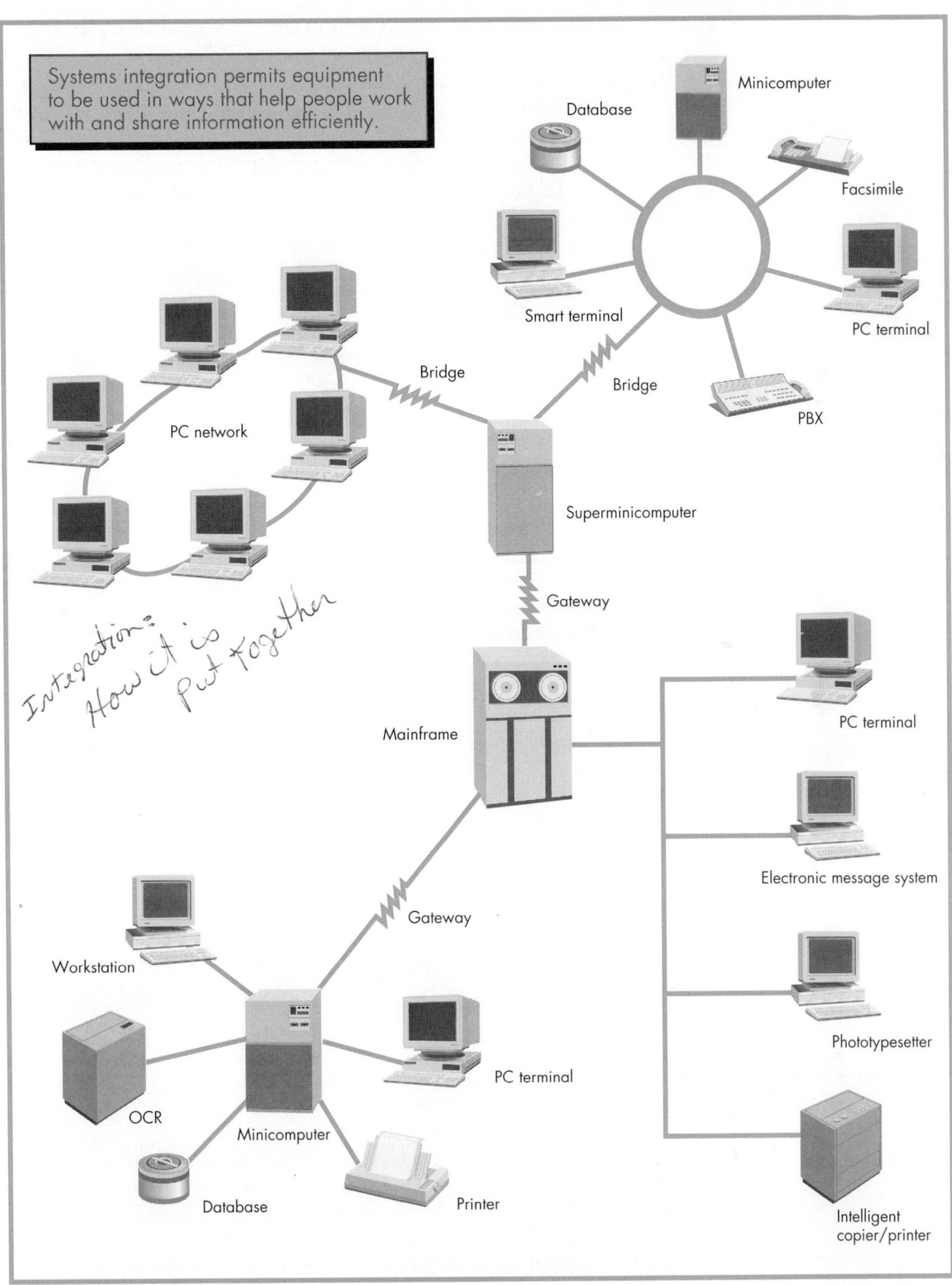
Systems integration permits equipment to be used in ways that help people work with and share information efficiently.
Database
Minicomputer
Facsimile
Smart terminal
PC terminal
PBX
Bridge
Bridge
PC network
Superminicomputer
Gateway
Integration: How it is put together
Mainframe
PC terminal
Electronic message system
Gateway
Workstation
Phototypesetter
PC terminal
OCR
Minicomputer
Database
Printer
Intelligent copier/printer

As time goes on, greater equipment compatibility is inevitable. Many components, including networks and interfaces, will help lessen this problem. Corporations are capitalizing on networks for linking all types of systems—from personal computers to minis and mainframes. The key is being able to access and interchange information among existing and added components.

For example, many corporations link a PC directly to a mainframe. The link can be as automatic as calling up a program stored in your computer. What happens may be illustrated as follows: The user who needs information from the mainframe keyboards in the request. The mainframe software finds the information in its database. The information is put into an intermediate file, called a notepad or **clipboard**. The program reformats the clipboard file so it is compatible with the personal computer software. At that point, any secretary or executive can download or transfer the information and use it with a PC spreadsheet, database, word processing, or other applications program.

Your Role in Systems Integration

On a day-to-day basis, most of us are concerned primarily with doing our own job. It may be to communicate more effectively with seven branch offices or to fax a ten-page report to the company headquarters across the country. We know we need accurate and precise information to make decisions. Our perspective often may not go beyond the limit of our own desk. Yet understanding how systems are integrated is important for everyone. Seeing how office systems interrelate will help you use the equipment effectively to access, generate, communicate, and manage information.

Of course, every office worker need not have access to every bit of information a company has generated or stored in a computer system. But it is important to keep in mind the overall interaction of equipment and systems. Interaction, integration, and connectivity will only increase as we move into the future. No piece of equipment or person in an office is isolated. You and the equipment you use are part of some type of integrated information system. In the systems approach to office automation, every bit of information, every task, every piece of equipment, and every person relates to all the others.

Your Workstation

Interrelatedness will take on greater significance with each new development that makes computer equipment more powerful, sophisticated, and versatile. As manufacturers find new capabilities to build into office equipment, we will find workstations (a separate category of computer equipment that can be similar or identical to some supermicros) designed more precisely to meet users' needs. The definition of a workstation continues to change as hardware gets more powerful and sophisticated. But many people refer to an office worker's entire work area, including the desk and equipment, as a workstation. Thus, for all practical purposes, secretarial and **executive workstations** may be whatever the users (frequently specialists and managers) need to perform work tasks in an information system.

Linked Equipment

For some employees, an executive workstation may include a word processor, a personal computer, or a "dumb" terminal that is linked to other equipment in the user's work area. The linking of equipment provides the user with multifunctioning and networking capabilities. The purpose of the executive workstation is to place within reach as much information as the employee needs to function effectively—whether it be through one piece of equipment or several pieces linked.

Many executive workstations provide the user with a variety of useful and interesting software for performing a wide range of functions. Software can make a workstation easy to use if "help" screens are incorporated into the programs. A help screen or menu provides detailed information to assist in making a decision on what step to take next. A help menu may take up several screens. To bring it onto the screen, you merely touch one or two keys. After reading the help screen, you press one key to make it disappear and are instantly returned to the screen you were working on. Help screens are useful to many computer users. Software with

An integrated information system includes workers, as well as the information and equipment they use.

The windowing feature available with many software programs enables a user to access several files at the same time.

help screens that permit a user to choose a function without extensive keyboarding are becoming more and more popular with executives and others who have limited keyboarding skill.

A workstation usually will have or support windowing capabilities. This allows a user to access several sources at the same time. **Windowing** is a feature of many software programs that may permit a user to work with several files at one time (**multitasking**) without having to exit and store each file. For example, a calendar may be brought to the screen while a report is being keyed. The report is kept in the background as you look at or change the calendar. **Calendaring** can give you a built-in alarm to remind you ahead of time when you have an appointment or something to do. If someone makes an appointment with you and it conflicts with your schedule, the computer will let you know.

Electronic phone directories and notebooks are two more examples of how windowing can be useful for a personal management workstation. An **electronic phone directory** enables you to keep your own personal list of phone numbers on a disk. Touching one key automatically dials the phone number. With an **electronic notebook**, you can interrupt whatever program you are working on and key a random thought into a separate file. Then, with a single key, you can return to your original program. You can forward items from calendar and notebook programs to a colleague by electronic mail, making it easy to schedule meetings. Other features include an electronic dictionary, other types of schedule planning, and personal filing.

Some workstations support more than one operating system, several programming languages, and graphics. Some support **computer-aided applications** such as computer-aided instruction (CAI) and computer-aided design (CAD), engineering (CAE), manufacturing (CAM), and publishing (CAP). Other systems have a dictation capability. You can send a voice message along with a document, and it is replayed in your own voice at another location. Several devices and input methods (such as a mouse, digitizing tablet, light pen, and touch-sensitive screen) are available to make workstations user-friendly.

Workstation users may access information from a CPU or mainframe, often called the **host system**. Being able to tap into every information area of company operations is important to top executives. Executives and managers need quick access to information in a readable, usable form from a great many sources. By having access to a wide range of information and the documents of many authors, an executive can manipulate raw data and create a report.

As voice processing is improved, more and more executives (especially those with limited keyboarding skills) can use dictation as input that a computer can translate into a document as easily as an OCR now reads a printed page. For example, a workstation user may input original information and extract data from several databases. It can be manipulated into a graphics presentation that may include some image processing. Then it can be transferred to other computer systems via one or more networks.

The Focus on Integrated Processing

Workstations, networking, and communications will take on even more importance as all types of inputs and outputs become more easily processed. One technology that has speed, flexibility, and accuracy for handling text, music, voice, images, and codes is **digital signal processing (DSP)** which changes or converts all signals to ones and zeros (digital form) to manipulate all types of information. Because a computer recognizes only digital signals, DSP has some important implications for integrated processing of text, data, voice, graphics, and images. Integrated processing offers multiple capabilities for information access and transmission. The key to integrating applications is providing fast, easy access to several types of networks and transmission methods that permit person-to-person, person-to-group, group-to-group, person-to-computer, and computer-to-computer communications.

No doubt the executive workstation will continue to be attractive for businesses because of its nearly limitless capabilities. Businesses will find these systems cost-effective, mainly because of a wide range of hardware and software precisely designed to match the information needs of employees at every level, from management to support personnel.

The Integrated Information Processing Cycle

An information system involves everything we have talked about thus far. Information processing (with or without computer technology) is central to an information system. Information processing can help businesses be efficient and effective with office automation equipment. Because information processing encompasses all the business and technical operations of an information system, integrating operations makes sense. Thus, integration takes on new meaning as we look again at the five stages of the information processing cycle:

1. Input
2. Processing
3. Storage and retrieval
4. Output
5. Distribution and communications

The way the information processing cycle operates can differ from one office to another. For example, one office may use pencil and paper for input; another may use dictation equipment. One type of information may be stored on magnetic media, another on microfilm, and another on optical disks. Whatever equipment and media are used, the goal is to make the office a more productive place. The information processing cycle is flexible. We have streamlined information processing so effectively that if "lines" separate one step of the cycle from another, they are blurred.

As office systems and communications evolve, information is no longer processed in the simple cycle described at the beginning of this book. This point is shown in the expanded illustration of the information processing cycle below. Each information processing phase is greatly affected by computer technology. The success of information processing, then, depends on how well each of its various parts is interconnected and integrated.

Multiuser Integrated Systems

Information processing involves several stages, sequenced procedures, and sometimes numerous people from document origination to its use for decision making. Networks can contribute to the ease in developing and processing a document. Networks or integrated systems usually permit databases to be accessed by more than one person at a time. Because many computer networked operations of a business can occur simultaneously, we frequently call an integrated system a **multiuser system**. Thus, a computer network (both LANs and WANs) is usually an integrated system that permits several operations by multiple users to occur simultaneously. Multiuser integrated systems depend on networks, storage, and communications capabilities.

Computer-aided instruction (CAI) is a good example of how a multiuser integrated system might work. Let's say that a teacher uses CAI to reinforce math concepts with a class of students. Each student can progress through the math program software at his or her individual rate. Students who need more drill and practice may work more slowly than those who have already mastered the subject matter.

Teachers may ask students to store their responses to certain math problems. If they print the results of their work, they may make a few keystrokes to send their files to a printer. The hard copy is printed for each student as it is received by the printer. If the printer is busy printing another student's work, it **queues** (pronounced "cues") or puts the file in order for printing. (Printer queuing also allows for prioritizing printing orders.)

What is important in this example is that a network, storage, and communications may be used by several students at the same time. The main math CAI program is not altered even though it too is accessed by several students. Also, students in other classrooms may be using CAI for history; and staff in the school's Accounting Department could be working on several different parts of the school's financial operations. This simple example shows how important multiuser integrated systems can be for businesses—no matter how small.

Timesharing Services

Many large companies are finding that microcomputer networked or multiuser systems can meet their needs as effectively as the larger systems. Computer equipment decisions are frequently made on the standard of power and speed for the lowest possible cost. However, if an organization does not wish to purchase equipment large enough to provide the speed, storage, and capabilities it needs for information processing, it may instead subscribe to a

timesharing system. Subscribers may pay fees for using time accessed from equipment owned by another organization. Because the subscribers usually are physically removed from the equipment, telephone lines and other networks are used to gain access to it. A tracking system knows how much time each keyboard operator spends using the system, and the subscriber receives a bill, usually monthly, for the total time spent online.

Timesharing systems are used by many organizations that have branches scattered around the country. When the branches and the home office are sharing the same computer, their information processing workstations can communicate with each other. A **shared-tenant service** usually is a type of timesharing system that involves several businesses occupying a single building or building complex. Subscribers to a shared-tenant service can be provided integrated information and communications services. The landlord of the building provides these services in the same way as electricity, heat, maintenance, and security are provided to several tenants in a building. A few years ago, buildings that offered shared-tenant services were referred to as "smart" or "intelligent" buildings because many of their systems were controlled by microprocessors.

A drawback of a timesharing system is that sometimes the service provider oversells it. If too many keyboard operators are using the system, you may get busy signals when trying to reach the computer. Another drawback is the fact that timesharing systems may not be user-friendly for every end user. For example, special instructions must be followed to **log on** and log off the system. Otherwise, from the user's point of view, a timesharing system operates in much the same way as a shared logic system, except that it probably has more capacity and capability.

Computer System Maintenance

Maintenance usually is not a concern of the subscriber to a timesharing system, unless the service provider does not keep the equipment in working order. In most cases, service providers have their own in-house or within company maintenance staff to minimize equipment downtime. Maintenance is added to the cost of subscribing to the service. Many businesses with large computer systems also have developed their own maintenance capabilities. Other businesses that buy or lease smaller computer systems usually purchase service and warranty agreements from the vendor. Another option is a **third-party maintenance** service, which gets its name from the fact that companies that did not manufacture computer equipment originally provided it. Maintenance of computer equipment is a costly matter for most businesses. A service agreement can easily amount to an annual cost of 10 percent or more of the initial price of the equipment.

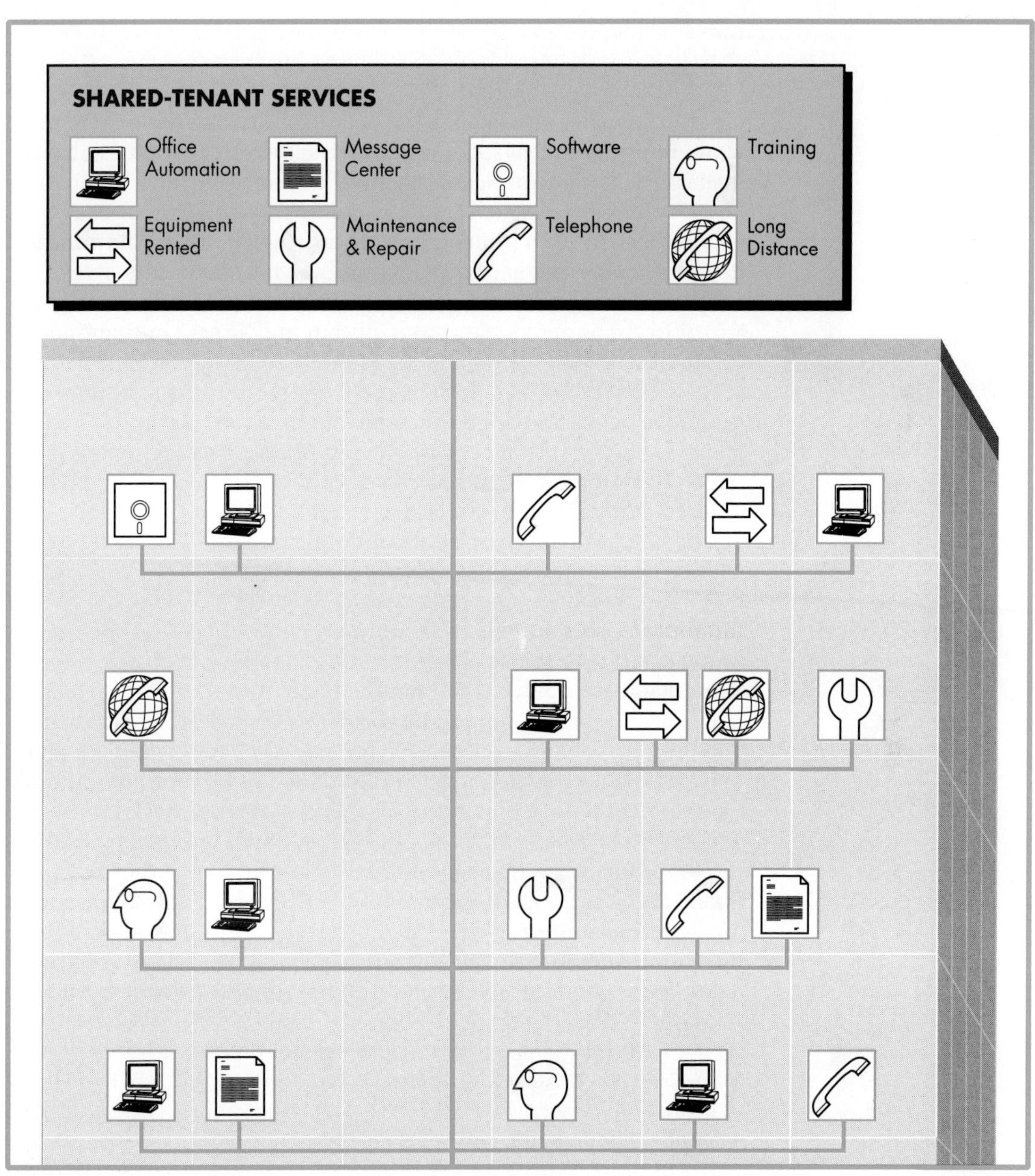

Shared-tenant service enables businesses occupying the same building or complex to share integrated information and communication systems.

Computer Security and Ethics

There are many advantages for organizations having totally integrated information systems. However, some safeguards usually are necessary to control access to information. One of a company's most valuable assets is its information, and most businesses take careful measures to protect their records, whatever media are used to store them. The security of computer information is a key element of information management. If an unauthorized person gains entry to a company's computer system and alters confidential information, the company can lose more than information.

Millions of dollars have been illegally transferred in the computers of banks and other financial and investment companies that store virtually all their records on computer-accessible media. In other instances, critical records have been lost because someone altered program commands that were central to operations. You should be aware of these problems and concerned about the security of your company's information.

Computer Crime

There are several types of **computer crime** (illegal use of a computer) and ways to use computer information unlawfully. Anyone who uses a computer is vulnerable to computer crime. Protecting computer information is as important as protecting paper files. In fact, it may be more so because you may not have as much control over who accesses the information you store in your computer as you do over who accesses the file cabinet by your desk.

As long as we have computers, we will probably have the threat of **viruses** ("damage-producing instructions" the computer reads and carries out). Viruses frequently are "planted" by someone adding or altering codes that can be harmful to your computer files and sometimes even to your hardware. An added or altered code in a program can create glitches in the program, causing

Some Kinds of Computer Crimes

- Copying information (including programs), frequently leaving the original intact
- Deleting from someone's files information valuable to the criminal or the business
- Changing or altering information in computer files
- Accessing files that are restricted to certain individuals
- Creating damage or implanting viruses (adding damage-causing codes to programs or software)
- Stealing money, information, or services

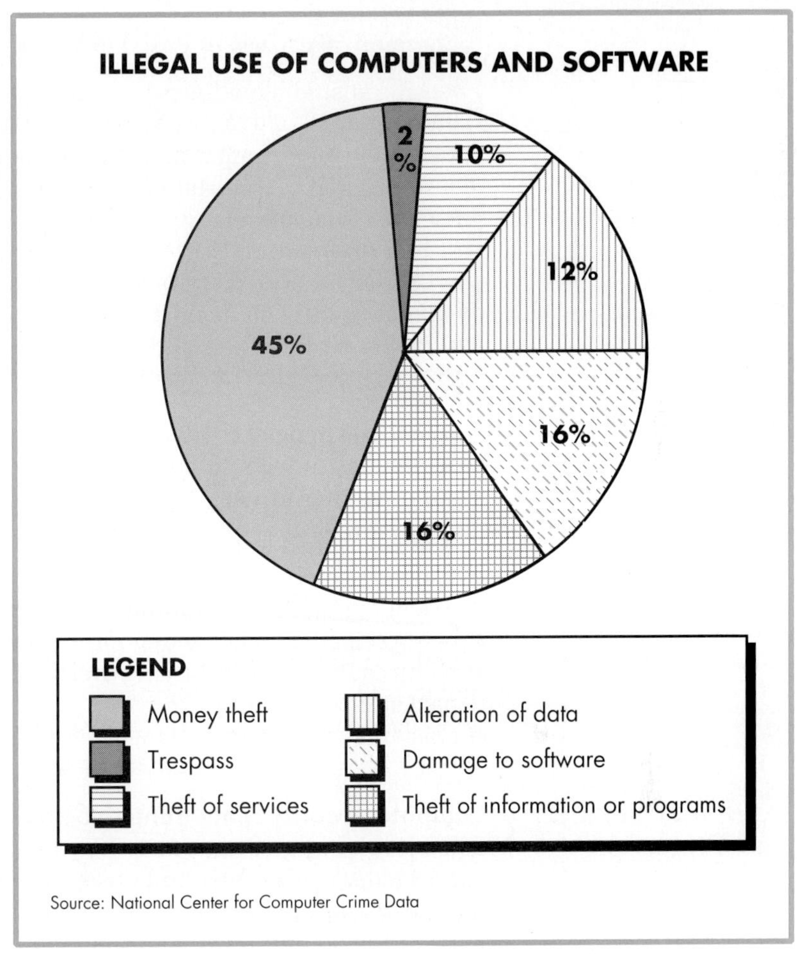

strange results from common operations. The presence of a virus sometimes shows up as frequent error messages on your screen. A virus may be like a "bug" or "worm" that finds its way into a part of a program and "eats away" or destroys your data. Other types of viruses may alter your files in some way each time they are accessed. Some viruses may erase entire programs and files.

Viruses are often planted by someone who is good at programming and breaking codes built into programs to protect files. There will always be people around who try to "break" or access protected programs. But there are ways to detect, avoid, and even "vaccinate" for viruses.

To combat these problems, members of the Computer Virus Industry Association and other software vendors are developing virus-detecting and antiviral software. Several software programs

Common Warnings of Possible Viruses

- An unusual slowdown in executing the operations of your computer
- Strange and frequent error messages appearing on your screen and at unusual places as you are working
- Other unusual changes occurring in operations as you process information
- Memory and disk storage appearing drastically reduced in an unusually short time
- Programs and files appearing unusually large or small

are available to detect viruses and to vaccinate against them. However, the best advice to computer users is to take precautions to avoid computer viruses. These include:

- limiting access to files
- making backup copies of files
- discouraging disk swapping
- being selective in accessing public bulletin boards
- being cautious about buying drastically reduced software packages
- checking for broken seals when buying software packages

Computer Security and Protection

Computer security is not limited to preventing crime, nor is it only a concern of large companies. Anyone using network services is susceptible, just as telephone users can be subjected to wiretaps and phonetaps. Because computer crime has become so widespread, the computer industry is seeking ways to help computer users with security as well as to control the nearly half a million viruses that creep into computer systems annually. Legislation has been initiated to promote computer security. For example, 1986 legislation brought about the **Computer Fraud and Abuse Act** to address many of the issues associated with computer crime. The 1986 **Electronic Communications Privacy Act** prohibits invasion of electronic mail. The 1976 **Federal Copyright Law** and related legislation restrict software copying just as there are restrictions for copying copyrighted materials.

Computer security involves other problems besides those criminal in nature. Computer system protection also is necessary because of environmental and related factors. There is a long list of dos and don'ts for software care (see Chapter 5). Many of the suggestions also apply to hardware security and protection. For example, place your computer away from direct sunlight, where temperatures can add significantly to the heat the system generates. Extreme cold, smoke, dust, and poor ventilation also should be avoided. Static caused by carpeting can be minimized by placing an antistatic mat under your desk. If you need to move your computer, follow the manufacturer's guidelines for doing so. Some computer systems are sensitive and need special handling if they are to be moved.

The biggest concern to many regular computer users may be the loss of information or system damage due to fluctuations in electrical power. You may have heard someone say that a computer system needs a "dedicated line" or its own electrical circuit. This is a good rule to follow. Having other equipment on the same circuit as your computer may cause changes in the power supply to your computer, resulting in the loss of information. Even more devastating may be an electrical surge or spike, which might be caused by a lightning storm. For a few dollars, you can add a **surge protector**, special power strip, or line protector to most systems to buffer power blasts that might not only destroy information, but burn out system circuitry.

In a similar manner, a loss of electricity while you are working on an important document can be devastating if you do not have your work stored. Storing information frequently and making backup copies are two of the best ways to combat this problem. Printing a document at predetermined times also will prevent the loss of great amounts of information. But remember that creating a pile of hard copy defeats one of the main advantages of your computer. If power loss is a real concern of yours, it may be worth the investment to purchase a standby or **uninterruptible power supply** (**UPS**) in case of a loss of electrical power while you are using your system. Uninterruptible power supplies range in price from a few hundred to several thousand dollars. The price is related to the standby supply operation time and the requirements of your system.

There are a few basic rules many companies follow in an attempt to avoid computer crime and to keep information securely protected.

Passwords and User IDs The use of passwords is common with many business computer systems. A **password** is a secret code assigned to each computer user. It can be an alphanumeric combination, unique to each user, that must be keyed in order to log on or gain access to a computer. Password letters and numbers do not appear on the screen.

Different employees in a company often have access to varying types and levels of computer information. In such a system with many terminals linked in a local area network (LAN), for example, each employee may be assigned a **user identification code**,

Recommendations for Avoiding Computer Crime and Keeping Information Protected

- Turn the system off when it is not in use.
- Install a lock that makes it impossible to use the system without a key.
- See that only authorized employees are given keys.
- Keep disk and other magnetic media files locked up.
- When the contents of a disk is confidential, do not label the disk with a description of its contents.
- Label disks with the owner's name.
- Put the company or firm name on a header or footer on every document—at least on the first and last pages.
- Include embedded errors in a document. Security consultants sometimes recommend that you intentionally include an occasional spelling error in a valuable document; thus, if a file is illegally printed or photocopied and not rekeyed, you can identify it.
- Make backup copies. Too often, nothing can replace information that is stolen, lost, or destroyed. Even if you have a hard copy and could scan or rekey information on disk if it is lost or stolen, it can save enormous amounts of time to keep at least one backup copy of every disk.
- Use an audit system. Monitor the use of your computer as closely as possible. There are software programs that keep a record of everyone who uses the computer, what time they sign on, and when they log off. Some programs even alert security officers if someone tries any unusual keyboarding procedures.
- Use passwords, user IDs, biometrics, and encryption measures for added security. (These are explained in the following section.)
- Change locks, passwords, and encryption codes whenever a key employee leaves the company or when security is threatened in any other way.
- Keep all company personnel informed of company security policies.
- Follow the company disaster and recovery plan.

or **user ID**, in addition to the password. Online information services also use passwords and give each subscriber an ID. After you key in the password that allows you entry into the system, you key your ID. This lets the system know more specifically whether you are entitled to use the system, whether you are an executive or administrative employee, what level of access you have, and what information you are permitted to access. Because passwords and user IDs are so vital to security, they are made as difficult as possible to decipher.

Another type of identification for computer security is called biometrics. **Biometrics** involves using devices that can identify some physical characteristics of authorized users. For example, your voice could be recorded as a **voice print** or a voice sample that is stored in the computer. Each time you log on the system, the computer compares the stored voice with a specified statement that you speak into a microphone of the computer. If the voice samples match, access is given to you. Some companies use biometric devices for fingerprints, palm or hand prints, retina scans, signatures, and writing samples. In some systems, the user's keying rhythm can be recorded and compared when logging onto the system.

Use of a special credit card or badge, sometimes with a microchip, is another security method for limiting computer access. The badge or credit card may be scanned or inserted into a device that reads it and permits or denies access. Because user cards, badges, and ID cards can be shared, they may not be as effective security measures as biometric devices. Another security alternative is to install automatic security systems that scan an area for movement. Surveillance cameras, for example, might be used to photograph people entering and exiting a restricted area. Other systems alert a central control area when movement occurs in a restricted area. Still other systems use a combination of photo, ID, and movement to record activity in an area.

This shows an encrypted message before and after decoding by the Datacryptor II.

No matter what system is used for access, the software of some systems is designed to give some users "read only" access to certain documents. This allows you to read a file but not to change it. Systems that provide **audit trails** or a record of users' activities (sometimes without the user knowing it) are popular with many businesses. Audit trails may be used to record only attempts to log on. In other cases, a computer record may be made of access, storing, copying, and naming of files.

Encryption Still more sophisticated measures of security are available to businesses that store and distribute highly confidential information. **Encryption** codes have been used by governments for thousands of years to keep valued information from getting into enemy hands in time of war. Various techniques are used for encryption. A typical encryption technique is to frequently switch the number of meaningless characters between the ones that count.

Companies often use software programs that change their encryption code automatically at preset intervals, such as once a week. To read encrypted files, a user must not only log on with a proper password and ID, but must use a special password to unscramble the secret code.

Software Piracy and Ethics

You may think that **software piracy** (copying or making unauthorized use of software) applies only to those who are known criminals and lawbreakers. Consider how Lucia Maldonado innocently became involved.

Ms. Maldonado has figured out the company's budget for the next quarter on her micro using Excel (a spreadsheet software program). She wants Gene Hayhurst in the Marketing Department to take a look at it. She feels he may want to comment on it or change the numbers. But Gene uses Lotus 1-2-3 on his personal computer, not Excel. Without a disk that contains the Excel program, he cannot run Lucia's budget on his computer. So she copies the Excel program disk. Then she prints out a copy of the budget and gives it to Gene, along with the Excel disk and the data disk that has the budget file stored on it.

Gene takes home the printout and the disks to work on the budget on his personal computer over the weekend. His son William is only in high school but already knows computers inside and out. William is fascinated by Excel. Gene makes a copy for William, who belongs to a bulletin board service. William tells all his friends on the BBS that he will send them Excel if they want to download it.

Before long a lawyer for Microsoft Corporation, the company that publishes Excel, is sitting in the reception room of Gene and Lucia's company. Lucia thought she was helping the company save money by giving Gene the copied disk.

William had no idea he was violating the law. But it is a crime to copy Excel and almost all other commercially produced software programs. Software is protected by the same federal laws that make it illegal to reproduce a textbook or any other copyrighted information without prior written permission from the publisher. This is stated clearly on every software package. Microcomputer users who copy software illegally are a serious problem for software manufacturers.

Often top management has no idea that its employees are committing software piracy. To prevent lawsuits, many corporations are now issuing statements for their employees to sign that make it clear the company does not condone unauthorized software copying and use. Once the company has these signed statements, disk copies become an employee's personal responsibility.

Future Computing of Dallas, Texas, found that, on average, for every legitimately purchased microcomputer software program, there is one illegal copy. The company estimates that if there were no illegal copies available, yearly software sales would increase 25 to 30 percent. That adds up to several hundred million dollars a year that software publishers are losing because of illegal copies.

The copyright law prohibits users from making copies of most software programs, whether the copies be for friends or for co-workers. However, the argument still exists among businesses that a software program is similar to a book copyright. Thus, if they can buy one dictionary and several secretaries are legally permitted to share it, they should be able to buy one software package, and their employees ought to be able to share it in the same way. Few people photocopy a dictionary when they need it. It is easier to go out and buy a dictionary. But you can copy a disk with just a few keystrokes. That makes it easier, and certainly less costly, to copy a disk than to buy one. Laws will continue to address these problems; but they almost always are in response to problems.

Software manufacturers have been forced to take steps to protect themselves from software piracy. Many include special programs on their disks that make it impossible for anyone but a computer expert to make copies. A number of program disks allow you to make one copy but no more. If you try to make additional copies, a prompt appears on the screen to tell you that you have made your copy. Other software companies give you one disk when you buy the package. The serial number that comes with your software identifies *you* as the purchaser. If the disk is damaged, stolen, or lost, you can contact the company and typically get a replacement disk free. If you need additional disks after that, you may be able to get them for a nominal fee.

These and similar measures are clear warnings that software piracy is no innocent matter. The packages of many software programs carry a sale and distribution warning, license agreement, and warranty to the purchaser. Read and become familiar with this information so you know the limitations the manufacturer has placed on the use of the software. Practicing good business ethics is as important as demonstrating excellent work skills and habits. To be an effective employee, you need to practice business ethics every day.

Continuing Changes in Technology

Today, information is the number one industry worldwide. In the United States, information is a valuable commodity. The technology for managing information is one of our most marketable assets. Computers have added significantly to our ability to manage information, and integrated information systems have become a necessity. Dimensions of change such as these are not always easily accepted. To change means to forget old ways and learn new ones.

Many people are reluctant to change—some because they simply cannot adapt. People have feelings and are creatures of habit. Technology does not recognize emotions and feelings. However, the computer revolution has affected our lives in a number of ways. Here are some of the factors that are important to businesses. Note how many of these factors are closely related to each other . . . and how they emphasize the importance of integrated information systems.

Training and Skills

Business and industry training amounts to over $60 million a year in addition to what the government spends on education and training programs to upgrade and retrain our work force. Many current jobs have specifications that reflect computerization. Old jobs will continue to be phased out as new ones are created. All levels of workers, including top executives, are pursuing retraining related to computer technology.

Communications Patterns

Electronic mail has changed how we communicate and has altered many business procedures. With more managers using applications software at executive workstations, information needs to be easily accessible. Organizational procedures, using local area networks and communications software, are being implemented to centralize information and keep it uniform for top management.

Rapid Communications

Electronic audio exchanges and calendaring software are helping executives avoid the game of "telephone tag." Teleconferencing is permitting managers to "meet" and communicate more often. Evolving communications systems are helping businesses run more efficiently. Digital signal processing (DSP), Integrated Services Digital Network (ISDN), and other developments are contributing to fast, accurate communications.

Organizational Roles

Many companies no longer have as many managerial levels or one secretary for each manager (except at the highest levels). Technology is giving secretaries more decision-making tasks and making it easier to perform more complex duties. Electronic information access is making it possible for managers to perform more independently in some areas yet interrelate more closely in others.

Data Management

Companies are growing increasingly dependent on databases, online information services, and other interactive systems rather than generating and maintaining data themselves internally. Database management and electronic filing systems are helping companies manage vast amounts of information and provide employees quick and easy access to it for informed decision making.

Privacy and Security

As information becomes more accessible, there are growing concerns for security measures. The use of passwords, biometrics, and encryption are contributing to better information security. Viruses and computer crime are problems most computer-based companies face. Copyright laws and other legislation have helped protect the rights of software manufacturers and electronic media users.

Managerial Techniques

Managers are making decisions with more complete and diverse information and often staying in touch with telecommunication systems. Top executives who believe in hands-on management are communicating with employees at every level directly rather than through reports forwarded to them by middle managers. **Simulations** or "what-if" programs are permitting companies to consider options before marketing a product.

Decision Support and Knowledge-Based Systems

Decision support systems (DSS) in the form of spreadsheets and database management are helping end users manage information and make business decisions. Progress is also being made with **artificial intelligence** (computers with humanlike intelligence). Some companies are using **knowledge-based systems** and **expert systems** to help them select alternatives to action and solve problems.

Industry Standards

Industry standards are contributing to connectivity and integrated systems of information transmission. Networks are improving communications both locally and worldwide. International markets are becoming closer because data links permit the transfer of information. Standards for facsimile transmission and electronic data interchange (EDI) are contributing to productivity in many facets of business enterprises.

The tremendous growth in electronic office technologies has generated a need to change the way we manage information and many of our traditional business procedures. We need to keep in balance the contradiction between the enthusiasm that makes us want to think the computer can solve all our problems and the unease we may feel in adapting to its use. Computers give us access to more information more quickly, to share with more people in more ways than ever before. Until machines with artificial intelligence can truly imitate human thinking and reasoning abilities, we will need people to solve problems. In a computerized society, only a business that has the human resources to use information creatively will have the competitive edge.

CHAPTER SUMMARY

- Systems integration is a way of looking not just at individual tasks but also at how those tasks go together and relate to other tasks.
- All offices are concerned with managing information, but the greatest efficiency in the information processing cycle is achieved by a systems approach.
- Integrated information processing refers to resources "working together"—which means that every person, every task, and every piece of equipment relates to all the others.
- An executive workstation is an electronically equipped work space designed for multitasking. It helps a user generate, process, store, distribute, and retrieve information rapidly and efficiently.
- Digital signal processing (DSP) converts information of all types into digital form for efficient, accurate, and quick processing.
- Information processing and management technology are so advanced now that it is often difficult to pinpoint where one step of the information processing cycle ends and another begins.
- Multiuser systems are integrated systems that capitalize on networking, storage, and communications capabilities.
- Subscribers to timesharing services usually do not have to buy costly, powerful processing equipment but use less expensive workstations tied to the central system to process information.
- Computer maintenance can be a costly part of a company's total budget for computing.
- Computer security systems keep unauthorized users from accessing information. Passwords, other identification codes, and biometric devices are used to control access to restricted information and areas.
- A more sophisticated computer security system is one that relies on encryption or the translation of confidential files into secret codes.
- The unauthorized copying of software—piracy—accounts for millions of dollars in lost revenues each year for software manufacturers.
- Devices like surge protectors and uninterruptible power supplies can prevent information loss and damage to a computer system.
- Business ethics are important to you and your organization. They should be practiced by all employees every day.
- As organizations continue to implement information technologies, dramatic changes in work environments may contribute to some people's reluctance to accept many of these changes.
- In an information society, human resources are the competitive edge; they're the key to any organization's growth.

VOCABULARY

artificial intelligence
audit trails
biometrics
clipboard
computer-aided instruction (CAI)
computer crime
Computer Fraud and Abuse Act
digital signal processing (DSP)
Electronic Communications Privacy Act
encryption
executive workstation
Federal Copyright Law
host system
integrated information system
knowledge-based system
log on
multiuser system
password
queues
shared-tenant service
software piracy
surge protector
systems approach
third-party maintenance
timesharing system
uninterruptible power supply (UPS)
user identification code
virus

CHAPTER QUESTIONS

1. Why is the integration of information processing equipment regarded as an extension of the systems approach?
2. In a large, integrated information system, how can other people be prevented from reading or changing your files?
3. Explain how an integrated information system can be beneficial to any type of business.
4. What is an executive workstation? Name some of its benefits and functions.
5. In a company fully equipped with an electronic office system, it may be difficult to distinguish between one step of the information processing cycle and another. Show how this can happen by tracing a document as it might move through a large corporation with many branch offices.
6. What are the advantages and disadvantages of a timesharing service?
7. What is computer crime? How do viruses creep into systems? List and explain five solutions firms are implementing to help control these problems.
8. Name some of the ways you can protect your computer system and its components.
9. What is meant by software piracy? How can employees stop it?
10. Within an organizational structure, identify at least five ways in which technology has changed our lives.

CASE STUDY

Kingsley, James, and Ellison, a brokerage firm with the latest in communications equipment, uses a word processing system to prepare letters and reports that are sent to investors, branch offices, and large companies around the world. Sometimes these letters and reports contain numeric data that changes minute by minute as the business day proceeds on Wall Street.

The firm has a large data-processing system it uses to make calculations needed to analyze stocks and bonds performance. It also uses this system to manage clients' accounts and to transfer funds. In analyzing investment potential for its clients, the firm uses information from outside sources such as financial news services. It also makes its own calculations and relies on its brokers' instincts.

Describe the integrated information processing system you might find in such an office. Explain how the system would perform some of the operations the firm carries out.

CHAPTER 10

The Office Environment

Jamie René Long is now back at her office at Michael & Sons after a one-year leave of absence. She is amazed at how much the company has changed. Last year the word processing operators worked in a centralized area. Most secretaries used electric typewriters; a few used word processors. Several secretaries had their own offices connected to their bosses' offices. Now each secretary has a workstation or a micro and works in a semiprivate partitioned area located close to the manager. Many of the executives also have workstations or personal computers. Much of the bulky, heavy furniture has been replaced. The decor looks as comfortable as it is efficient. In talking to co-worker Stacy Douglas about the office changes, Ms. Long is impressed by Ms. Douglas's enthusiasm for their new office environment.

Today most business people realize how important it is to use office automation technology for making their day-to-day operations efficient. Top executives and ***CIOs (chief information officers)*** *know that a successful information system depends on how well they can integrate the many and varied parts of their total operation. They know that information processing with automated equipment increases productivity and improves document quality. They are aware that office procedures within the organizational structure are very important. They also know that it takes people to make a system work. Taking all these elements into consideration, there are many ways an information system can be organized. Let's look at some of the the most common types of office settings in which people process information.*

Information Processing in a Traditional Setting

In a traditional office, a secretary works for one or more managers. Introducing information processing equipment into this kind of environment usually does not result in many major organizational or structural changes. The new equipment either replaces the old or is used in addition to it. In a traditional setting, secretarial stations (whether or not they have automated equipment) are typically located directly outside or near the manager's office. In some companies, they are clustered in one area, and managers are grouped in another. A good example of how automated information processing is integrated into a traditional setting is the Kringle Publishing Company.

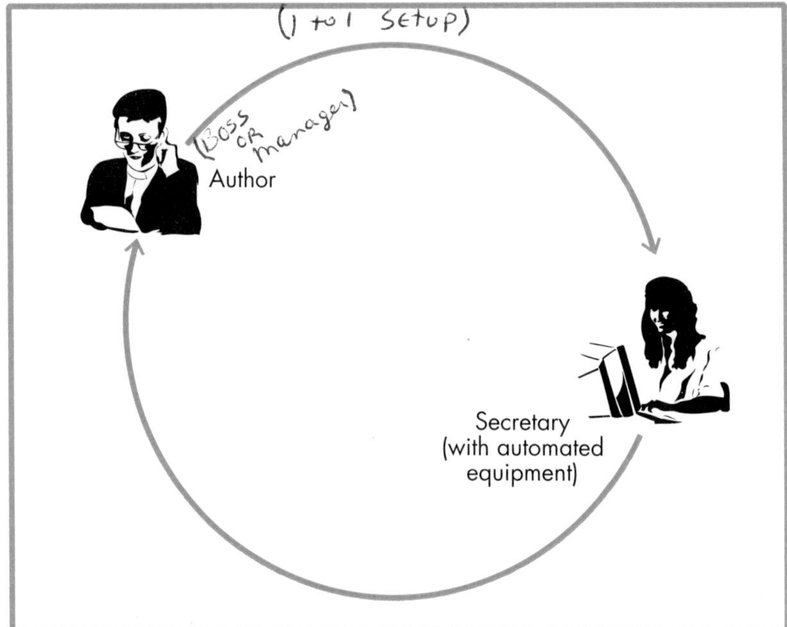

Work flow in a traditional setting.

A traditional office environment as compared to a more modern one.

Erica Beauvais is a secretary for Kringle Publishing Company. She recently transferred from the Marketing Department to the Editorial Department. The Editorial offices look similar to those in Marketing. The secretaries' responsibilities are basically the same. They include keyboarding, filing, taking dictation, answering telephones, greeting visitors, and handling general administrative responsibilities. The only difference is the equipment.

The equipment in Marketing includes two standalone word processors for keyboarding reports and budgets. The secretaries use electric or electronic typewriters. In Editorial, nearly everyone has a microcomputer, and the secretaries are trained to use word processing software. The authors of the books the company publishes usually submit their manuscripts both on disks and as hard

Characteristics of a Traditional System

- Information processing is available to all sizes and types of offices without restructuring staff or procedures or implementing a large-scale system.
- Work procedures may vary widely among departments because of office autonomy (being self-contained, with each department having its own controls).
- Secretaries work exclusively for their own managers and do not normally provide secretarial support for others in the company.
- Fewer instructions need to accompany a document for processing, since one person will see it through from beginning to end. Record keeping for tracking a document usually is less formal than when several people are involved in the information processing stages.
- Document turnaround time usually is very short.
- Emphasis is on efficient information flow rather than on the quantity of documents produced.
- Secretarial tasks usually are varied and involve a variety of office situations and pressures.
- A close working relationship with one or more authors is often fostered.
- The opportunity to follow most jobs through from beginning to end can bring greater worker satisfaction and pride in the work performed.
- Career paths may be limited if not clearly defined and often depend on the promotability of an employee's manager. Career mobility, especially seeking a job at another company, may be quite good because of the experience gained from using automated equipment to process a variety of documents.

copy. Sometimes an editor revises a document by keyboarding revisions at a terminal. Other times the editor asks a secretary to transfer any keyed or handwritten revisions to the disk.

Many companies like Kringle have chosen to integrate information processing equipment into a traditional office setting. For some companies, such integration is chiefly a means of "getting their feet wet" in modern technology. But many companies, including Kringle, select this setting because having several microcomputers is precisely what is required to meet their needs.

In an office where word processing equipment has been integrated into a traditional setting, input goes directly from manager to secretary. If automated equipment is shared, the secretary must decide whether to use the automated equipment or a typewriter. A three-line memo, for example, would probably be done most quickly on the typewriter. A lengthy statistical report would be prepared on the automated equipment. Availability of equipment is the key factor in determining equipment use. The more automated the pieces of equipment available, the greater the likelihood that most or all documents will be prepared on them.

Secretaries working in traditional offices equipped with personal computers and other computer equipment have basically the same responsibilities as secretaries in offices that do not have automated equipment—the day-to-day tasks are similar. What is different is that the electronic equipment generally enables the secretary to work more quickly and efficiently, and the department as a whole can be more productive. With manager and secretary located near each other, there are few logistics problems. Documents can easily go back and forth for revisions, proofreading, and signature.

Information Processing in a Centralized Setting

When word processing was first introduced in the 1960s, the tendency of many companies was to establish a centralized area for it. Dedicated word processing equipment was expensive, but many businesses could justify its cost if it was used extensively. The concern for equipment utilization was so great that some organizations initiated "shift work." That is, over a 24-hour period, two or three word processing specialists would rotate, with each working 8 hours on one machine. Although the trend is away from centralized settings, let's examine the components of such a system.

An **information processing center** is a centrally located room or area in which a group of information processing specialists handles all or most of the document preparation for an entire company. It is frequently referred to as a **document production center** and sometimes, more traditionally, as a **word processing center**. "Word processing" is being replaced with the broader term "information processing." ("Word processing center" is not used much any more because most companies do not confine themselves merely to "word" processing, but also process data, images, and other types of information.) The increased use of software programs for integrating word processing, spreadsheets, database management, and graphics has contributed to this trend.

Centralized information processing normally is found in a large organization rather than a small office. *Specialization* is a key word in centralized information processing systems because workers in an information processing center do only information processing. Each operator may have a different degree of responsibility within the center, but all operators prepare documents by using automated equipment.

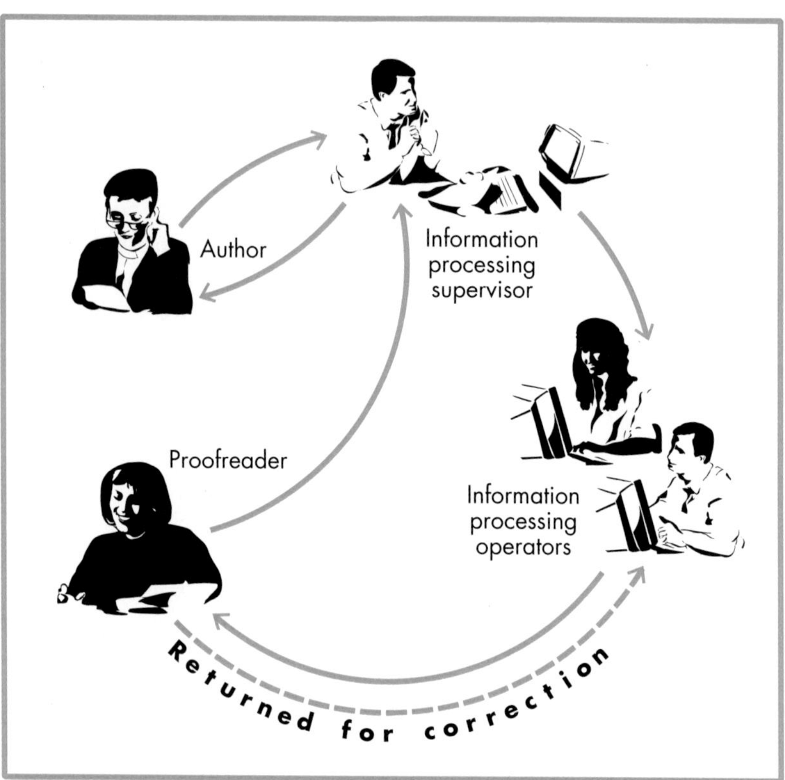

Work flow in a centralized information processing system.

In some companies, information processing operators specialize in handling certain types of documents or subject matter. Such is the case of Frank Reid, who has been working at Spiro & Edlemann Pharmaceuticals for over a year. He has spent most of that time in the information processing center, specializing in keyboarding statistics and tables for the company's numerous research reports on pain relievers. During that time, Mr. Reid has become familiar not only with the standardized formats for charts and tables used in the company's reports, but also with various pharmacological terminology. Whenever a chart or table has to be formatted, the center supervisor gives it to Mr. Reid.

As Mr. Reid's experience indicates, the specialization that comes with centralized information processing tends to increase efficiency and productivity. Specialization also allows better matching of employee skills with assignments.

However, operators in an information processing center, no matter how specialized, usually handle the work of many managers in all the company's various departments. This way, if one manager is away from the office, no operator's work comes to a standstill. The same is true when one of the operators is away. Furthermore, because operators prepare documents for such a large number of managers, there is a fairly continuous flow of work, and operators don't have to spend much time waiting for assignments.

Company work flow will determine the type of equipment needed in a centralized information processing system. For example, a company that produces several 75-page financial reports each month needs a system that allows operators to share the preparation of such large, tightly scheduled jobs. A company that regularly distributes lengthy documents updating repetitive statistical information requires a system that makes it possible for operators to share prestored text, mailing lists, and databases.

A **work order** or **requisition form** is usually sent with each document that enters a centralized information processing center.

Characteristics of a Centralized System

- Costly information processing equipment can be shared by several offices or departments.
- Workstations may be located near each other, enclosed with partitions, or contained within a large, open area for easy access to both employees and equipment.
- Large volumes of documents can be processed rapidly and efficiently, with several operators sometimes working simultaneously on a long, urgent document.
- Centers are often located a considerable distance from managers, which may possibly lead to problems in revising long, complicated documents.
- Managers depend on a center's efficiency for document processing. Poor center management can result in delays, misplaced documents, and other inefficiencies.
- File retrieval may be efficient because of standardized and consistent storage procedures. Also, central storage of repetitive paragraphs provides easy access to those who use them.
- **Specialization** (becoming an "expert" at a task) may provide desirable challenges to some people and may eliminate the stress of frequent switching among a variety of generalized tasks.
- Some workers may feel isolated from managers, resulting in diminished pride in work.
- Repetitive job tasks may cause some employees to become bored with their work, resulting in lower-quality work and a high rate of employee turnover in the center.
- Career paths for employees may be limited because of the lack of advancement opportunities within the center. However, a supervisory position in a center may lead to management positions at varying levels in other areas of the company.

A work order contains identifying information about the manager (department, office extension, mail station, and similar information) and special instructions on how the document is to be processed. The document may be sent electronically, by interoffice mail, or by hand delivery to the center.

A center supervisor will keep a record of the document, log it in and out of the center, give it a priority rating, and schedule it for processing by assigning it to a specialist. After the document is keyed, it may be read by a proofreader, corrected, and returned. Making copies may be handled from the center, but a company with an information processing center usually has a centralized reprographics center to handle copying. Careful records are kept of all these details to track a document. After the document is processed according to instructions, the center may store the file indefinitely or for a specified period of time. In general, smaller companies store files much longer than large companies.

Information Processing in a Decentralized Setting

Many companies have **decentralized information processing systems,** where documents are processed in close proximity to a few or several executives or managers. If it is a small information processing center that "reports to" or is an offshoot of a large center, it may be called a **satellite center** or **minicenter** (other names are used by different companies). However, a minicenter may be inde-

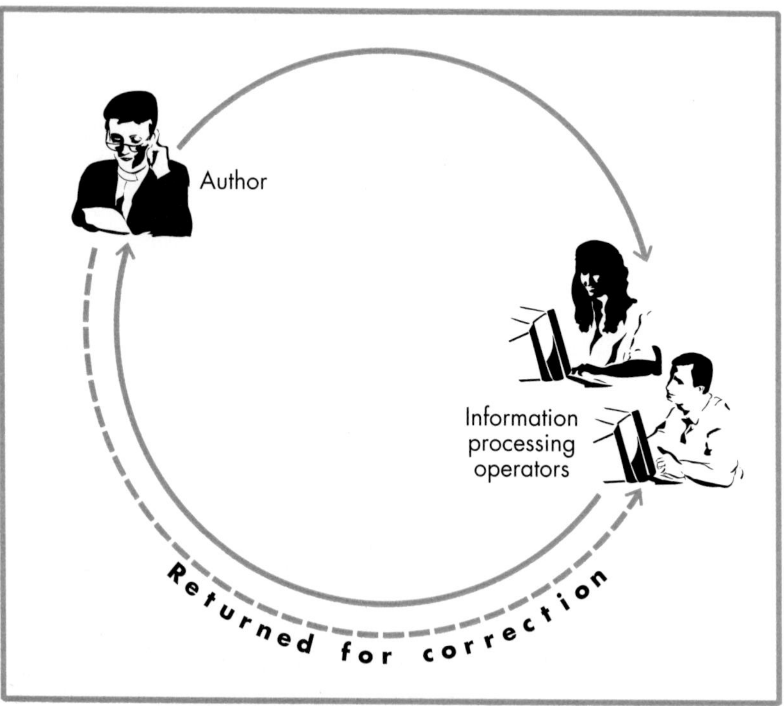

Work flow in a decentralized information processing system.

pendent of any large, centralized system. It may be set up to serve one or more specific departments or floors. Information processing operators prepare documents or other kinds of work for all the managers in the departments or floors served. The layout and design of the workstations in a minicenter may closely resemble those of the offices it serves so the total area appears attractive and coordinated.

Depending on the company, working in a traditional setting might be quite different from a decentralized setting. For example, here's how a move changed the life of Harvey Weinstein.

Mr. Weinstein has worked at two different companies. At his previous firm of Dalke, Anderson, and Renwick, he was secretary to three managers in the Accounting Department. He had many responsibilities, a heavy work load, and a lot of stress and pressure on the job. He saw no opportunity for advancement.

Now Mr. Weinstein works at Vanguard Software Products. After five months as an information processing specialist at Vanguard, he has come to a definite conclusion: He much prefers working at Vanguard. Today he produces documents for one department, the Legal Department. He does not have to deal with any of the administrative responsibilities associated with a secretary's job. He knows the managers, so he still feels involved.

Mr. Weinstein works in a minicenter that employs three operators. His friend, Arnold Tobias, works in another minicenter that processes documents for the Sales Department. The Sales Department satellite has six operators because it generates a much higher volume of paperwork than the Legal Department.

The managers in both departments are pleased that Vanguard adopted the decentralized system. Having their own information processing specialists who know the procedures and formatting requirements, as well as specialized software associated with the departments, is both efficient and productive for them. Also, having the equipment right in the department is convenient, especially when managers need to work directly with specialists in document preparation or revision. The attorneys in the Legal Department are particularly happy because the operators have become familiar with the legal terminology used, which helps in document preparation and revision.

The work flow in a decentralized information processing system may be similar to that in a centralized system. Input to a minicenter, for example, may vary from cassette dictation with dictated instructions or handwritten documents accompanied by a work order or document requisition form. A supervisor or lead operator of the satellite controls the flow of work by keeping a detailed log of all documents entering and leaving the satellite. The contact between specialists and managers varies from one center to another,

Characteristics of a Decentralized System

- Equipment purchased for a decentralized system may cost more than for a centralized system, but less than for a traditional system, especially if the company is large.
- Equipment and software selection can be based on the special needs of a department or unit.
- Turnaround time is relatively fast, since operators and managers usually work near each other. Some paperwork (work requests and work logs) usually is necessary.
- Close working relationships between managers and specialists depend on company procedures. Some operators may be assigned to certain managers.
- A strategically located satellite center may mean greater flexibility for operators and managers in handling documents.
- A lead operator who supervises satellite activities may have good equipment skills but lack the supervisory skills to manage a minicenter.
- Potential for efficiency and productivity should be high because specialists are familiar with department documents and vocabulary. However, having to work on the same kinds of documents day after day can be boring and result in poor quality work.
- The work flow and office environment may lessen the production pressures found in a centralized system.
- Specialists can become good at equipment operation, terminology, functions, and procedures of one particular unit, but lack a total, clear perspective of the organization as a whole.
- Career opportunities may be limited to positions available in the individual satellite or minicenter. However, the specialized skills gained may be helpful to operators who want to stay in a specialized area, such as the medical field, and seek such a job in another organization.

depending on the role, functions, size, and services of a center. For example, some centers may handle a manager's mail and telephone calls—as in a traditional office. These functions can be assigned to one operator or shared on a rotating basis.

A decentralized system may combine many of the features of both the traditional and centralized systems. Because of equipment integration and connectivity, the tendency of many businesses today is to decentralize their information processing operations. In fact, some have decentralized so much that they are on the fringes of a traditional system—a "traditional" system that incorporates networking and telecommunications from individual workstations.

Ergonomics

An office environment that considers the people who will work there can contribute significantly to worker efficiency and productivity. **Ergonomics** is the term given to the science of adapting the working environment, conditions, and equipment to suit the workers. Ergonomics is sometimes referred to as **human engineering**. If a company plans to change over to or enhance its current electronic office equipment, managers need to look closely at how their people will interact with the equipment and how the equipment will fit into their office environment. Workers' psychological and physical well-being is a very important consideration in planning an ergonomically designed office.

Purchasing equipment and setting it on people's desks does not in itself create an electronic office. Managers who introduce equipment without thinking through and planning how and where it will be used are letting themselves in for employee complaints that range from eyestrain, blurred vision, and concerns about radiation to numbness, headaches, backaches, and wrist problems. When employees feel discomfort about their work environment, absenteeism and workers' compensation claims increase, while productivity drops.

Office equipment and furniture designers have all but solved most of these problems. Designers are conforming to standards of such groups as the **American National Standards Institute (ANSI)**, the **Business and Institutional Manufacturer's Association (BIFMA)**, and the **Human Factors Society.** The results are interesting, exciting, and artistic. But as long as employees complain about aches and pains, we can count on designers and interested groups to study the issues and improve designs. No doubt vendors and employers will continue to keep an ear open to employees' health concerns.

The Office Landscape

Because most businesses are concerned about people, the environment in which people work is important. Designing an environment that is efficient, pleasing, and comfortable is not necessarily expensive. Many office buildings today are built with large open areas that a business can adapt to its individual needs. **Office landscaping** or the **open office plan** is one approach to office design. Office landscaping usually refers to an open layout of desks, equipment, and files arranged in free-standing clusters separated by screens or partitions. This design approach gives workers a feeling of space while suiting their work needs. Office landscaping replaces permanent walls and fixtures with an open area containing movable **modules** (partitions or parts that connect or fit together), modular furniture, and other adaptable features.

An open office plan offers flexibility in the way equipment and furnishings are arranged.

Office Design Considerations A key element of an office landscape is flexibility. Office furnishings and equipment are designed to be easily moved and put together in various ways. Work surfaces, storage facilities, and shelving units can all be rearranged to meet workers' changing needs. Such flexibility is particularly important at a time of rapid technological change. When a company needs to expand or alter its current system, the office setting must be able to accommodate not only sophisticated new equipment but also any reorganization of workers brought about by such equipment.

Besides being easy to construct and change, the modular open office plan saves space and energy over more traditional office plans. The open plan makes it possible to have good air flow, lighting, heating, and air conditioning because walls do not extend to the ceiling. However, the lack of permanent floor-to-ceiling walls contributes to higher noise levels, less privacy, and more security problems than in a traditional setting.

Planning considerations must address such issues as cables, wiring, hookups, and network concerns; storage space for office materials, supplies, and files (current as well as backup files); and other more "natural" environmental factors (electrical, heating, and lighting as well as fire and water protection). Location of light switches, temperature controls, and fire extinguishers must be planned for worker access and safety. An open concept contributes to less formality, more social interaction, and the need for work area neatness—factors that can be real concerns for a business as well as individual workers.

Aesthetics An optimum office landscape combines practicality with convenience and comfort. In other words, it should be a productive as well as an **aesthetically pleasing** (attractive) environment. The overall layout is designed to promote the efficient flow of paperwork from one department or work area to another. Individual areas are partitioned off by means of acoustical panels, which provide privacy while helping control the noise level. Desk tops, cabinets, drawers, and storage units all may be attached to these panels in a variety of configurations. Strategically placed plants help serve as partitions and help absorb noise; they also add to the pleasantness of the office environment.

Have you ever wondered why office equipment and furniture usually are quite basic in color? Why office walls, floors, and ceilings follow the same rule? Color has a tremendous effect on people. If you are surrounded by bold, bright colors for long periods of time, you may experience fatigue because of too much stimulation. A general rule is to use light, soothing colors (light blues, greens, grays, tans, or muted yellows) for large areas. Dark colors have a tendency to "draw in" or make an area appear smaller and may be good for making a large room appear smaller. Lighting and space should influence color choices in an office. For example, dark and bold colors might be effective as accents—just as they can be attractive accessories for a basic suit you wear.

Plants, colors, and accessories can add to the aesthetics of an office landscape. If they are selected carefully and tastefully, they can help create a pleasant and psychologically stimulating atmosphere. In turn, they can contribute to worker satisfaction and productivity.

Office Furniture

When the famous architect Louis Sullivan introduced the phrase "form follows function" in the late nineteenth century, who could have guessed that many architects and designers today would still be following his design rule? Office furniture designers in particu-

Factors Affecting Office Furniture and Equipment Design

- Office productivity levels must be raised to compete effectively in world markets.
- More people are working in offices than in any other kind of work environment.
- Many health complaints from office workers relate to back pain and fatigue.
- The growing market for products associated with office health risks is of interest to both office workers and employers.
- Legal issues are getting the attention of employers who want to reduce the possibility of liability claims.

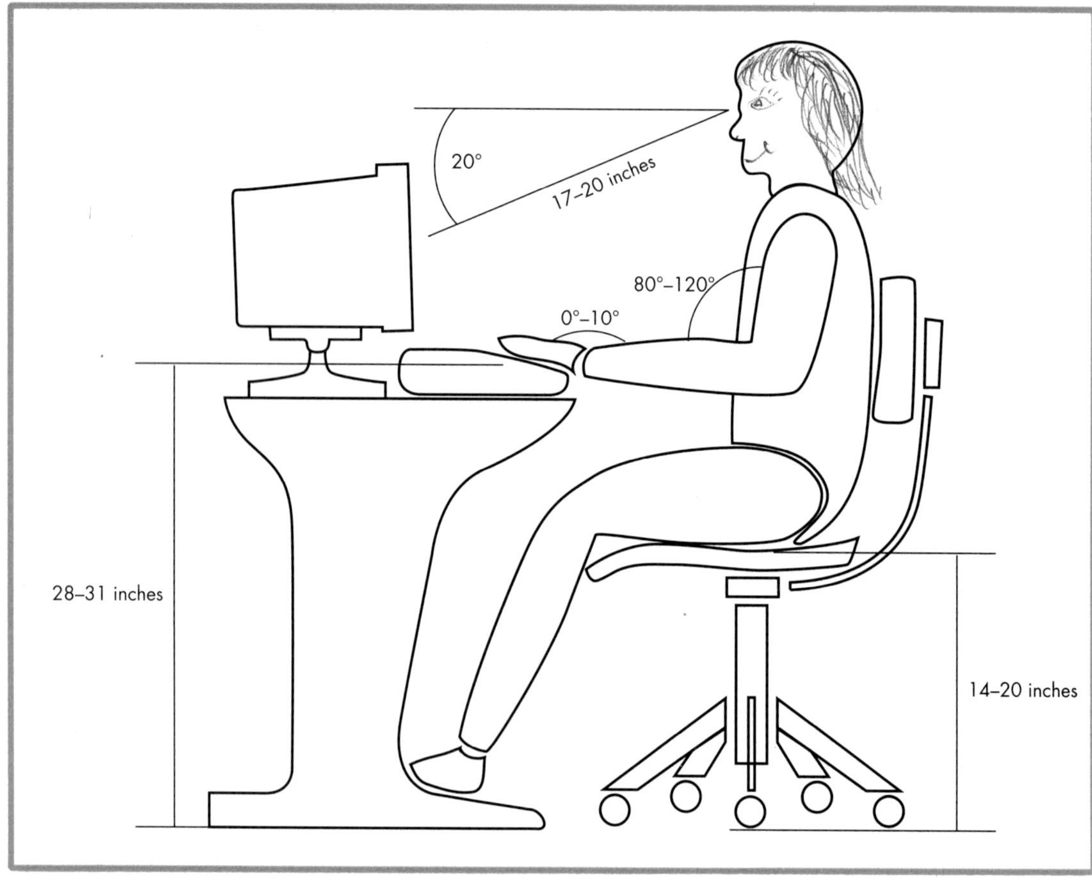

Equipment and furniture designed with the worker's well-being in mind help create a pleasant, comfortable, productive work environment.

lar are taking his advice seriously. Many designers know that the usefulness of a piece of furniture depends on whether a person feels comfortable using it. Thus, the human interface with technology is essential. As a result, designers today are applying their expertise to office furniture.

Designers and vendors are producing office furniture and equipment that is of different sizes and shapes to fit the various sizes and shapes of people. No longer are desks all one size. They have changed in many ways to match the changing needs of the office worker. No longer do people have to sit in uncomfortable chairs designed for the "average" person. A "one size fits all" design may make some of us bend, slouch, or squeeze into a chair, which can cause stiff muscles, tension, and anxiety.

The "form-follows-function" principle and ergonomic research have contributed to well-designed office furniture. The five-wheel chair is a good example of how ergonomic research can

This specially designed chair features a high degree of adjustability to provide comfort and protection for the lower back.

be applied. Designers in Europe learned that people like to lean back in their chairs and tend to push themselves suddenly away from a desk. They found that a chair with four wheels toppled too easily. A five-wheel chair rolls around just as well but does not tip over as easily.

An office chair should be important to every office worker who spends much time sitting. According to ANSI standards, the seat height should be adjustable from 16 to $20\frac{1}{2}$ inches, seat depth should be between 15 and 17 inches, and seat width should be at least 18 inches. If a chair height does not permit the user's feet to touch the floor, a footrest (placed at about a 60- to 90-degree angle to your lower legs) is recommended.

Researchers also determined that a backless kneeling chair relieves stress on your upper back. When you sit in a backless chair, your knees rest on a knee pad. When you want to lean forward, you are forced to arch your back at your hips. This eliminates pressure on your back. A chair with a backrest, however, is recommended for back support. A good backrest will provide support to the spine and will form about a 90-degree angle to the seat.

Sitting the wrong way can give you a backache. Some back experts think that up to one-third of all lower back injuries would be eliminated by giving workers ergonomically designed chairs. In this country, backache is the second most frequent reason people stay home from work (the common cold is first). Many different working conditions can contribute to backaches—lifting something heavy, moving the wrong way, and sitting in the wrong chair. Practicing good posture as you are sitting and working at a desk can make your back feel more comfortable and reduce fatigue while you keyboard.

Practicing Good Posture in Your Office

- Use a pillow if your chair does not support your lower back.
- Sit as straight as possible to distribute your weight evenly between both hips.
- Put your feet up on a small box or a phone book under your desk to take some of the weight off your lower back.
- Lean forward from your hips instead of bending your shoulders if you need to get closer to the screen.
- Position your body so you are looking straight ahead at the screen. Try not to twist to the right or left so you must look at the screen sideways.
- Keep your pockets free of objects (such as a wallet or an eyeglass case) that would make you change the way you normally sit.
- Adjust your chair so your thighs are approximately horizontal, your calves vertical, and your feet rest squarely on the floor or a footrest.
- Position the keyboard so your upper arms are hanging straight down, and your forearms are held comfortably at a slight angle.
- Stretch, flex, twist, and do other mild calisthenic exercises while sitting at your desk.
- Get up and move around, whenever you get the chance, to vary the stress on your muscles and back. Just sitting still is work and can increase the pressure on your spine by 40 percent.

Equipment Design

Just as the design of office furniture contributes to your health in the office, so does the design of office equipment. Office equipment, too, must fit its function. This human interface with technology is essential in equipment design.

Equipment designers, like designers of office furnishings, strive to combine practicality, convenience, and comfort. They recognize that computerized equipment has a unique set of features that can be adapted to meet employee needs. The **National Institute for Occupational Safety and Health (NIOSH)** is one of the concerned organizations that investigate health risks and safety of workers. It has studied working conditions in mines, factories, and mills, and has set new standards for industrial hygiene. Perhaps its best-known recommendation is the hard hat at construction sites.

Office worker health and safety are also being studied by NIOSH. Issues such as stress, fatigue, lighting, repetitive movements, air quality, and the effect of VDTs are of concern to NIOSH.

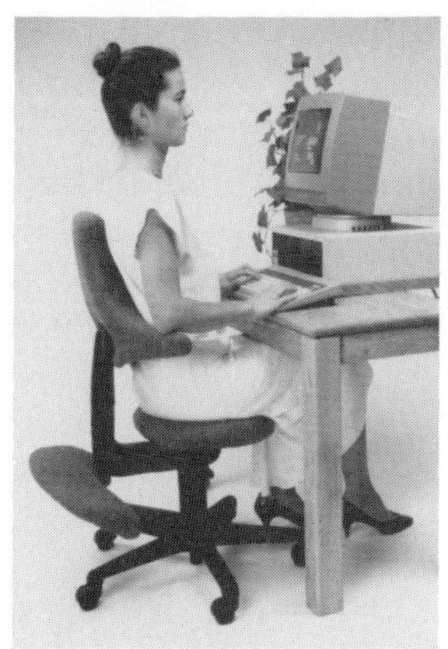

Good posture and proper positioning of equipment help prevent fatigue.

VDT Safety Some employees may find that a display screen of one color is easier on their eyes than one of another color. For example, display screens may use white, green, or yellow letters against a dark background or dark letters against a light background. They can be positioned at eye level or above or below it. Screens also can be set up at different angles and at varying distances from the user.

NIOSH studies have determined the best way to use a VDT. The angle from your eyes to the center of the screen should be no greater than 15 degrees, and you should sit at least 14 to 20 inches from the screen. Harvard University's Health Services group suggests a distance of at least 17 to 30 inches. Other groups suggest sitting as far away from the screen as you can while still seeing it comfortably.

Visual Fatigue If there is a question about the visual sharpness of a VDT, have it checked regularly. A flickering or blurred screen, for example, forces the eye to readjust continually, and this can cause fatigue over a period of time. Information processing operators sometimes complain of eyestrain and headaches after keyboarding for several hours. According to NIOSH and the National Center for Disease Control, there is still no real evidence that VDTs can harm your eyes or any other aspect of your health.

Many of us feel some eyestrain after doing any kind of close work for a long time. For this reason, if you can keep from gazing at the screen nonstop while you are keyboarding, it can help to relax your eyes. Take visual breaks every few minutes by looking at something else.

Glare and Radiation Some vendors recommend that a **screen shield** (a mesh or glass device with a special coating or conductive material) be used in the front of a monitor to reduce glare and/or radiation from the VDT. Although the effects of VDT use associated with eye problems and radiation levels have not been established, a concerned user may get peace of mind using such a device. Some have suggested that the amount of radiation from some home appliances can be just as great or even greater than from a VDT. But most home appliances are not used eight hours a day.

Keyboards and Repetitive Motion Keyboard design and position may have some adverse effects on some workers. Repetitive motion studies are dictating new keyboard designs and work patterns. A keyboard can be positioned at varying distances from a detached screen and at varying heights on a desk. Keyboard devices designed to protect against wrist and hand problems (such as carpal tunnel syndrome) are being marketed.

Rest Breaks Administrative employees, VDT operators, and secretaries have indicated that they like regular rest breaks during their working hours. There are several research studies that show breaks help keep you relaxed and increase your productivity. NIOSH recommends a break every hour for heavy keyboarding and every two hours for more moderate work. Managers add one note of caution: Employees who are permitted breaks should not skip them.

The Physical Environment

Control of lighting, noise, temperature, and humidity in the office environment is essential if people and equipment are to work most efficiently.

Lighting Lighting has always been one of the most important elements of the office environment, and with the introduction of automated electronic systems, it becomes even more important. Poor or inadequate lighting or lighting that is too bright or glaring can reduce both productivity and work quality and can even contribute to lower employee morale.

Ambient lighting, background or room illumination, is usually indirect lighting. In most offices ambient lighting is fluorescent lighting rather than incandescent lighting. Fluorescent lighting provides more light per watt, generates less heat, and produces less glare. Light fixtures, often built directly into modular furnishings, can provide direct (**task lighting**) or indirect lighting or a combination of both. When properly placed, such fixtures will adequately illuminate the work area without producing harsh or glaring light.

Proper office lighting can reduce glare from display screens and help avoid operator eyestrain and fatigue. Similarly, the intensity of the light on ergonomically designed screens can be adjusted to suit the overhead lighting and cut down on glare. Ideally, to be as readable as possible, your monitor should be three to five times brighter than the ambient light in the room. Screen glare can make screen editing impossible. Direct sunlight can cause glare. Where possible, screens should be positioned away from windows, or users should be given the option of masking sunlight with curtains or blinds.

The type and amount of lighting in an office should be based on the activities performed. For example, if your work requires that you read fine print, you should have direct or task lighting. More casual visual tasks may not require any special lighting other than that produced by the general or ambient room lighting.

Illuminating a paper copy while keeping the light away from the user's eyes without causing screen glare can be a problem in some offices. Dim ceiling light and a desk lamp with a 100-watt bulb and a parabolic or bowl-shaped reflector will eliminate this problem. An adjustable desk easel or work stand also helps make it easier to read a sheet of paper while you are keyboarding.

Noise Control Noise can be distracting as well as cause stress and fatigue. Noise levels can be a problem when using electronic office systems. The sounds of printers and other automated equipment located in an open space with freestanding partitions can create a difficult situation—so much noise that workers can neither concentrate well nor communicate effectively with one another.

Many offices have controlled distracting noises by installing **acoustical** (noise absorbent) ceilings. Specially designed sound-absorbing acoustic panels and partitions are also used to control noise. Carpeting, draperies, plants, and other accessories perform a similar function. Some office equipment, especially noisy impact printers, can create as much noise as a factory or a busy street with a lot of traffic—possibly as much as 80 to 90 **decibels** (the common measure for sound intensity). The recommendation from the **Occupational Safety and Health Act (OSHA)** is that noise on a daily basis must not exceed this decibel level for office workers.

The noise of impact printers can be reduced with special noise-reduction devices known as **acoustical hoods** or **shields.** Also this kind of equipment can be kept in a separate area within noise-absorbing modular enclosures. The trend toward use of laser and other nonimpact printers in offices is reducing this problem significantly.

Controlling sound does not mean eliminating all noise. Indeed, some office sounds are necessary in order to maintain the proper work environment. **White noise**, such as soft background music or the gentle hum of an air conditioner, can be soothing. White noise can also provide a low-level, continuous background sound that effectively masks other minor noise. Research has shown that white noise is preferred to a totally silent environment and that changes in background noise at different times during the day can contribute to office morale and productivity.

Temperature and Humidity Temperature, humidity, and air flow are other aspects of the office environment that must be controlled if automated equipment is to operate at peak efficiency. High temperatures can accelerate the deterioration of equipment, magnetic tape, floppy disks, ribbons, print elements, printer paper, and various other office materials and supplies. Rapid or extreme variations in temperature can have the same effect. For these reasons, temperature control, humidity, and ventilation are three factors that are important when automated office systems are considered for an office.

Electronic systems should not be placed in areas that receive a considerable amount of direct sunlight. Similarly, equipment should not be placed near heating or cooling ducts or large windows. For example, installation plans frequently provide for a clearance space of several inches to a few feet around the back and sides of information processing equipment (space varies according to the type of equipment). Vendor recommendations for space around equipment allow for adequate ventilation and air flow. Space also permits access for equipment servicing. Operator comfort can be affected by space allowances because the combination of equipment and body heat can raise the room temperature (especially in a small room or in crowded conditions).

Just as temperature extremes can cause electronic equipment to deteriorate, so can humidity that is too high or too low adversely affect equipment. High humidity leads to moisture absorption and dimensional changes in printer paper, floppy disks, and other magnetic media. Paper that has absorbed moisture and increased in weight can hinder the performance of paper feeders and jam printers and copiers. To avoid equipment problems, always store paper in a cool, dry place.

Low humidity allows static electricity to build up. Static electricity can cause logic errors in the memory of CPUs and even permanent damage to sensitive control and logic circuits. For these reasons, many vendors recommend certain environmental conditions for operating equipment. Some vendors also require that antistatic carpeting be laid down before installing their electronic equipment.

<table>
<tr><th colspan="5">RECOMMENDED EQUIPMENT ENVIRONMENT*</th></tr>
<tr><th rowspan="2"></th><th rowspan="2">Acceptable Temperature Range</th><th rowspan="2">Acceptable Humidity Range</th><th colspan="2">Acceptable Rate of Change per Hour</th></tr>
<tr><th>Temperature</th><th>Humidity</th></tr>
<tr><td>Recommended Range† for Optimum Performance</td><td>65–75°F
18–24°C</td><td>40% to 60%</td><td>Should not change more than 5°F (2.8°C) an hour, ideally.</td><td>Should not change more than 6% an hour, ideally.</td></tr>
<tr><td>Minimum</td><td>59°F (15°C)</td><td>40%</td><td rowspan="2">Change per hour should not exceed 10°F (5.5°C) or equipment problems may occur.</td><td rowspan="2">Change per hour should not exceed 12% or equipment problems may occur.</td></tr>
<tr><td>Maximum</td><td>80°F (27°C)</td><td>60%</td></tr>
<tr><td colspan="5">*For sea level to 8000 feet altitude.
†Staying within these limits ensures good system reliability and performance.</td></tr>
</table>

Feasibility Studies

Designing an integrated information system with proper attention given to the environmental concerns, equipment, procedures, and people making up the system takes careful consideration. Many companies find that it is well worth the time and cost to approach such an undertaking by first conducting a **feasibility study** (a detailed analysis of all company functions to determine the best way to handle information). A feasibility study involves gathering a great deal of information from employees and the company files. When all the facts are collected, the results are analyzed. A report of the findings is prepared and presented to management for action. The report should contain sufficient information for management to make a decision on the best system design for the needs of the company.

For a feasibility study to be successful, employees must understand its importance. It is difficult to conduct a feasibility study without employee support and involvement; thus, it makes sense to prepare employees for such a study and to seek their cooperation. Also, companies can benefit from discussing their goals with employees. Companies that communicate with employees about how change may affect them usually are successful in implementing change. Businesses that keep employees informed also usually get good cooperation from their employees.

Feasibility studies may be conducted by a company's own employees. Frequently, however, they are performed by specialized consultants who spend considerable time analyzing how workers currently handle document preparation and other tasks. The goal is the same: to determine if a company could benefit from an automated information system or from replacing or enhancing its current system. If such changes seem needed, an office systems consultant is generally brought in. Together, and often with an ergonomic specialist, the consultant and company management decide what kind of system the organization needs for optimum efficiency.

A Comfortable, Productive Office

Electronic office systems are making it possible to process information more quickly and in greater quantities than could be done even a few years ago. How people fit into this new environment, both physically and psychologically, is extremely important. Interest is coming from all levels of an organization—top execu-

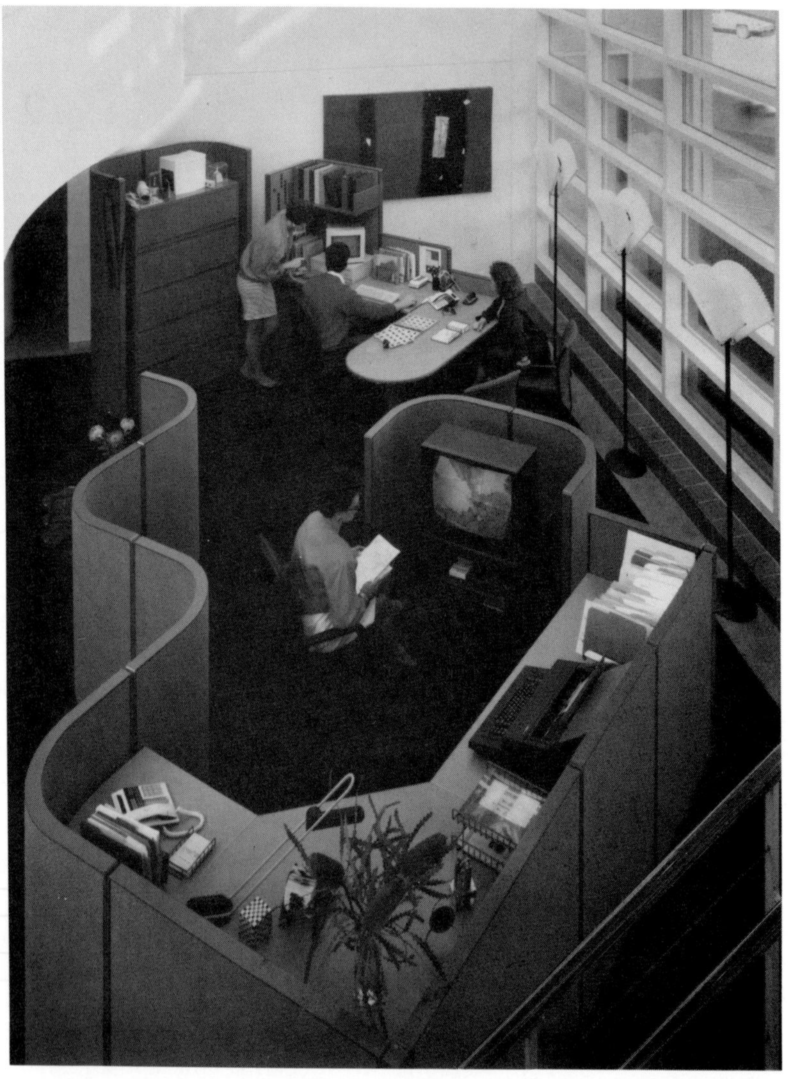

Creating a comfortable, productive place to work is key to the design of equipment and furniture for the automated office.

tives, managers, secretaries, and specialists using the equipment in ever-increasing numbers.

Many of the environmental issues associated with automated systems have been thoroughly researched. However, people are still having difficulty making the transition to electronic systems. As new environmental issues surface, studies of the physical and emotional stress experienced by many users of automated equipment will continue. Manufacturers, office ergonomists, and designers are keeping a close watch on developments. No doubt their conclusions will be reflected in the design of future office equipment and furniture to make the automated office an even more comfortable, efficient, and productive place to work.

The Human Interface With Technology

The human interface with technology is essential. Both productivity and aesthetics are considerations in creating efficient, pleasant work environments.

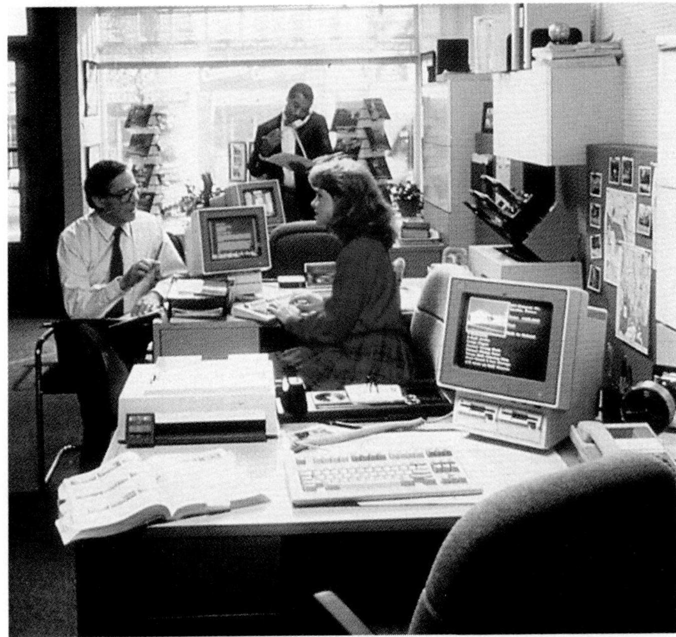

Practicality, convenience, and comfort are as important in a small office as they are in a much larger work setting.

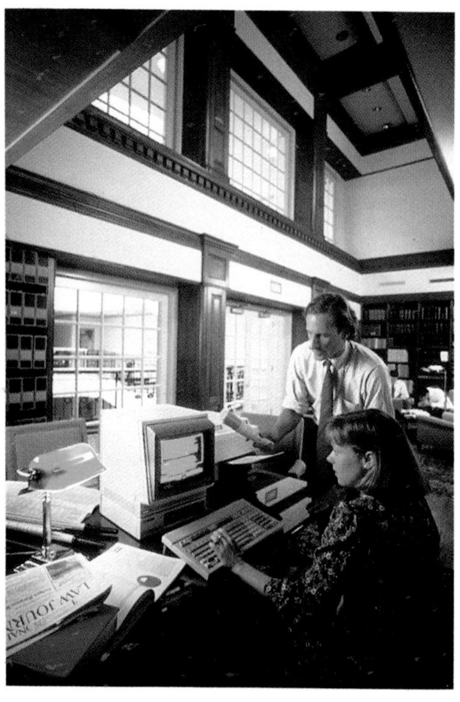

Information processing technology enables law firms to handle large amounts of paperwork quickly and efficiently.

Medical offices use information processing technology to maintain accurate patient records.

Banks use information processing technology to document financial transactions and maintain statistical records.

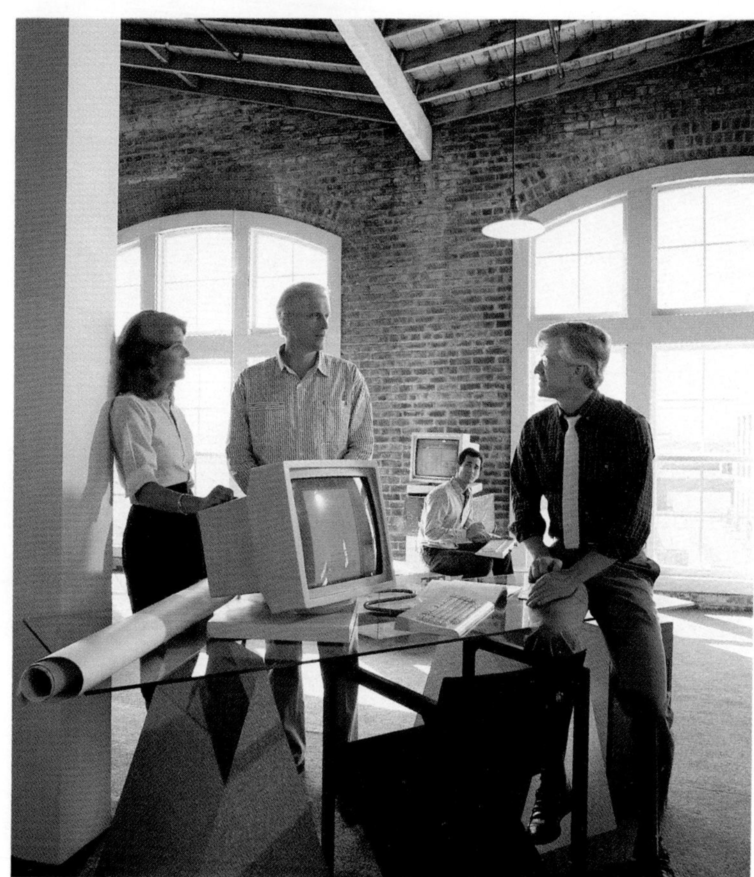

This design firm uses computers to create and modify architectural plans.

Corporate headquarters offices at Esprit in San Francisco.

CHAPTER SUMMARY

- Automated equipment generally enables a secretary in a traditional office setting to work more quickly and efficiently and enables the department as a whole to be more productive.
- Secretaries in a traditional office usually are assigned to one or a few managers and handle both keyboarding and nonkeyboarding tasks.
- The core of a centralized system is the information processing center, a centrally located area where operators handle all or most of a company's document preparation.
- Operators in an information processing center work for managers throughout the company and may be specialists in specific types of documents. Some employees enjoy working in a center; others feel isolation, boredom, and on-the-job pressure.
- Decentralized information processing systems are made up of satellites and minicenters located close to managers.
- In a decentralized or satellite system, information processing operators usually become specialists in the terminology and formatting of the documents produced by their department or floor.
- Ergonomics is the science of adapting working conditions, environment, and equipment design to meet workers' needs.
- An office landscape capitalizes on open space and modular office systems that are easily changed as an organization changes.
- Backaches, eyestrain, stiff muscles, stress, and fatigue are common ailments of office workers. Health complaints can result from poorly designed chairs and other office furniture and equipment.
- Readjusting body position, taking short rest breaks every hour or two, and changing to another task can reduce fatigue, monotony, and health risks for office workers.
- When you keyboard, sit as far away as possible from the screen and have your eyes level with the top of the screen.
- The ideal lighting when using a display screen is to have the screen three to five times brighter than the light in the room. Desk lamps can focus light on hard copy and prevent screen glare.
- "White noise" can contribute to office productivity.
- Temperature and humidity can adversely affect the performance of electronic systems and magnetic media.
- A feasibility study can be useful to determine the need for an information processing system and how people will implement it.
- People are valuable resources to a business and are key to its total operation. A pleasant office environment can contribute to their well-being and efficiency.

VOCABULARY

acoustical
aesthetics
ambient lighting
American National Standards Institute (ANSI)
centralized information processing system
decentralized information processing system
decibel
document production center
ergonomics
feasibility study
information processing center
modules
National Institute for Occupational Safety and Health (NIOSH)
office landscaping
satellite center
specialization
task lighting
white noise
work order

CHAPTER QUESTIONS

1. What are the three basic ways of organizing information processing equipment and employees? Explain the characteristics of each. Explain why companies prefer decentralized systems over centralized systems.
2. If you were a secretary using a personal computer in a traditional setting, name three kinds of tasks you might be expected to perform on the equipment.
3. If you worked in an information processing satellite, how would your work differ from that in a centralized system?
4. Suppose you worked in an information processing center in a large company. Describe how your work environment would differ from that of a secretary in a traditional setting.
5. What major factors do ergonomists consider when they plan an office environment? Why is flexibility so important in designing offices for electronic systems?
6. Discuss the importance of good furniture and equipment design in an office. Describe the ways designers have approached the problems of sitting.
7. Discuss the importance of lighting, noise, temperature, and humidity in today's office.
8. How can you help yourself stay relaxed and comfortable while at your desk? What is the value of rest breaks?
9. Your company has just hired a consultant to conduct a feasibility study. What kinds of information would you expect to get from the consultant's study?
10. Why are people so important to the success of an information system? Explain your reasons.

CASE STUDY

Samantha Iio is an experienced secretary who left the office a few years ago to raise a family. Now that her youngest child is in school, Ms. Iio is ready to return to a 9 to 5 job. For the past several years, she has worked part-time as a specialist in the information processing center of the Intercontinental Brokerage and Investment Corporation, a large investment firm in her community.

Ms. Iio enjoyed the new technology of the automated equipment, but she was glad she worked only half-days. By noon, she was often frazzled by the high pressure of turning out a specified number of documents each day.

When Intercontinental reorganized its information processing center into minicenters, Ms. Iio was offered a full-time position as a lead operator-supervisor of the new satellite center for the International Relations Department. Ms. Iio had been seeking a full-time job and recently received an offer from Randall T. Gross Clothiers, a medium-sized retail clothing firm. At Gross Clothiers, she would be a personal secretary to one of the six company managers. They have the latest office automation equipment, which is networked and integrated. She would use the databases of their network and telecommunications for distributing information to the four other company branches. She also would have filing, telephoning, and other tasks to perform for her boss.

Intercontinental has promised Ms. Iio that if she takes the center position, her chances for advancement will be excellent, and this is important to her. Her future at Gross Clothiers would be uncertain, probably depending on what happens in her boss's career.

What advice would you give Ms. Iio? Which of these jobs should she take? Or would it be better for her to continue to look around for another position? Explain your answers.

CHAPTER 11

Optimizing Productivity

Brian Satero recently began working as an information processing specialist in a satellite center at Legasé & Whitmire, a large law firm. On his first and second days of work, Mr. Satero attended an orientation program for new employees. On the third day, his supervisor, Camille Newman, gave him several office documents, including a procedures manual, a list of document and boilerplate codes, and a software vendor manual. Mr. Satero told Ms. Newman how pleased he was to be working for a company that provided its employees with so much information. Ms. Newman explained that the management at Legasé was very concerned about productivity, and all the help they could give new employees to make them as productive as possible was well worth the effort.

Word Processing Goals

To process words/information/paperwork:

- faster
- more accurately
- with improved quality
- with less physical + mental effort
- at a lower cost

than had been achieved by traditional WAYS

~~What coordinates~~

The law firm of Legasé & Whitmire is not alone in its concern for office productivity. Productivity is important to every organization concerned with competing in today's economy. Merely having automated equipment does not ensure optimum productivity. A business needs skilled employees to use equipment in efficient and productive ways. People are important for implementing procedures that are cost-effective and productive. People are vital for making decisions that contribute to an organized and productive environment. For these and other reasons, we have used the word ***productivity*** *throughout this book.*

People, Change, and Productivity

The way work was done ten years ago is not the same as it is today or will be in the future. Also, the amount of work that needs to be done daily in offices all over the country continues to increase. Although automated office equipment has become affordable for most businesses, the cost of equipment and maintenance is a major expense for many organizations. Information technology is affecting the entire structure of business organizations.

Change in the ways we process information is also influencing the relationship between employees and managers. Workers at all levels need skills that can be transferred from one job to another as well as from one career to another. Productive, skilled employees are in demand and will continue to be a valued resource as long as businesses compete with each other.

Computers can instantly gather and distribute information throughout a business organization. As employees on every level "plug into" and share information, each person knows more about what is going on in the company. To assure that employees understand the total system, some organizations provide **cross training** or instruction and work experience in all company operations.

Networking and multiuser systems, for example, are making cross training more important than ever before. Information access and exchange influence the kinds of decisions we make and the way we make them. As more information is available to people on all levels, many managers will no longer need to issue orders. Many managers are glad to give up this role, giving more responsibility and decision making to employees. Many executives prefer to work unseen in the background, as facilitators whose main task is to make the office the fully creative and productive environment it can be for others.

Although we can measure how many lines or documents an operator keyboards, "Nobody knows how to measure the worth of information," says IBM scientist Lewis M. Branscomb. It is un-

Having access to information affects decision making in an organization.

known at what point an operator's keystrokes cease to be merely an alphanumeric combination and become a new idea. Electronic systems enable us to expand knowledge by giving more people access to information, but our responsibility does not stop there. We must also protect the rights of the employee who can take information and change it into a new idea. It remains for us to maximize the return to the individual from information technology. Rewarding people for their work can contribute to making an organization profitable—and profitability usually depends on productivity.

Work Procedures and Methods

The office of today cannot operate profitably without careful planning, good organization, and sound management practices. Managers need to know how the work is performed in an office. As a result, office productivity has become an area of study. The primary focus, of course, for people who analyze the office environment is office workers themselves. (Recall the discussion of feasibility studies in Chapter 10.) Office systems analysts are interested in finding out how to get the most done with the technology and equipment available.

One way companies try to increase productivity and efficiency is by setting up work procedures. Following these procedures can improve your personal productivity and help you do well on the job. Good procedures can benefit both you and the company. Most companies have found that without standard or set procedures, the overall cost of document production—in time as well as money—tends to go up. When there are no procedures, an employee's job becomes more difficult.

In this chapter, we look at a variety of procedures and methods used to control the work flow in an information system. Note that these procedures are intended to guide both employer and employee. Because they may vary considerably from one company to the next, it is essential to learn and follow your particular company's procedures.

Standardized Formats

Managers and information processing specialists can be saved a great deal of time and trouble if there are guidelines for formatting documents. Instead of having to develop a new format for every document, managers and operators alike can focus their attention on content.

Can you imagine working in an information processing center and having to remember which of the company's many managers wants which letters or memos prepared in a special way? **Standardized formats** eliminate this problem by requiring that all documents be prepared according to prescribed formats. The fewer the number of standardized formats used in a company, the less time an operator needs to learn the approved style. For this reason, many companies use one, and only one, format for all business letters and a similar one for memos. This approach is both effi-

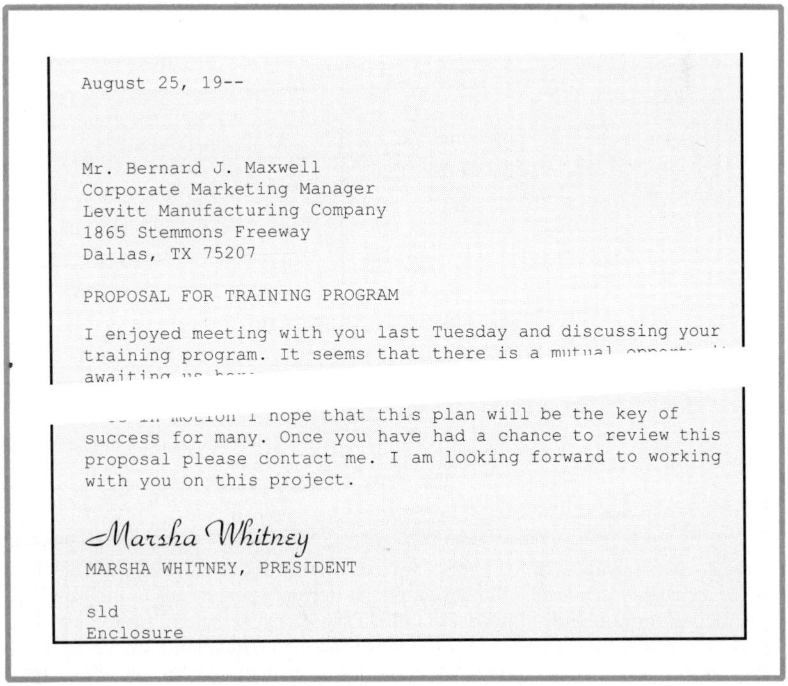

August 25, 19--

Mr. Bernard J. Maxwell
Corporate Marketing Manager
Levitt Manufacturing Company
1865 Stemmons Freeway
Dallas, TX 75207

PROPOSAL FOR TRAINING PROGRAM

I enjoyed meeting with you last Tuesday and discussing your training program. It seems that there is a mutual [illegible]

[illegible] I hope that this plan will be the key of success for many. Once you have had a chance to review this proposal please contact me. I am looking forward to working with you on this project.

Marsha Whitney
MARSHA WHITNEY, PRESIDENT

sld
Enclosure

A standardized format for business letters is a great timesaver. This illustrates a commonly used letter style in business, the simplified block.

cient and economical, particularly in view of the sophisticated formatting, storage, and retrieval capabilities of modern equipment. Standard formats or styles that everyone follows also contribute to productivity.

Document Coding

In an efficient information processing system, files are carefully coded. Once a document or paragraph has been coded and stored, it can be retrieved easily. A clear and systematic **document coding** system enables operators to retrieve standard paragraphs, repetitive letters, forms, and other recorded files whenever and as often as managers need them.

Document codes vary, depending on how a company has organized its electronic filing system. In some companies, the code

Job Request Form

Project No.: 7448
Author: R. Hazelwood
Ext. No.: 564 Date of Request 10/11

Job status		Spacing		Static
draft		single space	✓	8 1/
final	✓	double space		8 1/
revision		single and 1/2		letter
				mem

Date/time wanted 10/12—3 pm
Requested by R. Delagado

For Word Processing Center Use Only

Operator	Date	Time in/out

Work Order (Please print.)

Stored Document Reference No. 5469
Requested by R. DELGADO
Department MARKETING
Extension 250 Date 10/11
Date/time wanted 10/12 NOON
Addressee MR. J.C. NICKEL, SERVICE DIRECTOR, KEYSTONE CORP.
Address
10379 DARNESTOWN RD.
ROCKVILLE, MD. 20850

Variables
1. 06 4.
2. 11 5.
3. 12 6.

Signature/Title
David Holmes, VP
cc R. Hazelwood

Enclosures: 1 Photocopies: 1 Envelopes: 1

Here are two examples of work request forms. The work order shows which copy is to be changed in a form letter and which boilerplate paragraphs to include. The job request form includes information about the line spacing and stationery the author wishes to use. The copy for the letter is usually attached to the form by the author.

includes letters designating department and file type. For example, the code M-4-87 at the top of a hard copy of a letter (but not on the original) can indicate that the memorandum is the Legal Department's (department 4) standard memo number 87. Some companies find that having a document code is so helpful for locating the disk copy that they also include it on the original. The document code can be included as part of the reference initials. Thus, KWB/129 appearing at the bottom of a letter (on both the original and the copies) can indicate that Kirsten W. Brown prepared document number 129.

A manager working with a secretary or information processing specialist can request prerecorded documents or paragraphs by their assigned code numbers. Variable or specific information for processing a document also can be requested. These requests may be made using a work order form (discussed in Chapter 10) or a similar type of form, sometimes called a **variable sheet.**

A manager can indicate on the work request or variable sheet what stored paragraphs are to be used and what variables are needed to produce a complete document. Variables might include names, dates, dollar amounts, or just about anything else. In some companies, variable information is communicated by means of dictation rather than through a variable sheet. By combining variable information with boilerplate paragraphs, a manager can work with an operator to create an almost infinite number of "new" documents—provided, of course, that a sufficient number of boilerplate paragraphs has been coded and stored in the system (see Chapter 2).

Procedures Manuals

Office efficiency can be improved when office workers become familiar with and use standard procedures for completing tasks. That is, as procedures become routine, tasks can usually be done in a productive manner. However, some procedures may be needed only once in a while, and a **procedures manual** can be a good reference to explain how to perform certain office tasks. Directions provided in a well-written procedures manual can also be helpful to new employees and temporary workers.

Procedures manuals are usually prepared by a company because they are specific to its needs. They may be used with other, more general guides, including published reference manuals and desk guides for office workers. Companies may furnish their employees with procedures manuals for many reasons and to meet a number of needs.

Because businesses have different needs, the content of procedures manuals will vary from one to another. Manuals for centralized systems may provide a guide on everything from how to fill out a work order request form to how to send an electronic

An office procedures manual explains how to do certain office tasks.

Guidelines for Keying Tables

1. Identify each table as follows:

   Table title: Key in all caps and center.
   Table number: Key the word Table in caps/lower case letters, followed by the appropriate table number.

2. Treat all table numbers within a document the same way; for example, Table 1.1, Table 1.2; Table 2.2, Table 2.3, Table 2.4.

Guidelines for Taking Dictation

Begin each day's dictation on a new page of your notebook.

In the lower left corner of each page write in the date that you use during the day; for example, October 9, 19--.

Number the dictation notes for each letter, beginning each day with number 1. Also number any related material the author gives you.

Guidelines for Revising Work

Make a photocopy of the document before making any revisions. Mark all changes and inserts on the copy, not on the original.

Clearly mark all changes and inserts in ink.

Identify extracts, indicating the name and identification number of the document from which the extract is taken.

message to a branch office. Manuals for decentralized systems may furnish specific information relating to the document needs of the particular department served.

Some companies encourage their employees to play an active role in the creation, preparation, and revision of procedures manuals. In other companies, developing procedures manuals is exclusively a supervisory responsibility, although supervisors frequently ask information processing specialists and other end users for suggestions.

User Manuals

User manuals frequently are **vendor manuals** or instruction books published by a manufacturer to help you use its product or service. A user manual may contain documentation ranging from the operation and care of your computer to the use of a software program. User manuals with a good table of contents, index, and glossary can be especially useful in helping you find the section or page for solving a problem and in providing explanations for unfamiliar terminology. Many manuals are used as training guides. That is, they provide step-by-step instructions to learn how to do a specific application.

Consulting a user manual can be helpful in solving problems or learning unfamiliar terminology.

User manuals also may be prepared by the business rather than by a manufacturer. For example, when an organization purchases a large computer system, the equipment itself is not much more than a piece of hardware. It is still necessary to develop software so the computer can perform its work. Once the software is completed, the company needs documentation to explain to its employees how to use the system. The **documentation** is a user manual or guide to its operation.

You should be familiar with the user manuals for the hardware and software in your office. The better you understand the features and capabilities of your office resources, the more productive you should be. As you work with your equipment, refer to the manuals from time to time for answers to specific questions.

In-House Training

People are not only valuable; they are a costly company resource. Because employees who are productive as well as quality conscious can be real assets, many businesses invest a great deal in making their employees the best workers they can be. Naturally, employees are not expected to learn work procedures and methods solely from procedures or users manuals. Most companies realize that to maximize employee knowledge, ability, and productivity, they must provide **in-house training** (within company instruction).

In-house training can take several forms. New employees may attend a company orientation. The program is designed to inform new employees about the company as a whole, its various parts, and its products or services. An orientation program may consist of several sessions or only one, and the person or persons con-

Many companies provide in-house training for their employees.

ducting it may complement the presentation with handouts, slides, films, overhead transparencies, and other printed and audiovisual materials.

Beyond providing orientation, in-house training programs deal with job performance. They cover work procedures, the use of information processing equipment, personal computers, and any other equipment that will be used on the job. Frequently, they include human relations and communications development. Skill development also may be included in the training. Training may be formal and highly structured or informal and loosely organized, depending on the individual company and the job for which the employee is being trained.

In-house training programs may be conducted by company personnel, by outside consultants, or by hardware and software vendors. In some companies, all these may play a part in training. For instance, company personnel may teach employees about work flow and the basic procedures for document production, an outside consultant may conduct a workshop on time management, and vendors may help train operators in the use of new equipment.

Measuring Productivity

Productivity can be increased through standardized formats, coding, standardized procedures, manuals and documentation, and training. But the question of how much it can be increased still remains.

Work Measurement Standards

The issue of determining an employee's productivity or **work measurement** is one that company managers must address if they are to justify the large dollar outlay required to purchase information processing equipment. Computing and recording the amount of work employees produce can help managers operate their business and plan ahead.

Usually if workers know they are measured against other workers as well as against their own prior performance, quality and productivity go up. Most good workers take pride in their accomplishments and in their improvement on the job. Also, assuming that adjustments are made for the varying difficulty of different assignments, achievement factors can be judged. A system that evaluates employees on the same basis helps ensure that the best workers are rewarded. Productivity measurement is most common in large information processing centers.

Work Measurement Methods

There are no clear-cut standards to guide businesses in measuring productivity. Thus, companies use several methods of productiv-

Issues Work Measurement Can Address

- The effectiveness of an information processing system
- The capability of current equipment to meet paperwork demands
- Possible alternatives to equipment maintenance, time-sharing, and other strategies for cost-effectiveness
- The impact of variations in work flow on scheduling and distributing work
- Possible need for full-time, part-time, or temporary employees
- Employee productivity and the possible benefit of additional training
- The costs of operating an information processing center, satellite centers, or individual pieces of specialized equipment
- How much to "charge back" to customers (or the departments in the company for time spent using the information processing system)
- The relationship of employee productivity to job performance standards (For example, a specialist who processes general correspondence might produce many more documents than a specialist who works on highly technical, lengthy material.)
- Measuring production once a standard is set and outlining eligibility for possible salary increase or promotion

ity or work measurement. Two of the most common are work logs and production counts.

Work Log A **work log** (**log-in sheet, document log,** or **production log**) is a chart that records the work coming into and going out of an information processing center (or, in some cases, a satellite or minicenter). In some centers, a supervisor takes responsibility for keeping the work log current. In other centers, one operator may be assigned the task of keeping the log, or it may be up to each specialist to enter a document into the log when it is completed.

Each operator's work can be recorded on an individual document log, or everyone's work can be noted on one master log. Logs may be tabulated on a daily or weekly basis and then summarized in production reports. Such reports, which may be compiled monthly, quarterly, yearly, or all three, enable center or satellite supervisors to communicate to management such useful information as the average turnaround time for each kind of document produced, the total amount of work produced per department and per manager, and the amount of dictated input as opposed to handwritten or rough draft input.

Work logs are used to measure productivity, but that is by no means their sole purpose. Log sheets are used to manage, track, and coordinate the flow of work into and out of a center. They are used for charge-back purposes and to provide a concrete and detailed record of a company's document production. Logs also measure the overall productivity of a center or minicenter as well as the output of each operator in lines, pages, or documents.

Production Counts A number of different methods are used to measure a worker's productivity. Several involve **production counts** that tally the production quantity—**document count, page count,** and **line count.** Line counts are used more frequently than other types of production counts. Another method involves the manager or supervisor establishing a **production time estimate** (an estimate of how long it will take a specialist to do the job). It may be possible with such a system for operators to contract for the jobs. That is, operators are paid according to the job rather than an hourly wage.

One purpose of a work log is to measure productivity.

There are definite problems with these methods because they cannot always measure precisely the various jobs done. In some situations, all the documents produced are similar in format and

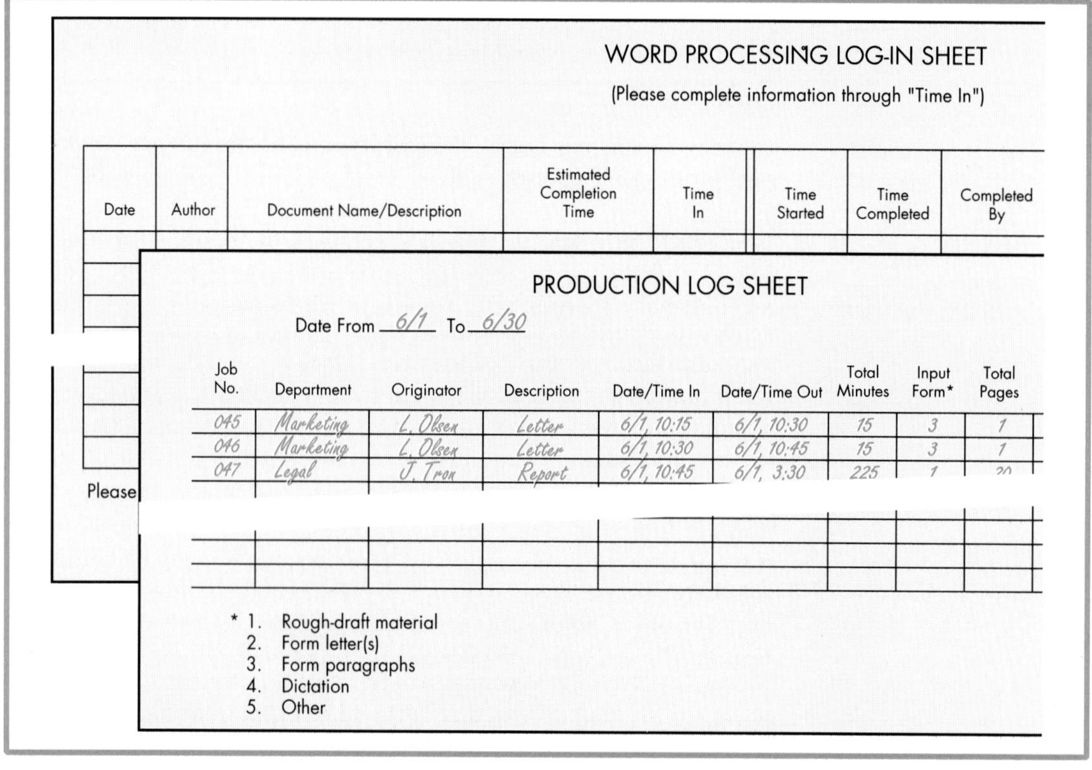

WORD PROCESSING LOG-IN SHEET

(Please complete information through "Time In")

Date	Author	Document Name/Description	Estimated Completion Time	Time In	Time Started	Time Completed	Completed By

Please

PRODUCTION LOG SHEET

Date From 6/1 To 6/30

Job No.	Department	Originator	Description	Date/Time In	Date/Time Out	Total Minutes	Input Form*	Total Pages
045	Marketing	L. Olsen	Letter	6/1, 10:15	6/1, 10:30	15	3	1
046	Marketing	L. Olsen	Letter	6/1, 10:30	6/1, 10:45	15	3	1
047	Legal	J. Tron	Report	6/1, 10:45	6/1, 3:30	225	1	20

* 1. Rough-draft material
2. Form letter(s)
3. Form paragraphs
4. Dictation
5. Other

Businesses continually seek more effective ways of measuring productivity while maintaining high standards of quality.

in the manner of input. But in other cases, documents are much more diverse. Some are dictated; others are rough drafts or handwritten. Some contain complicated statistical data; others are only brief letters and notes. Some documents are totally new; others are old documents with only minor revisions. Still other documents are forms or boilerplate that require only a few inserts and simple editing.

Establishing work production measures can be time-consuming and complicated for both managers and operators. Merely counting the total number of sheets of paper produced would lead to invalid comparisons. Some companies have devised systems that take into account not only the length of the document but also such factors as the complexity of format, difficulty of content, and manner of input. Under such a system, a two-page statistical table with a complicated format would count as far more work than a two-page prerecorded form letter.

Productivity and Quality Goals

Regardless of actual measurement methods used, all companies strive to streamline their productivity measurement procedures. When work measurement is coupled with maintaining high quality standards, the measurement task may not be easy. The process of measuring productivity can take a great deal of time. It also can become a hindrance to operators, leading to poor morale and lower-quality work. For these and other reasons, productivity measurement can become counterproductive. Management is always on the lookout for easier and quicker ways to compute and measure productivity based on quality.

There are no definite ways to guarantee productivity. Approaches to productivity measurement will continue to vary from company to company. Some establish highly structured measurement systems designed to calculate productivity with the utmost accuracy. Others take a more relaxed approach, with specialists recording line counts and a supervisor totaling and compiling the data into an overall production report.

Whatever the end result, many experts say that office productivity cannot be calculated. Such a statement makes it important for workers to be organized and skilled, and to take pride in work. As important as increasing production is, volume is only one aspect of information processing. If documents are not accurate, speed becomes meaningless. As one supervisor put it, "Better to produce 100 perfect documents than 200 imperfect ones."

CHAPTER SUMMARY

- People are valuable but costly assets to a business. If people are cross trained in all aspects of company operations, they may be able to contribute to high productivity.
- One way companies try to increase productivity and efficiency is by establishing certain work procedures.
- Standardized formats for documents save time and trouble for both information processing operators and managers by establishing a set style of document preparation for everyone to follow.
- Document coding enables operators to retrieve prerecorded files quickly and easily whenever a person needs them.
- A manager can request prerecorded documents by their assigned code numbers and then indicate specific variable information by using a variable sheet. The stored boilerplate paragraphs are combined with the information specified on the sheet to create a new document.
- Office procedures manuals are designed to guide and help employees perform their assignments.
- Measuring the productivity of information processing workers helps management evaluate current equipment and plan equipment changes according to need.
- Productivity measurement provides management with important information that can be used in planning and scheduling work and in identifying high and low producers.

- Productivity measurement is also used in financial recordkeeping and planning.
- Calculating and recording employee work production help managers and supervisors set performance standards tailored to the individual company or department.
- A work log is a chart that records work coming into and going out of an information processing center, minicenter, or satellite. Although they have other purposes, document logs are commonly used to measure productivity.
- Office productivity is at best difficult to measure. Quality must be considered in work measurement.

VOCABULARY

cross training
documentation
document coding
in-house training
line count
procedures manual
production counts
productivity
standardized format
user manual
variable sheet
work log
work measurement

CHAPTER QUESTIONS

1. Why are employers so concerned with productivity? Do you think their concern is justified? Why or why not?
2. Why might a company that has a standard format for letters be more productive than one that lacks this standardization?
3. What is a document code? Give an example. Why are document codes necessary?
4. Give three examples of how a procedures manual can help a new employee.
5. If you were a department supervisor, would you want to measure your operators' productivity? What would be the advantages and disadvantages?
6. What is a document log, and what uses does it include?
7. Why is it usually invalid to compare the work output of the operators in a center just by counting the number of sheets of paper each produces? How could this problem be remedied?
8. What is a variable sheet, and how is it used in an information processing center?
9. Explain how a company's orientation program differs from an in-house training program.
10. Why can productivity measurement be considered a good thing for employees as well as for management?

CASE STUDY

Michaelson and Cox is a large accounting firm that recently established four information processing minicenters to handle its huge volume of documents—correspondence, reports, statistical information, customer accounts, etc. Jasmine Knopf was made manager over the four satellite centers. She has been with the company for five years and was promoted to the position from her former job as administrative assistant to one of the firm's accountants.

After the satellite centers had been in operation for several months, it was apparent to management as well as to Ms. Knopf that things were not going well. Managers complained that document turnaround time was too long. They also didn't like the fact that similar documents were prepared differently by different operators. These operators were also having problems keeping track of the work they were supposed to do and in deciding which jobs had priority over others. Also, much time was being wasted in having operators keyboard from scratch documents that had like or similar elements. New operators had trouble learning equipment and procedures.

Management was concerned that the enormous investment they had made in expensive electronic equipment was not paying off in increased productivity. They wanted proof that the minicenters were a worthwhile investment.

In order to alleviate the problems with managers and operators, Ms. Knopf's manager, the director of Management Information Systems, decided to send Ms. Knopf to a five-day workshop for information processing managers and supervisors. She was eager to attend the workshop because she was naturally concerned about the problems the minicenters were having.

Based on what you have learned in this chapter, what do you expect Ms. Knopf learned at the workshop that would help end the problems in the satellite centers? Put yourself in her place, and develop a plan for eliminating the problems described.

CHAPTER 12

You and Your Career

As Angela Malek waited for her interview in the reception area of the law firm of Cartwell, Rothers, and Nimoy, she looked over her neatly formatted resumé. Her qualifications were strong. She had excellent keyboarding and proofreading skills. She also had just completed a word processing concepts and applications course. Still she was nervous. Would her communications and human relations skills come through to the interviewer? Would she be able to convey that she was highly dependable, reliable, flexible, and cooperative? Her nervousness lessened a bit as she thought, "I'll just be myself. I have excellent skills and a willing, positive attitude. I like people and I'm professional. I'm a hard worker. This is my career choice; I can do it."

Most people approach a new position hoping to like their job and do well at it. Ms. Malek was no exception. She made her decision to work in a career related to information processing because she liked the challenges it offered. She knew that her skills were good. She knew, too, that if she applied herself to her job and showed initiative and potential, she could look forward to other job opportunities.

There are many options open in the field of information processing that are available to you today. After you have worked at a job for a while, you may consider being promoted or changing from one kind of job to another in the same field. Technology advances also will provide new job opportunities for you to consider a few years from now—jobs that do not even exist today.

Developing Marketable Skills

The opportunities are great for people with good skills and for people who can adapt to changing times. Work force researchers tell us that most people will change careers two to four times within their working lifetimes—and that statistic does not include job changes. The average working person probably will make five, six, or even more job changes in addition to career changes.

To prepare for the changing job outlook, you will need several skills to be successfully employed in an occupation within an information system. Each of these skills (including knowledge, attitudes, and personal attributes and characteristics) has importance for the many kinds of job situations and careers available in an information system. How well you develop these skills will determine your success in the information processing field and the office job market.

Most employers agree that two main skill areas are vitally important to job success: (1) technology skills and (2) interpersonal (human relations) and communications skills. Many of these are called **transferability skills** or skills that permit you to move from one job to another. Having skills that transfer from one career to another is important because jobs do not remain constant. There are some basic skills that will be extremely valuable to you in competing in a changing job market. Assess your skills because they will influence your final decision about a career as well as your ultimate success on the job.

Technology and Related Skills

You must be able to apply the information processing concepts you have learned to office work. Your hands-on skills must be tied closely to the many components of productivity. For example, ex-

Technology and Related Skills for Office Workers

- **Keyboarding and document formatting** As a general rule, at least 50 words a minute with a high degree of accuracy is desirable. Keyboarding skill must be coupled with an ability to format and make decisions for producing an attractive end product.
- **Proofreading** Sharp proofreading skills are essential. A document with errors is an ineffective document. The work you produce reflects not only on you as an employee but on the image of the company. A business cannot tolerate errors and still remain competitive.
- **Transcription** Familiarity with transcription equipment is desired by many business executives. Actual training in operating transcription equipment will extend employability and also usually improve keyboarding skills.
- **Shorthand** Although shorthand is not as popular as it used to be, employers usually consider this skill a plus. Many companies hire employees who have shorthand because of the English grammar and usage-related communications skills that accompany it.
- **Mechanical aptitude** Working with automated equipment in today's office is a necessity. Employers want employees who not only have office equipment skills, but who also enjoy working with equipment and are able to do some "basic troubleshooting" when a problem arises.
- **Computer knowledge** Employers expect employees to know basic computer concepts and operations. Hands-on training, especially in word processing, is also very important. Information processing experience is always desirable.

cellent keyboarding skill is of little value unless the final product is error-free and neatly formatted.

Interpersonal Relations and Communications Skills

More people are fired from jobs because of poor human relations than for any other reason. Most jobs require "people skills" or good interpersonal skills. Employers want employees who can get along with co-workers and be able to communicate with people at all levels. Many qualities contribute to good human relations and communications skills. If you think about it, information processing involves "communications." For example, information processing is of little value if the information is not distributed and communicated for decisions to be made. Employers place great value on interpersonal skills that have a high degree of transferability.

Interpersonal and Communications Skills for Office Workers

- **Language** Solid language skills—a strong working knowledge of English grammar and usage, punctuation, and spelling—are an absolute necessity. Enrolling in a business English course or self-study program at home can help improve these skills.
- **Critical thinking and decision making** The ability to think abstractly, to organize material, and to follow instructions is essential to an office position. Workers who have developed their decision-making and critical thinking skills are valued employees.
- **Dependability** Workers who can be depended upon are valued workers. Dependable employees come to work every day and on time, follow through on projects, keep their word, and contribute their fair share to the work load. Enthusiasm for work and a cheerful and helpful attitude help enhance a worker's dependability.
- **Relating to others** Employers want employees who get along with their co-workers. Being able to work well with all types of people helps get a job done. Being happily involved with the people and the work in an office is important.
- **Good judgment** Using good judgment in the work environment is a must. All work should be accurate and logical. Learning to trust common sense and to start and complete projects on your own are essential.
- **Maturity** Employers want employees who can handle matters in an adult manner. Develop confidence in what you can do well. Show people they can depend on you to take responsibility. Exercise self-control with yourself and others.
- **Flexibility** Office workers must be willing to accept change. Keep an open mind and go with the flow. Be receptive to

Information Systems Careers

Self-evaluation is important to making the right career choice. You need to know yourself as an employee. You need to have a clear idea of your job skills. And you need to know in what type of working environment you would be happy. There are several additional things you need to consider.

You will be able to assess a job more easily if you have a general knowledge of the opportunities within the information processing field. One caution: Job titles do not necessarily mean the same thing to all businesses. They vary as widely as the duties one new ideas, procedures, tasks, and equipment. Learn to adapt easily and cheerfully to change.

- **Discretion** Professionalism in any setting is important. Avoid discussing the information with which you work—inside or outside the office—even if it is not labeled "confidential." Rumors and gossip have no place in business.
- **Receptiveness** No one expects a worker to know everything. Admit what you don't know and need to learn. Be receptive to others' advice and suggestions. An enthusiastic worker with an open mind is an asset to any employer.
- **Integrity** Loyalty to an employer is a desirable trait. Be on time—arrive on time and don't leave early. Take reasonable lunch breaks. In business, time is money. When you are prompt, it tells your boss that you like being at your place of work.
- **Personal appearance** Appearance and body language can say more about you than your words. The image you portray also reflects on your office. Be sure your dress is appropriate, neat, and clean. Watch your body language. Your movements and gestures also communicate a message.
- **Positive attitude** Employers like positive people because they usually generate positive results. Take a "can do" approach. If you think you can do something, you have a better chance of performing well than if you take a negative approach.
- **Team member** Running an effective information system takes group effort. Pitch in and help others when you are not busy. The team approach can be very effective. Offering help to a co-worker may yield you a return favor—and at a time when you need it most.

performs in various positions. Job titles and descriptions also change frequently. Be aware of these vast differences as you assess each job.

It is difficult at best to identify job titles and job descriptions in a changing information society. Experts suggest that new job titles with new job descriptions will comprise anywhere from 20 to 50 percent of the jobs 10 to 15 years from now. To assist businesses with job information, many professional organizations and groups conduct employee surveys. These groups also provide direction in identifying new developments in the specific fields they represent.

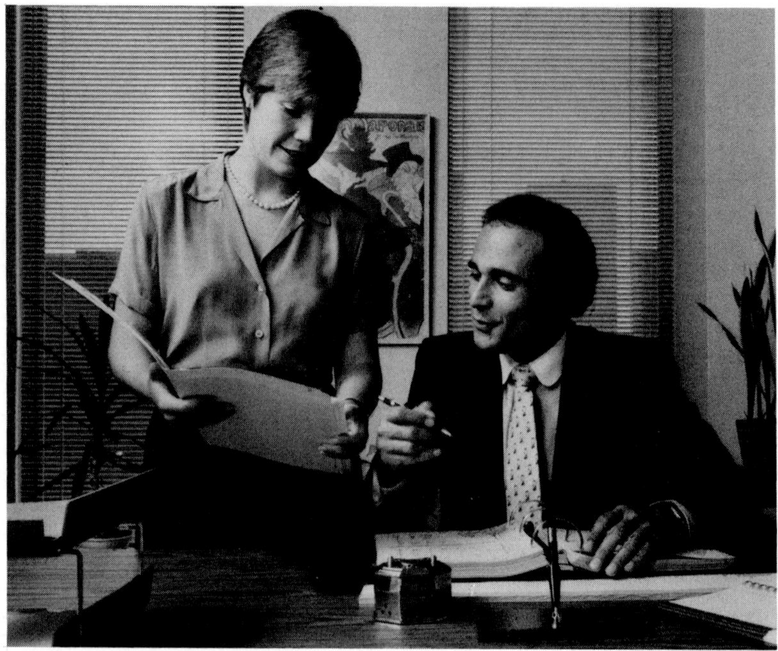

Employers value workers with good interpersonal skills and positive attitudes.

For example, the **Association of Information Systems Professionals (AISP)** is a professional organization that develops and disseminates information/word processing ideas, methods, and techniques. Founded in 1972, the AISP is made up of individuals working in information systems and related areas. Any person wishing to join the AISP can do so. Members receive the AISP regular publications, which focus on topics such as annual job survey data, technical information, and other material of interest to persons in the information systems field.

Based on these and other sources, the following titles and job descriptions will give you a general idea of what to expect in information processing and related jobs. They should help you gather more specific career information from businesses where you want to work.

Information Systems Specialists

Many kinds of specialists are needed to operate an information system. Individuals who mainly do keyboarding and document formatting are called information processing operators or specialists. In a centralized information processing system, specialists can be classified according to a number of different levels and specialties based on their degree of skill, seniority, and special aptitudes or interests. Here are a few of these classifications.

Information/Word Processing Trainee An information/word processing trainee position is usually for people just entering

Assessing Your Career Choice

- Do the skill requirements of the job match your abilities and training?
- Has the employer spelled out the duties you will be expected to carry out?
- Would you feel comfortable and yet reasonably challenged performing these duties, or is there another job that would be better for you?
- What advancement opportunities are available within the company or will this position prepare you for other jobs outside the company?
- Will you need retraining or further education to maintain this position or move to another position?
- Have you been realistic in prioritizing your capabilities and expectations for making a good career choice?

Working Environment Considerations

- **Company size** Weigh the advantages and disadvantages of working in various sizes of businesses (large, medium, small). Your happiness is important for optimizing your work.
- **Company type** Determine if there are kinds of businesses (law firm, manufacturer, advertising agency, retail chain) where you want to work. Weigh your choices in determining job success.
- **Company structure** How comfortable you are in a job may depend on the way a company is organized. For example, the work you would do in one word processing center can be quite different from that in another or in a traditional office.

the job market. A trainee may have no work experience or possibly as much as a year of work experience. An entry-level trainee needs good keyboarding and formatting skills; a good knowledge of grammar, punctuation, and spelling; and the ability to use dictionaries, handbooks, and other reference materials such as vendor manuals.

A trainee should like working with machines and should have a spirit of teamwork. Trainee duties include routine transcription and manipulation of text from dictation, rough drafts, and other raw material. Trainees usually keep their own production records and may be required to proofread their own work.

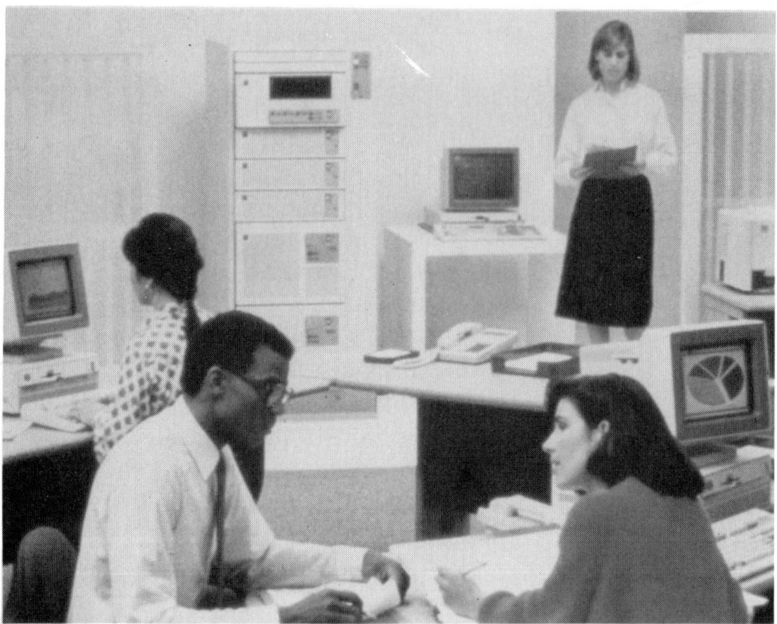

An entry-level trainee should have effective interpersonal skills as well as good information processing skills.

Proofreading Specialist A proofreader checks documents for content, grammar, spelling, punctuation, and keying errors. Many proofreaders key the final corrections on the specialist's copy and print the document. Thus, proofreaders need good machine skills. Proofreaders also may be asked to set standards for grammar and formatting and to guide authors and secretaries in their effort to meet them.

Information/Word Processing Operator/Specialist A specialist position (sometimes called a Specialist I) is for people with about six months to two years of word processing experience. In addition to meeting all the requirements and performing all the duties of a trainee, an operator handles special documents, meets established quality standards, uses all the text-editing functions of word processing equipment, and is familiar with any special terminology or practices associated with the organization.

There may be two or three levels within this category. For example, a Specialist II (intermediate level) will be skilled at formatting, producing, and revising complicated documents, such as lengthy technical and statistical reports. The specialist may have to assemble these documents from complex sources, sometimes retrieving information from electronic files. Specialists must understand proofreading and editing symbols. They must be fully acquainted with procedures and records maintenance.

A Specialist II requires the ability and confidence to act independently when interpreting instructions. At this intermediate level, the specialist assumes full responsibility for the accuracy and completeness of a document. Information processing specialists sometimes operate telecommunications equipment.

Information Processing Lead Operator or Assistant Supervisor As experience is gained, some companies have career opportunities for specialists to move into supervisory positions. Such an advanced position may be referred to as a Specialist III, lead operator, or assistant supervisor. At this advanced level, a person usually knows how to operate all the equipment and perform all the jobs within an information processing center. The person may be responsible for coordinating and assigning work, compiling production statistics, and recommending changes in procedure. Some specialists in these positions may be involved in training new employees.

Data-Entry Operator/Specialist Similar to information processing specialists, there may be several levels of data-entry operator positions. The level depends on experience and skills. Data-entry clerk and operator duties include entry and retrieval of data in a computer system through the use of terminal devices and/or keypunch equipment. A data-entry specialist works with statistical data, codes input, and receives and sorts data. At advanced levels, a data-entry specialist may be classified as a supervisor. In a supervisory position, the person would plan, schedule, and direct all data-entry and related activities.

Data Control Clerk and Coding Specialist Both data control clerks and data coding specialists receive and input data into a computer system. Original documents are coded for processing and are checked for correctness and completeness in the input and output stages. Inventory and records lists are maintained for access and review of stored records. In some companies, there is a wide range of data control and coding of jobs, from entry-level to advanced positions.

Phototypesetting Specialist A specialist or operator who keys and revises text for use in a photocomposition system, such as that used to print magazines, is called a phototypesetting specialist. This job requires a knowledge of fonts (type sizes and faces) and other aspects of printing and typesetting, as well as general proficiency on a microcomputer or similar equipment.

Peripheral Equipment Operator/Specialist Many companies need specialists to operate various kinds of equipment. For example, a duplicating specialist may operate all types of duplicating and photocopy equipment. Some peripheral equipment specialists operate only one very specialized type of equipment, such as an intelligent photocopier. Other specialists may operate several types of peripherals, including OCRs and other scanning devices, printers and plotters, microform readers and copiers, backup card and tape systems, and similar peripherals. Peripheral equipment operators need machine skills to perform necessary equipment operations to input, output, and store documents. Usually, some technical knowledge of the equipment is required of a peripheral equipment specialist.

Telecommunications Specialist A telecommunications or teleprocessing specialist is an equipment operator who has specialized skills in sending and receiving documents. These skills include how to key and code information that is to be transmitted. A teleprocessing specialist verifies protocols and procedures. The specialist also must know procedures for logging and monitoring transmissions. A specialist in telecommunications also must maintain security as information and files are distributed. The specialist makes decisions on transmission modes and directs all the distribution of a system.

Secretaries or Administrative Assistants In many businesses, secretaries or administrative assistants may be involved with information processing in addition to their other duties. An administrative secretary works as part of an administrative support team to handle information processing, takes dictation, does filing and photocopying, makes schedules, and performs other tasks for one or more executives. If you work in the smallest of offices, of course, the support team may consist of one person—you!

As a secretary moves up the career ladder, the position may carry a "status" title with it. Like information processing specialists, secretarial positions may be designated by level with such titles as senior administrative secretary, administrative officer, or executive assistant. A person in this type of position is qualified to compose and edit documents for executives. Senior positions require several years of experience. People in executive assistant positions may handle special projects, assist a supervisor, and help executives with research.

Many executive assistants have started their careers in entry-level positions. If your goal is to reach the executive assistant level, you more than likely will be an exceptional secretary who is fully aware of the organization's practices and standards. You will have excellent decision-making and organizational skills as well as information processing skills.

Supervisors and Managers

There are many different levels and specialties among information systems specialists/operators and secretaries/administrative assistants. There also are wide differences among the various levels of supervisors and managers, usually based on experience and responsibility. Management steps and levels vary widely among businesses. For example, some do not distinguish between supervisory, managerial, and/or administrative levels. However, to help you understand the difference, supervisory and managerial positions for information processing and administrative support services are noted here.

Information/Word Processing Supervisor An information processing supervisor is responsible for the day-to-day operation of a department, minicenter, or center. The supervisor does training, makes assignments, establishes and maintains quality standards, sets priorities, and helps operators process documents. Supervisors also analyze production procedures and suggest ways of improving them. They sometimes make recommendations for equipment purchases, and they help prepare budgets.

Information/Word Processing Manager An information processing manager usually has more responsibility than a supervisor. A manager is responsible for the entire information processing center or operations of a company, including the design of the system.

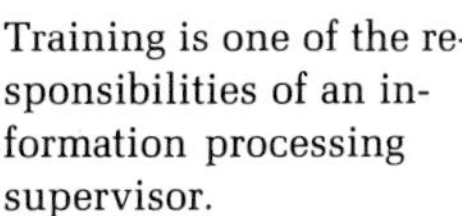

Training is one of the responsibilities of an information processing supervisor.

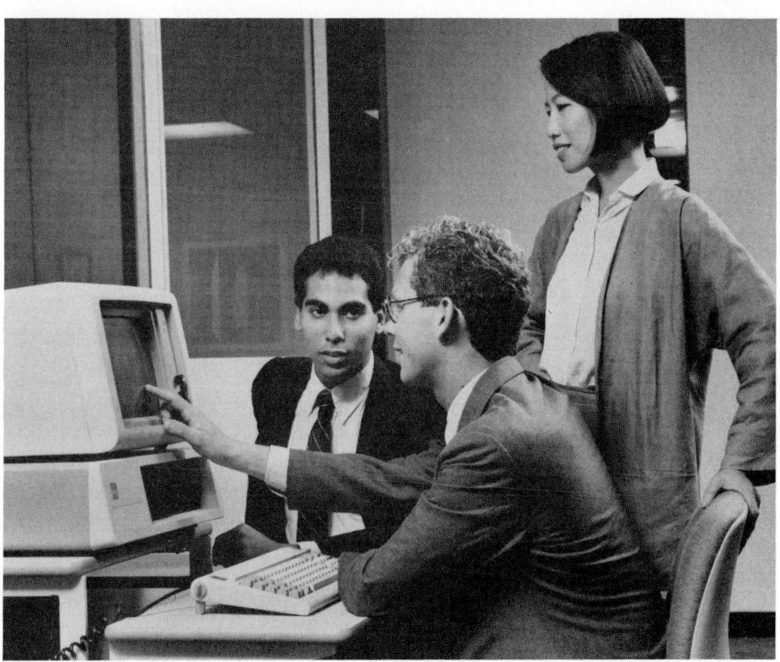

The manager is in charge of staffing decisions and budgets and coordinates the work of authors, specialists, and the administrative support staff. In addition, the manager may oversee the operation of reproduction, graphics, printing, and distribution.

Administrative Support Supervisor An administrative support or administrative services supervisor coordinates the secretarial team's work flow. The supervisor has similar responsibilities to an information/word processing supervisor, making sure day-to-day operations of administrative support run smoothly. Administrative support supervisors act as go-betweens for secretaries and executives. The supervisor evaluates staffing requirements and recommends improvements in the administrative support system.

Administrative Support Manager An administrative support manager is responsible for the development, maintenance, and evaluation of all administrative support services, such as records management, staffing, distribution, and paraprofessional aid. The support manager works closely with the information processing manager to coordinate the work of their staffs. In addition, the support manager may be in charge of other administrative functions, such as printing and purchasing.

Chief Information Officer A chief information officer (CIO) also may be called the director of information support systems. This person has total responsibility for all aspects of an organization's office system. The CIO's responsibilities have significance to all employees, whether they are involved in information processing, administrative support, or other related functions.

Other Specialists in an Information System

There may be more job levels in large companies than in small ones. Some companies have **horizontal career paths,** which may permit you to select from several jobs with about the same level of responsibility. Horizontal paths usually provide diversity in job duties. It is also important to know the steps or levels in a **vertical** or **upward career path.** The presence of several levels in a vertical path, for example, does not necessarily mean it will take you longer to advance in your career. Each company will have its own promotion and career enrichment policy. You should become familiar with the career options of your company. Here are several other jobs that you may consider as you gain experience and advance in your career.

Staff Analyst A staff analyst requires good organizational and analytical skills. The responsibility of the staff analyst is to consult and assist information processing and administrative support

Some larger companies have their own training department.

supervisors and managers. In doing this, the staff analyst conducts studies, reviews operations, and recommends appropriate staffing, procedures, and equipment.

Trainer An information processing specialist is a good candidate to become a trainer. A trainer's chief responsibility is usually to teach new operators how to use software applications such as word processing, spreadsheets, and database management. However, a trainer may instruct in many areas, such as computer and peripheral equipment, office procedures, or machine-dictation skills. Training depends on company needs. Before purchasing information processing equipment, managers may ask a trainer to make recommendations based on personal experience or knowledge of what equipment is available.

Some trainers are in-house trainers or employees of a company. Large companies may even have their own training department. Other trainers are employed by a vendor. Vendor trainers may offer instruction at the vendor location or within a company on an as-needed basis. Vendor trainers usually need greater expertise than in-house trainers because many of them also sell equipment and software.

Computer Applications Specialist Purchasing applications software is a significant expense for companies that furnish many of their employees with personal computers. These businesses often hire an applications specialist whose job is to test applications packages and decide which ones work best for the company. Applications specialists also help teach employees to use software packages. Specialists need to have a good working knowledge of both hardware and software. An interest in learning new software and in troubleshooting problems is a common requirement for a computer applications specialist.

Systems Analyst Selecting the appropriate computer system is not an easy task for a company. Some have in-house systems analysts to help them make this decision. In other cases, a systems analyst will be called in to help with the task. A systems analyst needs to work closely with managers and employees to design a system that precisely fits their needs. Software and hardware decisions must be made. Then the kind and number of operators needed must be determined. Once the system is in place, there may be operator training and orientation. A systems analyst will work with the employees who will use the system and continue to make changes until the system is operating smoothly.

Many large companies employ a full-time systems analyst in each department. Some companies employ a part-time analyst on

A systems analyst helps select the most appropriate computer system for a company and ensures that the system operates properly after it is in place.

a project-by-project basis. Systems analysts like solving computer problems logically. They must have good oral and written communications skills. Systems analysts need to be able to explain the technical aspect of computers in a meaningful way to people in the business environment.

Programmer Organizations that use mainframes, minicomputers, or a sizable number of microcomputers often cannot find prepackaged software programs that satisfy their need for a particular business operation. They hire a programmer, full- or part-time, to design and write programs that will perform specific functions. Programmers often work with systems analysts as part of a team.

Concentration is essential for programmers because programming can be tedious. It is detailed and precise; it requires logical thinking. Many programmers have mathematics backgrounds in addition to computer training and they may know a number of programming languages, including BASIC, COBOL, FORTRAN, Pascal, and Assembler.

A records clerk must have good organizational skills.

Records Analyst/Database Specialist Information handling has become a concern to most companies. If a company's databases are large enough, or if many or widely dispersed sources are used to update them, records analysts and database specialists can help organize and manage them. Large companies that create and maintain their own databases often employ a records manager.

The records management field has entry-level positions such as records clerks, as well as advanced positions such as records managers. Many records professionals are records analysts and database specialists. Some jobs are highly specialized (such as retention analysts and archive specialists). People in the records management field must like detail and organization. Data manage-

A sales representative must be knowledgeable about the vendor's product.

ment in an automated system can be very interesting because of the networking and online communications possibilities.

Vendor Sales Representative Many vendors that sell software and hardware employ people to sell, demonstrate, and provide training for the products they sell. Sales representatives, trainers, and marketing support staff need technical expertise about a variety of computers and peripherals. They also need to be familiar with the software packages designed for office computers. As a sales representative, you must be able to deal with many kinds of people in a variety of business settings, and you may have to travel extensively. In addition, you need a thorough knowledge of the vendor's product line and of how its products compare with those of the competition.

Vendors are especially eager to hire sales representatives who can operate their equipment and who have learned from experience how the equipment performs during routine use. If you are aggressive and knowledgeable, you can earn excellent money as a vendor sales representative.

Your Working Environment

Knowing about the skills required of you can help you succeed on a job. As you assess your skills, also assess the kind of working environment in which you will work. Your skills, attitudes, likes, and dislikes will be important to the success of your career choice.

The company size, type, and structure are important to you. If you do not like working on team projects, you may not be happy in a setting where several persons contribute to a finished product. You may find you like specified, detailed job tasks rather than more global general duties where there are few defined guidelines. If you prefer working alone, there are many jobs that permit and even demand a degree of isolation. If you enjoy personal interaction in accomplishing tasks, you will want to look for a job that provides it.

You also should consider several other things as you assess your work habits. For example, if you are ambitious, seek a job that has a good chance of leading to a higher position. If security is more important to you, you may want to forgo advancement opportunities for the greater safety of a stable position. If you like working with machines, you have many options. If you don't, you may want to find a job that is more involved with people than equipment. If you are flexible, you should look for a position that gives rein to your flexibility. If you aren't, you will want a structured job with definite, prescribed duties. Remember, the more versatile and flexible you are, the more jobs you will find to mesh with your skills and work habits.

Although you may have heard about certain "secrets" of success, there actually are no secrets. Most employees soon learn that the factors for determining how well they do on a job are quite straightforward. Job success is the result of a combination of factors. The ability to carry out tasks to your employer's satisfaction is, of course, the key element.

Making a Career Choice

Judi Parks has been an information processing specialist at Broderick & Sons for two years. She has learned a great deal working for the sales department. Her keyboarding speed and accuracy and her ability to make formatting decisions have increased considerably. But Ms. Parks is eager to develop her skills further, to acquire more knowledge, and to maximize her potential. The question is how.

This question is, of course, a common one. Throughout your working life, you will be faced with decisions similar to the ones Judi Parks must make. Should I stay at my present company or look for a job elsewhere? Should I continue as an information processing specialist, consider moving on to a similar position, or try to move up to some other kind of position?

Making a career choice is not easy. You are the only one who can answer such questions, because you know best what your career goals are. But there is seldom one correct answer. There are many options, and these may change from one month to the next. Knowing what your options are is the first step toward making wise decisions about your career. In addition, talk to as many qualified people as you can to find out what they think are your strengths and abilities. Once you have a realistic sense of yourself, you will be equipped to choose intelligently from among your career options.

However, if you like many career fields, it may be difficult to narrow down just one that suits your personality. If you feel you do not know enough about a career, you may want to find a part-time or temporary job that will give you more information about a job field. Another way to help you make a career choice is to get further education. Let's look briefly at some of the options that will help you make a career choice.

Temporary Employment

Temporary jobs provide an excellent way to evaluate what you like and dislike about a career. They also are a good way to gain experience before making a long-term career commitment. Temporary agencies need people with good skills. They look for, and supply companies with, people who know information processing and can work with microcomputer applications programs. Assignments can be quite varied. You may work as a secretary, specialist, or in any other area for which you are qualified. An assignment may last a day, a week, a month, or longer. Because you can choose from the assignments that are offered, your work hours may be more flexible than if you worked full-time for one employer.

Some temporary agencies offer a variety of opportunities. For example, Manpower, Inc., the largest temporary agency, has offices all over the world. Manpower employs more than 125,000 people a year. The company will test your skills on validated tests to assure that you are properly placed in a job. If you need or want additional specialized training to upgrade your skills or even retrain, you can get it. Some agencies like Manpower also offer excellent benefits, including paid holidays, health and accident insurance, child care discounts, vacation bonuses, and personal counseling.

If you are uncertain about what kind of environment you want to work in permanently, signing up with a temporary agency could give you a chance to sample the possibilities. Many times a temporary assignment even leads to a full-time job offer.

Education

The value of education cannot be overemphasized. Whether you want to move up in the information processing field or use your information processing experience as a stepping-stone to some other job, education can help you attain your goal. Many com-

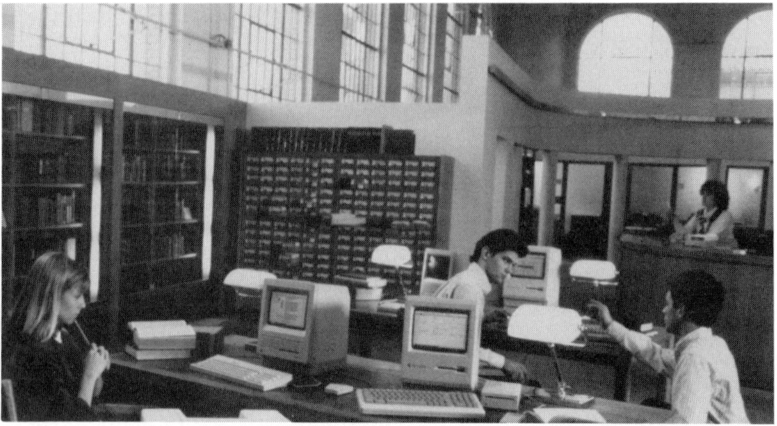

Additional education and training can be valuable in achieving your career goals.

panies recognize the value of advanced or continuing education, and to encourage their employees to take courses, they will pay part or all of the tuition fees. Some companies pay for any type of course; others pay only for courses directly related to an employee's job. Your company's orientation manuals probably explain its policies in this area.

Professional Organizations and Certification

Your personal and professional growth and development can be enhanced by joining a professional organization, such as the Association of Information Systems Professionals, mentioned earlier. Some organizations, such as the AISP, have periodic publications as well as local meetings that you can attend. Meetings may feature speakers on current information systems topics and provide a good way to meet and talk with other people who share your interests and concerns.

Besides the AISP, you may wish to consider joining such organizations as the Office Systems Research Association (OSRA), Professional Secretaries International (PSI), American Society of Training and Development (ASTD), American Federation of Information Processing Societies (AFIPS), or Association of Records Managers and Administrators (ARMA).

Some of these, including the Institute for the Certification of Computer Professionals (ICCP), sponsor prestigious certification. Certification means you have passed an exam indicating you have a high degree of skill or expertise in a certain area. For example, passing the **Certified Systems Professional** (**CSP**) exam indicates you have passed a series of tests proving competency in information systems. Other certifications include **Certified Professional Secretary** (**CPS**), **Certified Records Manager** (**CRM**), **Associate Computer Professional** (**ACP**), and **Certified Data Processor** (**CDP**). The status attained by earning one of these ratings is highly valued by many employers. Also, your rating may earn you credit at some colleges and universities.

Performance Appraisals

Continuing to assess your abilities on your job will help improve your work. Your supervisor will also periodically review how well you are doing on the job. A **performance appraisal** is an excellent way for you to learn more about your strengths and weaknesses. Every company has its own approach to performance appraisals. The approach may also vary from one department to another. Some supervisors, for example, evaluate their employees' performance in writing every six months. Other supervisors conduct informal review sessions every quarter and then do formal performance appraisals once each year. In some offices, performance appraisals are conducted on the basis of a series of performance goals agreed on in advance by employer and employee.

Performance appraisals should help you plan your future. Thus, to get the most from them, view performance appraisals as an opportunity. Your supervisor can tell you what your best areas are and where you can improve. If there is anything about the appraisal that you don't understand, ask your supervisor to talk about it in more detail. If your supervisor suggests that you improve your performance in certain ways, try to get specific recommendations on what to do. Maybe a recommendation will involve a better work procedure or even a training course in a specific area. Try to come away from the appraisal sessions knowing more about your-

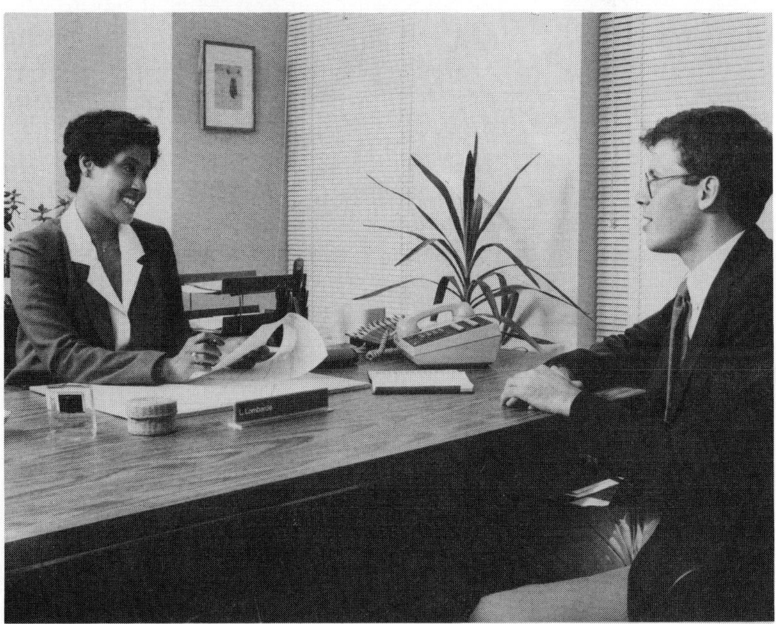

The information you obtain in a performance appraisal can help you plan your future.

self so you will have a clearer idea of where you are headed on the job.

Growing With Your Company

Many companies provide advancement for their employees to grow with the business. If you are happy working at a particular company but want to move to a new or more challenging position, don't assume that you must change companies. In most companies, especially larger ones, there may be more job opportunities than you imagine, and a good work history with the company can put you one step ahead of the competition.

Some businesses have a policy of **job posting,** in which they list job openings on a bulletin board or in the company newspaper several weeks before outside applicants are interviewed. Whether or not your company posts job openings, you can investigate other in-house positions by talking with someone in the Personnel Department. A personnel specialist can make you aware of what is required to climb various career ladders (for example, how many years of service and what skills are generally needed to move from an entry-level word processing operator to an information processing supervisor). Information from personnel also can be helpful in determining what in-house training or outside education might help you develop the additional skills you need for the position.

Your supervisor can be one of your best sources of assistance in planning your future with a company. As you learn more about your company and what it has to offer, get to know your supervisor. Developing a friendly, open, and mutually respectful relationship with your supervisor can be a great help to you in several ways. Your supervisor may, for example, be able to advise you about newly available positions for which you are qualified—or for which you could become qualified. Through performance appraisals, both formal and informal, your supervisor also can guide your improvement in such a way as to increase the likelihood that you will be promoted. Your supervisor may have the knowledge and experience for making suggestions to help you develop long-range career plans. Tap the sources available to you.

Your Future in an Information System

Information processing systems have developed at an amazing rate. All signs point to this trend continuing for many years. Electric typewriters are being replaced with electronic typewriters, and dedicated word processors are nearly extinct. The greatest growth in information processing equipment has been with microcomputers and sophisticated workstations that can perform multi-functions with great speed. It is a familiar process, one repeated with each new wave of information technology. Things we formerly did by hand we can suddenly do automatically. Functions we performed electrically are made more efficient and productive with electronic tools. Machines are making decisions, and the processing of all kinds of inputs and outputs is possible.

Integrated information systems have become a necessity with so much information close at hand. Integration, interrelatedness, and connectivity provide answers for the growing need to manage information. They have contributed to a great many developments that have significance for wide and local area networks. Mass storage and memory devices are making information access and management easier than ever before.

Telecommunications has brought peoples of the world much closer. The lines for most of the technologies are blurring as faster and more powerful information system components are introduced. And these technologies are becoming more affordable as their sophistication increases.

Undoubtedly, the integrated automated office is an exciting, stimulating, and challenging place to work. It is a place where modern technology gives us the opportunity for professional and personal growth. It promises a bright future for you if you choose to be a part of it.

CHAPTER SUMMARY

- Your career opportunities will depend largely on your skills. Transferability skills are important to permit you to make job and career moves as changes occur in information systems.
- The key element of your career success is to carry out the job tasks and responsibilities required by your employer.
- Before you apply for a job in information processing, you should have good keyboarding and document formatting skills.
- Proofreading and shorthand skills and the ability to think in abstract terms, organize material, and follow instructions increase your chances for career success.
- Training on or at least familiarity with transcription equipment and some aptitude for mechanical equipment are additional career qualifications in information processing.
- You will benefit from hands-on training, even if it is not on the specific equipment you will use on the job.
- If you plan to work in information processing, it is absolutely essential that you have a solid sense of English grammar and word usage, punctuation, and spelling.

- Success on the job results from a combination of factors: the ability to carry out assignments and relate to others, good judgment, maturity, flexibility, discretion, personal appearance, a positive attitude, and a conscientious approach to the job.
- The size of a company, the type of business, and the specific information processing environment in which you work all help determine whether the position is right for you.
- When you apply for a job, try to find a position that fits your skills, offers opportunity for advancement, and challenges your career goals.
- The range of career choices and levels are numerous in an information system. Some of these include specialists of all types, secretaries, managers, trainers, sales representatives, and consultants.
- Temporary agencies offer short-term assignments that can lead to full-time employment. Temporary work gives you a chance to explore a number of different organizations.
- Education and job training can help you immeasurably in getting ahead. It is also important to understand the value of performance appraisals in preparing for career advancement.
- Joining professional organizations and earning certification by examination are two excellent ways to stay up-to-date and advance in your chosen career.
- Employees should make the most of the opportunities in their company before changing employers. Reading posted job descriptions, talking to personnel specialists, and consulting with supervisors are three ways to explore in-house options.
- The future in an information system is extremely bright for workers with good skills.

VOCABULARY

Association of Information Systems Professionals (AISP)
Certified Systems Professional (CSP)
job posting
performance appraisal
transferability skills

CHAPTER QUESTIONS

1. What are the two basic skill areas employers seek in office employees? Why are these skills so important?
2. Describe the technology skills you have to offer an employer.
3. Name and discuss at least three interpersonal and communications skills that are expected from employees and that are important to success on a job. In what ways do job skills and qualities, especially attitude, directly affect job performance? Give an example.

4. What is probably the key factor to success on the job?
5. Knowing your own temperament and qualifications, describe the type of company where you would be happiest working. What do you have to offer such a company?
6. Discuss the responsibilities, functions, and pros and cons of at least four of the following career categories in information systems. Describe a career path that is realistic for you.

applications specialist	trainer
staff analyst	programmer
database specialist	peripheral equipment specialist
systems analyst	vendor sales representative

7. What are the advantages of working for a temporary agency?
8. How can further education help you reach your career goals?
9. Name at least three ways to stay up-to-date or advance in your career.
10. What are some arguments in favor of staying with an employer rather than switching companies? How can employees use performance appraisals to their advantage?

CASE STUDY

Kylie Collingsworth has worked as an information processing specialist in a satellite center at Ivanhoe Institute for the Performing Arts for over three years, ever since she graduated from business school. Ms. Collingsworth enjoys many aspects of her job. She works with fine people for a reputable company, earns decent wages, and enjoys excellent benefits. But lately she has begun to feel restless on the job.

Ms. Collingsworth is considering changing jobs. Ivanhoe has three satellite centers, but she isn't sure that she merely wants to transfer to another satellite. She has begun looking at newspaper ads for openings at other companies. At the same time, she has ordered the current catalog of the community college she attended and is studying course offerings in management training.

Ms. Collingsworth has not yet approached her supervisor to discuss her feelings. At her last performance appraisal, she was told that she was "outstanding in most respects," especially in organizational ability. However, she was told she could still improve the speed at which she works.

Last week during her lunch break, Ms. Collingsworth noticed an announcement that described an opening for an administrative assistant posted on the company's "Ivanhoe Opportunities" bulletin board. She wondered whether she would qualify for that job and whether she should apply for it.

Based on what you have read in this chapter and speaking as one friend to another, what advice would you give Ms. Collingsworth? What would you do if you were Ms. Collingsworth?

Hands-On Applications

Part 1 Knowing Your Computer

Before you can actually begin working on a computer, it's important to familiarize yourself with the equipment you will be using. The following applications will help you to do that. Although the makes and models of computers vary, the basic components of most systems will be the same.

Application 1

Computer Hardware

Label the parts of a microcomputer.

Number a sheet of paper from 1 to 5 or use the "Student Reference Guide" supplied by your instructor. Identify the five parts of the computer hardware shown in the drawing below.

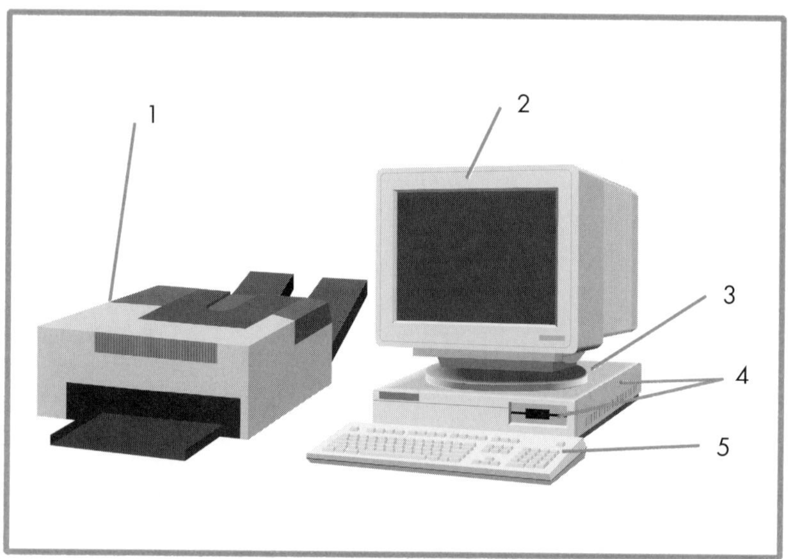

Application 2

Hardware Description

Gather information about your computer system.

Record the following facts about your computer system.

1. Brand and model
2. Number and type of disk drives

3. Capacity of internal memory
4. Size and type of floppy disk required
5. Brand and model of printer
6. Type of printer (dot matrix, laser, pin, etc.)
7. Other separate components (mouse, ten-key pad, etc.)

Application 3

Keyboard

Label the parts of a computer keyboard.

Number your paper from 1 to 10 or use the "Student Reference Guide" supplied by your instructor. Identify the ten parts of the computer keyboard shown in the drawing on page 316. If your keyboard differs from this one, make a mental note of where the keys are located on your keyboard.

Application 4

Monitor Adjustments

Locate the controls for your monitor (as appropriate for your system).

Make the following adjustments to your monitor.

1. Turn the power on or off.
2. Adjust brightness.
3. Adjust contrast.
4. Change the tilt.
5. If using a color monitor, switch the color "off" (as appropriate for your system).

Caution: Turning the power "on" is hard on the circuitry of an electronic system. If you have turned the power "off," wait at least a minute before turning it "on" again.

Application 5

Boot

Start up (boot) the computer.

Write down the sequence of keys to press to start up (boot) your computer.

Application 6

Insert/Remove Floppy Disk

Insert a floppy disk into the disk drive.

Write down the steps to follow to insert and remove a floppy disk.

1. Watch a demo and note how a disk is inserted in and removed from a disk drive.
2. Have someone watch as you insert and remove a disk the first time.
3. Practice inserting and removing a floppy disk.

Application 7

View Directory

View a directory of a disk.

Write down the steps to call up your directory. Call up your directory and view the contents.

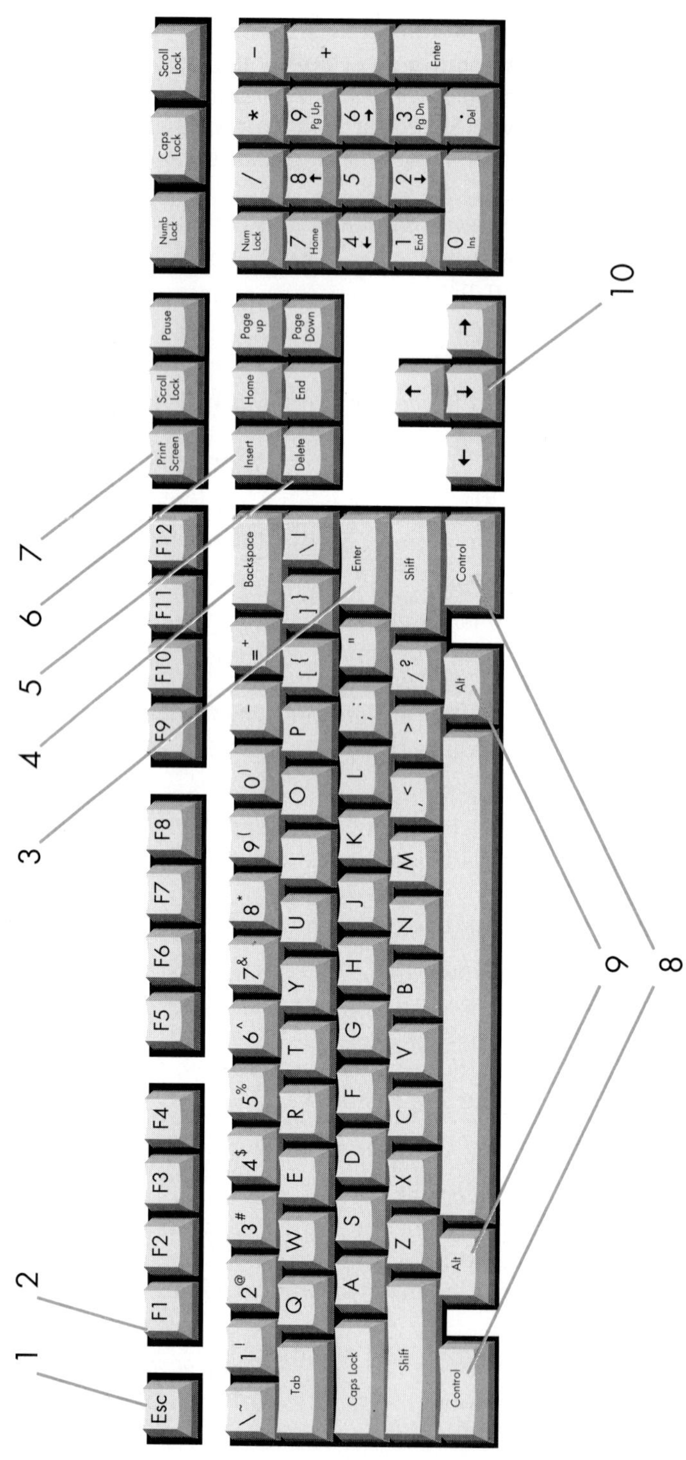
1
2
3
4
5
6
7
8
9
10

Application 8

Initialize Disk

Initialize (format) a blank disk.

Warning: If you initialize a disk that has files stored on it, all files will be lost. Initialization is crucial, so follow instructions carefully.

Write down the steps to initialize (format) a disk.

1. Initialize (format) a disk.
2. Make and affix a label to your disk called *WORKDISK*. Add your name.

Part 2 Knowing Your Software

Application 9

Load Program

Load a word processing program.

Write down the keys you press to load a word processing software program on your computer.

Load your word processing software program.

Record the following information about your software:

1. Name and version
2. Number, type, and size of disks
3. Amount of memory required
4. Operating system needed
5. Licensing requirements

Application 10

Create File

Create a file called *NAME.XX*.

1. Create a file called *NAME.XX* (substitute your first and last name initials for *XX*).
2. Key in your name and address, using the ⟨Backspace⟩ key to correct errors as you key and using the ⟨Return/Enter⟩ key at the end of each line.

Application 11

Save File

Save your file NAME.XX.

Write down the steps to save your work from this first word processing activity. Save your file NAME.XX to your WORKDISK.

Application 12

Retrieve (Recall) File

Retrieve (recall) your file NAME.XX.

Write down the steps to recall (retrieve) a file from disk.

1. Recall your file NAME.XX.
2. View your file and save it back to disk under NAME.XX.

Application 13

Print File

Print your file NAME.XX.

Write down the steps to print your file. Print your file NAME.XX using the default printer setting.

Application 14

Exit Program

Exit from your word processing program.

Write down the steps to exit your word processing program. Exit from your word processing program.

Application 15

Power Down

Finish your work and, as appropriate, power down.

As appropriate for your system:

1. Remove your work disk from its disk drive and store it in its protective jacket.
2. Remove the word processing program disk from its disk drive and store it in its protective jacket.
3. Turn off the system power switches.

Part 3 Basic Editing and Formatting of Files

You are now ready to explore some of the features of a word processing program. Before beginning these activities, use your "Student Reference Guide" to review the steps you already know for using your computer system.

Note: In the remaining applications, you will create files, save them to disk, retrieve (recall) them, and print them. Because these operations are basic, they will not always be repeated in your instructions. Follow the steps you have learned or refer back to Applications 10–13 for creating, saving, recalling, and printing files.

Application 16

Word Wrap

Key in a paragraph using word wrap in new file WRAP.

1. Create a file WRAP.
2. Key in the following paragraph, using the ⟨Backspace⟩ key to correct errors as you key and using the ⟨Return/Enter⟩ key at the end of the paragraph.

```
The word processing feature that automatically breaks
the end of a line after a complete word and begins the
next word on the next line is called word wrap.  Word
wrap is a powerful word processing feature.  It is
one of the ways word processing is very different from
operating a typewriter.
```

3. Save your file to your work disk under the name WRAP.

Application 17

Cursor Keys

Use the arrow keys to move the cursor in the file WRAP.

Write down the special keys (other than cursor arrow keys) or commands to move the cursor.

Recall the file WRAP.

Use the arrow keys and cursor function keys to move the cursor to the

1. First letter of the fourth word of the fourth line
2. Last letter of the word *begins*
3. Beginning of the current line
4. End of the current line
5. End of the file
6. Beginning of the file

Application 18

Return/Enter Key

Use the ⟨Return/Enter⟩ key to create paragraphs and blank lines in new file REUNION.

1. Create a file REUNION.
2. Key in the following paragraphs, using the ⟨Return/Enter⟩ key to end each paragraph.
3. Create a blank line between paragraphs.
4. Create a blank line at the beginning of the file.

```
It is 19xx! That means it has been five years since we
were the members of the Class of 19xx of West Ridge
High School.  It is hard to believe!  Haven't five
years passed by quickly?
     (1 BLANK LINE)
You are invited to a five-year class reunion to catch
up with what has happened to your classmates after
their high school days.
```

Application 19

Delete

Delete text from file REUNION.

Use the ⟨Delete⟩ key to delete (erase) text.

1. Erase (delete) the word *by* in front of *quickly* in the file REUNION.
2. Erase the words *days* and *their* in the last sentence.
3. Delete the sentence, *It is hard to believe!*

Application 20

Insert

Insert information in file REUNION.

Write down the key to insert text into your letter.

1. Insert (add) the following date and greeting above the two paragraphs (in letter format) in the file REUNION.

```
January 15, 19xx
     (3 BLANK LINES)
Dear Classmate
     (1 BLANK LINE)
```

2. Add *cordially* before the word *invited* in the last sentence.
3. Add *party* after the word *reunion* in the last sentence.

Application 21

Typeover (Replace)

Make changes in file REUNION.

Practice with typeover (or replace) by making these changes to file REUNION. Write down the keys to press for typeover or replace.

1. Change the date to January 17, 19xx in the file REUNION.
2. Change the word *after* in the last sentence to *since*.

Application 22

Margins

Change the left and right margins in the file REUNION.

Write down the steps to change the left and right margin settings.

1. Set 1-inch (10-space) left and right margins, if they are not already set, in the file REUNION.
2. Move the cursor to the left margin, after the last line, and reset the left and right margins to 2 inches (20 spaces).
3. Within your new margins, add a blank line and the following four lines of information.

```
What:  a dinner party and dance
Where:  West Ridge Inn, 777 Sunset Drive
When:  Saturday, June 24, 19xx, at 6 PM
Who:  class members and spouses or guests
```

4. After the "what-where-when-who" information, reset the margins to 1 inch (10 spaces) left and right, add a blank line, and key in the rest of the file (letter) as follows:

```
The total cost of the event is $22.50 per person.  If you plan to
attend, please RSVP with a deposit of $10 per person to me at the
above address.
     (1 BLANK LINE)
I look forward to seeing you.  Your classmates are counting on
you to be there, too.
     (1 BLANK LINE)
Sincerely
     (3 BLANK LINES)
M. K. Fernweiller
Class President
```

Application 23

Insert Text

Insert more text in file REUNION.

1. Insert the following new paragraph right after the "what-where-when-who" information (within the 1-inch margins) in the REUNION letter.

```
The after-dinner speech will be an inspirational talk
by West Ridge's volleyball coach, Pat ''Spike'' New-
bury.  If you ever attended pep rallies at West Ridge,
I don't have to tell you how fortunate we are to have
Coach Newbury as our speaker.
```

2. After the title *Class President*, create one blank line and add

```
PS Please RSVP by February 28, 19xx
```

Application 24

Block Move

Move blocks of text in file REUNION.

Write down the keys or commands that are used to move a defined block of text to another position in the document. Use "block move" to move the paragraph about Coach Newbury's talk so that it follows the paragraph about costs in the REUNION letter.

Application 25

Underline

Underline text in file REUNION.

Write down the steps for underlining text.

1. Underline *per person* in the paragraph on costs in the REUNION letter.
2. Underline the *PS* line to highlight the deadline for classmates to respond.

Application 26

Bold

Boldface text in file REUNION.

Write down the steps to change from normal print to boldface. Make the words *What, Where, When,* and *Who* boldface in the REUNION letter.

Application 27

Proofread

Proofread and print file REUNION.

1. Proofread and correct all keyboarding and formatting errors in your file REUNION.
2. Save and print your file (letter).

Application 28

Center

Center text in file NAME.XX.

Write down the keys you must press to center a line of text.

1. Recall the file NAME.XX.
2. Center each line of your name and address.
3. Save and print your file.

Application 29

Caps Lock

Insert and capitalize text in file WRAP.

Note the key(s) you must press to activate and deactivate the ⟨Caps Lock⟩ function.

1. Recall the file WRAP.
2. Use ⟨Caps Lock⟩ to key in the title WORD WRAP at the left margin above the text.

Application 30

Tab

Indent text, using tab in file WRAP.

Write down the steps needed to change the tab settings to values other than the default settings.

1. Indent the first sentence, using the ⟨Tab⟩ key in the file WRAP.
2. Create a new paragraph with the second sentence.
3. Indent the new paragraph, using the ⟨Tab⟩ key.
4. Add a blank line between paragraphs.
5. Save your file.

Application 31

Special Functions

Add special functions in new file CODES.

1. Create a file CODES.
2. Key in the following paragraph as it appears:

DELETING CODES

(1 BLANK LINE)

Many word processing functions are accomplished by embedding special codes into a document. Underlining, **bold**, centering, and capitalization are a few of these common functions. These functions can be removed by deleting the embedded codes.

(1 BLANK LINE)

When you select a code to be deleted, a message usually will appear on your screen warning you of your intended action. A warning message will not appear on your screen when you delete some codes, such as tabs or returns.

Application 32

View Codes

View the codes in file CODES.

Write down the steps to view and hide the function codes.

1. View the codes in file CODES.
2. Write down the codes along with any special symbols that identify the special codes.

Application 33

Block Indent

Indent blocks of text in file CODES.

Write down the steps to activate and deactivate the block indent function.

1. Use "block indent" to create hanging indent paragraphs in file CODES.
2. View the code for "block indent" and add it to the list you made in Application 32.
3. Save your file.

Application 34

Required Spaces

Add required spaces for new file LIST.

Write down the steps to activate and deactivate the required space feature.

1. Create a file LIST.
2. Using the "required space" (hard space) function between the colon (:) and the beginning of each underline, key the following text as it appears:

```
Name:          ______________________________
Address:       ______________________________
City, State:   ______________________________
Zip Code:      ______________________________
```

3. Create two or three blank lines at the end of the file.
4. View the code for "required space" (hard space) function and add it to the list you made in Application 32.

Application 35

Block Copy

Copy a block of text in file LIST.

Write down the steps to identify and copy a block of text to a new location in the document.

1. Use "block copy" to make a duplicate copy of the form (text plus one blank line).
2. Insert the copy directly below the original form to create two forms on the page.
3. Use "block copy" to make a duplicate copy of the two identical forms (text plus one blank line after the second form).
4. Insert the copy directly below the second form to create four forms on the page.
5. Is there one blank line between each of the forms? If not, add or delete lines as necessary.
6. Save your file.

Application 36

Delete Codes

Delete special codes in file CODES.

Write down the keys to delete embedded codes.

Recall your file CODES.

Delete all the special codes for:

1. Hanging indents
2. Underline
3. Bold
4. Centering

Save your file.

Application 37

Block Delete

Delete blocks of text in file REUNION.

Write down the steps to delete blocks of text.

1. Recall your file REUNION.
2. Use "block delete" to delete the last sentence in the letter.

Application 38

Search and Replace

Search and replace text in file REUNION.

Write down the steps to search for a word and to search and replace a word.

1. Use the "search" function to find the word *cost* in the file REUNION. How many times does it appear in the letter?
2. Search for the word *all*. How many times does it appear in the letter?
3. Use the "search and replace" function to change the abbreviation *RSVP* to *respond*.

Application 39

Spell Check

Check spelling in file REUNION.

Write down the steps to spell check your document.

1. Use the "spell check" function to check the spelling in the file REUNION.
2. How many words did it find? Make a list of the words it found.
3. Were any of the words the spell checker found correctly spelled? Write down why the spell checker may find correctly spelled words.
4. Use the "spell check" function to find all the spelling errors.
5. Does your "spell check" function correct all errors that may be in a file? Write down as many kinds of errors as you can think of that your "spell check" function may not find.
6. Save your file.

Application 40

Print Directory

Print a directory of a disk.

Write down the steps to print a copy of your disk directory.

1. View your directory. How many files do you have stored on your disk?
2. Print the directory.
3. Note the percentage of disk space you have available for storing more files.

Part 4 Managing Your Files

Managing your files is important for ease and speed in recalling your files when they are needed. Storing your files under logical names and using consistent, standard procedures are two ways to add to the efficiency of managing your files.

There are several techniques to help you manage your files, depending on the system you are using. For example, similar files can be grouped together into directories to save a great deal of time when you need to find files. Floppy disk users will probably need several work disks, which requires that files be further organized. In most cases, good file management requires some periodic reorganization and deletion of files.

Note: The following applications are for floppy disk users. If you are using a hard disk or nonfloppy disk system, check with your instructor before starting this applications section.

Application 41

Copy Disk

Copy a work disk.

Write down the steps to copy all files from your work disk to a new disk using your word processing "copy disk" function.

1. Format (initialize) a new work disk.
2. Using the "copy disk" function, copy the entire contents of your original work disk to your new work disk (work disk #2).
3. View and compare the directories of both disks to assure they are the same.

Application 42

Rename File

Rename file WRAP on work disk #2.

Write down the steps to rename an existing file.

1. Rename the file WRAP on work disk #2 to WRAP2.
2. View the directory to assure you have WRAP2 on your work disk #2.
3. Recall your file WRAP2.
4. Key the following as a new ending paragraph:

```
     This file has been copied and renamed.  If I am
using a floppy disk, I have copied this file from my
original work disk to a second work disk (work disk #2).
```

5. Center the heading and add two blank lines between the heading and the first paragraph.
6. Save your file (to work disk #2).

Application 43

Delete File

Delete file WRAP from original work disk.

Write down the steps to delete a file from your disk.

1. Delete the file WRAP from your original work disk.
2. View your directory, noting that the file has been deleted.

Application 44

Copy File

Copy file WRAP2 to original work disk.

Write down the steps to copy a file from one disk to another.

1. Copy the file WRAP2 from work disk #2 to your original work disk.
2. Key the following text to WRAP2 on your original work disk, adding a new ending paragraph:

```
    This revised file has been copied again.  If I am
using a floppy disk, it has been copied from my work
disk #2 back to my original work disk.
```

3. Save your file (on original work disk).

Application 45

Merge Files

Merge file LIST with new file GOLF on original work disk.

Write down the steps to merge one file into another file.

1. Create a file GOLF on your original work disk.
2. Key the following text, adding two blank lines after the text:

```
       ROSTER FOR CHAMPIONS GOLF TOURNAMENT
    (1 BLANK LINE)
                 Murfield, Scotland
                  August 15, 19xx
    (1 BLANK LINE)
The following tournament participants are eligible to
register for the next round of the Champions Golf
Tournament:
    (ADD 2 BLANK LINES)
```

3. Working from your original work disk, use the "merge" function to add the file LIST to the bottom of your file GOLF.
4. Save your new file GOLF.
5. Proofread and print your file.

Application 46

Erase Disk

Erase work disk #2.

Write down the steps to erase all files on a disk.

1. Erase (delete all files from) your work disk #2.
2. View the directory, noting that all files have been deleted.

Part 5 Extending Your Editing and Formatting Skills

Formatting a document usually requires more than just setting margins and tabs. In the following applications you will learn how to change the defaults (preset values for document layout) for many formatting functions. A few of these include line spacing, page lengths, pitch, justification, and headers.

Application 47

Pagination

Paginate a file.

Some word processing programs require a file (document) to be paginated before certain other functions can be accomplished.

1. If your program requires pagination for such functions, write down the steps you must follow to paginate a document.
2. Make sure you use these steps each time you activate a new formatting feature requiring pagination.

Application 48

Hyphenation

Use hyphenation in new file CAFE.

Write down the steps to both manually insert soft hyphens and to automatically insert soft hyphens.

1. Create a file CAFE.
2. Set 3-inch (30-space) margins left and right.
3. Using the "automatic hyphenation" feature (soft hyphen), key in the following text:

```
     Next week the Towers Cafeteria will be opening
to employees of our organization.  The Towers'
attractive menu of culinary delights will feature low-
cholesterol breakfast and luncheon selections for the
most discriminating guest.  Additionally, an extensive
buffet and tempting house specialties will be offered
daily.
     We hope you will plan to join us for our grand
opening celebration in the Towers Cafeteria on
Wednesday, October 16.
```

4. Print your file.
5. How many hyphens appeared in your copy? (If none, reset margins and reprint.)
6. Recall your file and manually insert soft hyphens wherever the lines would be better filled with text than with blank space.
7. Print your file and compare it with your first copy.
8. Recall your file and turn off the "automatic hyphenation" feature.

Application 49

Required Page End

Insert required page ends in file CAFE.

Write down the steps to insert a required page end code.

1. Reset margins to 1 inch (10 spaces) left and right in the file CAFE.
2. Add a "required page end" code after the first paragraph.
3. View the page end code and add it to the list you made in Application 32.
4. Print your file, noting that you have two short pages of text.
5. Recall your file and delete the "required page end" code so both paragraphs will be on one page.

Application 50

Line Spacing

Change line spacing in file CAFE.

Write down the steps to set line spacing.

1. Delete any blank lines between the two paragraphs in the file CAFE.
2. Change the line spacing to double spacing in file CAFE.
3. Print your file, noting the change in line spacing.

Application 51

Justification

Justify the margins in file CAFE.

Write down the steps to automatically justify margins.

1. Recall the file CAFE.
2. Activate the "automatic justification" feature.
3. Print your file, noting the even left and right margins.

Application 52

Pitch

Change the pitch in file CAFE.

Write down the steps to change pitch.

1. Recall the file CAFE.
2. Change the pitch (type or font size) from 10 to 12 characters per inch. (If you are already at 12 pitch, change to 10 pitch. Make paragraph adjustments as appropriate.)

Application 53

Page Length

Change page lengths in new file CAREER.

Write down the steps to change the page length.

1. Create a file CAREER.
2. Set 2-inch (20-space) margins left and right.
3. Set line spacing to double spacing; 12 pitch.
4. Access your page length feature and set the page length to 55 lines.
5. Key in the text from your textbook, beginning on page 296 with **Information/Word Processing Trainee** and ending after the first paragraph on page 298.
6. Save your file.

Application 54

Header

Add a header in file CAREER.

Write down the steps to add a title using the "header" function.

1. Recall your file CAREER.
2. Access your "header" function and key the words *Career Opportunities* at the left margin.
3. Save your file.

Application 55

Footer

Add a footer in file CAREER.

Write down the steps to add text using the "footer" function.

1. Recall your file CAREER.
2. Access your footer function and key the word *Page* at the left margin.
3. Save your file.

Application 56

Page Number

Add a page number in file CAREER.

Write down the steps to add page numbers using the "footer" function.

1. Access your "footer" function in file CAREER.
2. Add a system page number code one space after the word *Page*.
3. Position the footer on line 58.
4. Save your file.
5. Proofread, spell check, and print your file.

Application 57

Tabbed Columns

Add columns using tabs in file CAFE.

Review the steps to change tab settings (Application 30).

1. Recall your file CAFE.
2. Change the line spacing to single spacing adding a blank line before and after the second paragraph.
3. Using your ⟨Tab⟩ key to set up columns, key in the following text:

```
Monday      Flemish Game Hen
Tuesday     Fajitas al Carbon
Wednesday   Curried Chicken
Thursday    Quiche Lorraine
Friday      Baked Red Snapper
```

4. Save and print your file.

Application 58

Text Columns

Create text columns in new file COLUMNS.

Write down the steps to create text columns.

1. Create a file COLUMNS.
2. Set columns to 27 characters.

3. Using the "text column" feature, key in the following text as two columns:

```
Creating text columns is a con-      grams. As you become more experi-
venient way to enter text into       enced in using word processing
newspaper-like columns. That is,     software, you will discover that
as you enter text, the words flow    the text column feature has many
from one column to the next, just as applications. In addition to
the word wrap feature allows words   creating newspaper columns and
to "wrap" from one line to the       decimal columns, you can also use
next. If you enter more text         the text column feature to create
in the middle, the first column      block columns. These are often
will "snake" to the second col-      used in documents containing short
umn. The capability to produce       blocks of text that need to remain
columns of text is a useful feature  next to each other on the page.
found in many word processing pro-
```

4. Save and print your file.

Application 59

Decimal Columns

Create decimal columns in new file BUDGET.

Write down the steps to set up decimal columns.

1. Create a file BUDGET.
2. Set decimal tabs (tab align) for three columns.
3. Using the "decimal tabs" function, key the following numbers:

```
 38.97     46.79     16.89
  1.16    394.33      4.00
671.09     22.78      8.95
 55.20      2.15    498.77
```

4. Save and print your file.

Part 6 Creating Office Documents

In the remaining applications you will process office correspondence while practicing your editing and formatting skills. You will format a memo, letters, and a report from existing files and also format and compose new documents. Refer to your "Student Reference Guide" or other reference sources for a review of the basic office document formats.

Application 60

Format Letter

Format a letter in new file REUNION1.

1. Copy the file REUNION and name the new file REUNION1.
2. Set 1½-inch (15-space) margins for the body of the letter; do not change the margins for the "what-where-when-who" information.
3. Reformat the letter in modified block format; use the current date; the class president is Marjorie Williams.

4. Unbold and underline the "what-where-when-who" information.
5. Proofread, correct errors, save, and print file.

Application 61

Compose Letter

Compose a letter reply in new file REPLY.

1. Create a file REPLY.
2. Compose a short letter in block format answering the REUNION1 letter; say you will attend the function.

Application 62

Format Report

Format a report, using file CAREER.

1. Reformat the file CAREER into a report.
2. Set $1\frac{1}{2}$-inch margins left and right; justify; set page lengths of 60.
3. Center, bold, and cap the heading INFORMATION SYSTEMS SPECIALISTS; leave one blank line between the heading and the first line of the text.
4. Delete the header and footer; create a new header with the report heading at the left margin and PAGE (with system "page number" code) ending at the right margin.

Application 63

Form Letter

Create a form letter in new file LETTER.

Write the steps to insert "mail-merge" codes into a form letter.

1. Create a file LETTER.
2. Key the following text, including appropriate "merge" codes for the inside address (A1) and greeting (A2).

```
May 16, 19xx
     (4 BLANK LINES)
(A1)
     (1 BLANK LINE)
Dear (A2)
     (1 BLANK LINE)
Congratulations!  Your name has been entered in our SKI SUNNY
COLORADO sweepstakes.
     (1 BLANK LINE)
As an entrant, you are guaranteed to win one of the 10,000
prizes and may win the grand prize of a one-week vacation in
Vail, Colorado.  The final drawing will be held next month at
our corporate headquarters in San Francisco.  Good luck!
     (1 BLANK LINE)
Sincerely
     (3 BLANK LINES)
Peter G. Martin
President
     (1 BLANK LINE)
xx
```

3. Proofread, spell check, and save your file.

Application 64

Mailing List

Create a mailing list with codes for merging in new file ADDRESS.

Write down the steps to add appropriate "merge" and "end of record" codes to your mailing list file.

1. Create a file ADDRESS.
2. Key the following names and addresses, using the appropriate "merge" and "end of record" codes for each new entry.

```
Ms. Martha R. Blackman
312 Oak Street West
Boston, MA 02166
     (1 BLANK LINE)
Ms. Blackman

Mr. Billy Ray Johnson
29038 Runnels Avenue
El Paso, TX 79951
     (1 BLANK LINE)
Mr. Johnson

Ms. Evelyn Warner
P.O. Box 9203
Kansas City, MO 64132
     (1 BLANK LINE)
Ms. Warner
```

3. Proofread, correct errors, and save your file.

Application 65

Mail Merge

Create form letters by merging file ADDRESS with file LETTER.

Write down the steps to mail merge an address file (ADDRESS) with a form letter file (LETTER).

1. Set up the system to merge file ADDRESS into file LETTER.
2. Merge and print the letters.

GLOSSARY

acoustical Noise-absorbent.
acoustic coupler A communications device that converts electrical data signals to tones for transmission over telephone lines by using a conventional telephone handset. The tones are converted back to electrical signals at the other end of the line.
ambient lighting Background or room illumination.
American Standard Code for Information Interchange (ASCII) A code devised for data communication between equipment of different manufacturers, with alphanumeric characters, punctuation marks, and various control codes represented by ASCII characters; the standard code for digital asynchronous communications over telephone lines.
analog signals Continuous electrical signals or voltages (rather than on/off digital signals or impulses) during transmission; contrast with *digital signals*.
aperture card A type of keypunch card with a rectangular opening that holds one or more frames of microfilm.
applications software Computer programs designed for a specific purpose, including word processing, spreadsheets, databases, graphics, communications, integrated tasks, and desktop publishing.
architecture See *topology*.
archive Storage of backup, or duplicate, text on disks.
artificial intelligence Computer systems with human-like intelligence.
ASCII See *American Standard Code for Information Interchange*.
assembly language A coded language similar to machine language but using abbreviations of words as codes.
asynchronous transmission A type of data communication in which characters are sent one at a time at uneven intervals.
audit trails A record of users' activities.
author The creator of a document; also called *word originator* or *principal*.
automated office An office that has adopted the systems approach through the use of electronic equipment to make office work faster, thus improving productivity.
automatic recalculation A procedure in a programmed spreadsheet whereby all entries in the other related cells are automatically refigured to conform to new information whenever one number has been changed.
automation A system of production that uses automated machines.

background printing A feature of some information processing systems that enables users to work on one document while another is being printed.
backup Duplicate text that is magnetically stored.
band printer See *line printer*.
BASIC The simplest of all computer languages.
baud rate A measure of transmission speed at which data is sent through communication lines; also called *bits per second (bps)*.
bidirectional printing A method of printing in which the type element moves from left to right and from right to left.
binary code On/off electrical signals that a computer understands; also see *bit*.
binary digit See *bit*.
biometrics The use of special devices to recognize authorized computer users by one or more of their physical characteristics.
bisynchronous transmission A type of data communication in which characters are sent in a steady stream, also called *synchronous transmission*.
bit The smallest unit of information recognized by a computer, represented by a single one (on) or a single zero (off); stands for *BInary digiT*.
bits per second (bps) See *baud rate*.

boilerplate Stored text that can be rearranged or combined with new material to produce tailor-made documents.
boot To turn on a computer in preparation for keyboarding or other uses.
bridge Connects the components of two similar LANs so they can communicate; contrast with *gateway.*
bubble memory See *solid-state storage.*
buffer An area of memory used to temporarily store data.
bulletin board service (BBS) A computerized service, accessible by modem, that provides different kinds of information, such as announcements, schedules, notices, or product descriptions.
bundled software A system built into the ROM of a computer that combines DOS with other applications, and that works automatically when the machine is turned on.
burster A device that separates continuous-form paper into individual sheets.
bus or tree network The most flexible local area network, with only one cable and any number of nodes plugged into it anywhere along its length. The best-known bus network is Xerox's Ethernet.
byte A group of bits strung together to form a character (letter, number, symbol, etc.). Programmers string bits to form characters just as people combine letters to form words.

cassette A magnetic recording tape permanently encased in a small plastic container.
cathode-ray tube (CRT) An electronic vacuum tube that can be used to display text and graphic images; a type of *video display terminal.*
CCITT (Consultative Committee for International Telephone and Telegraph) A group that recommends international standards for communications equipment. Also see *Integrated Services Digital Network.*
cell The location at which a row and a column intersect on a spreadsheet.
central controller See *hub.*
central processing unit (CPU) The component of a word or data processing system containing the operating instructions; acts as the "brains," "logic," or "intelligence" of the unit; sometimes called the *internal processor* or *microprocessor.*
central recording system A system in which all dictation is channeled (usually over telephone lines) into a central location, where it is recorded and transcribed.
centralized information processing system A centrally located area where documents are processed by information processing specialists to make maximum use of personnel and equipment, thus improving productivity.
centralized records management system A management system in which the records of a company are kept in one place.
centralized reprographics A grouping of reprographics staff and equipment in one location for duplicating and assembling documents for an entire company.
character printer An impact printer that prints one letter, symbol, or figure at a time.
chip A miniature integrated circuit on a thin slice of supporting material, usually silicon.
clock speed See *cycle time.*
clustered system An arrangement in which word processing units or microcomputers share one or more components, such as a printer or hard disk; also known as a *shared system.*
coaxial cable A multilayered transmission medium developed to minimize noise interference; consists of copper wire surrounded by an insulating layer of air or plastic, a layer of aluminum or copper mesh, and a protective cover.
COBOL A computer language mainly used for business.
coded system Software without a menu to guide the user through its operation; requires the user to key in codes, using function keys or combinations of function and character keys; also called *command-driven system.*
code keys Function keys common to many types of computer equipment.
collating Gathering and arranging in order the separate sheets of a multipage document.
command-driven system See *coded system.*
communications channels Used to transmit data from one place to another.
compact disk–read only memory (CD-ROM) A type of disk that can be read but not written upon.
compatibility The capability of equipment to interact successfully with other equipment.
computer-aided design (CAD) A process for manipulating drawings on a computer screen.
computer-aided transcription The use of a com-

puter to transcribe sound impulses recorded on magnetic tape by a shorthand machine.

computer-assisted retrieval (CAR) Retrieval of documents stored on microform, using computers linked to central file systems.

computer-based message system A communications system using computers to send person-to-person messages.

computer-based voice message system See *electronic audio communications.*

computer crime Use of a computer to commit crimes such as illegally copying information from a copyrighted disk, or deleting or altering valuable information from another user's disk.

computer output microfilm (COM) A process by which a printout is produced directly on microform; an integration of computer and microform technologies.

configuration The manner in which several components are arranged. For example, the arrangement of a computer system and its peripherals.

connectivity The capability of different kinds of equipment to communicate with each other on public or private networks.

constant A part of a document that does not change for each recipient; sometimes called *repetitive text* or *standard text.*

continuous-form paper A roll of single-ply or multiple-ply paper with horizontal perforations separating each sheet.

control characters Codes sent in message transmission to indicate spacing, carrier returns, formatting keystrokes, and printing directions; also called *control codes.*

CPU See *central processing unit.*

crash The inability of a computer system to function because of failure in either the hardware, software, or power supply.

crosstalk A noise problem during data communication caused by electrical interference, causing the transmitted signal to be distorted so that information is lost.

cross training Instruction and work experience in all company operations.

cursor A spot of light on a display screen indicating where in the text the user is working.

cursor keys Keys generally marked with arrows; used to move the cursor up, down, and to the right or left on the display screen; also see *cursor.*

cut-sheet feeder An automatic sheet feeder that holds paper in a bin, aligns it, and inserts it one sheet at a time into a printer.

cycle time The time a computer takes to execute an instruction; ranges from 2 to 33 million instructions per second in most microcomputers.

cycles per second (cps) The number of cycles a computer can perform in one second; a measure of CPU speed; also called *hertz.*

daisy wheel A spoke-shaped element on some character printers.

database A collection of related files (items) stored in a system and available for different uses; also see *online information service.*

database management system (DBMS) A combination of hardware and software used to set up and maintain a database and manage the information stored.

database service A provider or supplier of database access to one or more databases; also see *online information service.*

data communications (data comm) A system for exchanging data within or among organizations; also see *electronic mail.*

data processing The manipulation of information in numeric form by a computer; frequently included under the information processing umbrella, yet is usually a distinct component of an information system.

decentralized information processing system A system in which documents are processed in proximity to executives or managers.

decentralized records management system A system in which records are kept in several areas throughout the company.

decentralized reprographics The placement of reprographics equipment in several areas throughout a company to make duplicating more convenient.

decision support system (DSS) Information systems that help users manage information needed to make business decisions.

dedicated word processor Electronic equipment designed to be used specifically for word processing.

default Function settings for keys that have been preset by the manufacturer.

desktop publishing (DTP) A system for combining text and graphics to create special presentations such as advertisements and brochures.

digital audio tapes (DAT) A magnetic cassette tape used to store audio information (sounds) in digital form (digital signals).
digital media See *magnetic media.*
digital signal processing (DSP) The conversion of input into digital form (digital signals), which permits the integrated processing of text, music, voice, graphics, and images for information access and transmission.
digital signals On/off signals or impulses (ones and zeros represented by binary code) used for transmission; signals a computer understands.
digital voice exchange (DVX) A system in which voice messages are converted to digital form and stored for playback.
digitizer Scanning device used to change words, graphs, images, etc., into signals that a computer can understand.
discrete media Recording media, such as cards, disks, and cassettes, that can be detached easily from dictation machines and used on other dictation or transcription equipment. Also known as *external media.*
disk See *floppy disk* and *hard disk.*
disk drive The unit in a word processor or microcomputer into which the floppy disk is inserted to program the machine.
disk operating system (DOS) The system software that manages the resources and functions of the computer, such as the keyboard and the transfer of information from soft copy to disk.
display screen See *video display terminal.*
distribution and communication One of five stages in the information processing cycle; ensures that information is available to the people who need it. The method of distribution and communication depends on the form in which the information is needed and the location of the recipients.
document Any business communication that contains information; includes correspondence, reports, statistical tables, and forms.
document assembly The creation of a document by combining stored paragraphs, sometimes with new material added.
document coding A number or a combination of numbers and letters assigned to a document to facilitate storage and retrieval.
document production center See *information processing center.*
documentation The operating instructions for equipment or software; also called *user manual* or *vendor manual.*
DOS See *disk operating system.*
dot matrix A printing pattern in which a group of closely spaced dots is used to represent a character.
dots per inch A standard for screen clarity and type quality; see *resolution.*
downloading Transferring information from a communications network to a computer.
dual display A feature of some systems that permits two screens of data to appear at the same time; also referred to as a *split screen.*
dual-sheet feeder A device that feeds paper automatically into a printer from two separate stacks.
duplex A protocol that allows data to be communicated between two computers in both directions at the same time; also referred to as *full-duplex.*

electronic audio communications A technology by which telephone calls can be recorded, stored electronically, and delivered at designated times; also known as *voice mail* and *voice store and forward,* and, if computer-based, *computer-based voice message system.*
electronic copier/printer A machine that combines the technologies of printer, office copier, and facsimile machine.
electronic data communication See *electronic mail.*
electronic data interchange (EDI) A process similar to facsimile, except that documents are transferred from one point to another in their original computer-readable form.
electronic filing system A standardized system for filing documents and records on magnetic media.
electronic imaging See *image scanning.*
electronic mail (E-mail) Electronic transfer of information over communications channels at very high speeds; sometimes referred to as *electronic data communication.*
electronic private automatic branch exchange (EPABX) Routes telephone calls to the phone extensions within an organization.
electronic shorthand See *machine shorthand.*
electronic typewriter (ET) A word processor with all its components housed in one unit or with add-on modules such as a display screen to make it more user-friendly.

emulation Programming a terminal to carry out instructions from another computer; for example, a PC can be programmed to perform as the terminal of a mainframe.
encryption Putting confidential computer files into code so that only receiving terminals with the correct decoding program can unscramble the message.
endless loop A long loop of recording tape used in some dictation machines; often used as the voice storage medium in central recording systems.
end user An operator or other person who uses computer equipment.
erasable optical disks A type of optical disk that can be used for recording, erasing, and reading data.
erasable programmable read only memory (EPROM) Chips designed to allow erasing of programs and reprogramming of the system to fit specific needs.
ergonomics The science of adapting the working environment, conditions, and equipment to suit workers; also called *human engineering.*
executive workstation A self-contained, electronically equipped work area designed to help managers generate and retrieve information efficiently; also see *workstation.*
expert systems See *knowledge-based systems.*
external modem A unit separate from the computer that connects to the phone and CPU with cables and jacks; also see *modem.*

facsimile (fax) A copy of a document transmitted electronically from one machine to another, usually via telephone lines.
feasibility study A detailed analysis undertaken by a company to determine how it might be reorganized or how equipment might be used to increase productivity.
fiber optics The use of light-conducting glass or plastic rods to transmit information coded as light signals.
field A single item of information stored in a database.
file A group of related pieces of information stored together in a database.
file server A workgroup computer that acts as a file or software depository and a hub for E-mail.
firmware The operating instructions or programs of a computer that are permanently installed as a basic part of the hardware.
fixed disk A hard disk for a microcomputer encased and fixed in its drive.
floppy disk A magnetic storage medium for word processors and microcomputers that looks like a small phonograph record in its protective jacket.
font Typeface style.
form letter A letter containing few variables and many constants, or sections of repetitive or standard text.
format The page margin, spacing, and indentation requirements of a document.
format keys Function keys that control the physical layout of a document, such as margins, page length, vertical line spacing, printing requirements, tabs, and indentations.
full duplex See *duplex.*
function keys Special keys on word processing and microcomputer keyboards used to communicate instructions to the central processing unit.

gateway Connects components of two dissimilar LANs or connects a LAN to a main computer not in the LAN so they can communicate; contrast with *bridge.*
graphics tablet An input device used in conjunction with a stylus for sketching and drawing.

hard copy A paper copy of a document; also called *printout.*
hard disk A magnetic storage medium with a large storage capacity; used with word processors and microcomputers.
hardware The physical equipment of a computer or word processor.
head The mechanism on a disk drive that reads recorded information to find the data desired and that writes data to the disk.
holography A laser (light) photographic technology that produces images in three-dimensional form.
horizontal applications software Software that can be used by any business.
host system The central computer to which smaller computers, minicomputers, or microcomputers are connected.
hub The controlling node in a star network serving as a central switching device through which

all messages are routed to the receiving node; also called *central controller.*

human engineering See *ergonomics.*

hypermedia The linking of related information by association from all types of media.

icon A picture or symbol of a function.

image scanning Using an electronic device that "sees" or scans letters, memos, graphs, illustrations, and other forms of information for electronic reproduction, transmission, or storage.

impact printer A printer that strikes type against a ribbon and paper to produce a character.

in-house training Orientation and hands-on equipment programs provided by companies to enhance employee knowledge, ability, and productivity.

index code A method of coding images to simplify finding a specific document on a roll of microfilm.

information The orderly and useful arrangement of facts, or data, so that they are accurate, timely, complete, and concise.

information processing The coordination of people, equipment, and procedures to handle information; includes word and data processing, administrative support, the storage and retrieval of information, and the distribution and communication of information.

information processing center A centrally located area in which a group of information processing specialists handle all or most of the document preparation for an entire company.

information processing cycle A sequence of five stages—input, processing, storage and retrieval, output (including printing and reprographics), and distribution and communication—that occurs repeatedly in the processing of information in an office.

information specialists People who know how to manage information and use it to make decisions.

information system An integration of the technology, people, procedures, and other components of a business that make it work effectively.

ink-jet printer A nonimpact printer that sprays electrically charged ink particles onto paper to form characters.

input Entering facts or data into a system for processing; one of five stages in the information processing cycle.

inscribed media Voice storage media, such as plastic belts, cylinders, and disks, that cannot be erased or reused.

integrated information system A system in which different computer-based functions and equipment—such as word processing, data processing, and telecommunications—are linked electronically.

Integrated Services Digital Network (ISDN) A standardized communications network in which data is transmitted in digital form to permit communications between dissimilar equipment.

integrated software An applications program designed to link several applications so that a variety of tasks can be performed without changing the software program.

intelligent copier/printer An electronic copier/printer that can manipulate data.

interface An electrical or mechanical link connecting two or more physical units or systems. Standardized interfaces make different kinds of equipment compatible.

internal modem A modem installed inside the CPU; usually cannot be seen. See also *modem.*

internal processor See *central processing unit.*

internal storage media The storage of text or data inside the word processor or microcomputer.

joystick A hand-held input device used to manipulate characters on the display; used most frequently with video games.

keyboard A component of a computer or word processing system resembling a typewriter keyboard but usually having additional keys for special functions.

keyboarding Entering data into the memory of word processors, microcomputers, and other electronic equipment by pressing keys on a keyboard.

knowledge workers Information specialists who make up the majority of the work force.

knowledge-based system A system designed to offer a selection of alternatives that managers can use in making decisions and solving problems; often called expert system.

LAN See *local area network.*

laser printer A printer that uses a laser beam—a

ray of pure, red light—to burn images onto light-sensitive paper.

letter quality (LQ) A type of printing consisting of whole, fully formed images; contrast with *dot matrix*.

light pen An input device resembling a standard writing pen with a light-sensitive cell at the tip; used to enter or create data and graphics on a display screen.

line printer A printer that prints one entire line, rather than one character, at a time; sometimes called a *band printer*.

linear display A feature of some electronic typewriters that enables the user to view a single line of type.

link The connecting path between two nodes in a local area network.

local area network (LAN) A system of communication among various kinds of electronic equipment within a small distance, usually up to 50 miles.

log on Establishing a connection to another system.

machine language The language understood by computers, written in combinations of ones and zeros (bytes) into which programs are translated.

machine or electronic shorthand The process of keying symbols and/or letters (and/or combinations of them) into a machine.

macro A file of stored keystrokes that can be accessed later using one or two commands.

magnetic media Media, such as cards, disks, and cassettes, that record dictation or keystrokes by means of electrical impulses and magnetism.

magnetographic printer Uses magnetic charges with pressure and/or heat to bind images to the paper.

Mailgram A form of electronic mail sent via Western Union's telecommunications equipment and delivered the following day as regular first-class mail.

mainframe A high-powered, expensive computer used primarily by businesses for large-scale information processing.

management information systems (MIS) An information system that provides information to all levels of management in a timely manner.

mass storage A collection or library of storage media.

media Recording materials, such as cards, disks, and cassettes, commonly used with information processing equipment.

media compatibility The capability of different memory devices to share each other's disks or tapes.

media conversion Changing one medium into another.

megahertz (MHz) One million hertz (cycles per second). See *cycles per second*.

memory An integral component of computers where input is temporarily stored during program execution (RAM) and where permanently installed instructions are located (ROM); see *random-access memory* and *read-only memory*.

menu A list of processing options (tasks or functions) displayed on some word processing equipment and on microcomputers using certain applications software packages.

microcassette A type of tape cassette (voice storage medium) that can record up to 120 minutes of dictation time.

microcomputer The smallest type of computer powered by one or more microprocessors that can be programmed to perform a variety of tasks; also called *personal computer, professional computer, PC*, and *micro*.

microfiche A small sheet of film on which reduced images are arranged in rows and columns; used for records storage.

microfilm A continuous roll of film containing reduced images of text or graphics; used for records storage.

microfilm jacket A set of plastic or acetate sheets for holding strips of microfilm.

microform A miniaturized image of a document.

microform reader A device that enlarges and projects microform images for viewing.

micrographics The technology by which images of text and graphic information are photographically reduced and stored on film.

micro-opaque A small sheet of photographic paper on which reduced images are arranged in rows and columns; used for records storage.

microprocessor A tiny digital computer, usually consisting of a single, very small silicon chip; also see *central processing unit*.

microwave (relay) A transmission medium similar to high-frequency radio wave signals; used to send data between relay stations.

miniaturization The re-creation of objects in a smaller size.
minicassette A cassette smaller than a standard cassette, with a recording capacity of 120 minutes to a side.
minicenter See *satellite center* and *decentralized information processing system*.
minicomputer A medium-sized computer that is less costly and less powerful than a mainframe.
MIPS (millions of instructions per second) A measure of the information processing capabilities of a microchip.
MIS See *management information system*.
modem Short for *MOdulator/DEModulator;* a device that converts electrical signals into tones for transmission over phone lines.
modules Consisting of interchangeable or compatible plug-in items or other "building blocks" to expand capacity.
mouse A hand-held input device with a free-rolling magnetic ball on the bottom. Moving the mouse causes the cursor to move on the screen. Menus are displayed and files are opened by pressing a button on the mouse.
multiple cassette system A central recording system in which dictation from multiple authors may be recorded on cassettes at the same time.
multiple sheet feeder A feeder with three or four trays of paper.
multitasking The ability of a computer system to perform a variety of tasks or applications simultaneously.

multiuser system A computer system that can be used simultaneously by several people.

NCR ("no carbon required") pack A copy pack that uses chemically treated paper instead of carbon sheets.
near-letter quality (NLQ) A type of printing produced by high-quality dot matrix printers; the images resemble those printed by character element printers.
network topology See *topology*.
networking The linking together electronically of computer and other office equipment for processing data, words, graphics, image, and voice for the purpose of enabling people and machines to communicate and interact.
NIOSH (National Institute for Occupational Safety and Health) An organization that investigates worker health and safety issues.
node The location of each terminal, printer, or peripheral connected to a local area network by a separate cable.
nonimpact printer A printer that uses a mechanism other than a device that strikes the paper or ribbon to produce images.

OCR See *optical character recognition*.
office automation See *automated office*.
office landscaping A type of office design featuring freestanding clusters of equipment and furnishings surrounded by large, open areas.
omnifont optical character reader An optical character reader capable of reading any standard typeface.
online information service A service that enables users online access to one or more databases by connecting a personal computer to a telephone with a modem; also called *online database*.
operating system Manages the various functions of a computer and is often housed in the computer's permanent memory.
operation keys Special keys on a word processor that control other components such as the storage unit, printer, or other terminals (for sending and receiving keyboarded documents).
optical character recognition (OCR) A device or scanner that reads printed characters and converts them into signals for input.
optical (laser) disk A record-like device on which information is stored (recorded) through the use of laser beams.
output The production of soft copy or typed or printed copies in an information processing system; one of the stages in the information processing cycle.

page printer An impact printer that assembles and prints entire pages at a time.
paper shredder A device used to destroy large amounts of paper documents that are no longer needed.
parity bit A control code used in data communication as a check bit, sent along with the groups of alphanumeric bits, to determine the accuracy of data during transmission.
Pascal A popular, sophisticated computer language used for statistical and graphic applications.

password An identification code (ID) known only to authorized users of a computer; frequently called *user ID;* also see *biometrics.*

performance appraisal An evaluation of an employee's performance conducted by his or her supervisor.

peripheral Any device that extends the capabilities of a word processing system or microcomputer but that is not necessary for its operation.

permanent memory The set of instructions, or program, built into word processing equipment or a microcomputer by the manufacturer; also called *read-only memory (ROM).*

personal computer (PC) See *microcomputer.*

photocopying A reproduction process in which copies are produced directly from an original by photographic means.

phototypesetting The process of setting text into type by using a computer-controlled printing device that generates characters and records them photographically on film or paper.

picocassette A cassette the size of a small matchbox; can hold 60 minutes of dictation.

pinfeed platen See *tractor.*

plain-paper copiers Copiers that do not require special paper for reproducing.

plotter A printer that uses colored inks to produce documents containing graphics and other types of artwork.

point-multipoint communication An audiovisual system allowing one-way communication between two or more locations.

point-of-sale terminal (POS) A type of cash register with a keyboard for keying in and displaying prices and additional coded data printed on price tags.

presentation graphics The use of graphics, such as drawings, charts, and pictures, to make a written document more interesting.

printer An output device that produces copy on paper.

printout See *hard copy.*

private branch exchange (PBX) A telephone system for managing and transmitting incoming and outgoing calls both within and outside an organization.

procedures manual A book containing descriptions and explanations of office jobs, tasks, or systems that is prepared by a company for use by its employees.

processing The sorting, classifying, or editing of input to organize it into information; one of the stages of the information processing cycle.

production counts A work measurement method. For example, the counting of documents, pages, or lines to measure productivity.

productivity The output per employee.

program A sequence of instructions used by a computer to process information; see *software.*

programmable read-only memory (PROM) Chips designed to allow the user to program ROM for applications that are used frequently.

programming language Language used, following a specified set of rules, for developing software. For example, assembly language, BASIC, COBOL, and Pascal.

protocol A technique or procedure for transmitting data that governs the format and control of data transmitted.

protocol convertor A device that enables machines with different sets of operating procedures to communicate with each other.

queues Priorities among printing orders.

RAM See *random-access memory.*

RAM chips See *solid-state storage.*

random-access memory (RAM) The temporary memory of a word processor or microcomputer.

read-only memory (ROM) The permanent memory of a word processor or microcomputer.

reader/printer A microform reader capable of printing hard copies of documents stored on the microform.

record A collection of information stored in a database.

records management system The entire process of organizing, handling, and controlling all information (records or files) of a business; includes records inventory, retention schedules, and disaster recovery plans.

repetitive printing The printing of more than one original hard copy.

repetitive text Duplicate information contained in documents intended for different recipients; sometimes called *standard text;* see *constant* and *form letter.*

reprographics The processes, methods, and equipment used to produce copies.

resident software See *software.*

resolution The quality or readability of a VDT or of printed copy; sharpness usually increases as the resolution (dots per inch) of the image or character increases.

ring network A local area network topology resembling a ring, with messages passed along a closed loop from one node to the next until they reach the addressee; an example is IBM's token ring network.

ROM See *read-only memory.*

satellite center A small concentration of word or information processing operators and equipment (linked administratively to a larger center) serving specific departments or floors of an organization. See also *decentralized information processing system.*

satellite communications The transmission of information to geographically distant locations via satellite.

scanning An optical input method.

screenload The amount of text that can appear on a video display terminal at one time.

screen prompt An on-screen message that asks questions about what functions the user wishes to have performed.

scroll To move stored text vertically or horizontally so that it can be viewed on the video display terminal.

shared logic A system in which a number of word processors or microcomputers share the processing and storage capabilities of one central processing unit.

shared resource A word or information processing system in which workstations with their own internal processors share resources such as printers and central storage; also known as *multiuser, multiterminal,* or *multistation configuration.*

shared-tenant service A type of timesharing system that allows several departments within a business to share resources, for example, a computer, storage, or even a telephone system.

soft copy Text displayed on the screen of a video display terminal.

soft keys Keys to which different functions can be assigned.

software The operating instructions or program of a computer (called *resident software* when the instructions are built into the hardware); also see *applications software* and *system software.*

software piracy The illegal copying of commercially produced software packages.

solid-state storage A rigid storage device with electrical circuits rather than moveable parts that permits extremely fast access. Two types of solid-state storage are RAM chips (plugged into the CPU) and bubble memory (permanent memory that is very reliable).

sorter Equipment attached to a copier that routes copies to separate bins to assemble sets of multipage documents.

source document Any business correspondence originated by an author; also see *document.*

spreadsheet An accounting application that arranges data in columns and rows.

standard cassette A $2\frac{1}{2}$- by 4-inch cassette, usually with a recording capacity of 60 minutes or more, with some cassettes holding up to 180 minutes, 90 minutes on each side of the tape.

standardization The process by which equipment manufacturers agree on a standard design for a specific piece of equipment, such as the arrangement of letters on a typewriter keyboard.

standardized format An established style of document preparation.

standardized procedures Guidelines set up to ensure consistency in the way certain office tasks are performed.

star network A local area network with a topology somewhat like a star with all lines converging into a hub (central controller).

storage The component of an information processing system that holds the media on which information is stored; one of the stages in the information processing cycle.

supercomputer The most powerful and expensive computer; performs high-speed numerical calculations (number crunching).

synchronous transmission See *bisynchronous transmission.*

system software Coordinates all the other software and manages computer operations; also see *operating system.*

systems approach The examination not only of individual tasks but also of the way those tasks go together and fit in with other related tasks.

telecommunications Transmission and reception of communications, usually electronic, from one location to another.

teleconference A meeting of geographically separated participants connected via a telecommunications system using two-way voice, text, or video communication; sometimes called *videoconference.*
teletypewriter A keyboard terminal used in the transmission of hard copy over telecommunications lines.
Telex An automatic switching service with information transmitted worldwide over telecommunications lines between teletypewriters.
templates Key guides or function strips that can be placed near the keyboard to help the operator remember what the keys do.
temporary memory See *random-access memory (RAM).*
ten-key numeric keypad Similar to a calculator's keys; may be used along with the keyboard.
thermal transfer A nonimpact method of printing or copying using ink and heat to produce clear, sharp output resembling a photocopy.
thimble A thimble-shaped type element on some character printers.
third-party maintenance The provision of computer service or maintenance by a vendor who is not the original manufacturer of the equipment.
tiling A windowing technique that limits the size of each window in proportion to the total number of windows on the screen.
time-sharing system A system in which an organization pays a fee for using time on a computer owned by another organization.
topology The arrangement, or configuration, of electronic equipment in a local area network; also called *architecture.*
touch-sensitive screen An input method which allows the user to touch the screen to operate the system and the application programs.
tractor A device that guides continuous-form paper through a printer.
transmission system The communication methods, mechanisms, and devices that transfer information from one location or piece of equipment to another.
turnaround time The time information takes to be processed and returned to the author.
twisted-pair cable An inexpensive transmission medium used for transmitting data; consists of two insulated wires twisted together.
ultrafiche A small sheet of film containing extremely reduced images; used for records storage.
unified command structure When using integrated software, the ability to perform all tasks (word processing, spreadsheet, database, etc.) in a similar way by using the same commands.
unitized microform A reduced image on cards or sheets of film rather than on a continuous roll; can be stored like index cards.
upgrade To enhance or add to the features and capabilities of information processing equipment.
uploading Transferring information from a computer to a communications network.
user manual See *documentation.*
user-friendly Easy to use and operate.

variable An item that differs from document to document.
variable sheet A sheet prepared by an author containing information to be combined with prerecorded documents.
VDT See *video display terminal.*
vendor A supplier of office equipment, often the manufacturer.
vendor manual See *documentation.*
vertical applications software Software designed to meet the specific requirements of a particular business or industry.
video display terminal (VDT) A component of information processing or computer equipment that displays text on a screen for ease in editing before production of printed copy.
videoconference See *teleconference.*
videotex A public computer network that provides visual information, for example, the TV monitors in airports showing flight schedules.
virus A damage-producing instruction which may affect both software and hardware.
voice/data integration Transmission of voice and data at the same time.
voice mail (VM) or voice message system (VMS) See *electronic audio communications.*
voice message system (VMS) See *electronic audio communications.*
voice or speech recognition equipment Machines utilizing technology that can recognize and convert human speech into written form.
voice synthesizer Equipment used to convert written, stored words into "speech."
voice-operated relay (VOR) A feature of some

dictation systems in which the voice activates the recording mechanism.

white noise A low-level, continuous background sound, such as the hum of an air-conditioner, that effectively masks other minor noises in an electronic office environment.

wide area network (WAN) A system for computer communication over long distances.

windowing Viewing multiple functions simultaneously; the layering of separate areas of the screen on which different aspects of work can be displayed.

word processing center See *information processing center.*

work flow The path from the start to the finish of a task, for example, the path a document takes through the information processing cycle.

work log A chart that records the work coming into and going out of an information processing center.

workstation Traditionally, the equipment, furnishings, and other tools an employee uses to perform job functions; also refers to a specific type of computer hardware, with speedy multitasking capabilities, multiuser functions, and a large memory and storage capacity.

WORM (write-once read many times) disk A type of optical disk on which data can be read and written but usually cannot be erased.

Index